THE LOGIC OF
ACCIDENTAL
NUCLEAR WAR

BRUCE G. BLAIR

THE LOGIC OF ACCIDENTAL NUCLEAR WAR

THE BROOKINGS INSTITUTION
Washington, D.C.

Copyright © 1993 by
THE BROOKINGS INSTITUTION
1775 Massachusetts Avenue, N.W., Washington, D.C. 20036

Library of Congress Cataloging-in-Publication data:
Blair, Bruce G., 1947–
The logic of accidental nuclear war / Bruce G. Blair.
    p. cm.
    Includes bibliographical references and index.
    ISBN 0-8157-0984-6—ISBN 0-8157-0983-8 (pbk.)
    1. Nuclear warfare. 2. Nuclear crisis control.
    3. Command and control systems. I. Title.
    U263.B57   1993
    355.02′17—dc20   92-41301
                                          CIP

9 8 7 6 5 4 3 2 1

The paper in this publication meets the minimum requirements of the American National Standard for Information Sciences—Permanence of paper for Printed Library Materials, ANSI Z39.48-1984.

ⒷTHE BROOKINGS INSTITUTION

The Brookings Institution is an independent organization devoted to nonpartisan research, education, and publication in economics, government, foreign policy, and the social sciences generally. Its principal purposes are to aid in the development of sound public policies and to promote public understanding of issues of national importance.

The Institution was founded on December 8, 1927, to merge the activities of the Institute for Government Research, founded in 1916, the Institute of Economics, founded in 1922, and the Robert Brookings Graduate School of Economics and Government, founded in 1924.

The Board of Trustees is responsible for the general administration of the Institution, while the immediate direction of the policies, program, and staff is vested in the President, assisted by an advisory committee of the officers and staff. The by-laws of the Institution state: "It is the function of the Trustees to make possible the conduct of scientific research, and publication, under the most favorable conditions, and to safeguard the independence of the research staff in the pursuit of their studies and in the publication of the results of such studies. It is not a part of their function to determine, control, or influence the conduct of particular investigations or the conclusions reached."

The President bears final responsibility for the decision to publish a manuscript as a Brookings book. In reaching his judgment on the competence, accuracy, and objectivity of each study, the President is advised by the director of the appropriate research program and weighs the views of a panel of expert outside readers who report to him in confidence on the quality of the work. Publication of a work signifies that it is deemed a competent treatment worthy of public consideration but does not imply endorsement of conclusions or recommendations.

The Institution maintains its position of neutrality on issues of public policy in order to safeguard the intellectual freedom of the staff. Hence interpretations or conclusions in Brookings publications should be understood to be solely those of the authors and should not be attributed to the Institution, to its trustees, officers, or other staff members, or to the organizations that support its research.

Foreword

THE legacy of the cold war includes a vast repository of nuclear weapons whose dependable control cannot be taken for granted. The political revolution in the former Soviet bloc may have ended the cold war, but it also subjected the Russian nuclear command and control system to unprecedented stress. The 1991 Moscow coup, the disintegration of the Soviet Union, and the ongoing political, economic, and social crisis throughout the region seemed to be pushing the system to the brink of nuclear anarchy. Apprehension grew over the prospects of the splintering of nuclear control among various successor states, of the accidental or unauthorized use of weapons, of the leakage of nuclear warheads, technology, or expertise to the third world, or of some hitherto unimaginable nuclear catastrophe.

This book analyzes these and other threats to the cohesion and effectiveness of the command and control systems of the former Soviet Union and the United States. Bruce G. Blair, a senior fellow in the Brookings Foreign Policy Studies program, identifies the cold war roots as well as the more recent causes of nuclear control problems. His examination shows grounds for both genuine concern and reassurance. He contends that during the cold war the command and control systems were more volatile and prone to inadvertence than was generally believed. Having been carried over to the post–cold war era, these systems pose a latent or residual danger that warrants remedial attention. Blair does not subscribe, however, to the more alarmist assessments that portray a growing danger of nuclear anarchy in the former Soviet Union. He disputes the prevalent opinion that the risk of accidental or unauthorized use of Russian nuclear weapons is increasing, arguing that such opinion overstates the weaknesses and understates the strengths of Russian safeguards.

Finally, he outlines a comprehensive policy agenda that addresses deficiencies in the systems of both Russia and the United States. The purpose of this agenda is not only to reduce the risk of nuclear inadvertence between the two nuclear superpowers, but also to set an example of responsible nuclear custodianship for the rest of the world.

A draft of this book was reviewed by a study group that met at Brookings in the spring of 1991, a group consisting of Mark Bing, Robert Einhorn, Raymond Garthoff, the late Doug George, Rose Gottemoeller, Peter Hauslohner, Janne Nolan, Leon Sloss, John Steinbruner, Edward Warner, and General (ret.) Larry Welch. Ashton Carter and Howard Stoertz also read the entire manuscript and provided thoughtful comments. Warner Schilling gave an exhaustive critique that greatly improved the study. Harold Feiveson, who reviewed part of the manuscript, provided helpful suggestions. Scott Sagan and Raymond Garthoff generously shared documents collected during their own research. The author is particularly indebted to several colleagues who supported this research endeavor from its inception to completion and made unique contributions in ways too numerous to mention: John Steinbruner, who collaborated with the author on the original draft of chapter 7, Sherman Frankel, Richard Garwin, Kurt Gottfried, Henry Kendall, and Frank von Hippel.

The author is also grateful to the many U.S. experts whose contributions cannot be individually attributed by name. The sensitivity of the subject necessitates anonymity for many persons who gave generously of their time and insight. In addition, the author wishes to thank several organizations and individuals for facilitating meetings with Russian experts. Of special value were meetings in Moscow and Washington arranged under the auspices of the International Foundation by Daniel Matuszewski, Frank von Hippel, Tony Byrne, William Miller, and Yevgeni Velikhov. Thanks to these colleagues, and interpreters Sally Onesti Blair, Nikolai Kapranov, and Tatiana Hudson, the author conducted extensive interviews yielding invaluable insight. Other productive meetings were arranged by Roald Sagdeev and Susan Eisenhower of the Center for Post-Soviet Studies, Howard Ris of the Union of Concerned Scientists, Sergei Kortunov of the Russian Foreign Ministry, and Mark Stiffler of the U.S. Department of the Navy.

Joseph Fennell and Ethan Guttmann assisted in computer modeling. Jeffrey Porro and Caroline Lalire edited the book. Adrianne Goins, aided by Drew Portocarrerro and Sarah Chilton, verified its factual content; and Caroline Pecquet provided administrative support. Susan Woollen prepared the manuscript for typesetting, and Julia Petrakis provided the index. Finally, the author appreciates the many contributions of Brookings colleagues and support staff to the project. They include Melanie Allen, Joshua Epstein, Alf Hutter, William Kaufmann, Catherine Kelleher, Michael Levin, Scott Parrish, and Paul Stares.

Brookings gratefully acknowledges the Carnegie Corporation of New York, the W. Alton Jones Foundation, and the John D. and Catherine T. MacArthur Foundation for providing financial support for this project.

The views expressed in this book are solely those of the author and should not be ascribed to the persons or organizations acknowledged above, or to the trustees, officers, or other staff members of the Brookings Institution.

BRUCE K. MACLAURY
President

February 1993
Washington, D.C.

To
my parents, Betty and Donald Blair,
and
my wife, Sally Onesti Blair

Contents

   Tables

Figures

Abbreviations and Acronyms

ABM	antiballistic missile
ADCOM	Air Defense Command
ALCC	airborne launch control center
ALCM	air-launched cruise missile
ANMCC	Alternate National Military Command Center
ASAT	antisatellite
ASW	antisubmarine warfare
BMEWS	ballistic missile early-warning system
CASMS	Center for Analysis of Space and Missile Situation (Soviet/Russian)
CGS	commander in chief, general staff (Soviet/Russian)
CIA	Central Intelligence Agency
CINCs	commanders in chief
CINCEUR	commander in chief, Europe
CINCLANT	commander in chief, Altantic
CINCNORAD	commander in chief, North American Aerospace Defense Command
CINCPAC	commander in chief, Pacific
CINCSAC	commander in chief, Strategic Air Command
CINC SRF	commander in chief, strategic rocket forces (Soviet/Russian)
CIS	Commonwealth of Independent States
DAL	destruct after launch
DE	damage expectancy
DEFCON	defense condition (U.S.)
DGZ	desired ground zero
DSP	defense support program
EAM	emergency action message
ELF	extremely low frequency
EMP	electromagnetic pulse
ERCS	emergency rocket communication system

ESD	environmental sensing device
FSU	former Soviet Union
GLCM	ground-launched cruise missile
GPALS	global protection against limited strikes
GPS	global positioning system
GRU	Chief Intelligence Directorate of the General Staff (Soviet/Russian)
HEU	highly enriched uranium
HF	high frequency
IAEA	International Atomic Energy Agency
ICBM	intercontinental ballistic missile
INF	intermediate-range nuclear forces
IRBM	intermediate-range ballistic missile
JCS	Joint Chiefs of Staff
JSTPS	Joint Strategic Target Planning Staff
KGB	Committee for State Security (Soviet/Russian)
LCC	launch control center
LDT	launch at designated time (Soviet/Russian)
LF	low frequency
LNO	limited nuclear option
LOW	launch on warning
LPAR	large phased-array radar
LUA	launch under attack
MF	medium frequency
MIRV	multiple independently targeted reentry vehicle
MPA	Main Political Administration (Soviet)
MRBM	medium-range ballistic missile
MVD	Ministry of Interior Affairs (Soviet)
NATO	North Atlantic Treaty Organization
NCA	National Command Authorities
NDS	nuclear detection system
NEACP	national emergency airborne command post
NMCC	National Military Command Center
NMCS	National Military Command System
NORAD	North American Aerospace Defense Command
NPT	Non-Proliferation Treaty
NSA	National Security Agency
NSDD	National Security Decision Directive
NUWEP	Nuclear Weapons Employment Policy
OTH	over-the-horizon radar
PACCS	postattack command and control system
PAL	permissive action link
PARCS	perimeter acquisition radar attack characterization system
PAVE PAWS	precision acquisition of vehicle entry phased-array warning system
PCL	positive control launch

PVO	air defense forces (Soviet/Russian)
QRA	quick reaction alert
RVSN	strategic rocket forces (Soviet/Russian acronym)
SAC	Strategic Air Command
SACCS	SAC automated command and control system
SDI	strategic defense initiative
SHF	superhigh frequency
SIOP	single integrated operational plan
SLBM	submarine-launched ballistic missile
SLCM	sea-launched cruise missile
SRF	strategic rocket forces (Soviet/Russian)
SSBN	nuclear ballistic missile submarine
SSN	nuclear attack submarine
START	strategic arms reduction talks
STAVKA	Headquarters to the Supreme High Command (Soviet/Russian)
TACAMO	take charge and move out
TNF	theater nuclear forces
TVD	theater of military operation (Soviet/Russian)
UHF	ultrahigh frequency
VGK	Supreme High Command (Soviet/Russian)
VHF	very high frequency
VLF	very low frequency
WTO	Warsaw Treaty Organization

THE LOGIC OF
ACCIDENTAL
NUCLEAR WAR

CHAPTER ONE

Introduction

WHEN nuclear tensions between the United States and the former Soviet Union ran high, the risk of nuclear inadvertence was much greater than has generally been recognized. The danger lurked in the command and control systems governing the forces. While managing tens of thousands of nuclear weapons for the purpose of deterring each other from launching a deliberate attack, the systems simultaneously posed a threat of launching an attack by accident. The distinct possibility existed that a nuclear war could begin through unauthorized use, by accident, or, more likely, because of erroneous information about the other side's nuclear intentions or actions.

This book analyzes the command and control systems of the nuclear superpowers and explains how they created such a threat during the era of confrontation. Previous studies have not rigorously established the magnitude of this danger, the lessening of which is among the main reasons to celebrate the end of the cold war. This book thus clarifies an obscure but important part of our nuclear history.

It is much more than a historical study, however, even though the Soviet Union no longer exists, the cold war is over, and relations between the United States and its former adversary are friendly. Nuclear inadvertence remains an issue of contemporary relevance, for several reasons.

First, the end of the cold war did not bring the nuclear stand-off to a final, irreversible end. Two states with huge nuclear arsenals still face each other. Poised even in peacetime for rapid use, the arsenals are inherently dangerous. In a crisis, an unlikely event whose probability is nonetheless unmeasurable, the risk of inadvertence would markedly increase. Though the possibility of nuclear confrontation between the United States and Russia is remote, it cannot be ruled out, any more than a sharp deterioration of U.S.-Russian relations or a return of hard-liners to power in Moscow can be ruled out.

Second, the U.S.-Soviet nuclear rivalry during the cold war contains lessons that apply to the rivalries among the emerging nuclear states. The book's title refers to the fact that inadvertence is an inherent risk in any relationship strained by nuclear antagonism. It is the common fate of nuclear archenemies everywhere that their operational postures evolve in ways that increase the risk.

Third, while generally easing nuclear tensions between the superpow-ers, the end of the cold war brought with it sociopolitical instabilities within the USSR that raise the specter of nuclear anarchy. The breakup of the Soviet Union cast doubt on the efficacy of nuclear safeguards in the new Commonwealth of Independent States (CIS), as did confusion over the control of nuclear weapons during the attempted coup of August 1991. A close analysis of the functioning of the Soviet Union's command and control system can inform our judgments about the adequacy of the systems of its successors. In short, this book is an analysis of the past and a guide to the future.[1]

Deterrence at the Crossroads

Before the end of the cold war most strategic analysis assumed that nuclear conflict could occur in one of two ways: through a failure of deterrence (an aggressor would calculate that the benefits of an attack outweighed the costs) or through inadvertence. A failure of deterrence was by far the dominant model; indeed it could be called the standard perspective on nuclear security.

According to deterrence theory, war is to be prevented by threatening a potential aggressor with retaliation destructive enough and credible enough to outweigh any benefit the potential aggressor could expect to gain. It is a theory that works for a coherent, calculating decisionmaker; Americans became heavily invested in perceiving the opposing nuclear forces as if they were the equivalent of rational individuals. Though spirited debates about this deterrent logic are ongoing, the principles of a stable nuclear balance have nonetheless been established reasonably well. For deterrence to hold, the opposing forces are each to be conceded a bedrock capability to carry out effective retaliation, which ensures the deterrent effect; each is to be denied, however, the ability to destroy the other's retaliatory capability in an initial attack, which prevents an incentive to initiate war.

This conception of stability became widely accepted during the cold war, and analysts working within its framework devised sophisticated models with which to assess existing and alternative force structures. Technical calculations of nuclear force exchanges provided the means and benchmarks by which to test whether deployments fit the principles of stability.

After the breakup of the former Soviet Union, the idea that war is to be prevented by a mutual threat of nuclear retaliation rang hollow. Deterrence and stability lost resonance as the images of malign adversaries dissolved, as the background fear of premeditated nuclear attack receded along with it, and as new security issues—notably, nuclear proliferation—competed for attention.

The standard perspective, however, has survived the end of the cold war. Nuclear deterrence is not as salient, but it has not dropped off the agenda of security policy. Both defense establishments, including their arms control components, still view the nuclear situation partly through the old prism. Most of the security community continues to endorse the importance of nuclear deterrence and to apply the standard benchmark tests. Each side will retain a potent capacity for retaliation to nuclear attack as long as total nuclear disarmament remains a chimera and as long as the slightest danger exists of regression in the relationship between the United States and its former adversary.

Despite the deepening bonds of cooperation between the traditional rivals, the revolutionary change sweeping the former Soviet Union remains partially undigested by the West, sustaining at least the Western desire for a nuclear insurance policy. The August 1991 attempt by Soviet hard-liners to overthrow President Mikhail Gorbachev, and the reactionary attitudes that still permeate a sizable portion of the population, have strengthened that desire. This is to say nothing of the corrosive effects on mutual confidence caused by the inherent capacity of each side's immense forces to initiate an attack at any time. The mere presence of such annihilating power continues to cause some degree of mutual suspicion. In sum, both sides consider it an imprudent leap of faith to assume that all risk of purposeful nuclear use has been forever extinguished. Nuclear deterrence remains a precept of both sides' security. To hedge an uncertain future, attention and resources will continue to be invested in its maintenance.

The nuclear superpowers nonetheless consider the requirements of deterrence to be easing. Both concede that existing nuclear arsenals are far larger and combat alert levels are far higher than necessary. It is widely recognized that by dint of inertia two large strategic organizations stand guard today against implausible scenarios, with arsenals befitting a bygone era.

To bring these monuments to the cold war obsession with premeditated attack into accord with political reality, the respective defense establishments recently began to make far-reaching adjustments to the nuclear postures. Nuclear war plans have been reviewed and extensively modified, at least in the United States. The modernization of nuclear forces was drastically curtailed and redirected. The alert level of a substantial portion of the forces and command and control systems was lowered. With the strategic arms reduction talks (START) agreement as the point of departure, both governments embarked in the fall of 1991 on a bold course of sweeping unilateral reductions in strategic and tactical nuclear arms. Additional large cuts in strategic arsenals were negotiated in 1992 and codified in the START II agreement. From the 1992 level of about 10,000 strategic nuclear warheads on each side, the United States and Russia agreed to pare back to 3,500 by the year 2003. In addition, they pledged to entirely eliminate the single most destabilizing weapon system in the arsenals—the accurate, multiple warhead missiles housed in land-based silos.

Deeper reductions to a level of 1,000 or fewer strategic warheads on each side are politically feasible in the post–cold war era. While no consensus on the minimum force level required to deter has been reached, most analysts hold that deterrence will be overdetermined for the indefinite future, allowing for the continuing downsizing of the arsenals.

Although stable deterrence remains a guiding principle for shaping the reductions, scenarios featuring deliberate attack so strain credulity that increasing attention is being paid to the problem of inadvertence. The ascendant view is that deterrence can be adequately served by much smaller arsenals under increasingly strict operational control to prevent their accidental or illicit use.

Inadvertence

During the cold war, the fear of premeditated attack overshadowed the danger of unpremeditated attack. A failure of deterrence thus received far more attention as a path to war than did a breakdown of command and control functions. Mainstream strategic thought and analysis emphasized the unresolved theoretical and practical issues of deterrence, and the tools of the trade were honed exclusively to deal with them. The standard tack was to treat nuclear forces as the equivalent of rational individuals, an obvious simplification that sharply limited its usefulness for analyzing problems of inadvertence. Studies yielded no conclusions about the ability of the elaborate command and control systems to preserve strict operational control over nuclear weapons.

The standard perspective, however, invoked the threat of inadvertence when it was expedient. Ironically, deterrence theory used this threat to shore itself up in areas of logical weakness. The notion that dysfunctional command and control or some other nonrational factor could affect the use of nuclear weapons in fact became a crucial underpinning for a theory that works only for rationally calculating decisionmakers. In a clever twist of reasoning, the theory of deterrence converted what seemed to be a flaw in its logic to a strength. The apparent flaw, which an aggressor might recognize and try to exploit, was that if deterrence based on the threat of massive retaliation should fail, it would not always be rational for the victim to carry out the threat.[2] The primary aim of the retaliatory threat was to deter, and if deterrence crumbled for some reason, retaliation would serve little rational purpose.

This internal contradiction, accorded the status of a genuine paradox, undermined the theory. But by invoking "the threat that leaves something to chance" (which presumes the existence of an inherent, irreducible risk of inadvertence), arguing that a potential aggressor could not count on pure reason to dictate its victim's response,[3] the theory disposed of the conundrum. Rational decisionmakers, so went the argument, realize that the laws of reason are unlikely to be obeyed strictly in nuclear war. Even if circumstances logically compelled a rational victim of nuclear aggression to withhold a retaliatory strike, an aggressor would run a risk of inducing spasmodic (irrational) retribution. The damage inflicted on the victim's command and control system by the aggressor's attack might in fact preclude any chance of rational behavior.

The risk of inadvertence was also invoked as a threat that inhibits a crisis from escalating. In this view, recognizing that command and control dysfunctions or other nonrational factors could cause states to blunder into war would motivate rational actors to step back from the precipice. Their fear that a confrontation could slip out of control and stumble across the nuclear threshold would cause them to be extremely cautious and more conciliatory. Paradoxically, such prudence could be exploited in a crisis. The party that acts with reckless abandon may get its way by playing on a more cautious opponent's fear of inadvertent escalation.

Nuclear roulette and all it connotes—risk, gambling, inadvertence—thus contributed, oddly enough, to nuclear security in the abstract. The standard perspective cast those dangers in a positive light, as theoretical virtues when cold-blooded nuclear aggression loomed large in the collective mind and deterring that aggression justified extreme measures. But at the end of the cold war they became liabilities. States that share an overriding interest in avoiding all military confrontation, to say nothing of nuclear war, wish to leave nothing to chance. Consequently, no defensible rationale exists for running the same risk of inadvertence today that was run in the past.

Nuclear Rivalry and Inadvertence

This risk stemmed mainly from the influence of four interrelated factors on the evolving nuclear postures of the cold war antagonists. And the case history of the superpowers can reasonably be generalized to apply to any nuclear rivalry.

First, the tremendous destructiveness of nuclear weapons meant that even a small number threatened the coherence of vital command posts and communications networks. The adversaries were driven to invest heavily in various schemes—combinations of active defenses, hardening, mobility, and redundancy—to protect their command and control systems. The return on such investments proved unsatisfactory, however. The systems were intrinsically susceptible to severe disruption from the effects of nuclear weapons. Even massive investment, a luxury beyond the means of most nuclear states, could not have entirely eliminated the problem. Retaliation, strictly defined, was thus a particularly demanding task, not so much because an initial attack might have destroyed all the individual weapons required but because an attack threatened the command and control system necessary to provide coherent direction. Nuclear forces were not unitary rational actors but large organizations whose internal procedures made it difficult to carry out the expectations that the standard perspective depended on. Standard assessments of the U.S.-Soviet strategic balance glossed over this vulnerability, calling into serious question their conclusions about the stability of deterrence during the cold war.

Second, the vulnerability of command and control systems to nuclear attack created strong pressure to buttress the credibility of the retaliatory threat by delegating alert and launch authority and shortening the reaction time of the nuclear postures. Nuclear states feel compelled to establish an operational-alert stance to hedge against the threat of a sudden nuclear attack by an adversary. It is not enough to have nuclear weapons, their delivery systems, and command infrastructure in storage or some other inactive status under tightly centralized civilian control if an opponent's nuclear offensive forces are ready for combat or can quickly be made ready. The nuclear superpowers thus pursued quick reaction postures that required the transfer of weapons from civilian to military custody and the thorough integration of warheads, delivery systems, and command channels. Strategic military organizations strived to match or exceed their opponent's combat readiness, a competitive dynamic that proved mutually reinforcing and essentially self-defeating in that it left both sides in an even better position to mount a sudden surprise attack using forces on routine day-to-day alert.

Third, fast reaction postures rely heavily on early warning, which imposed another huge burden on the command and control systems. The two-sided deployment of forces with very short delivery times required each side to monitor the opponent's forces on a near real-time basis, to detect both preparations for attack and actual launches. The United States and the Soviet Union thus acquired an extensive and costly reconnaissance infrastructure that also had to be linked to the command and control systems to permit timely decisions and rapid military responses. The result was a pair of command and control systems with a strong propensity to raise alert levels during a period of crisis as they interacted with each other. Both systems also became more prone to react quickly to the first signs of enemy launches, rendering them vulnerable to faulty warning indicators. Unmanageable crisis interactions, aggravated by erroneous early warning that at the extreme could trigger the dissemination of launch authorization, became more likely.

Fourth, the rapid reaction postures imposed on the command and control systems a requirement for ironclad safeguards that reliably prevented the accidental or illicit firing of even a single nuclear weapon (negative control). Unlike the previous requirements, this one was relatively inexpensive, but it nonetheless represented a daunting challenge.

Negative control was the dominant peacetime function, and elaborate safeguards were incorporated in the systems. But for all their sophistication and stringency, these technical and organizational measures were not tested and proved in every situation the cold war might have presented. This is particularly true for crisis situations, which could have severely strained safeguards because of the competing demands of exercising positive control (the requirement to dispatch forces on authoritative command) under severe time constraints. Negative control was counterpoised to the positive function associated with the central strategic purpose of nuclear forces: preparing to carry out enough destruction to deter the enemy. The challenge to the command systems was to preserve strict operational control while ensuring a convincing performance of the wartime mission. These requirements clashed, especially in crisis circumstances. Measures that would facilitate the speedy, deliberate use of nuclear weapons competed with measures that would minimize the risk of their aberrant use, and vice versa.

New evidence presented in this book substantiates the postulated effect of each of these four factors on the postures of the nuclear superpowers. It strongly supports the central thesis that the postures evolved under the influence of these factors to produce a much greater danger of inadvertence than has previously been established. The analysis backs the following specific conclusions:

—The Soviet command and control system, which Western observers generally portrayed as a highly survivable wartime system, was actually quite vulnerable to nuclear attack and probably just as fragile as the U.S. system.

—The Soviet system, contrary to widespread belief, undertook emergency preparations for nuclear combat on many occasions. Because both sides had this strong propensity to raise alert levels even when tensions were only slightly heightened, the crisis threshold at which the two systems could have become entwined in escalatory nuclear alerting could have been crossed much earlier than is commonly assumed.

—The U.S. and Soviet systems, again contrary to widespread belief, were geared for launch on warning. This became the primary mode of command system operation for both postures, placing both nations at risk of going to war on the basis of false early warning information. In pursuing a rapid reaction posture, the United States delegated nuclear launch authority to military commanders during the entire cold war era.

—The rapid reaction postures of both adversaries depended on early warning systems of dubious reliability. The questionable performance of the warning networks created a greater danger of inadvertence during a crisis than was recognized. The United States was especially prone to misinterpret events because its command system allowed the relatively unreliable pre-attack indicators of Soviet intent (strategic warning) to play a large role in the U.S. launch decision process. But both sides relied on strategic as well as tactical warning to guide launch decisions, a reliance that put them deeper into a preemptive stance than they realized themselves.

—The Soviet Union went to extraordinary lengths to ensure strict centralized control over strategic nuclear weapons. Its system of safeguards compared favorably with the less stringent regime imposed on U.S. weapons.

Taken as a whole, these summary findings drive home the broader conclusion: cold war antagonism became embodied in command and control systems that put the nuclear superpowers at substantial mutual risk of a catastrophic failure of negative control as they strived to fulfill the difficult operational demands of positive control—notably the demand to project a credible capability to perform the retaliatory mission. In sum, their nuclear postures were accidents waiting to happen.

The demise of the cold war is allowing the traditional rivals to reduce this danger without concern for its effect on deterrence. Considerable progress toward that end is being made, though final success is a long way off. A residual risk of inadvertence, stemming from the four factors discussed earlier, still lurks in their command and control systems. The danger is associated with a crisis, the likelihood of which has presumably decreased, but by how much nobody knows. The danger should diminish as relations continue to improve, but meanwhile steps could be taken to mitigate it.

The situation is less sanguine for the emerging nuclear powers, whose futures harbor the same dilemmas as those faced by their predecessors during the cold war. A similar evolution of their nuclear postures and an attendant increase in the risk of inadvertence are predictable. Prospective nuclear rivals with fewer resources to lavish on command and control systems indeed face even higher risks. Their safeguards are bound to be cruder and weaker and are likely to be tested more often. The volatile relations between many of these states have a large potential to erupt into a full-blown military confrontation, intensifying the trade-off between positive and negative control and creating more opportunities for weaknesses in safeguards to emerge.

Internal Threats and Inadvertence: The Domestic Wild Card

Besides the inherent danger of inadvertence stemming from the antagonistic postures of nuclear rivals, some states face domestic threats to their command and control systems. The former Soviet Union falls into this category. The danger of nuclear anarchy within its former borders is in fact largely responsible for the growing popular and governmental awareness of the problem of inadvertence. The political revolution that dissolved the USSR, ended the cold war, and relieved Western fear of premeditated attack simultaneously engendered fear of the unpremeditated use of nuclear force.

SCENARIOS FOR NUCLEAR ANARCHY. As the former Soviet Union fragmented, it appeared to be fertile ground for an outbreak of "loose nukes." Several different strains of the virus were anticipated. One was the outbreak of multiple nuclear successor states. The unraveling of the USSR boded ill for preserving a single nuclear weapon state within its former borders. Nuclear weapons were believed to be deployed on the territory of about ten republics, four of which were home to various units of the strategic nuclear forces. (The Soviets had repatriated the last of their nuclear weapons located outside of Soviet territory in about August 1991, with the return of those based in East Germany.)

The ingredients for instant proliferation were thus available, posing a temptation for the leaders of some republics, which made certain legal claims to them. Nuclear weapons were valued as sources of international prestige, bargaining leverage, and money (especially from the potential sale of uranium extracted from dismantled weapons) and as military counterbalance to Russian hegemony. The specter of proliferation loomed ever larger as Ukraine and Kazakhstan, in particular, started haggling with Russia over their roles in governing such forces. That multiple nuclear successor states would emerge was almost a forgone conclusion to many Western observers, notably the neorealists, who saw this as a classic case of states in search of security in an anarchic situation. This drive, together with other incentives, portended not only a custody fight but, worse, one with the potential to turn violent.

Another "loose nukes" scenario was a simple breakdown of operational control. It was feared that, whichever state or states inherited the weapons, the operational control over them might degenerate, allowing irresponsible parties to gain control over some portion of the arsenal. Variations on the theme included the capture, theft, purchase, or other appropriation of nuclear weapons by "renegades" within the former Soviet Union, who might then try to sell them on an international black market. This danger seem especially acute because large numbers of tactical nuclear weapons were being relocated at the time. Literally thousands of small nuclear warheads were being packed up and shipped back to Russia, a process that exposed them to diversion from within or interdiction from without. Some warned of heightened risks of accidents during the mass exodus of weapons from the outlying republics to Russia; others feared the unauthorized use of weapons.

Another variation on the theme was inspired by the attempted coup in August 1991; it was feared that a second coup could severely compromise the integrity and coherence of the nuclear command system. That weapons might even be used in some of these circumstances became a genuine concern. Perhaps the worst-case scenario was the unauthorized launch of strategic nuclear weapons by disaffected low-level crews within the nuclear chain of command.

The third prevalent fear of "loose nukes" stemmed from doubt about the virtue of the broader nuclear establishment in the Soviet Union— nuclear weapons design laboratories, research and production facilities for fissile materials and other bomb components, the civilian nuclear power industry, and so forth. Social upheaval and severe economic austerity could erode the safeguards in place that had prevented sensitive nuclear technology, fissile material, or expertise from leaking out to a proliferator state. Estimates varied widely, but there were hundreds to many thousands of former Soviet nuclear scientists, engineers, and technicians who could offer very useful assistance to countries like Iran, Iraq, and Libya in developing nuclear weapons. Because of the growing ease of emigration and the economic hardship facing many of these individuals, the prospect that some could be lured into supporting would-be proliferators became a serious concern. As for sensitive technologies like nuclear detonators ("triggers") leaking out, that likelihood also seemed greater as the military-industrial sector decentralized, pursued profits, and sought new customers.

In 1991 none of these gloomy scenarios seemed fanciful. It really was uncertain whether nuclear safeguards were reliably effective and whether lines of nuclear authority remained clear, intact, and stable as powerful centrifugal forces tore apart the USSR and its traditional institutions. Given the level of distress—political, social, and economic—the situation seemed fraught with danger. Few observers dismissed the notion that, even without the additional strains of widespread civil war, the command system could lose control over at least some portion of the roughly 30,000 weapons scattered across the vast expanse of the country.

WESTERN POLICY RESPONSES. Western reaction to the prospect of nuclear anarchy took the form of several major policy initiatives linked to the general issue of nuclear control in the former Soviet Union.

Among its effects on U.S. policy, the specter of the unauthorized or accidental use of long-range ballistic missiles gave fresh impetus to the missile defense program of the Strategic Defense Initiative Organization. The danger boosted support for the proposal to amend the ABM (Antiballistic Missile) Treaty and deploy some variant of the antimissile system called global protection against limited strikes (GPALS). A consensus formed within the U.S. Congress in 1991 to back these initiatives and the GPALS' budget grew significantly.[4]

A more preventive approach to the threat of nuclear inadvertence and proliferation was taken by President George Bush and President Gorbachev in the wake of the failed coup and just prior to the dissolution of the Soviet Union. In September and October 1991 they announced plans for drastically reducing the tactical nuclear arsenals, removing the vast majority from far-flung combat units and consolidating them in central storage depots. They also declared that the combat readiness of hundreds of strategic nuclear formations would be lowered, effective immediately. All long-range bombers were taken off alert, as were about five hundred ICBMs on each side.[5] Although Bush and Gorbachev did not explicitly say that these actions were intended to enhance weapons security at home, the most important effect was to alleviate the danger of the illicit seizure of some portion of the far-flung Soviet arsenal.

A preventive approach was also promoted by advocates of Western economic assistance to the former Soviet Union. They argued that without a large infusion of aid, the emerging Commonwealth would slide deeper into chaos and lose control over nuclear forces. On these plausible grounds, the U.S. Congress earmarked $800 million of the defense budget for use, at the president's discretion, in helping the former Soviet states to dismantle nuclear warheads and in providing humanitarian aid. International assistance in converting the military-industrial sector to nonmilitary pursuits includes the financial support of joint projects to divert the work of nuclear weapons scientists into such areas as nuclear weapons destruction, design and safety of civilian nuclear reactors, and controlled fusion research. In this vein, the United States, the European Community, Japan, and other participating governments have pledged about $75 million for an international science and technology center based in Moscow for the CIS (plus Georgia) and in Kiev for Ukraine. These funds will support weapons scientists who agree to work on non-military scientific and commercial projects. Such subsidies are intended to help keep weapons scientists gainfully employed inside the former Soviet Union.[6]

The United States will also donate hundreds of millions of dollars to assist the CIS in eliminating the thousands of nuclear weapons slated for deactivation under the various arms control agreements currently in force. The bulk of the assistance is likely to support construction of a facility to store plutonium extracted from the weapons. Unless this bottleneck is removed, a backlog of weapons awaiting dismantling will remain exposed to potential diversion.[7]

In addition, the United States took a preventive tack to deal with the threat of proliferation in the former Soviet republics on whose territory nuclear weapons were stationed. To ensure that a single nuclear successor state (Russia) emerged in place of its predecessor (the USSR), the United States predicated political support and financial assistance to the new republics in part on their willingness to accede to the Nuclear Non-Proliferation Treaty (NPT) as non-nuclear weapon states and to forswear an independent launch capability for any nuclear weapons remaining on their soil. At the same time, several of these former republics, those with strategic forces on their territory, came under strong U.S. diplomatic pressure to abide by the terms and help carry out the obligations of the START I agreement.

Lastly, the issue of nuclear control rapidly gained influence in the arena of U.S.-Russian arms control negotiations. In June 1992 President Bush and President Boris Yeltsin announced further cuts in strategic arms beyond START I, cuts whose effect was to ensure the eventual elimination of strategic missile forces from the territories of Ukraine and Kazakhstan. The key provision is the elimination of all multiple-warhead ICBMs (intercontinental ballistic missiles), which covers all missile fields in those regions. Also, under the rubric of "operational arms control," the United States and Russia plan to discuss additional steps for improving warning, nuclear safety and security, and other aspects of command and control to help prevent an unintended nuclear catastrophe. One effort likely to come to early fruition is to establish a joint early-warning center.

THE CURRENT SITUATION. The situation in mid-1992 seemed less bleak than it was during the previous year. The threats of nuclear inadvertence and proliferation had ebbed. The risk that nuclear successor states would proliferate after the breakup of the Soviet Union proved more manageable than was generally expected. All tactical nuclear weapons had been removed from non-Russian territory by July 1992. Strategic nuclear forces remain in Ukraine, Belarus, and Kazakhstan, but all three states signed a START I protocol with the United States in which they agreed to adhere to the NPT as non-nuclear weapons states "in the shortest possible time," keep nuclear weapons under "a single unified authority," and implement the limits and restrictions of START.[8]

In separate letters, the leaders of all three states pledged to eliminate all nuclear weapons from their territory within the seven-year period provided by the START I agreement. They attached conditions to their commitments, however, and the seven-year time span for implementing them leaves plenty of time for nuclear gamesmanship to give birth to more nuclear successor states. In its letter, Ukraine also reiterated its long-standing position, insisting on the "right to control over the non-use of nuclear weapons deployed in its territory."[9] Ukraine claims the right to have a physical veto over the use of nuclear weapons, and it also seeks administrative control over all such forces on its soil. As of fall 1992, all CIS nuclear forces were still firmly in the control of Russian President Yeltsin, the Russian minister of defense (Pavel Grachev), the chief of the Russian general staff, and the commander in chief of the Russian strategic rocket forces. Yeltsin has agreed to consult the other states of the Commonwealth, and to obtain permission from the leaders of Ukraine, Belarus, and Kazakhstan before launching any nuclear forces.

The past year also witnessed a flawless performance in maintaining nuclear safety and security. The gloomy predictions of nuclear accidents, thefts, and even unauthorized use during the mass relocation of weapons from the outlying former republics to Russia never materialized. As best as one can judge from available sources, not a single incident of loss of control occurred. Control over the strategic nuclear forces also appears to be as strict as ever.

Nor has the social, economic, and political turmoil resulted in any known leakage of nuclear expertise or technology to the fledgling nuclear states. During the past year the West has enjoyed extensive contact with the directors and staff of the former Soviet nuclear weapons laboratories, missile design bureaus, ministry of atomic energy, organizations responsible for safeguarding fissile materials, and related agencies. Those persons affiliated with Russian programs have greatly allayed, if not laid to rest, Western fears about nuclear leakage. Russian officials and scientists do not appear to be any less motivated than their Western counterparts to try to prevent the spread of nuclear weapons. That nuclear proliferation indeed poses a more immediate and direct threat to Russia than it does to the United States is not lost on them. Nevertheless, the fear of leakage of nuclear technology from Ukraine has not been allayed, and the concern about Russia over the long term is warranted.

This generally comforting record mainly reflects the Soviet penchant for tight central control over the entire life cycle of nuclear weapons, from design research to combat-alert operations to dismantlement. Imbued with a long-standing and deep-seated obsession with controlling nuclear weapons, the Soviet Union historically went to great lengths to ensure tight central control over them. The command system deserved greater credit that it received in the West for its ability to deal effectively with aberrant behavior within the chain of command and with threats stemming from social upheaval. The West also deserves some credit, especially for its role in persuading the non-Russian republics not to seek nuclear status. U.S. diplomatic pressure may have been critical in getting Ukraine and Kazakhstan to sign the START I protocol, pledge to join the NPT as non-nuclear weapons states, and cooperate with Russia in removing strategic and tactical nuclear weapons from their territories.

This admirable performance to date cannot, however, be confidently extrapolated into the future. The safeguards imposed on the nuclear weapons establishment in the former Soviet Union are strict but far from foolproof. Ample room for strengthening safeguards against domestic turbulence exists both on a unilateral basis and in coordination with others, including in particular the United States.

Double Whammy: Simultaneous Domestic and International Crisis

The current state of affairs in the former Soviet Union sets the stage for a nuclear crisis involving acute domestic *and* international tension.

This combination would create unprecedented difficulties for the command and control system were it to occur. While not a likely scenario, since a nuclear crisis triggered by a conflict of interest between the former Soviet Union and its traditional adversary is increasingly far-fetched, it merits serious consideration. The potential exists for a domestic nuclear crisis to engage the command and control systems on both sides (not to mention the possibility of other nuclear states becoming involved). A failure, or the threat of imminent failure, of negative control because of domestic turmoil could plausibly spark an international reaction that initiates crisis interaction between the command systems. For instance, if the August 1991 coup had degraded nuclear safeguards and projected an increased nuclear threat beyond the Soviet borders, it might have triggered a heightened state of U.S. (or Chinese) nuclear readiness. If this reaction in turn caused enough concern within the Soviet command system to produce a counteralert, then the danger of nuclear inadvertence would have grown. The rising priority of the wartime mission would have put additional stress on the command systems, making their negative function more difficult to perform, especially in the context of internal threats to the Soviet command system.

The risk of inadvertence has thus grown more complex. Domestic threats to nuclear control and security have the potential to spill over into the international arena and to reverberate back and forth between the internal and external environments.

Analyzing the Historical and Present Risk of Inadvertence

What makes a catastrophic failure of nuclear command and control particularly disturbing is that no credible estimate of the risk exists. Little more than the rough outlines of the danger is understood. A whole new kit bag of theories, tools of analysis, and data bases is needed.

The standard deterrence perspective is more a hindrance than a help because positive rather than negative control is its main concern. Its traditional calculus emphasizes the vulnerabilities of the forces to deliberate attack, and by the same token treats the sources of unintentional attack superficially.

The shortcomings of that perspective can be overcome only by replacing it with a new conception of nuclear security. If the improper or accidental employment of nuclear weapons defines the greater danger, and if ensuring the safe operation of forces is the ascendant priority of the security agenda, then the essential task is to closely examine the command and control systems with a view to identifying failure modes that could produce nuclear disaster. Past and existing nuclear safeguards need to be evaluated in the context of threats posed by the domestic and external environments.

The ability of the command systems to operate nuclear forces in a safe manner has depended on the immediate state of politico-military relations between the rival nuclear states. An evaluation of safeguards should treat the state of tension between them as a variable instead of a constant. An assessment should indicate, for example, the extent to which the risk of unauthorized missile launches rises or falls with the level of tension; or the extent to which crisis tensions compound the problem of early warning malfunction or error, thereby increasing the risk that a false alarm would induce a command system to order the use of weapons.

Methodology

The core analytic task of this book is to identify and elucidate the dominant failure modes of the command systems as they labor to perform the functions of negative and positive control during periods of acute tension. Such crisis scenarios hardly require any justification for the historical assessment; the cold war produced conditions ripe for nuclear crises. Such scenarios are an essential methodological device for exposing dangers that might have emerged during the era of confrontation. They similarly help expose deficiencies in safeguards that might emerge in a future crisis.

Projecting the abnormal modes of command system operations under conditions of domestic stress also depends on this methodological device. Such analysis requires an understanding of how the systems are supposed to work in a conflict—their normal or prescribed operations including the planned sequence of actions involved in the intentional firing of nuclear weapons. For example, the established procedures for launching missiles reveal a great deal about who possesses authorizing and enabling codes, information crucial to appreciating the potential for these codes to be disseminated improperly.[10]

This approach to the analysis of command system operations, furthermore, facilitates the separation of the effects of crisis interaction—that is, the role of the external environment—from the effects of domestic stress on the safety of nuclear operations. This study suggests, though it cannot prove, that the dangers of inadvertence stemming from a possible future international crisis are still much more serious than the dangers that derive solely from domestic threats to the command and control systems. The most plausible breaches of negative control arising from internal turmoil—for instance, the theft of a tactical nuclear weapon from a Russian depot—have far less catastrophic consequences, while the more dreadful scenarios growing out of internal disintegration—for instance, the unauthorized launch of a boat load of submarine missiles— have far less plausibility. If the risk of an event is defined as its probability combined with its consequences, then the risks associated with the crisis interaction of the strategic command organizations appear to be considerably greater than the risks created by domestic upheaval in the former Soviet Union. This conclusion underscores the importance of improving relations and making a future crisis even less likely. The benefits of cooperative security, and the costs of a relapse, are clearly high.

The basic task of this book—assessing the efficacy of safeguards in various international and domestic contexts—requires analysis that delves deeply into the design of the nuclear command and control systems. Therein lies a great difficulty. Both the physical infrastructure and procedures of these systems are obscured by secrecy. The Soviet system was particularly shrouded in secrecy. Although the successor system is now more accessible to examination, it still remains opaque to outside view. The public record contains sparse, uneven, and contradictory material on the peacetime operations of the system; it is even less useful for analyzing crisis and wartime operations.[11]

The assessment here, therefore, draws heavily on information gathered through interviews with individuals professionally involved in the study or operation of the nuclear command and control systems. Their expertise proved indispensable to the analysis of the past and present system in the former Soviet Union. Persons with backgrounds in the Soviet nuclear armed forces, particularly those who served in combat roles in the land-based strategic rocket forces and in the submarine ballistic missile forces, provided invaluable data. Many U.S. and foreign government analysts also shared crucial insights. In addition, their dissection of Soviet nuclear exercises allowed information collected from Soviet sources to be cross-checked, and suggested new avenues of inquiry.

Although every effort was made to cross-check information, distinguishing fact from fiction ultimately depended on my subjective filter. The store of reliable knowledge of Soviet command is sufficient to warrant tentative judgments but too meager to support many firm conclusions. The fast-changing situation in the former USSR adds to the difficulty. It is almost impossible even to keep the shifting political and military landscape under constant surveillance, much less to absorb its implications. The portrayal of the respective systems, past and present, is thus highly interpretive.

Such bridled speculation is of course no stranger to the field of nuclear studies. Although it is a mature discipline that has produced a coherent logic and set of principles–many consider it to be tilled to the point of exhaustion–it rests on a foundation of conjecture. While this justifies skepticism, it does not warrant condemnation. On the contrary, it is the constant interplay of speculation and skepticism that germinates new insight in this and every other field of intellectual inquiry. Most of the history of science consists of a succession of new conjectures and hypotheses. One conjecture reigns until another overthrows it. Such is the nature of the enterprise.[12]

Scope of the Book

The key hypotheses of this book do not concern the gritty details so much as the essential nature of the command and control systems. Some of the basic features appear to shed light on the difficulties these systems have in managing nuclear forces safely under conditions of stress, whether domestic or international. A model isolating such basic features is outlined in chapter 2 and fleshed out for the U.S. and Soviet command systems in chapters 3 and 4, respectively. Briefly, the model captures (a) the operative goals of the systems, and (b) the balance between centralization and decentralization in the managerial practices of the systems. The U.S. and Soviet systems were (and are) very different in these two respects, suggesting different susceptibilities to and causes for a breakdown of negative control.

The model produces two major propositions about the danger of nuclear inadvertence. First, the Soviet command system was better designed to prevent the unauthorized use of nuclear weapons. The pertinent safeguards on the U.S. side were less impressive. Second, a crisis that was perceived to pose a nuclear threat would have immediately produced two serious unintended consequences that in turn would have increased the risk of inadvertent war. In a crisis, command and control vulnerability and launch on warning immediately assumed, for different reasons, great importance in the decision process on each side. The acute vulnerability of command and control that existed on both sides changed from a latent to a salient factor, and to compensate, both command systems adopted a stance of launch on warning. Classic preemptive instability resulted, and the command and control systems became prone to overreaction to erroneous indications of enemy attack. The systems prepared to disseminate launch authorization immediately on receiving warning of the launch of opposing forces, and decisionmakers became more disposed to believe attack indications issued by the warning system. Launch on warning thus entered the foreground at the onset of a crisis, as an unintended effect of the crisis, to create a still greater danger of inadvertence.

Chapter 5 assesses in detail the vulnerability of the command systems, particularly the Soviet system, and points up the classic preemptive instability that emerged from it. The analysis contests the prevalent view that the Soviet system was so resilient that decisionmakers did not fear its collapse under attack. It is argued that such confidence did not exist and that it would have been unwarranted in any case.

The evolution of both command systems toward the adoption of launch on warning as the primary mode of strategic operation is documented in chapter 6. The risk of inadvertent war created by such a posture is qualitatively assessed.

Chapter 7 presents a formal model whose illustrative calculations gauge the danger that erroneous attack indications would produce an inadvertent war. It shows why the reliance of the command systems on launch on warning requires early warning networks to perform almost flawlessly, and argues that such standards of performance are unrealistic in crisis situations.

Chapter 8 proposes a set of policy remedies to reduce the risk of nuclear inadvertence and set an example of responsible nuclear custodianship for the rest of the world. The proposals require a sharp reorientation of the axes of security policies, with the emphasis tilting further away from the traditional preoccupation with calculated aggression and closer to the strengthening of safeguards against major sources of inadvertent conflict. Such rotation acknowledges that the deterrence of premeditated attack has been firmly established and that the primary threat of war arises from lapses of strict operational control over nuclear weapons.

The recommendations include encouraging Ukraine to repudiate an independent nuclear capability and impose strict export controls on nuclear-related technologies; removing the commitment to attack opposing strategic weapons and command systems from U.S. and Russian mission requirements; protecting the command systems from attack; revoking the predelegation of nuclear launch authority granted to military authorities; reducing the day-to-day combat readiness of the strategic forces; curbing nuclear exercises; reducing reliance on the option of launch on warning; improving the performance of early-warning networks; establishing a joint U.S.-Russian early-warning center; installing foolproof locks on all nuclear weapons; destroying all weapons that cannot meet high standards of safety; and forming a joint U.S.-Russian nuclear emergency response team. Some of these measures can be implemented unilaterally, while others warrant bilateral negotiation.

If the reader believes that deliberate nuclear aggression by the traditional adversaries remains the principal threat and uppermost priority of nuclear security policy, this book's recommendations will strike a discordant note. It is hoped that the book will at least subject this belief to critical reevaluation.

Some important topics have been excluded because of limitations of space and scope. Among other omissions is the large subject of the danger of nuclear accidents (pure accidents) posed by the design of the safety features on the nuclear weapons themselves. The reader is referred elsewhere for such analysis.[13]

Other omissions include the vast and insightful literature on civil-military relations in the former Soviet Union. This book does not begin to do justice to the important relationship between the political leadership and the military-industrial complex. Instead, the book concentrates on the techno-organizational and doctrinal components of Soviet command and control.[14]

The content of this book overlaps that of two recent superb studies by Scott Sagan and Peter Feaver.[15] The penetrating analysis of U.S. nuclear command and control provided by these authors covers topics that are central to this book—notably, the civilian control of nuclear weapons and the risk of nuclear accidents. Their approach to those subjects is quite different from mine, but all three studies are companionable.

CHAPTER TWO

Perspectives on Nuclear Crisis Dynamics

CENTRAL to the arguments advanced in this book is the thesis that rival strategic command and control organizations in the course of their evolution acquire a sense of vulnerability that causes them to adopt rapid reaction postures. They deploy combat-ready nuclear forces in peacetime, and in periods of acute tension with a nuclear rival, jittery organizations further shorten the fuses on their nuclear forces and prime themselves for responding rapidly to signs of impending attack. The potentially dangerous consequences of such behavior are well appreciated. Escalating alerts, were they to occur, would put additional strain on safeguards and could initiate unmanageable interaction between the opposing forces.

But the thesis seems to founder for want of evidence showing this kind of alerting interaction between the U.S. and Soviet nuclear forces during the Cuban missile crisis or any other moment of acute cold war tension. It takes two to spar, and one of them—the Soviet Union—is alleged to have stayed completely out of the ring. Researchers have reported no evidence to suggest that the Soviet Union ever initiated a nuclear alert or ever reacted with an alert to any of the global nuclear alerts instituted by the United States in 1960, 1962, and 1973.[1] On the basis of this apparent restraint, American scholarship inferred a deep-seated Soviet reluctance to increase the combat readiness of nuclear forces or for that matter even to conduct large-scale nuclear exercises that include such extraordinary measures as the surging of strategic submarines from port. It was thus reasoned that nuclear tensions would have to cross a high threshold before the command and control systems would begin to interact.

Those inferences are wrong. The historical record is in fact replete with episodes of Soviet nuclear alerts that substantiate the thesis advanced here. The Soviet reputation for abstinence is undeserved.[2] All three of the global U.S. nuclear alerts caused a nuclear reaction in the Soviet Union, and the Soviets initiated nuclear alerts on other occasions. The principal known episodes are recounted below. Additional details of these cases and brief accounts of minor incidents that may have occurred at other times are interspersed throughout this book. Although an escalatory dynamic either never occurred, or quickly fizzled, the potential for reactive alerting was significant. The episodes reveal enough of an alerting impulse on the Soviet side to support the contention that the command and control systems were liable to move rapidly toward their wartime missions in time of crisis.

History of Soviet Nuclear Alerts

The chronology of Soviet nuclear alerts began in 1960. At the time strategic aviation was the only branch of the Soviet armed forces equipped with strategic nuclear weapons.[3] The fleet of long-range bombers conducted routine airborne patrols and supported a ground alert posture, but they were unarmed in peacetime. When the United States declared a worldwide nuclear alert during the Paris summit in May 1960, the Soviet air force commander ordered the airborne planes to return to their bases, where they could be loaded with nuclear bombs if such a decision were taken by the chief of the general staff. (Approval from the chief, given by the issuance of a so-called preliminary command, was required to load the aircraft with nuclear weapons.) The U.S. alert lasted only a brief time, however, and the preparations to load weapons onto Soviet bombers did not move beyond returning the bombers to base. Nonetheless, a prolonged U.S. alert would probably have moved the Soviets to the next phase. In any event it is fair to say that the alert induced a nuclear reaction, albeit a low-key and short-lived one.

The intense U.S. nuclear alert of 1962 during the Cuban missile crisis induced a much stronger reaction, according to a former career officer in the Soviet strategic rocket forces (SRF). His account rebuts the voluminous academic literature on the crisis, which finds no evidence that nuclear steps of any kind were taken by the Soviet Union other than the activities inside Cuba itself[4]—presumably out of fear that a nuclear counteralert involving home-based strategic forces might provoke an American attack.[5] Pronouncements to the contrary made by the Soviet leadership shortly after the crisis ended have been widely dismissed as self-serving rhetoric.[6] Richard Betts characterized Soviet military activity this way: "The remarkable Soviet nonalert was equivalent to a threatened dog's rolling over belly-up."[7] This academic skepticism has been at least partially supported by the U.S. intelligence community, which by all previously declassified accounts did not detect any signs of a Soviet nuclear alert during the crisis.[8]

At least one circumspect former intelligence officer on duty at the time, however, readily concedes that alert activity simply might have escaped notice.[9] That a general nuclear alert occurred but went largely unnoticed is quite plausible in the light of the information gleaned from interviews with the Soviet source mentioned above. He claims that after the United States put its nuclear forces on defense condition two, which involved extensive preparations for an immediate large-scale nuclear strike, the Soviet Union increased the combat readiness of its strategic land-based missile and aviation forces. (The Soviet navy did not have strategic nuclear weapons then.) The operational arsenal was small, but all available forces were made ready for combat.[10] The top state and military leadership, including the general secretary and chief of the general staff, decided to put the SRF on a war footing that would permit them to be launched within a few hours of a decision to fire. This meant raising the alert level by one notch, going from *constant* to *increased* readiness, which put the missiles in a configuration to be launched within two to four hours after receiving the order to fire.

The missiles were not fueled or raised to the vertical fire position but all were loaded with high-yield nuclear warheads. The normal practice of keeping all warheads in depots separate from the missiles (a negative control measure) yielded to the imperative of the wartime mission and the requirement to mate the missiles and warheads (a positive control measure). Such preparations for war were undoubtedly difficult for U.S. reconnaissance to detect. Similarly the leadership ordered a *stand-down* of the strategic aviation forces; that is, the termination of routine training and maintenance and above all the assumption of a runway alert posture that allowed for a quick takeoff.[11] None of the planes ever took off during the crisis, but they could have been loaded and launched very quickly if circumstances had required it. Nuclear weapons for the bombers were located nearby, and some were probably loaded, according to the Soviet source. These steps probably were not readily detectable, which may explain why U.S. senior military officers later claimed that Khrushchev never even put any bombers on alert.[12]

The next episode in the chronology of Soviet nuclear alerting is linked to the 1968 invasion of Czechoslovakia.[13] This one also evidently escaped the notice of U.S. intelligence. It involved the intermediate-range ballistic missiles of the SRF in the Ukraine, Byelorussia, and the Baltics. In Byelorussia launch personnel at the missile sites received alert orders a half hour before the invasion was launched. Their orders, which came from the SRF main headquarters in Moscow as well as from Smolensk (the main SRF army headquarters with jurisdiction over these missile forces), moved the missiles from a routine condition of readiness to a condition known as *vysshaia*, usually translated as *increased* in English. Maximum alert status lay only a notch higher. At this middle rung on the ladder a number of quite serious preparations were undertaken, including marrying nuclear warheads with missiles, as was done during the Cuban crisis. The affected forces maintained a tense vigil for three weeks. Strategic rocket forces in other regions of the country apparently were exempted, though they were notified of the possibility of conflict. And the Soviets are alleged to have increased the combat readiness of some ballistic missile submarines.[14]

There was a hiatus in Soviet nuclear alerts until the 1973 Arab-Israeli conflict, except for a minor episode in 1969 when border clashes with China prompted the Soviets to declare a countrywide alert of their air force—much of which was dual capable (that is, capable of delivering conventional or nuclear arms).[15] The deep involvement of the United States in the 1973 war acquired a nuclear dimension when the United States declared a global strategic alert that reportedly went unanswered by the Soviet Union. Press reports and subsequent academic studies of the nuclear aspect of the crisis once again found no signs of any Soviet nuclear reaction, and hence gave no hint of any interaction between the two sides' strategic organizations. But again the conventional wisdom is contradicted by new evidence. The Soviets took steps, according to a Soviet source familiar with the episode, to increase the combat readiness of some groups of the Soviet SRF. A preliminary command was issued to the portion of the rocket forces that needed the most time to prepare for combat. This order was canceled before the procedures were completed, because the U.S. nuclear alert was short.[16] But there is little doubt that an interactive dynamic between the two strategic organizations had been briefly sparked and fueled for a short period.

This litany of alerts of Soviet nuclear forces is probably incomplete. Some thin evidence suggests unusual nuclear activity at the time of the invasion of Afghanistan in 1979, the Polish crisis of 1981, and the period of acute U.S.-Soviet tensions between 1982 and 1984.[17] In addition, as will be discussed in later chapters, the Soviets often conducted large-scale exercises of their nuclear forces, some of which appeared unusual enough to generate apprehension among U.S. government observers. In sum, the strategic organizations' history reveals a propensity to raise the alert level of nuclear forces in real emergencies and emergency exercises. This inclination has led to far more interaction between the organizations than the historical record has revealed. The risk of escalatory interaction is not just an abstract idea; it was a real phenomenon during the cold war.

Analyzing the Historical and Contemporary Risk

The danger of nuclear inadvertence carried in such crisis dynamics was actually considered by practitioners of cold war diplomacy to be exploitable. Henry Kissinger argued that what seems balanced and safe in a crisis is often the most risky because a too temperate, deliberate, and predictable course allows the adversary to match every move, thereby prolonging the conditions of inherent risk. His prescription was to exploit the adversary's reluctance to play nuclear roulette: by escalating "rapidly and brutally to a point where the opponent can no longer afford to experiment," the crisis may be brought to a quick and favorable resolution.[18] Kissinger practiced this philosophy of crisis management during the 1973 Middle East crisis by declaring a global U.S. nuclear alert in the hope that it would deter the Soviets from intervening unilaterally to save the trapped Egyptian army. The alert appeared less a threat to start a nuclear war should the Soviets land troops than a ploy to convince the Soviets of our willingness, if necessary, to run a risk of nuclear war in order to prevail.[19]

In the post–cold war era, the traditional rivals aspire to minimize the risk of nuclear inadvertence by avoiding crises, strengthening safeguards, and making their vast strategic organizations less prone to volatile interaction in a crisis.

This transformation of the cold war political and military rivalry makes it difficult indeed to conjure up a plausible scenario of a future crisis that would bring the old adversaries to the brink of nuclear war. Yet caution is in order. Past crises have erupted with sudden unexpectedness, and scripts of those historical surprises would also have been difficult to write beforehand. The peculiar character and causes of these events have been understood only in hindsight.

The domestic crisis inside the former Soviet Union might be one potential source of rising nuclear tensions. The cohesion of what was once the Soviet nuclear command and control system depends in part on the ability of the Soviet Union's successor states and the military to cope with their severe social, economic, and political problems. The present prognosis is somewhat gloomy. Festering disputes between the governments increasingly threaten to dismember the Commonwealth of Independent States and break up the unified nuclear command system. Other fissures in the system that might occur would cause even greater alarm in the West—irreconcilable disputes among the various leaders over their relative command authority; the illicit seizure of nuclear control during a coup, especially if accompanied by unusual changes in the combat disposition of strategic nuclear forces; lapses of control down the chain of command; and worst of all, the illicit firing of nuclear weapons.

Such developments would undoubtedly cause the United States to consider taking military precautions. From a strictly military standpoint, it would seem only prudent to heighten the alert status of U.S. forces if CIS nuclear forces appeared to be spinning out of control. In the extreme case of the actual use of even a single weapon because of a failure of negative control, the U.S. command and control system would be strongly inclined to adopt the maximum alert stance.

In considering such contemporary scenarios and their implications, or in analyzing the historical risk of inadvertence, the two models discussed next are helpful.

Models I and II: Basic Models of Unstable Crisis Interactions

Understanding a problem invariably begins with a simple model that usually contains a sizable element of speculation. Two such models that have been developed shed considerable light on the instability of crisis interaction.

SECURITY DILEMMA MODEL. One of the models builds on a popular academic thesis known as the *security dilemma*, which helps explain the phenomenon of arms racing.[20] Adversaries exist in an anarchic, Hobbesian world. One state's gain in security achieved through growth in its armaments is another state's loss. The second state is compelled to fortify its strength, which then redounds to the first state's disadvantage. That spurs another round of arms expansion. The cycle repeats itself endlessly, leaving all sides worse off than they were at the start. Although each increase in armaments is deliberate and rational from the standpoint of each state, the collective dynamic is unmanageable and irrational.

States cannot exit from this spiral model's structural predicament. An analogous process occurs between the command and control systems of nuclear-armed adversaries. As command and control systems strive to project a credible threat of retaliation to deter an enemy attack, the combat readiness of opposing forces inexorably creeps upward. The result is a growing capability to mount a sudden attack, even in peacetime, that threatens the command and control systems themselves. The systems react by further shortening their reaction times. This cycle of mutually reactive escalation in peacetime combat readiness is far easier to start than stop. In a crisis, the process intensifies until states reach the flashpoint of preemption. Sheer momentum is the predominant force, not statecraft.

This tidy model, the security dilemma, doubtless contains a grain of truth and probably captures a major dynamic of crisis interaction. However, it takes an overly mechanistic, reductionist view of policymaking. The destinies of states are sealed by rigid rules of choice that invariably produce spiraling escalation.[21]

This excessive determinism threatens the validity of the model's predictions. Virtuous leaders in real life not only seek an escape from constraints but frequently succeed, particularly in time of severe stress. Flexibility remains the watchword during such periods. Policymakers are sometimes keenly aware of the security dilemma and actually weigh the trade-off between preparing for war and not provoking it. In some crisis situations, they may resist pressure to raise alert levels in order to reassure an adversary of nonaggressive intent.

At any rate, decisions affecting preparations for war are unlikely to conform to any theory as deterministic as the security dilemma. It banishes the cunning political animal from the scene, leaving no room for the uncertainties of political reaction to strategic warning or for unexpected twists and turns in crisis interactions. At the same time, its parsimony ignores all of the mundane real-world mechanisms that regulate the activities of nuclear forces.

ORGANIZATIONAL MODEL. The second mainstream model that purports to illuminate the difficulties command and control systems would have in preventing the outbreak of inadvertent war during a crisis is the organizational model.[22] It skirts the dilemmas of choice facing policymakers and focuses instead on the complexities of aligning military operations with formulated policy. While leaders struggle to craft policies that strike an appropriate balance between reassurance and threat, large military organizations must somehow be harnessed to the chosen course.

In order for a nation's leaders to balance reassurance and threat, the leaders must be able to exercise both negative and positive control over the nuclear command and control system. As discussed in chapter 1, the aim of negative control is to prevent the unintended use of nuclear weapons. Unauthorized launch of nuclear weapons is the most extreme example. A mishap resulting in accidental detonation of a nuclear weapon is another example. Authorized launch induced by faulty intelligence—for instance, spurious indications of nuclear attack generated by early-warning sensors—can also be understood as a failure of negative control; national policy hardly sanctions the use of nuclear weapons in response to electronic apparitions. Loss of negative control can occur in numerous other ways, sometimes in a rather subtle fashion; for example, military organizations generating their forces to peak readiness might take extreme measures that overstep the bounds envisaged, much less approved, by higher authority.

Positive control requires the command and control systems to project a convincing performance of the wartime mission and to prosecute the mission if ordered by proper national authority. Failure to perform this positive function might stem from subordinates' disbelief when given orders, or from insubordination. A host of other command dysfunctions are more probable causes of such lapses: military planners misinterpret guidance or draw up infeasible plans, plans derail because of bad intelligence on the adversary's strength and reaction, unforeseen complications disrupt force coordination, and so forth. An untimely communications outage is perhaps the best example. Positive control over emergency military operations would obviously suffer if policymakers were unable to disseminate orders setting the terms of alert, rules of engagement, or other operational parameters. It would fail catastrophically in the event of an enemy attack that decapitated the command system or destroyed communications needed to disseminate launch authorization. Positive control is the critical linchpin of deterrence.

The organizational model sees the risk of inadvertent war depending on the ability of command systems to preserve strict operational control (negative control) while simultaneously undertaking preparations for war (positive control). The model sees many hazards in the tension between these twin aims of crisis operations. The main hazard lies in the scale and complexity of combat preparations.

Serious preparation for war imposes elaborate and time-consuming requirements on the military establishments. From a military standpoint preparations should begin early into a crisis and should conform to preestablished plans of action. Efficient management of the details furthermore depends on substantial decentralization of authority down the chain of command. In contrast, political leaders wrestle with the inevitable mismatch between preplanned military options and the broader exigencies of an unfolding crisis. A suitable response could from a political standpoint require plans to be drawn up from scratch.[23]

Policymakers also hesitate to delegate authority. Decentralization reduces almost by definition political influence over the priorities assigned to positive and negative control. And policymakers worry that military organizations if left to their own devices tend to skew the balance toward getting ready for war at the expense of safety. The risk of a failure of negative control increases, and at the same time the noisy background of energetic military preparations for war drowns out or discredits political signals meant to allay the adversary's fear of attack. Political leaders therefore habitually seek to impose sharp constraints on military autonomy during a crisis.

It is not easy, however, to accommodate the political desire for flexibility and ensure strict military adherence to the precise formulations of policymakers. Except in a narrow legal sense national policy officials do not possess total control over the conduct of large-scale military organizations. They can set only the general terms of emergency operations. The operational details that affect the balance between positive and negative control (and between reassurance and threat) are too extensive, too diverse, and too remote to be regulated by executive edict. With respect to the United States in particular, subordinate commanders manage most of the details, and as a crisis intensifies, the details get bumped further down the chain of command for digestion.[24]

Although the Soviet nuclear forces were kept under tighter central control (in both the positive and negative senses) than their U.S. counterparts, managing them in a crisis would undoubtedly have posed similar difficulties. Performing the twin tasks of negative and positive control would have been even harder if political dissension had been rife among top leaders as it was in 1991.

From the perspective of the organizational model the specter of inadvertent war appears in the form of dynamic interactions between semiautonomous units of the opposing military establishments. These diffuse operations inevitably deviate from intended patterns. As units depart from familiar peacetime routines designed mainly to ensure negative control and institute less familiar procedures designed to ensure combat readiness, the internal priorities of the military postures begin to shift from negative to positive control in a way that is too diffuse to manage or even to monitor centrally. Furthermore, the transition degrades both types of control because the military units involved lack the experience to solve the novel problems that new situations present. Their repertoire of emergency procedures is not adequately suited to the circumstances, or the procedures might never have been practiced under realistic conditions. Inappropriate procedures and rules of engagement or flawed implementation, combined with a strong instinct for military units to preserve themselves at all costs, lead to a loss of control by political leaders. The delicate diplomacy of policymakers seeking a way out of the security dilemma is imperiled, overridden, and wrecked in the substratum of operational interaction between jittery combatant organizations.

Model III: Toward a Command System Model of Nuclear Inadvertence

A model is needed that captures more of the actual command and control systems that mold the operational behavior on each side. An overview of such a model follows. It is fleshed out in the next two chapters with richer descriptions of the U.S. and Soviet systems. This model represents the adverse effects of crisis conditions on negative control. Crisis here simply means heightened tensions caused by some confluence of events or even a single major shock that creates a distinct possibility of direct conflict between the opposing strategic organizations. Although it seems most likely that a future crisis would be triggered by some nuclear incident inside the former Soviet Union that spills over into the international arena, the model does not rest on a specific scenario, and it applies to the past as well as the future.

The model has each of the command and control systems exhibiting a distinctive pattern of behavior reflecting its basic attributes. The behavior pattern is produced by two key attributes. The first concerns the *operative goals* of the respective command systems. The second concerns the *balance between centralization and decentralization* in the managerial practices of the systems.

At the most general level, the operative goals of both systems coincide. Each is designed to ensure both negative and positive control.

These twin requirements interfere with each other to a considerable extent, forcing the respective systems to choose a point on the continuum between "guns tight" and "guns ready." During the cold war that point of compromise was closer to guns ready in the U.S. case, though in both systems the balance between the aims leaned strongly toward negative control in peacetime. Strategic organizations on both sides supported positive control through training, war games and readiness exercises, maintenance, and combat-alert operations, but the normal regimen fell far below maximum capacity. Economic and safety considerations took precedence over constant high readiness to prosecute wartime missions.

The point of compromise also varies with circumstances. If the international situation makes military conflict a distinct if not an imminent possibility, the prevailing priority will shift quite sharply in the direction of positive control. Once it does, this priority activates a set of specific wartime goals that were markedly different in each command system before the end of the cold war. Each system also pursued these goals in a markedly different way.

U.S. strategic forces had to be prepared to inflict severe, comprehensive damage to the array of targets in the former Soviet Union in four distinct categories formally established by national guidance. Target coverage constituted the critical variable in the U.S. command system during a crisis. It was the raison d'être of the strategic nuclear organization of the United States.

Command functions serving negative control took precedence over target coverage in peacetime operations. Functions serving positive control—routine training, alert operations, and maintenance—were modest in scope and tempo. A serious crisis would have elevated the priority of target coverage. During a crisis the principal function of the U.S. nuclear command and control system was to act as a force multiplier in the obliteration of enemy targets.

As discussed in the following chapters, the immediate consequences of imbuing the U.S. strategic organization with this purpose were (1) the rapid generation of nonalert strategic forces to full alert status; and (2) the adoption of launch on warning. Both consequences reflect the demanding requirements of target coverage levied on the organization. The requirements were so ambitious that the full inventory of strategic weapons had to be readied for combat. In the same vein, if the organization attempted to ride out an attack before retaliating, it would have suffered such severe command disruption and force attrition that it would have been effectively neutralized in terms of target coverage, the core value against which it evaluated its performance. To fulfill its mission, therefore, the U.S. command system had to anticipate an enemy attack in time to put all strategic forces on alert and prevent their destruction on the ground.

The simplicity, singularity, and constancy of the organization's goal (maintaining comprehensive target coverage regardless of the situation and fulfilling the targeting objectives in wartime) heavily skewed U.S. command and control system toward decentralization.[25] Because there was no doubt about the U.S. response to nuclear attack, the organization could preprogram the responses of subunits and distribute authority down the chain of command.

The organization evolved a chain of authority over nuclear combat operations running directly from the National Command Authorities— the president or the secretary of defense or their duly constituted successors—to the nuclear combat commanders in the field, a chain that diminished the ability of the highest military body (the Joint Chiefs of Staff) to replan and redirect nuclear operations. It also vested its intermediate- and low-level nuclear commanders with wide discretion to change the disposition of their forces in anticipation of possible conflict. As will be discussed in the next chapter, regardless of the alert terms set by national leaders, every combat commander in the field bore responsibility for the survival of his forces and the success of his mission if war broke out. Considerable discretionary authority to implement alert measures in fact extended down to the lowest echelon in the chain of nuclear command. In certain circumstances the individual weapon commanders had the independent authority to take all of the steps on all of the alert checklists applicable to their particular units. All this diffuse alert activity in a crisis served explicitly or implicitly the larger goal of the organization: blanket coverage of enemy targets.

U.S. command arrangements were highly decentralized and permissive compared with the Soviet arrangements. In stark contrast to the U.S. nuclear command and control system, the top echelon of Soviet politico-military command retained virtually complete control over nuclear operations (see chapter 4). Negative control was strict, if not ironclad, and positive control was centrally exercised. No significant authority to alert or maneuver, much less fire, nuclear forces resided below the top leadership. The top echelon controlled even the premises of decision throughout the command system. It was also physically harder for a solitary node of the Soviet command system to issue alert or launch orders than it was in the U.S. system.

The intense concentration of authority and operational control of Soviet nuclear forces was not just a microcosm of Soviet political culture or a simple reflection of stylistic preference. Unlike the U.S. system, which tended to invoke spontaneously a preestablished objective (comprehensive target coverage) and plan (the single integrated operational plan, or SIOP) at the onset of a crisis, the Soviet system assumed that preplanned options had a short shelf life. The system considered them so perishable in a crisis that the organization's highest priority was to tailor a new menu of options to suit the particulars of the situation.[26]

This approach to security planning demanded a centralized command structure with a large support staff and a vast infrastructure at the top. The Soviet politico-military leadership bore full responsibility for monitoring the international situation and the status of enemy and friendly forces, for formulating politico-military strategy, and for coordinating the actions of subordinate units down the chain of command in rather minute detail. For subordinate commanders to show much initiative would have meant arrogating to themselves a security burden that only the highest levels of government could properly shoulder. Only the U.S. command system, with its rigid nuclear missions and plans, benefited from such decentralization. The Soviet command, therefore, used elaborate technical and organizational mechanisms to ensure that orders sent to combat units were scrupulously implemented, and received extensive feedback (quite automated in the case of land-based strategic missile forces) with which to monitor the implementation of prescribed tasks. Tremendous inertia tranquilized the subordinate echelons, which only detailed instructions and blessings from the top could overcome.

As discussed in chapter 4, the paramount goal of the Soviet command system was thus simply to protect itself from attack and strictly preserve the leadership's prerogatives to direct operations. The system thus devoted vast resources to preserving its vital functions—intelligence collection, warning, decisionmaking, operational planning, dissemination of instructions, and enforcement of directives—so that it could respond flexibly to abrupt changes in its operating environment.

The nuclear forces themselves, though assigned wartime missions in peacetime, were only provisionally committed to the missions. Unlike the vast majority of U.S. strategic forces, they were not wedded to an established objective and plan of execution. The Soviet command system valued the nuclear arsenal far more as a reserve stockpile that could be tapped to support new objectives as they emerged.

Soviet nuclear forces thus represented a command multiplier, the inverse of the U.S. case, in which command served as a force multiplier. In the U.S. posture command and control increased the utility of the forces in carrying out a one-time, prearranged plan whose essential objective was to destroy a long list of targets. In the Soviet posture the forces increased the elasticity of command—the retention, elaboration, and wholesale reconstruction of response options according to the evolving demands of the situation.

Revised View of Nuclear Crisis Dynamics

This comparative sketch, which is elaborated on in the next two chapters, points up more inadequacies in the first two models of crisis instability. The organizational model assumes a dynamic interaction fueled by highly decentralized decisionmaking on both sides. It accurately portrays the U.S. side as decentralized, but incorrectly attributes this trait to Soviet command and control.

The security dilemma model also slides past an important difference between the two systems. The model pictures the adversaries as two command and control systems with the same goals and perceptual filters in a hypersensitive dynamic of mutual reactive escalation. In reality, the systems pursued dissimilar goals and would have exhibited more complex and asymmetrical behavior. U.S. nuclear operations were driven by targeting requirements. The paramount priority of Soviet crisis operations was to preserve a functional command and control system with strict central control. The respective systems' interaction defied easy prediction. The crisis actions of one side may or may not have impinged on the other side's dominant security objective, and hence may or may not have induced a reaction.

Model III, by contrast, predicts that military operations undertaken by the United States that put in jeopardy the Soviet command and control system, or any other environmental condition that produced this result (including domestic stress), would have been especially disturbing to the Soviet system. Such a threat would have run the greatest risk of inducing a spontaneous, volatile reaction. The sensitivity of the Soviets to a growing threat to their command system was greater than their sensitivity to other types of threats. The specter of a sudden collapse of command was their worst fear and could have provoked them to take drastic action even if their force structure remained secure. By the same token the Soviets could tolerate growing threats to their force structure so long as the situation posed no serious threat to their command system.

Regarding the United States, Model III predicts that the most spontaneous, energetic U.S. reaction would have occurred when Soviet operations or other factors drove U.S. coverage of targets below the required minimum. Such operations could have ranged from crisis dispersal of mobile nuclear forces from their peacetime garrison locations, a procedure that would have diminished the effectiveness of U.S. nuclear strikes, to preparations for the immediate launch of strategic forces against U.S. strategic forces. The latter would have threatened the survival and coordination of U.S. retaliatory forces, jeopardizing their ability to ensure the systematic destruction of Soviet targets. A growing threat to the U.S. command system and force structure could have been tolerated so long as U.S. decisionmakers could have counteracted it with such palliatives as the predelegation of release authority and launch on warning. Analysis clearly indicates, however, that under no circumstances could the U.S. strategic organization have met its requirements for target coverage if either the command system or the force structure rode out a significant portion of a Soviet attack before initiating retaliation, let alone if both absorbed the full weight of an attack before attempting to strike back.

There are other implications of the basic dissimilarities in U.S. and Soviet command structure that increase our understanding of their crisis interaction. It appears that U.S. alerting was more rigid but faster than Soviet alerting, mainly because of the greater decentralization of U.S. nuclear command. The centralization of Soviet command and control rendered the system relatively ponderous, but it afforded greater capacity to tailor the Soviet posture to fit national objectives.

The U.S. strategic command organization was more narrowly attuned to the adversary's military disposition and was inclined to react quickly to changes that adversely affected target coverage, so much so that it could direct energetic responses long before U.S. political leaders had fashioned a coherent crisis policy. The U.S. system was also more likely than its Soviet counterpart to shed safeguards as it labored to project a convincing performance of its wartime mission, and more likely to do so without informing the political leadership. Its preoccupation with comprehensive target coverage also made it a blunt instrument for dealing with smaller contingencies.

CHAPTER THREE

Characteristic Behavior of the U.S. Command System

FOR THE U.S. command and control system the paramount mission in time of crisis was to achieve a high level of what military planners call *damage expectancy*:[1] the ability in the face of any adversity to demolish the full spectrum of targets in the former Soviet Union.[2]

Damage expectancy was defined in specific quantitative terms. Top U.S. civilian and military officials stipulated target coverage requirements, which were laid out in broad outline in national policy guidance documents. Military planners converted the general prose of the guidance into specific quantitative damage expectancy requirements for all major categories of targets in the single integrated operational plan (SIOP).[3]

These specific requirements constituted the essence of U.S. nuclear strategy. They were binding on and pivotal to U.S. strategic assessment, planning, and operations. When American military officials reported on the overall state of deterrence, their bottom line was a summary of the ability of SIOP forces to meet the damage expectancy obligations. The Reagan era "window of vulnerability," for example, represented the declining ability of SIOP forces to destroy the required number of targets in one of the four major categories—namely, Soviet nuclear forces. When U.S. officials raised an alarm over threats to some component of the U.S. nuclear posture—for instance, the SS-18 ICBM Mod 5 threat to Minuteman silos—their frame of reference was the adverse impact on U.S. coverage of targets in the former Soviet Union. When they testified on behalf of new weapons programs, they stressed the weapon's potential contribution to damage expectancy. The MX missile, for example, was highly touted as a means of rejuvenating damage expectancy against Soviet nuclear forces (very hard ICBM silos in particular) and thereby closing the "window of vulnerability." And when the U.S. command and control system operated its deployed combat forces, its almost exclusive goal through the spectrum of conflict from simple political crisis to wartime implementation of the SIOP was to be able to meet its narrow, technical damage expectancy requirements.

The hallmark of the U.S. command and control system, therefore, was its acute sensitivity to any changes in damage expectancy. It regarded a crisis situation as truly critical and unstable when events drove, or threatened to drive, damage expectancy below minimum acceptability. When target coverage dipped below this minimum for whatever reasons, the system was designed to sound the tocsin and act promptly to bring coverage back within tolerance. The system also monitored the environment for signs of imminent enemy attack and other adverse developments that needed to be anticipated and acted upon lest the unfolding events degrade target coverage.

When a drop (actual or imminent) occurred in the coverage of any of the four target categories delineated in the war plan, the command and control system followed a set of decision rules to select one of the preprogrammed action sequences in its response repertory. After performing this procedure, it monitored any changes. If damage expectancy did not return to its proper level, the bad reading triggered a different preprogrammed operation. The trial and error process would continue until a response that restored target coverage to normal was found or until the system ran out of options.[4]

Unlike the Soviet posture, the U.S. posture enslaved command to the goals of a master target plan. The elegance of the SIOP and of the supporting command arrangements lay in this simplicity; they were dedicated to ensuring that the strategic forces fulfilled their single, narrowly defined technical objective: blanket coverage of the Soviet target base. Command and control was not operationally saddled with other functions.[5] It was therefore able to cope with the pervasive confusion of complex crisis situations simply by ignoring information that was not pertinent to its critical mission. The system obviously required a rich menu of responses in order to adapt in crisis environments. Its repertory must have included a set of responses that matched the variety of environmental disturbances it could encounter. But the system's narrow focus enabled it to prepare contingency plans for many such disturbances.

Tensions in the System: Target Coverage versus Crisis Management

Implicit in this characterization of U.S. operational behavior is the possibility that successful adaptation by the command and control system could have heightened tensions and made a crisis less manageable. Dexterity in preserving target coverage might have provoked hostile Soviet reactions. The command and control system was in fact so rigid along dimensions other than target coverage that it was not adept in managing crises. Thus certain action sequences may have proved maladaptive vis-à-vis the United States' other security objectives or vis-à-vis the goal of multistate stability. For example, circumstances might have warranted a moderation of threat for the sake of mutual reassurance; establishing or maintaining blanket coverage of Soviet targets would have had the opposite effect.

U.S. political leaders occasionally complained about the system's bias toward large strike options designed for the wholesale obliteration of targets and pressed for modifications that provided greater flexibility to pursue other goals such as preventing escalation and terminating conflict. But with rare exceptions such modifications never took root in command system procedures. This reflected a schism between the civilians, who were concerned with matters of crisis diplomacy and conflict resolution, and the military planners, who emphasized projecting a convincing performance of the wartime mission.

The tension between political flexibility and damage expectancy was intensified by the approach taken by the command and control system to the operational requirements of SIOP targeting.[6] The system was not configured to deliver just a few weapons in retaliation against whatever targets commanders choose to select. To achieve comprehensive and efficient coverage of the targets it deemed important, the command and control system worked out systematic target assignments for all deployed weapons on active status except for a relatively small portion in the strategic reserve force (about 1,000 warheads in 1990). Moreover, the strategic command system was committed to producing an attack sequence that enhanced the penetration of piloted aircraft (involving more than 100 defense suppression warheads on land- and sea-based ballistic missiles in 1990) and to minimizing the destruction its own weapons might have done to one another.[7]

Because systematic target allocation and attack sequencing involve large-scale integration of information, they require considerable time and a substantial flow of information. Preparations must be made in advance of any crisis, and the resulting plans cannot be rapidly altered. Since it is very unlikely that the planning and communications capability of a command system could survive direct assault, the effectiveness of SIOP retaliation depended on the U.S. command and control system's adherence to previously established plans. These must have been executed before disruption of the command system and widespread damage to U.S. individual weapons. Similarly, the established plans could not have been rapidly altered to accommodate the ad hoc targeting schemes of political authorities without compromising the basic mission of U.S. nuclear forces.

The most noteworthy episodes in the clash between political flexibility and damage expectancy were the efforts to program mini-options (called limited nuclear options, or LNOs) into the war plans, to provide for their rapid implementation in a crisis, and to move a small contingent of strategic nuclear forces out of the SIOP and into a special reserve force. Limited nuclear options were envisaged as a menu of preplanned but small-scale pre-SIOP operations (a single weapon to many tens of weapons against predetermined targets, as opposed to the many hundreds of weapons released under the smallest SIOP option). The special reserve force (variously called an elite or ad hoc force) was to be put at the disposal of the national command authorities for use whenever and however they deemed fit. These efforts were not very successful, however, even though they entailed only a slight modification of command arrangements. Earmarking a portion of the strategic forces for purposes other than damage expectancy in order to increase political flexibility during a crisis (any time prior to the exercise of the SIOP) met strenuous resistance from military quarters.[8]

Despite some pressure, admittedly inconstant, from political leaders over the past three decades, the command and control system retained its narrow compass. Military planners conceded little. At the time of this writing, only a handful of alert weapons had been set aside for limited nuclear options.[9] Most of these options existed only on paper. Only a few had been assigned alert forces and programmed operationally to permit rapid and smooth execution on command. Similarly, planners recently set aside only a nominal ad hoc reserve force (about 150 weapons in 1990).

The lion's share of the strategic forces continued to be rigidly committed to preplanned SIOP missions and to fulfilling the corresponding requirements of damage expectancy. Of the remainder, which was a potential source of weapons for fashioning additional limited or ad hoc options, most belonged to the strategic reserve force. Military planners, however, did not create the strategic reserves to support pre-SIOP missions and might have objected to tapping into it for that purpose. The strategic reserve force was earmarked for use only following a strategic nuclear exchange. Furthermore, the few hundred weapons in this reserve status in peacetime were actually assigned SIOP targets, though targets of relatively low priority—for instance, factories in Eastern Europe. (This reserve force grew severalfold under conditions of generated alert. The force would then have included dedicated land- and sea-based missile forces and crisis-generated bomber forces plus some bomber forces that would have joined the ready reserve after completing and recovering from an initial SIOP mission.) The strategic reserve force was provisionally committed to the SIOP and was arguably off limits for pre-SIOP operations.[10]

In theory, of course, the National Command Authorities had the legal right to tap into any and all of the forces, including those that were integral to the SIOP, and demand their reallocation to limited nuclear options or ad hoc missions. Nevertheless, political actors had been reluctant to meddle in this arena of nuclear planning. Moreover, any successful attempt to exercise their legitimate prerogatives in the midst of crisis would have required considerable political will.

Military planners made some additional, albeit minor, concessions to civilian concerns about flexibility. By arranging for damage to be inflicted in stages instead of all at once and by offering options in the SIOP designed to limit collateral casualties among noncombatants, military planners enlarged the scope for politico-diplomatic maneuvering to control escalation and terminate conflict short of all-out war. Still, the established SIOP mission—target coverage—took absolute priority over such "extraneous" considerations. Political authorities would thus have been bound by the contours of the war plan rather than the other way around.

SIOP flexibility was essentially reduced to dispatching large groupings of forces aimed at one or another of the target categories while withholding large groupings aimed at the rest, and to overlaying some politico-diplomatic rationale onto the chosen combination. The command system further reduced the latitude for choice by disallowing many hypothetical combinations. For instance, an attack solely on war-supporting industrial targets was not an option. This target category could not be attacked except as part of a comprehensive strike against the full array of military targets. Similarly, the menu of SIOP options did not include a surgical strike at the Soviet leadership. A full counterforce strike had to accompany it. Moreover, no option had been created to limit noncombatant casualties in an attack on Soviet leadership.

Such rigid structuring implicitly acknowledged the strong prior commitment of the strategic organization to preexisting plans. There was little expectation that a nuclear war would involve extensive mission replanning to accommodate any novel notions of intra-war diplomacy. The operational plan was virtually etched in stone and the mode of execution was preordained. Such arrangements ensured systematic target coverage, but severely constrained political choices.

These constraints on flexibility were minor, however, compared with the constraint the obsession with damage expectancy imposed on the timing of nuclear release. The gravest consequence of allowing damage expectancy to govern the U.S. strategic posture was the tremendous pressure it put on the command and control system to deliver a preemptive blow based on strategic warning, or to launch the forces on tactical warning of an enemy strike. As argued later in this chapter, and in chapter 7, the pressure for rapid reaction or literal launch on warning not only drastically reduced flexibility but also increased the risk of nuclear inadvertence.

Decentralization of Mission Planning and Execution

That these constraints on political flexibility during a crisis remained in place throughout the cold war was a manifestation of the second basic feature of U.S. command and control that had systematic effects on behavior: the diffusion of authority. The command system was a highly decentralized, loose confederation of semiautonomous subsystems.

Oversight from the top civilian authorities has never been strict in the arena of nuclear operations.[11] By inattention civilian leaders surrendered most of their prerogatives to the professional military. Military planners perpetuated the dominance of target coverage over other goals, set the damage requirements, fashioned the operational plan for meeting the requirements, and governed combat activities in support of the plan.

The Joint Strategic Targeting Planning Staff in Omaha, in consultation with the Joint Chiefs of Staff, built the strategic war plan.[12] One division of the JSTPS specified the target base (the so-called National Strategic Target List) and the "ground zero" locations that ensured full coverage of the target base. Another division—the SIOP division—assigned strategic weapons and scheduled their appointments with the ground zero locations. The war planners of JSTPS and JCS basically determined whether the SIOP provided for enough damage to the Soviet target base to satisfy national guidance. They would examine the issue every year and on occasion make necessary changes to operational plans.[13] The strategic war planners also strongly influenced the number and type of targets put into the SIOP and the allocation of U.S. forces to SIOP versus non-SIOP missions. Control over any one of these variables—damage expectancy requirements, the SIOP target list, or assets assigned to the SIOP—would give military planners enormous influence on how forces are generated in a crisis and how they are employed in wartime.

Military planners also protected the high priority given to target coverage in nuclear operations by zealously guarding their monopoly on mission planning. Although their dominance in this sphere stemmed partially from statutory restrictions that limited civilian access to war plans,[14] civilian leaders had long deferred to the military in drawing up the plans. According to Janne Nolan, civilians were cut out of the loop on such important matters as the periodic SIOP revisions that often expanded the target list. She found that the "revisions reports" that explained changes in the SIOP, changes that required approval by the secretary of defense or even the president, had never actually been delivered to political authorities until the late 1980s.[15] The damage expectancy criteria used at the JSTPS were also allegedly closely held in Omaha.[16] As a consequence, the consonance of the SIOP with political guidance, or the lack thereof, was opaque from the viewpoint of top political leaders. This left the president and his civilian advisers at the mercy of contingency plans over which they had little intellectual mastery or practical leverage in a crisis. Senior policy officials were not sufficiently tu-

tored in the plans that regulated nuclear operations and were not sufficiently equipped to bend the operations to their will.

In a crisis civilian authorities had the formal right to dictate the terms
of alerting and executing the forces. In a nuclear emergency, though,
preestablished plans for a strike against a full array of Soviet targets
would have taken precedence down the chain of command unless the
civilian leaders actively intervened to override the process.

Vast latitude existed throughout the nuclear chain of command to
prepare units for a comprehensive strike. As argued above, the generation of dormant forces to high-alert status and other changes in force
disposition would have largely been semiautomatic, programmed responses to the threat of war. They were designed to establish and preserve
target coverage and could occur with little oversight from civilian leaders.

Senior military commanders have always had almost carte blanche to
set the alert levels of forces under their control.[17] These commanders
received the intelligence and warning data on which to base such decisions at the same time the data flowed to political authorities, and they
were ultimately responsible for determining whether to increase combat
readiness. Using his own alert code words and communications, the
commander of the Strategic Air Command, for example, had the authority to flush the entire bomber force into the air and send it half the
distance to its targets in the Soviet Union. The senior duty controller in
the SAC command post had the authority to order the bomber crews to
scramble to their planes and start their engines. The protective launch
of the crucial airborne command posts in SAC as well as other commands
could be flushed on the authority of relatively junior commanders.[18] The
decentralized U.S. command system permitted even individual weapons
commanders to take virtually all alert steps short of firing weapons.[19]
And orders affecting the disposition of U.S. nuclear forces flowed
through military channels with marginal civilian oversight. Central control over these adjustments rested on the principle of negative rather than
positive control. That is, the diffuse adaptations occurred unless explicitly prohibited by political authority. Yet the existing arrangements did
not provide extensive feedback to the political leaders.

Decentralization was not without its virtues, chiefly its adaptability,
so long as target coverage remained the overarching objective. The distribution down the entire chain of command of provisional authority,
along with conditional rules of action, was probably the optimal command and control structure for fulfilling a one-dimensional wartime mis-

sion. Furthermore, the assimilation of this single purpose by the entire strategic organization facilitated tacit coordination of activities. It even permitted units to independently improvise judicious responses when established procedures failed to maintain damage expectancy, without sacrificing overall coordination.

The virtues of decentralization can become liabilities, however. The president and his top advisers would have experienced enormous frustration if they had tried to substitute new goals—for instance, preventing further escalation in alert readiness, or reinstating the tightest possible safeguards against unauthorized launch—for the goal of preserving target coverage. The U.S. command and control system lacked the internal logic and procedural mechanisms to switch gears. The potential existed for the preprogrammed and preauthorized process of organizational adaptation to gain irreversible momentum.

The lineage of the strategic war plan goes back many administrations. Successive political generations vetted and endorsed (though all too perfunctorily) the same basic policies that governed strategic operations. Through repeated reviews and affirmations over the span of several decades, the long-standing policies, which included contingency plans for devolving nuclear release authority to military commanders, gained legitimacy. Civilian leaders would have found it difficult to challenge this legacy without incurring high political costs.

Nuclear Predelegation

The command and control system's devotion to damage expectancy and the consequent undermining of political flexibility and negative control are clearly illustrated by the long-standing policy of predelegation. Although the evidence is somewhat sketchy, little doubt exists that past presidents, beginning with Dwight D. Eisenhower, delegated to key military commanders the authority to carry out nuclear war plans under some circumstances. Predelegated nuclear authority ensured that nuclear weapons could be used in the absence of a direct, timely order from the president or his successor.

Analyst Scott Sagan has unearthed documents pertaining to an extended "negotiation" among key military officials over the terms of predelegation in the Eisenhower administration.[20] The maneuvering appears to have led to a consensus for giving discretionary release authority to the major nuclear commands—the Air Defense Command (ADCOM), commander in chief, Strategic Air Command (CINCSAC), commander in chief, Atlantic (CINCLANT), commander in chief, Pacific (CINCPAC), and commander in chief, Europe (CINCEUR)—though the Navy initially balked at accepting the policy that "authority to order retaliatory attack may be exercised by CINCSAC if time or circumstances would not permit a decision by the president."[21] (The Army endorsed CINCSAC's rule.) Opinion apparently was badly divided over how far below the level of those commands the authority should be allowed to devolve. However, it is very doubtful that anyone advocated giving the individual launch crews any independent launch authority.

Contrary to some popular opinion, the discretionary authority to fire surely did not devolve to the SSBN, ICBM, or bomber commanders.[22] There were many good reasons for this exclusion. So many loose cannons in the field would have created an unacceptable risk that a nuclear war could begin with an unsanctioned act. Moreover, should deterrence have failed and a nuclear war begun, the goal of terminating it without further escalation would have been severely undercut if such wholesale delegation were permitted. In the same vein, the SSBN crews, for instance, labored under the assumption that their wartime effectiveness depended crucially on hewing to instructions from higher authority. Their counter-value targets (war-supporting industries located mostly in cities) were slated for destruction only as a last resort, and such attacks were likely to be withheld for a lengthy period of time. To take matters into their own hands during a communications outage would have directly contravened established policy, which emphasized the importance of retaining the countervalue option indefinitely to deter Soviet strikes against U.S. cities.

Similarly, SSBN crews with the counterforce mission at the time of war's outbreak understood that the military utility of their weapons would decline if they fired them without orders after waiting in vain for say, several days, for launch orders. Approximately 70 percent of the U.S. arsenal of SLBMs were assigned to nuclear and other military targets in the Soviet Union. The counterforce utility of these weapons would have been much greater if the crews patiently waited for targeting instructions from higher authority. In general, the wholesale delegation of launch authority carries extremely adverse implications for positive as well as negative control. Senior military officials would not have countenanced such arrangements, which threatened their own authority and their ability to ensure uniform coverage of the entire target base. Delegating target selection to the bottom echelon thus ran counter to the one coherent national war aim in existence.

On the other hand, the nuclear command system was so decentralized that individual weapons commanders had considerable latitude not only in deciding to go to maximum alert but also in determining the validity of launch orders that may have arrived incomplete or garbled. The stitching together of message fragments and interpretation of their validity as launch orders were two especially fine arts in U.S. SSBN operations. The ICBM and bomber crews had similar responsibilities.

It was thus likely that nuclear authority was delegated to a level below the CINCs (the unified and specified commanders) but well above the bottom level. During the Eisenhower administration, the CINCSAC, General Thomas Power, lobbied for the right to delegate his release authority to SAC's numbered Air Force commanders (just one level below the CINCSAC). Air Force Chief of Staff General Thomas White assured Power that despite resistance from other services, "we still consider that the president's instructions would permit specific delegation to your Air Force commanders."[23] Meanwhile the CINCPAC pressed for the right to give his subordinate unified commanders and Joint Task Force commanders the authority to initiate atomic strikes in the event of enemy attack by atomic weapons.[24] Furthermore, "they may launch strikes without specific approval from higher authority only after the nationality of the enemy has been positively identified. . . . Atomic strikes will be limited to the geographic area of the probable launching sites and/or attacking forces and to the territory of the nation making the attack." The CINCPAC also sought to give the numbered fleet or numbered Air Force commanders the authority to initiate atomic strikes under the terms described above if friendly ground forces were subjected to enemy atomic attack and numbered Army commanders requested atomic support from the Navy or Air Force.[25]

Reliable confirmation that certain major commands eventually were entrusted with predelegated authority to expend nuclear weapons without the specific approval of the president comes from several sources, including *U.S. Air Force Oral History Interviews*. In an interview in 1978 General Horace Wade said he used to worry that General Power was not stable, a matter of concern to Wade because of "the fact that he had control of so many weapons and weapon systems and could, under certain conditions, launch the force. Back in the days before we had real positive control, SAC had the power to do a lot of things, and it was in his hands, and he knew it."[26] General Power himself testified to Congress in 1960 that arrangements existed for him to launch a retaliatory strike after verifying that an enemy nuclear strike was under way in circumstances in which the president was not available.[27]

In interviews in 1979 with General Lauris Norstad (the CINCEUR through the early 1960s), Norstad said his authority to employ nuclear weapons without the approval of the president was based on an unwritten understanding, and that for him to launch on his own authority "it would have had to be pretty damn serious and urgent because every instinct would have been against it." He further acknowledged that he might not have waited for the enemy to use atomic weapons before he ordered friendly forces to use them. When asked about waiting for enemy use, he responded: "Well, I wouldn't have waited, necessarily, for them to use—I would have waited for them . . . to make a clear, overt act stating that they were going to attack us and destroy us with all means."[28]

In July 1961 President John F. Kennedy received explicit warning that Eisenhower's delegation of authority to use nuclear weapons created "a situation today in which a subordinate commander faced with a substantial Russian military action could start the thermonuclear holocaust on his own initiative if he could not reach you [by failure of communication at either end of the line]."[29] Kennedy did not revoke his predecessor's policy, however. Because he had only been a lieutenant in World War II, he was hesitant to overrule the wisdom of a famous general. A decree from an inexperienced president might appear cavalier and would have courted political disaccreditation by his military establishment, recounted one of Kennedy's key advisers.[30] But, the adviser said, Kennedy also did not renew the previous arrangements, leaving the situation ambiguous during his tenure. During the Cuban missile crisis, the SAC commander, General Power, who apparently had been delegated nuclear authority by Eisenhower, might have believed he possessed emergency nuclear power to launch the SIOP.

Although it cannot be authoritatively established from the public record that nuclear release authority continued to be delegated down the military chain of command during subsequent administrations, there is substantial evidence that it was. In 1976 a retired senior military officer testified to Congress that the commander of the ADCOM possessed authority to use nuclear weapons without the express approval of the president "only under severe restrictions and specific conditions of attack."[31] Interviews with a high-ranking military official conducted for this book revealed more. The authority to use nuclear weapons, indeed to implement the SIOP, was delegated to senior military commanders during the Carter and Reagan administrations. These nuclear CINCs were given the status of "pre-positioned national command authority." They were empowered to authorize a SIOP retaliatory strike and to select the SIOP option to execute. The existence of this arrangement was broadly hinted at by President Jimmy Carter's defense secretary, Harold Brown, who wrote in 1983 that "a decapitating attack should have the effect of making the response an all-out, unrestrained one."[32]

The authority of senior military commanders was reinforced by the fact that President Carter withheld codes from political officials in the chain of presidential succession stipulated by the Presidential Succession Act of 1947, codes they needed to identify themselves as commander in chief. The only exceptions were Vice President Walter Mondale and presumably the secretary of defense, who was a statutory national command authority.[33] By thwarting a legitimate presidential successor's ability to identify himself or herself properly as commander in chief during a crisis, Carter's action would have greatly weakened the functioning of the presidential successor system while empowering the military commanders picked to have predelegated nuclear authority.[34] A former senior civilian official in the Reagan administration, who supported the contention by a high-ranking military official that predelegation still existed during Reagan's second term in office, expressed concern over the fact that the instructions giving SIOP release authority to certain military commanders left the choice of retaliatory options entirely up to their judgment.[35]

The ability of top civilian officials to override such long-standing policies in the midst of a crisis was questionable at best. Doing so would have been complicated by the fact that numerous U.S. military installations possessed all the codes needed to disseminate valid launch orders. The civilian national command authorities did not carry or generate actual launch codes. They merely carried identification codes to be used to establish their identity when in contact with the military.[36] Key command centers of the national military command system actually held the launch authorization codes that would have been sent to the firing units. Furthermore, these centers alone possessed the combinations (the enabling codes) needed by that portion of the U.S. nuclear arsenal that was restrained by hardware locks. Many duplicates of all these authorization and enabling codes were distributed throughout the nuclear command system.[37] In sum, the nation's political leadership had widely dispersed the physical control over the unlocking and firing of nuclear weapons.

Although it is uncertain whether the structure, procedures, and biases of the U.S. command system would have overridden policy direction from political quarters, the potential for political and military purposes to collide was substantial. Reconciling divergent aims could have been a serious problem of crisis management. As a crisis deepened, this tension would have intensified as the command and control system encountered more threats to its critical variable, target coverage, and sought to overcome them through highly decentralized responses. This diffuse activity was less and less likely to be governed by timely guidance from an increasingly overloaded and sluggish civilian leadership.

Since the president and his civilian staff could not easily have orchestrated the extensive operational activity under way during a major crisis, their ability to govern the forces depended on other means. In particular, the way in which top leaders framed the core security problem at hand and characterized the threat to U.S. national interests could have been crucially important. Civilian leaders could have influenced the U.S. military establishment's perception of threat and thereby affected the command system's propensity to begin serious preparations for war. If policymakers discounted the danger of war, then military organizations would have tended to remain calm. For instance, the CINCPAC realized that the 1973 global nuclear alert was not serious after he received instructions not to take any alert measures that would incur economic costs, such as generating nuclear forces undergoing overhaul at the time.[38]

If, on the other hand, policymakers made clear they feared war in a brewing crisis, the command and control system would have been encouraged to focus on its wartime mission, generate forces, and prepare for the quick release of weapons. The steep ascent to the summit of combat readiness would have strained the ability of the command system to preserve strict operational control.

The savvy manipulation of these cues early into a crisis arguably offered civilian officials the most political leverage over the U.S. strategic organization. Despite this leverage the extensive decentralization of authority over U.S. military forces ran inherent risks that operations would deviate from the top leadership's desired course. In a comparative analysis of the Cuban missile crisis and the 1973 Middle East conflict John D. Steinbruner found that national officials managed to set a general political construction on the course of events that shaped the alert operations undertaken by attentive U.S. military organizations during both crises, but certain military actions clearly diverged from the intent of national leaders during the Cuban episode.[39] Indeed, military actions began to diverge even before the October 14 discovery of missiles in Cuba, as the U.S. Air Force undertook elaborate preparations for an attack on Cuba in anticipation of a confrontation. The Air Force effort quietly and apparently unbeknownst to political leaders began months before the crisis erupted.[40] In the midst of the crisis, U.S. political leaders also were scarcely aware of how ripe conditions had become for a catastrophic accident, unauthorized use of nuclear weapons, or other lapses of nuclear control as the U.S. command and control system shifted its priority from negative to positive control.[41] Recall also that the U.S. nuclear alert had sparked a reactive Soviet nuclear alert that might have been misconstrued by the United States, and that U.S. military commanders' nuclear authority was ambiguous.

The lesson drawn from this history: preparations for comprehensive attack could proceed further and faster than intended, interaction between command and control systems could grow volatile, and safeguards against unsanctioned attack or premature release on false warning could weaken.

Summary and Propositions: U.S. Operations

During the cold war, U.S. military planners imposed very ambitious tasks on themselves. When Mikhail Gorbachev became the general secretary in 1985, the number of Soviet targets in the SIOP was about 16,000.[42] The level of target damage demanded of the SIOP forces was high: nominally in the range of 70 to 90 percent damage expectancy for each of the four target categories, with a median level of approximately 80 percent.[43] Furthermore, the number of U.S. forces assigned to the SIOP mission, though large in absolute terms, was only a fraction of the total nuclear inventory from which weapons could be drawn. This underutilization of the nuclear arsenal, coupled with a bookkeeping device used by military planners that ignored the extensive damage that non-SIOP nuclear forces prosecuting theater missions would have inflicted on SIOP targets, understated the capacity of U.S. forces to destroy the target base.[44]

As soon as the U.S. strategic organization perceived a serious threat of nuclear attack, the three key variables—the list of SIOP targets, the level of damage required for each target, and the prior allocation of weapons systems to SIOP targets—would have combined with a decentralized command system to transform a strategic posture geared to safety into a posture geared to comprehensive target coverage. Driven by the requirements of damage expectancy, the strong propensity of the command and control system was to bring all SIOP forces to a state of wartime readiness.

More important, damage expectancy drove the timing of nuclear release. If deterrence buckled and a strategic war seemed imminent, the system was strongly predisposed to ensure that the SIOP forces suffered negligible prelaunch attrition and that their offensive operations conformed strictly to preprogrammed strike schedules against a large array of preassigned targets. The imperative of comprehensive target coverage would have primed the command system for launch on warning.

The simplest calculations quickly point up the absolute necessity for the U.S. command system to generate virtually all forces to a state of high launch readiness, to avoid attrition by launching before the impact of incoming Soviet forces, and to allocate weapons according to an integrated target plan and arrival schedule. Without these measures it would not have been possible for the SIOP forces (roughly 12,000 warheads in 1990 after full alert generation) to achieve 70 to 90 percent levels of destruction against either the 1985 target base, comprising some 16,000 Soviet targets, or the 1990 target base, comprising 10,000 targets.

The peacetime SIOP alert force, consisting of about 5,000 warheads, obviously could not even cover the smaller 1990 target base even if all warheads were successfully delivered to their targets and all attacked targets were completely destroyed. Under such conditions, the maximum overall damage expectancy was about 50 percent. This performance unrealistically assumes that the reliability of U.S. weapons was 100 percent; that none of the U.S. alert forces were destroyed before or after launch; and that each U.S. warhead destroyed its assigned target, regardless of the latter's hardness or mobility. Under more realistic assumptions, the overall damage expectancy would have been about 40 percent, far below the required level. This performance assumes that U.S. preemption or launch on warning occurred (none of the U.S. alert forces were destroyed on the ground); that 85 percent of the alert U.S. strategic bombers penetrated Soviet air defenses; that weapons systems reliability was 85 percent; that each delivered warhead had a high probability (83 percent) of destroying its assigned target, regardless of the latter's protection from nuclear effects; and that 850 delivered U.S. warheads were able to destroy 1,700 "soft" targets by judiciously targeting so that each explosion would have obliterated more than one target (multiple targets were within the lethal radius of each "desired ground zero").

Under the same basic assumptions, the U.S. command and control system could have increased the overall damage expectancy to about 83 percent of the 1990 Soviet target base, including 90 percent of the 2,000 hardened strategic force installations, by generating the full strategic arsenal in a crisis. But this performance still depended on launching U.S. SIOP forces quickly. The U.S. posture could have realized only a small fraction of the damage potential of U.S. forces if a Soviet attack had been ridden out before retaliation was authorized. Given theoretical vulnerabilities in command and control and force structure, Soviet attack would have compelled the U.S. command system to unleash the strategic forces immediately, particularly the land-based missiles in theoretically vulnerable silos. Even if the command system could have survived, its failure to launch a massive salvo before the arrival of incoming Soviet missiles would have resulted in an overall low damage expectancy below 70 percent, and in a very low damage expectancy against the targets with the highest priority: Soviet nuclear forces. The counterstrategic mission would have been negated, and the U.S. strategic organization would have suffered a defeat according to its own criteria for assessing mission performance. It could not have rebounded from this blow, which the organization would have perceived as fatal despite its residual SIOP capacity (not to mention the residual capacity of thousands of long-range nuclear forces excluded from the SIOP) to cause grave injury to the adversary after the absorption of its first strike.

Several subsidiary propositions emerge. First, the SIOP did not provide for the complete satisfaction of targeting requirements even under optimal conditions, a fact that implicitly promoted vigorous force modernization to close the gap. By controlling the main factors that determine the level of feasible target coverage, military planners thus not only defined the norms for crisis nuclear alerting and release timing but also created an impetus for the procurement of new weapons systems. That impetus of course has been dampened by the end of the cold war and shrinking defense budgets.

Second, U.S. forces had to be launched before the Soviet target base dispersed in order to achieve maximum target coverage. The importance of damage expectancy thus created an incentive to strike preemptively if certain classes of Soviet targets such as mobile ICBMs, submarines in port, and mobile command posts began to disperse in a crisis. The U.S. command and control system therefore surely possessed an option tailored expressly for preemptive attack.[45] Such an option would have represented a focal contingency in the system's repertory.

Third, U.S. reliance on rapid reaction or literal launch on warning created strong pressures to establish redundant authority over the release of SIOP forces so that a disruption of the nominal chain of command could not block the swift dissemination of launch authorization. In the event of a precursor attack that decapitated the civilian leadership, the pre-positioned release authorities in the military chain of command were likely to be prone to authorize retaliation before the thirty-minute flight time of Soviet land-based missiles elapsed. If they had not already done so, they were virtually certain to issue launch orders to the forces as soon as the first incoming ICBMs began to arrive.

Fourth, conditions that diminished the feasibility of launch on warning—for instance, disruptions in the flow of tactical warning information caused by technical malfunctions, natural disturbances, or damage suffered in the course of hostilities that preceded a nuclear strike—increased the utility of preemption and the command system's reliance on it.

Lastly, the wartime mission of the system required such fast action and involved such decentralized control that safeguards against improper release would have been placed under severe strain. The command and control system made subtle compromises in negative control procedures for the sake of ensuring a rapid transition to positive control. As discussed in chapter seven, an especially dangerous compromise was made in the early-warning subsystem to facilitate launch on warning. In typical fashion, this occurred deep within the bowels of a strategic organization without the benefit of top-level civilian participation or approval.

Such were the characteristics of and perils lurking in the U.S. command and control system designed to deal with nuclear contingencies during the cold war.

Implications for the Post–Cold War Era

This analysis of the U.S. command system should not be consigned to the annals of cold war history. The system has been carried over, essentially intact, into the post–cold war era. Damage expectancy is still its core value and its operational representation of deterrence, which remains its central purpose. The crisis operating characteristics that grew out of the underlying requirements of target coverage remain firmly in place: rapid force generation, decentralized control, and launch on warning.

The system did not change so much as the international context in which it operates. The traditional underlying causes of U.S.-Russian conflict have practically been removed. The likelihood of a nuclear crisis thus seems negligible. This represents a radical change that profoundly affects the outlook if it is permanent. As long as nuclear tensions continue to decline, the dangers of nuclear inadvertence lurking in the command system are more hypothetical than real and present concerns.

But the remission of nuclear tension may not be permanent. Tension could plausibly rise again, especially given the prospect that the nuclear command and control system of the former Soviet Union will crack under political, economic, and social duress. While the distress of the Commonwealth has not yet gravely weakened nuclear safeguards, no one can offer absolute assurance that control over the vast nuclear arsenal will remain reliably effective for an indefinite period of acute domestic strife. The specter of chaos, accompanied by the disintegration of the military leading to an outbreak of "loose nukes," is not a baseless fear. Moreover, real potential exists for a deteriorating situation to project a global nuclear threat.

The U.S. command and control system is unfortunately ill designed to cope with such events. Since its propensities and procedures were not altered to deal with the changing nature of nuclear danger in the post-cold war era, it would be prone to react to a threat of unpremeditated attack caused by a breakdown of command and control in the former Soviet Union in much the same manner it would have reacted to a cold war threat of deliberate attack. Crisis-alerting procedures under dispersed control would be triggered in the absence of high-level political guidance meant to dampen such responses.

The behavior of the U.S. system during the 1991 coup attempt appears to support these speculations. Although it was short lived and resonated only slightly in the Soviet nuclear posture, the Moscow coup nearly induced characteristic alerting behavior by the U.S. system. Despite President Bush's refrain that the coup posed no military threat to the United States, and the Joint Chiefs' reluctance to raise the alert level of U.S. forces out of fear that such a move might alarm the Soviets and provoke inadvertent hostilities, the U.S. military reportedly "took hundreds of quiet steps around the world to heighten readiness."[46] This diffuse activity reportedly involved all four military services and their joint combat commands, each of which "took numerous steps informally to anticipate potential threats and ensure that they were prepared to respond."[47] Many elements of the U.S. command system filtered their perceptions of the unfolding events through the conceptual lens of the cold war. From the system's perspective, the situation closely resembled the war scenarios during the cold war. As one career military intelligence officer put it, "Many of the [war] scenarios started with these kinds of things: a breakdown of the political system of the Soviet Union, some kind of internal instability which led then to regional instability."[48]

Despite uncertainty about the cohesion of the Soviet command system, the senior U.S. political and military leadership set a general political construction on the events that downplayed the nuclear ramifications of the coup. U.S. strategic organizations, though stirred by the events in Moscow, took their cues from this calm assessment and acted accordingly. Subordinate echelons of the decentralized U.S. command system were inhibited from initiating crisis alert procedures. A more alarmist assessment would have risked triggering a worldwide U.S. nuclear alert, heightening tensions and possibly sparking a full-blown U.S.-Soviet nuclear crisis.[49] If U.S. nuclear forces had been placed on a wartime footing, the Soviet command system would have felt pressure to increase the readiness of its forces. This cycle of interactive alerts would have only worsened the conditions that set off the cycle in the first place.

The U.S. command and control system requires major modifications to bring it into proper alignment with the international context in which it operates. In the event of another coup, the seizure of nuclear weapons by state actors in Ukraine or elsewhere, unauthorized actions by launch crews, or other nuclear emergencies in the former Soviet Union, the characteristic reaction of the U.S. system should be to eschew a knee-jerk response that invokes the strategic war plan. Deterrence would be a peripheral issue; the traditional emphasis on target coverage would be misplaced under these circumstances. The system should instead offer a set of responses designed to help restore legitimate, ironclad control over Commonwealth nuclear weapons and to mitigate the consequences of their illicit use. Steps taken should be defensive and nonprovocative. Some responses would involve joint U.S.-Russian actions, according to contingency plans drawn up in advance. Specific proposals are presented in the final chapter. They all presuppose a revamping of the U.S. command and control system.

Major modifications of the system would also be required to accommodate the growing demand for flexible nuclear options. One recent study of future nuclear policy by an influential group of strategists advocates new command and control capabilities for updating an existing strike plan in near-real time for operational reasons ("adaptive planning"), and for developing completely new plans in near-real time for policy reasons ("contingency planning").[50] As an example of contingency planning, the study envisions the sudden emergence of threats from non-Soviet sources, identified as China or the third world, to which the United States should be able to respond by improvising a strike plan for a "Nuclear Expeditionary Force" composed of some mix of B-2 bombers, SLBMs, sea-based cruise missiles, and short-range aircraft.[51]

For dealing with the former Soviet Union, a range of options are considered necessary. In the view of the study group, the threat posed by the former Soviet armed forces justifies retaining the SIOP's preplanned "Major Attack Options" inherited from the cold war ("with a full panoply of Republic and leadership withholds").[52] From the group's perspective of the new world order, however, the SIOP needs additional limited options. They recommend a series of new, preplanned "Limited Attack Options" involving fewer than 100 weapons in total (1 to 10 each) targeted at conventional offensive forces outside Commonwealth cities.[53]

This variation on the cold war theme of deterrence, updated to account for threats allegedly emerging from China and the third world, reflects the U.S. command system's obsession with targeting issues. It represents a digression from the real issues of command system modernization. The system needs to be modified to handle threats of inadvertence. Modifying it to support a "nuclear expeditionary force" for use against the third world is arguably an antediluvian proposal of secondary importance.

CHAPTER FOUR

Characteristic Behavior of the Soviet Command System

ALTHOUGH it bore superficial similarities to the U.S. system, the Soviet nuclear command and control system differed markedly in both respects that frame this analysis: operative goals and the balance between centralization and decentralization. First, whereas U.S. operative goals revolved around the hallowed value of target coverage, the Soviet system kept many variables in focus. It attached as much weight to geopolitical considerations, self-preservation, and negative control as to damage expectancy.

Compared with the U.S. system it had a weaker propensity to react to a threat by immediately instituting a worldwide alert that projected the maximum threat at all potential enemy targets in all theaters. Soviet command bounded threats in geopolitical terms and put a high premium on flexibility of response. It regarded a security crisis as a complex problem requiring a unique politico-military strategy and a customized operational plan to solve it.

Centralization was the style of command that best served this principle of flexible response. It comes as no surprise that in terms of the centralization-decentralization balance, strictly centralized control both positive *and* negative was a basic feature of the Soviet system that distinguished it from U.S. arrangements.

Nuclear Strategy: Fluid Aims and Rigid Implementation

Although a Soviet strategy replete with prepackaged options doubtless existed for waging intercontinental war, it is highly significant that there

59

was "no strategic doctrine for waging intercontinental war in the available military strategic literature, open or closed. . . . In professional elaboration of military doctrine, the 'intercontinental theater of military operations [TVD]' is little more than mentioned (except for allocation to it of most ICBMs, SLBMs, and heavy bombers)."[1] The absence of such doctrine in a strategic culture that placed great emphasis on doctrine and strategy is conspicuous. The best explanation is that the missions of Soviet strategic weapons were highly conditional.

It appears that the Soviet system was far less wedded to a previously concocted plan than the U.S. system, in part because the presumed antecedent conflict—war in the continental theater of operations, particularly war with NATO countries—was seen as having an enormous yet unpredictable impact on the objectives and capabilities of Soviet intercontinental operations. Until the recent dissolution of the Warsaw Treaty Organization, the continental theaters dominated Soviet contingency planning for both conventional and nuclear war. It was most difficult to see beyond that horizon. A conventional, let alone a theater nuclear, war could have resulted in the substantial attrition of forward-based strategic forces, particularly submarines and land missile installations in the Ukraine and Byelorussia. Strategic early warning systems and air defenses could have been knocked out. The support infrastructure used to maintain the combat readiness of strategic forces could have been severely degraded. Soviet planners also anticipated the need to expend a portion of the strategic nuclear forces to augment other firepower in a war that remained confined to the contiguous theaters. To make matters worse, Soviet planners expected a very difficult transition from theater to intercontinental war, one that the West could initiate with sudden and possibly devastating impact on Soviet capabilities for intercontinental retaliation.

Soviet planning for general nuclear war, therefore, might have prudently limited itself primarily to disrupting a massive U.S. first strike, deferring other operations until the consequences of the U.S. strike were thoroughly assessed and friendly strategic capabilities were reconstituted.

This is not to diminish the role of war planning for intercontinental operations involving homeland-to-homeland nuclear exchanges. Such strategic planning was doubtless a serious exercise, conducted by the general staff, that systematically related long-range nuclear forces to intercontinental targets and scheduled the sequence of strikes to achieve specific levels of target coverage. As best as one can surmise from sparse data, Soviet planners, like their U.S. counterparts, divided targets into four broad categories: (1) nuclear forces, (2) other military targets, (3) political and administrative centers, and (4) war-supporting industry. But the Soviet and U.S. categories did not correspond exactly. The first Soviet category, nuclear forces, was apparently more inclusive of nuclear infrastructure than was the analogous U.S. category. Soviet planners thus included, whereas U.S. planners excluded, the top rungs of the nuclear chain of command. Soviet attack on U.S. nuclear forces would not have spared the national command authorities, the command posts of the Joint Chiefs of Staff, or the headquarters of the nuclear commanders in chief. Soviet planners also put nuclear weapons production and assembly facilities in the same category as nuclear forces, whereas the U.S. strategic plan listed analogous targets under war-supporting industry. The Soviet category of political-administrative centers also differed from the U.S. category of leadership. The former were large cities such as Atlanta and Chicago rather than discrete political targets such as government and KGB facilities.

The relative priorities among these four target sets are fairly easy to infer. There is no doubt that Western nuclear forces received the highest priority. The secret Voroshilov course materials state categorically that "the most important mission is the destruction of enemy nuclear weapons."[2] According to a U.S. official interviewed for this study, Soviet planners pursued comprehensive coverage of this category, requiring perhaps a 90 percent probability of damage against the targets. This level of desired damage contrasts with an estimated 70 percent for other military targets and 50 percent for each of the remaining categories.[3]

Soviet strategic nuclear exercises indicated the existence of plans allowing for an assault on all targets in all categories at once. A bias toward massive initial salvos of ICBMs aimed at the complete spectrum of targets did seem to exist. Such a targeting policy also squared with a sizable body of Soviet literature that excoriated Western notions of intrawar signaling and coercion in which intercontinental strikes began with limited nuclear options and, absent a diplomatic resolution, escalated to the level of major attack options. Taken at face value, the Soviets' rhetoric rejected the idea of strategic nuclear flexibility, implying that their strategic war plan was a blunt instrument, quite inflexible and indiscriminant.

The preponderance of evidence derived from Soviet operational practices supports the opposite conclusion, however. The Soviet strategic command and control system was designed to offer a wide menu of options to deal with the nuclear unknown. The targeting permutations possible in the Soviet system were in fact vastly greater than in the U.S. system. Whereas the latter allowed for strikes against certain predefined target categories to be selectively withheld, the Soviet system allowed for selective strikes to be mounted against targets that had not previously been grouped together. The Soviets could designate novel groupings of targets for attack, *and* could release the unlock codes (the enabling codes) for the affected strike weapons with corresponding flexibility. Unlike the U.S. system, the Soviet enabling code system permitted individual weapons, groups of weapons, or all weapons to be unlocked in novel combinations, depending on the preference of the leadership. Because of inferior technology, however, the Soviet system was less flexible than its U.S. counterpart in aiming missiles at targets that had not been previously programmed in the missiles' memories.

Abundant evidence also shows that the Soviets had a doctrinal obligation to let the politico-military authorities bend nuclear operations to their will. If design principles are any indication, the system had to possess what the Soviets called "requisite variety"; that is, its repertory of responses was required to be large enough to handle a wide range of contingencies, depending on a kaleidoscope of political and military variables. The Soviet system was therefore sensitive to a broad range of factors and valued the process of planning above all else. The crux of effective command was the ability to "abandon quickly and decisively the previously adopted plan" and formulate a new one.[4]

The philosophical roots of this view were the simple beliefs that the essence of the command and control problem is uncertainty and that the copestone of command is foresight, or forecasting: "Forecasting in the control of the Armed Forces is the ability of the commander and staff to foresee and forecast, rationally and elaborately, the possible changes in politico-military and military situations, and to determine accordingly the most appropriate form of action for the Armed Forces."[5] The Soviet command and control system owed its distinctive character and physical configuration to this dictum. The high command always had a voracious appetite for fresh intelligence on the adversary's political bent and force disposition, particularly as regards the fluid threats present along the Soviet defense perimeter and in the adjacent theaters of continental operations. To keep the spectrum of threats under constant surveillance (a prerequisite of accurate forecasting), the Soviet high command placed the levers of an elaborate intelligence apparatus at its fingertips. The general staff directed strategic reconnaissance and made products available for direct consumption by the top echelons of command. The resultant forecast formed the basis for tailoring a strike plan to suit the circumstances, a process that was also centrally managed by the high command and the huge support apparatus of the general staff.

To increase its ability to adapt to dynamic change, the system also strove to maintain a sizable pool of reserve nuclear forces. A microcosm of this general approach was the organization of strategic forces into first-echelon forces, operational reserves, and uncommitted reserves.[6] The operational reserves covered targets missed by first-echelon forces because of losses from attrition and launch unreliability. The backup forces were designed to compensate for these random losses. This adaptive approach to strategic weapons allocation could husband scarce resources in a potentially vastly more efficient and economical way than could an approach that failed to capitalize on reprogramming.[7] The uncommitted reserves constituted the third strategic echelon, which had not been assigned any immediate mission and represented an important surplus capability at the disposal of the supreme high command. Strategic reserves as a generic category of forces were credited as a decisive factor in the Soviet defeat of Germany during World War II.[8]

In the Soviet scheme of things, protecting the command and control system itself, especially the upper layers, and preserving firm operational control from the center while ruling out aberrant actions by lower echelons constituted the critical variables—the overriding aim—of the Soviet strategic organization in time of crisis.[9] The ability to direct strategic forces flexibly to coherent national purposes obviously presupposed the existence of survivable forces, but preserving strict top-down control was both more important and more difficult. Command and control even took precedence over protecting forces from attack, an order of priorities most clearly evident in the 1960s, when the Soviets normally kept all their strategic nuclear warheads separate from all the delivery vehicles.[10] Acute force vulnerability was tolerated to ensure strict control over nuclear operations. The high priority of tight central control was also evident during the 1991 coup attempt, when the mobile ICBM force was moved from covert field locations back to its main garrisons.[11] It was evident even after the breakup of the Soviet Union, when tactical nuclear weapons were withdrawn from the outlying former republics, nuclear armaments for the long-range bombers stationed in Ukraine were disabled in place and those in Kazakhstan were removed to central storage, and all intercontinental missile forces in the non-Russian Commonwealth states were taken off launch-ready alert status. These moves reflected the overriding importance of ensuring that the top of the nuclear command and control system retained reliable negative control and that the lower echelons of the hierarchy lacked the means to assert positive launch control.

The role of the top leadership went well beyond granting or withholding approval to employ nuclear weapons, although that was certainly one of its exclusive prerogatives: "The major responsibility is borne by the political authorities, who make the decisions to use nuclear weapons."[12] The command and control system was also required to enable the Soviet leaders to orchestrate nuclear operations in a detailed way. Political authorities were expected to set the terms of nuclear alerting, to choose the objectives and damage requirements of nuclear strikes, to determine what specific restrictions on the employment of nuclear weapons to impose, and to firmly control the process of releasing unlock codes that were physically integral to the launching of forces. There is some evidence that the highest politico-military authorities (or the supreme high command in Soviet military parlance) reserved to themselves the responsibility for deciding such fine-grained details as the yield and height of burst of weapons to be employed, not to mention the allocation of forces to targets. (As discussed later, special channels of control were used to ensure strict wartime implementation of such details.) The rationale for "maximum centralization" was articulated authoritatively at the outset of the ballistic missile age and has not been markedly revised since then.[13]

Central Control of the Strategic Triad in Peacetime and Crisis

All three components of the strategic nuclear forces of the former Soviet Union were reserved exclusively for and subject to direct operational control by the supreme high command (VGK), composed of the top political leader (the general secretary until superseded by the president under Mikhail Gorbachev) and the defense minister. This authority was exercised through either the general staff or the commander in chief of the strategic rocket forces (CINC SRF).[14] The sacrosanct principle of centralization was thoroughly embodied in the positive and negative control regime imposed on actual operations.

In peacetime the general staff normally served as the controlling agency. It regulated the deployed strategic forces by means of either a *manual* or *automatic* mode of positive control. The normal peacetime mode was manual. In this case, operational orders flowed from the strategic nuclear section of the main operations directorate of the general staff headquarters in Moscow to the subordinate commanders in chief— namely, CINC SRF, CINC navy, and CINC air force (all of whose main headquarters were near Moscow)—and then through intermediate echelons such as SRF army headquarters to the individual combat crews of the far-flung land-, sea-, and air-based strategic forces. If the general staff elected to switch over to the automatic mode, a transition affected by transmitting a special preliminary command down the chain of command, emergency instructions such as launch orders may have flowed directly from the general staff to the combat crews, bypassing the CINCs and other intermediate levels of command.[15]

Alternatively, as the secret Voroshilov lectures say, the supreme high command could command the strategic rocket forces through the CINC SRF.[16] The SRF commander historically enjoyed an exalted status in the nuclear command and control system. Besides providing an alternate route for directing the SRF land missile forces, he possessed nuclear authority over strategic units of the navy and air force.[17] In an emergency, the SRF commander could have controlled the alerting and launch of Soviet SSBNs and long-range bombers, passing the orders through or around the CINCs of those forces.[18] In an extreme emergency—for instance, a nuclear attack that decapitated the general staff navy and air force headquarters and their alternates—the CINC SRF could himself have switched over to the automatic mode of command and control and assumed direct control over the entire strategic arsenal.

These organizations were nonetheless highly interdependent. A functioning general staff was able to block or override the CINC SRF if nuclear actions had been ordered without proper authorization. By the same token, the CINCs of the three branches of the strategic forces evidently could have thwarted an effort by the general staff to unilaterally exercise control over nuclear forces. For instance, the CINCs could block the transition from the manual to the automatic mode to prevent being shunted aside. During the summer 1991 coup attempt, the senior commanders of those branches—Y. P. Maksimov (SRF), V. N. Chernavin (navy), and Y. I. Shaposhnikov (air force)—decided among themselves to disobey any nuclear orders that the coup plotters (who included the then chief of the general staff) might issue. Accordingly, they almost certainly would have resisted any attempt to switch the command system out of the manual mode.[19] The CINCs surely would not have allowed the switchover because it would have meant relinquishing their de facto veto power over the employment of strategic nuclear forces and thereby enabling the conspiratorial, illegitimate leaders to gain total control over the forces. Such defiance would have been treasonous but technically in their power.

The key role of the general staff in managing the operations of strategic nuclear forces in peacetime was evident in the pattern of day-to-day communications. Acting as the executive agent of the supreme high command, the general staff from its main war room in Moscow periodically sent instructions to alert missile forces in the field. For instance, it often electronically seized the navy fleet broadcast network (very low frequency [VLF] and high frequency [HF] transmitters) to send messages to SSBNs on combat patrol at sea (and used radio and land-line communications to transmit orders to launch-ready subs at dockside). SSBNs were "chopped" to the general staff soon after embarking on a combat patrol (after submerging, the sub captain gave a short speech to the crew on the occasion of this transfer of operational control from a navy fleet command to the general staff), whereupon they tuned into general staff frequencies to listen for nuclear orders. The submarines also sometimes sent messages directly to the general staff. At other times the navy main headquarters near Moscow keyed the broadcast transmitters either to relay general staff instructions or to convey its own. Either the general staff or naval headquarters could transmit orders that affected the combat readiness of ballistic missile submarines.[20]

Both the general staff and the SRF headquarters also engaged in periodic two-way communications (primarily via land lines and high-frequency radio) with the launch crews of the land-based strategic missile forces. Parallel links with the strategic bomber forces surely existed. Although bomber aircraft did not maintain a short-warning alert status in peacetime,[21] the general staff operations directorate almost certainly interacted on a routine basis with the air army headquarters of long-range bomber fleets to regulate their combat readiness.

In a crisis, the general staff played an especially critical role in managing the combat readiness of nuclear forces on behalf of the supreme command. Raising the level of readiness was considered an exclusive prerogative of the top leadership. In principle, alerting was initiated only at the behest of the political leadership: "the decision for strategic deployment and transition of the Armed Forces from a peacetime to wartime standing is made by the political authorities of the State."[22] Central control over the alerting process was safeguarded in part by the practice of tightly restricting access to strategic intelligence on the political and military posture of potential adversaries. Strategic warning and reconnaissance information flowed directly and almost exclusively to the top layer of the command and control system—namely, through the KGB and GRU (military intelligence) to the general staff, giving the leadership control over the very premises of the decision process. Other military commands were kept largely in the dark, although in recent years more strategic intelligence had begun to flow with less restriction down to the level of fleet and army headquarters.

Elaborate feedback loops also existed, running from the lower to the upper rungs of the chain of command. The leadership was especially well equipped to monitor actions taken by subordinate echelons that altered the combat disposition of land-based strategic rocket forces. Automatic electronic reporting from missile silos instantly informed the general staff of improper changes of missile status, and using special technical means at their disposal, the higher command posts could quickly countermand the changes while isolating and neutralizing the lower command centers responsible for the violation.

The Soviet alerting process was designed to move the armed forces gradually through a series of measures according to specific instructions from the minister of defense and the general staff.[23] Most of the alert steps were of course preplanned and probably required only a brief signal to trigger their implementation. Alternatively, the general staff could send detailed instructions.[24] Established procedures for alerting the troops fell, with an important exception discussed later, into three levels of combat readiness: constant or routine, increased, and full. Changing these levels mainly affected the status of personnel, as opposed to weapons. In the strategic forces it affected the vigilance of the launch crews and initiated some prelaunch preparations. For instance, an increased alert message could have designated which envelopes the local commanders should retrieve from their safes to determine their missions and target aimpoints.[25] Some special measures that affected the status of the weapons themselves were also associated with each level.[26] Some of the personnel weapons measures associated with each alert level are outlined in general terms in the Voroshilov lectures. Although the correspondence was inexact, Soviet nuclear alert activity undertaken during past crises generally matched the measures associated with increased combat readiness.

Besides the above-mentioned alert levels, a special alerting order existed to move nuclear weapons and their operators to their most advanced state of combat readiness. This urgent order fell under a heading known as danger of war, which connoted a threat of imminent attack and was associated with tactical-like warning indicators—for example, the interception of Western messages authorizing nuclear use. If enemy attack appeared imminent, Soviet forces could be raised to a state of utmost readiness as rapidly as possible by declaring a combat alert (*boyevaya trevoga*), which might have been accompanied by additional guidance, such as instructions for transferring nuclear ammunition to the delivery units.[27] For the strategic nuclear forces, the notification by alert (*opoveshcheniye po trevoge*) brought them to full combat readiness in "only some minutes."[28] It took considerably longer to generate the SSBN and bomber legs to full readiness from their peacetime alert status, which historically had been very low. By contrast, a substantial fraction of the land-based strategic rocket force were, even in peacetime, "ready to begin action on the signal given to them by the Supreme High Command."[29]

The alert command that brought nuclear weapons and their operators to the brink of war was known to them as a *preliminary* (or sometimes a *prepare*) command (*predvaritel'naya komanda*).[30] The short-coded order (which was changed on a regularly scheduled, sometimes daily, basis) used to have several distinct sublevels to permit the launch readiness of strategic forces to be raised in discrete stages as the danger of war grew. Thus preliminary commands were issued on strategic warning during past nuclear crises to strategic missiles that required extensive, time-consuming launch preparations. Modern Soviet strategic forces did not require as much preparation. They achieved such an advanced state of combat readiness in peacetime that in recent years the stages of preparation were collapsed into one. A preliminary command thus triggered combat crews in the strategic forces to take a few short steps that prepared them to receive and implement the next order, the *direct* command (*neposredstvennaya komanda*, the fire order or go-code in the popular vernacular). The preliminary command was closely associated with the last-minute ICBM launch preparations that would be undertaken in response to tactical warning of an incoming enemy missile strike.

A preliminary command normally must have been issued jointly by the CGS and the CINC of the forces to be alerted. Special codes held by the CGS and CINC SRF, for example, had to be separately generated and combined by a special algorithm to create a valid preliminary command for SRF units.[31]

In the SRF the preliminary command gave the launch crews in the missile fields access to the communications channel through which a direct command could flow. This launch channel was normally disconnected at each echelon of SRF command (SRF headquarters, army, division, and regiment) as a peacetime safeguard. The channel was effectively blocked at several locations to prevent its misuse at any level of the SRF hierarchy. A preliminary command from the general staff electronically closed the circuits at each layer and thereby connected both the general staff and the SRF hierarchy to the channel used for disseminating the direct command. The preliminary command also gave launch crews access to the equipment that directly governed the launch of their formation of nuclear missiles and access to the special documentation used to authenticate a subsequent direct command. The preliminary command not only conveyed approval for such access to equipment and documentation but also electronically switched the circuits that provided the access. The recipients of this order could of course be selectively included or excluded by the general staff to allow for flexible alerting.

The preliminary command accompanied rather than preceded a direct command in some scenarios. In the SRF the preliminary command preceded the direct command in launch-on-warning scenarios. According to Soviet military sources, no preliminary command was ever issued on the basis of false tactical warning. In other retaliatory scenarios or in preemptive strike scenarios the two commands were likely to be issued together as a double message.

The preliminary command was optional in the control of ballistic missile submarines. If used, it was to be formed by combining the codes held separately by the CGS and CINC navy, though the CINC SRF could serve in place of the CINC navy should circumstances necessitate. If used, the preliminary command either preceded or accompanied a direct command. In exercises a series of short messages usually preceded the direct command. In any case, both preliminary and direct command messages to the Soviet SSBN force were identified during Soviet exercises. It is plausible that targeting instructions and a designated time of launch were contained in the preliminary message, followed by a separate short message (the direct command) containing the unlock codes and launch codeword. In some exercises the designated time of launch was subsequently canceled. SSBN forces then launched on command according to a new message containing the launch codeword and often a date-time group that designated the moment of release. In other SSBN exercises the preliminary and direct commands were folded into a single longer message. One explanation for the large variation in the message formats was that the SSBNs could be released in rather peculiar ways under special circumstances, as discussed later.

Soviet tactical nuclear weapons, unlike modern strategic forces, still went through a series of stages in the alerting process, and hence the preliminary command for these forces could specify what stage of preparation to implement.[32] For instance, a preliminary command issued by the chief of the general staff might start the process of transporting tactical nuclear ammunition from depots to field locations. In such cases a subsequent preliminary command called for the warheads to be moved close to the delivery means. In the final preliminary command the special custodians for the warheads would unlock the warheads using codes sent by higher authority and load them onto the delivery systems controlled by the regular military units. The secret Voroshilov lectures disclosed that in preparation for a nuclear strike in the European theater of operations, tactical nuclear weapons were to be turned over to delivery units about three hours before the planned strike.[33] A Soviet source with first-hand experience in FROG missile units estimated that the warheads could have been delivered to the field from division headquarters in about thirty minutes. In some Soviet exercises authorization to arm the delivery vehicles with tactical nuclear weapons was disseminated only after warning of Western preemptive nuclear attack became available (typically about two to three hours advance warning of tactical nuclear strikes against Soviet forces).[34]

Issuing the preliminary command to all or a subset of the nuclear forces was a profound act that normally required the consent of the top leadership. The general staff was ultimately responsible for its dissemination. In fact, the lectures say that "bringing the Armed Forces to a level of full combat readiness" was the most important responsibility of the general staff in a crisis.[35] For the strategic forces, however, the general staff and the strategic CINCs normally participated jointly in its dissemination. Both organizations apparently had to approve the order for it to pass muster at the receiving end.[36] This requirement provided a strong organizational safeguard during peacetime.

To handle contingencies involving breaks in the command chain from wartime stress, the physical capability and procedures existed at each echelon of the chain to issue the preliminary order to its respective subordinate formations. But if the command system remained intact, an improperly issued order would have been reported up the chain of command, where steps would have been immediately taken to cancel it. Interviews with Soviet military sources revealed that preliminary commands had occasionally been disseminated in error by echelons below the general staff level and that the mistakes had been rectified by high level intervention. Such concentration of authority and regulation of operational activity at the apex square with Voroshilov principles:

> In the transition of the Armed Forces to the highest level of combat readiness, their firm and continuous control is of particular importance. Control should ensure centralized and simultaneous communication of signals and instructions by the specification of proper measures from the General Staff and their direct communication to the troops. Higher staffs are to strictly control the actions of the troops.[37]

Centralized Procedures for Nuclear Launch

The procedures for authorizing the use of nuclear weapons embodied a core value of Russian political culture, collective centralized decision-making. No individual, regardless of rank or position, could alone issue the authorization to employ nuclear weapons.[38] This power was less concentrated than it is in the United States, where the president is entitled to authorize the use of nuclear weapons. The U.S. president also can and did predelegate his release authority to others, including military commanders. There is almost no evidence of any comparable predelegation of nuclear authority to Soviet military commanders.

First Stage: Permission Command

The procedures for releasing Soviet nuclear weapons were carried out in two stages. During the first stage the key persons who composed the supreme high command formed a special order, called a permission command (*razreshayushaya komanda*), which allowed the use of only those nuclear forces previously specified in the preliminary command. (As already noted, despite its name the preliminary command did not always precede the permission command.) This permission command was then transmitted to the CINCs of the strategic forces designated for release. The message established the legality of the attack order in the eyes of the CINCs of the SRF, navy, and air force.[39] A permission command satisfied the CINCs' requirement to ensure that a nuclear attack order was in fact a legal directive from the supreme high command.

Until the failed coup of 1991 the permission command was intended to be formed jointly by the USSR president (Mikhail Gorbachev), minister of defense (Dmitriy Yazov), and chief of the general staff (CGS) (Gen. Mikhail Moiseyev) after conferring with one another either face-to-face or by special telecommunications. In a nuclear crisis they were likely to go to wartime command posts and confer directly. In peacetime they were likely to be apart but always connected by a communications system designed for emergency conferences. (By monitoring this critical channel, the West was able to keep track of the location and activities of the three key nuclear authorities.) In addition, while away from their wartime duty posts in peacetime, these persons were tied into the missile attack early-warning network and equipped at all times with special devices (so-called footballs or nuclear suitcases) designed to enable them to generate and transmit their portions of the permission command rapidly. The nuclear suitcases (sometimes carried by an aide called a *Shurika*), part of a system called *Kazbek*, were wired into the offices, residences, dachas, and possibly the planes and other vehicles of the three key officials.[40] The separate codes sent by the president and defense minister traveled over a dedicated communications channel to an electronic device with a special algorithm that validated the two code halves, combined them, and passed them to another device that integrated the permission code input of the CGS. Then the composite permission code would travel to the CINCs of the strategic forces designated for launch.

A major underlying assumption of the Kazbek system, which earned its developers Lenin and other state prizes after it became operational in the early 1980s, was the threat of a surprise U.S. nuclear attack that caught the leaders while away from their wartime bunkers. Hence the permission command was supposed to be generated by the nuclear suitcases only when there was evidence of enemy nuclear attack. Detection of an enemy missile attack was supposed to be confirmed by two different sensor systems before the footballs were activated and the permission was sent. (The preliminary command could be triggered by initial, unconfirmed tactical warning signals.) In principle and by design, the use of Kazbek was strictly devoted to facilitating prompt retaliation under conditions of surprise attack. The early-warning sensors detect an attack, the center for processing early warning notifies the key decisionmakers (defense minister and CGS, who in turn inform the president[41]), and the decisionmakers authorize retaliation using the footballs kept on-line by a special section of the general staff.

If the Soviets initiated an attack or launched on warning in the midst of a nuclear crisis, the leadership would already have evacuated to wartime command posts, where the footballs or nuclear suitcases would have been superfluous, because their functional equivalents for issuing the permission command were built into equipment inside the wartime command posts.

As an alternative or supplementary measure, the Soviet command system put additional nuclear suitcases in reserve for top leaders who had been designated as presidential successors. Under the old communist system headed by the general secretary, two Politburo members were assigned this responsibility on a rotating daily basis. After the adoption of the presidential system under Gorbachev, the vice president was put second in line in the chain of succession, followed by the chairman of the Supreme Soviet.[42] Plans existed to activate the footballs assigned to these potential successors. Similar procedures and footballs doubtless exist to support Russian President Boris Yeltsin's successors in the event of his incapacitation. Such transfers of nuclear authority to the successors, and the activation of their reserve footballs, can be affected only under special conditions, however, and the successors do not themselves decide when the conditions are met. The responsibility for making the determination and putting a successor's football on-line rests with special units of the general staff and an organization that manages the footballs.[43]

Soviet arrangements for succession were akin to U.S. arrangements for presidential succession, but the United States went one step further by establishing an additional mechanism that provided for the delegation of nuclear command authority to people outside the chain of presidential succession: military commanders designated as pre-positioned national command authorities. The Soviet command system seemed to abhor the idea of delegating conditional authority below the level of the supreme high command. In the event of a decapitating attack on Soviet command, retaliation would likely have been delayed until a presidential successor had been installed and was able to generate his portion of the permission command.[44] By contrast, in an analogous situation, a single pre-positioned nuclear release authority in the U.S. military chain of command could have disseminated the go-code to all U.S. SIOP forces long before a presidential successor was even found.

The CGS, as first deputy minister of defense, probably played a critical role if the defense minister was unable to act, for whatever reason. It seems likely that the president and the CGS alone, without the defense minister, could have jointly formed the complete permission command under some emergency conditions.[45] The advantage of this technical arrangement—it reinforced positive control under conditions of a surprise attack that had disabled the defense minister—was apparently outweighed by its disadvantage: the defense minister could have been improperly cut out of the loop of nuclear decisionmaking. He might have been disregarded and stymied in some scenarios that warranted his casting a vote. Post-coup investigations indeed exposed, if not this particular loophole in the safeguards, considerable ambiguity in the nuclear rights and responsibilities at the interfaces of the three key positions.

After the Soviet Union split up and Boris Yeltsin took power, the CGS's footballs and associated communications networks were taken off line and put in reserve. Although the Commonwealth CGS (Viktor Nikolayevich Samsonov) apparently retained some backup role in generating permission codes in an emergency, he could not perform this function in peacetime. Special measures had to be taken to generate his reserve football.

As the peacetime nuclear role of the CGS was downgraded from active to reserve, the role of the CINC SRF (Yuriy Maksimov) was upgraded from reserve to primary. The SRF commander acquired a football, and his associated communications networks, formerly maintained as a reserve backup to the CGS, became the primary on-line channel for disseminating nuclear orders. At the same time, nuclear release authority was inherited by Russian president Yeltsin and the CINC of the Commonwealth armed forces (Yevgeny Ivanovich Shaposhnikov, the former USSR defense minister). Yeltsin, however, pledged to consult with the leaders of the other Commonwealth states and to obtain permission from the heads of state of Ukraine, Belarus, and Kazakhstan before authorizing the use of any nuclear weapons. To this end, a communications network linking those three heads of state with the president of Russia and the CINC Commonwealth was established. An emergency teleconference was supposed to be convened and a unanimous decision reached by the four state leaders as well as the CINC Commonwealth before any permission command was jointly issued by the president of Russia, the CINC Commonwealth, and the CINC SRF (backed up by the Commonwealth CGS) through their footballs.[46] This policy obligation was technically violable, however. The heads of the non-Russian governments could withhold their permission, but they could not exercise any technical veto that physically prevented the dissemination and implementation of a permission, preliminary, or direct command.

Another shuffling of personnel during the fall of 1992 elevated the status of the Russian defense minister (Pavel S. Grachev) and the Russian chief of the general staff (V. Dubynin) over the CINC Commonwealth, and replaced numerous senior commanders including the CINC SRF and CINC navy. In all likelihood the nuclear apex shed the Commonwealth fig leaf and became an all-Russian entity by October 1992. The Russian president and defense minister probably carried nuclear footballs; a third football and responsibility for disseminating orders probably resided with the new CINC of the Russian SRF, or reverted back to the CGS (probably the Russian CGS).[47] In late 1992, however, the president of Ukraine evidently acquired a primitive capability to physically block the transmission of launch orders (preliminary and direct commands) to missiles on Ukrainian soil.

Second Stage: Direct Command

The general staff's traditional role as the primary executive agent for disseminating the nuclear orders of the supreme high command (the president and defense minister, or their successors) is revealed in the Voroshilov lectures: "At the beginning of a nuclear war the most important mission of the General Staff is to ensure transmission of the signal for the launch of the initial nuclear strike to the executing elements and to ensure control of its execution."[48] The launch signal in question actually consisted of two distinct orders: the permission command sent to the nuclear CINCs in the first stage and the *direct* command sent to the individual launch crews in the second stage.

In the Soviet command and control system, during the second stage the CGS and the CINCs of the strategic forces, galvanized into action by the permission directive of the supreme authorities, independently formed and sent their respective halves of the direct command to a third node, which in turn validated, combined, and retransmitted them as a whole direct command to the launch crews. This order directed the crews to fire their weapons at the designated targets at the designated time. Only the crews of the forces previously specified by the preliminary and permission commands received the order.[49] The direct command came over special communications networks called, according to Soviet military sources, *signal* for the SRF, *wave* for the Navy, and *wing* for the Air Force.

The procedures for disseminating the direct command through these networks are important to understand. The command was composed of two codes, one traditionally injected by the general staff and the other by the CINCs. The two codes were electronically validated, combined, and reencrypted by the systems. Then a composite order was disseminated to the individual launch crews. Thus, for example, a decision in the 1980s to launch strategic rocket forces would have been carried out by the general staff and the CINC SRF. They performed mutually dependent, though interchangeable, tasks. Acting separately but in concert, each party would have formed its part of the direct command and sent it to a particular node in the Signal network, where the two parts would have been combined into the composite direct order for dissemination to the launch crews in the battalion command posts over the Signal communications system.[50] Analogous procedures would have been followed if the strategic submarine or bomber forces had been designated for release.

Continuing with the example of the land-based strategic rocket forces, the direct command once received by the launch control posts in the missile fields underwent special processing by electronic and organizational means to verify its authenticity. If the electronic verification was positive, certain symbols would appear on the computer monitors in the control posts, which the crews would then compare against documentation from their safes. This visual examination provided an additional check of the order's validity and also provided instructions to the crew. The direct command conveyed codes needed to determine targets and establish the time of launch and remove the blocking devices that prevented illicit launches.

The launch time for strategic forces could be set for some time in the future, or they could be launched immediately upon receipt of the direct command. The delayed launch procedure—known as launch at designated time (LDT)—was routinely used in exercises, with delays sometimes extending twelve hours for strategic submarines. Strategic rocket forces also used this procedure, though somewhat less frequently.[51] Although many U.S. government analysts interviewed for this study seemed fixated on the LDT option in Soviet planning because of its association with a cold-blooded first strike, Soviet officers who served in the strategic rocket and submarine forces downplayed its significance. They alleged that Soviet nuclear strategy, and crew training, strongly emphasized the launching of forces without delay.

After verifying the order and completing the targeting procedures, the launch crew, acting in unison within a strictly limited time span, formed and sent a launch command to its formation of strategic rockets (typically ten missiles). This command also underwent special control by electronic means on the delivery vehicles. A black box at each silo for example lifted the blocking devices to activate the launch if the result of the electronic verification was positive. When the allowed time span expired, the blocking system was automatically reactivated, and any future launches required altogether new orders from higher authority.[52]

As this second-stage got under way the requirement for centralized control over the operation was a basic principle of Soviet nuclear command and control.[53] This centralized coordination was primarily the responsibility of the general staff, which ensured it by its integral participation in the formation and issuance of preliminary, permission, and direct commands. The general staff's essential coordinating role was underpinned by its possession of the unlock codes that had to accompany the direct command. As discussed below, the launch crews in submarines and SRF facilities could not physically fire their missiles if they failed to receive the unlock codes that lifted the blocking devices on the missiles.

Strict centralization was also applied to subsequent phases of nuclear operations, when "in accordance with the instructions of the Supreme High Command, after the initial nuclear strike the General Staff assigns new missions to the Strategic Rocket Forces which are conducted in the course of the war. The main activity of the General Staff is the collection and processing of data on the situation after the initial nuclear strikes of both sides, and the restoration of the combat capabilities of the groupings of the Armed Forces in a way to enable them to accomplish their assigned missions, despite losses."[54]

As the initial or subsequent phases of execution got under way, the general staff and CINC SRF could coordinate a switch from the manual mode of operation to a fully automatic mode of nuclear release. This transition was designed to expedite a retaliatory launch and work around damage sustained by the chain of command. The switchover directly connected the top leaders with the strategic forces in the field. It could be instituted by special preliminary commands disseminated down the chain of command, or it could occur spontaneously if certain conditions obtained, particularly extensive damage to the chain of command caused by nuclear detonations on Soviet soil.

This automatic mode of operation was extremely centralized in that it transferred physical launch control of SRF missiles to key command centers reserved for the top politico-military leadership. One form this took is quite astonishing. From a select subset of the central command posts in the Moscow vicinity—for example, the installations near Chekhov[55]—top leaders could remotely load a nuclear attack order into emergency communications rockets deployed around the country and then remotely launch the rockets using land-line communications and automatic control equipment. The Soviets reportedly allocated SL-7 boosters and SS-17 missiles to this mission.[56] Typically the missiles were trundled onto launch pads at Soviet test sites such as Tyuratam, but they apparently could also be fired from silos at the test facilities or from certain silos located in SS-17 ICBM missile complexes.[57]

The Soviet emergency rocket communications system (ERCS) might well have been modeled on its U.S. counterpart, in which case silo-based SS-17 missiles with communications payloads would have been interspersed among indistinguishable silos housing nuclear-tipped SS-17 missiles. The loading and firing of communications rockets by remote control from central command posts was a uniquely Soviet twist on the theme, however. The proximity of the SS-17 ICBM fields to Moscow should have ensured reliable communications. These fields belonged to the Moscow-region army of the SRF, and unlike ICBM fields located east of the Ural Mountains could be hard-wired to the national centers.[58] The dismantling of the last SS-17 forces by 1995 would suggest that ERCS will be abandoned or shifted to other types of missiles, though the mission might still be performed from the missile test facilities.[59]

An even more unusual feature, revealed in interviews by Soviet military sources with direct knowledge of the system, was that the ERCS missiles transmitted fire signals directly to unmanned ICBMs, bypassing the launch crews in the field. This claim is not corroborated by evidence gathered by the United States during Soviet ERCS missile tests. In some thirty ERCS tests conducted over the past several years, all from the test facilities, none was accompanied by a subsequent firing of an ICBM during the one-hour period of ERCS flight.[60]

In the same vein some of the underground command posts reserved for the supreme high command as well as the headquarters facilities of the SRF were equipped with a remote-launch capability that permitted them to bypass lower echelons and fire the widely dispersed nuclear-tipped ICBMs directly. The special feature of this arrangement was equivalent to that described earlier: the central posts physically actuated the switches that fired the missiles. Bypassing everyone between them and the unmanned missile silos, these posts exercised remote robotic-like control over the far-flung ICBMs. The Soviets first tested this capability, called an unattended launch, in the late 1970s. It probably used automatic control equipment linking the central posts with the silos of fourth-generation ICBMs—namely, the SS-17, SS-18, and SS-19 forces. The SS-25 mobile ICBMs could also be fired by this remote-control method. The procedure required that a special preliminary command be sent to the ICBM launch crews, who then performed a procedure to transfer direct control to higher authority. The whole procedure took about ten minutes, after which the missiles could be fired by the politico-military leadership without any further participation by the local launch teams.[61]

Such an arrangement presumably meant to ensure both rapid launch on warning and tight political control over Soviet nuclear forces, would in all likelihood have involved general staff participation in the unlock procedures performed at the central posts and in the activation of asso-ciated communications links to the missiles. The commander of the stra-tegic rocket forces was also involved in the preparation for remote auto-matic launch. In exercises the SRF headquarters itself demonstrated a capability for remotely launching mobile missiles in the field. The links between higher authority and the fixed or mobile missiles used under-ground cable, terrestrial land-line, and low-frequency radio communi-cations.

U.S. analysts appear to hold a range of opinion on the maturity of the remote-launch technology and the extent of its application. At one end of the spectrum is the view that systems designed for the unattended launching of communications or nuclear-armed rockets were experimen-tal. At the other end is the view that the systems were fully operational, at least for a substantial portion of the strategic missile force, relegating the SRF personnel at subordinate echelons—SRF army, division, regiment, and battalion—to housekeeping duties as far as the ICBM forces from the fourth generation on were concerned. Field personnel maintained the missiles' readiness; the central command posts in the Moscow area pushed the buttons that ignited their motors. Several senior U.S. government analysts stressed that the Soviets prized this streamlined release apparatus because it provided an all-important capability for rapid launch on warning.

Another variation on the theme was that the remote-control system permitted the central command posts to remove the safety catches (the electro-mechanical coded switch devices or permissive action links discussed below) in the launch centers or perhaps in the missile silos themselves, but that the actual firing of the missiles could still have been left to the fire control teams at the local battalion command posts. The SRF military crews would have implemented launch orders sent from the Moscow-area central command posts, but the electro-mechanical safeguards against the unauthorized launch of missiles would have been shed by the central posts themselves using automated systems linked directly to the local manned command posts or the unmanned silos or both.[62] By the same means the high command could have remotely reactivated the safeguards and thereby reimposed negative control if desired, though absolutely no evidence of that exists. The reactivation of blocking devices apparently occurred automatically in the local command posts by electronic means after a short time.

Soviet military officers interviewed for this study adamantly affirmed the existence of an operational capability for remotely firing modern ICBMs. One SRF career officer emphasized its importance in expediting a launch-on-warning response to U.S. attack. The most representative view held that the primary, normal method of release was to disseminate launch authorization (the direct command) to the crews in the missile fields. The command and control system resorted to the remote system of launch only if leaders feared that this normal mode would malfunction because of enemy strikes against the chain of command. It was asserted that the remote launch of ERCS missiles, as opposed to nuclear-armed missiles, was strictly limited to retaliatory operations after nuclear explosions on Soviet territory and that even then other conditions had to be met within a specified period of time in order to use this last-ditch tool of strike execution.[63]

Soviet efforts along these lines raised the question whether a comparable system had been developed to bring the sea-based missiles under the direct fire control of the Moscow command posts. Devising a reliable means for unlocking, much less firing, ballistic missiles on submarines submerged at sea (as opposed to those on alert on the surface at dockside, a common practice) from command posts on land, much less from deep underground centers as far away as Moscow, is of course a problematic technical feat. No evidence has turned up to suggest the existence of a system that allowed for remote unlocking and firing of SLBMs by the unattended launch procedure. Available evidence strongly suggests that Soviet SLBM launch procedures were similar to U.S. procedures. An order sent to the submarine was validated by a few crew members who then coordinated the firing of the vessel's missiles. In the case of Soviet but not U.S. submarines, as discussed later, the crews normally needed to receive unlock codes that enabled them to fire the weapons.

Authority and operational control at key command centers would still have been quite concentrated if, as seems likely, the primary method of disseminating launch authority to the strategic forces was simply to send short messages to the individual weapons commanders. The central authorities disseminated orders raising the level of combat readiness. Then they sent launch authorization, unlock codes, targeting instructions, and launch times in short, coded messages, galvanizing the launch teams into action to fire their weapons. This process was partly automated. For example, the Signal land-line communications link used to deliver the strike orders to launch crews in the ICBM battalion command posts, particularly those associated with fourth-generation forces, employed automation.[64] The physical act of firing the missiles, however, normally fell to the crews. Similarly, the Soviet fleet broadcast communications network (HF and VLF radio towers on shore) was an automated system for transmitting orders to the SSBN crews, who then manually carried out the launch procedures.

Nuclear Safeguards at the Top

Nuclear command and control systems are political, social, and cultural structures embedded in a larger socio-politico-cultural setting. Assessment that focuses narrowly on techno-organizational safeguards would exclude some potentially major sources of both cohesion and dysfunction in the systems.

Coup Dangers

Consider the abortive coup in August 1991 and the strain it put on the nuclear command system. The stresses were essentially socio-political in nature, as was the system's reaction. Questions about the status of the nuclear launch codes (the so-called nuclear suitcases, or footballs), though not unimportant, trivialize the command system's performance as it labored to preserve negative control. The established techno-organizational procedures had not been designed to cope with such upheaval at the apex of command and could not by themselves resist the designs of the coup leaders. Spontaneously improvised actions that deviated from established procedures had to be taken by second-echelon military commanders—people in key positions within the nuclear command system—to buttress negative control. Socio-political factors motivated these remedial actions. By the same coin, deviations from established procedures could undermine the negative function. The effects of socio-political factors on control can cut either way. They may be beneficial or harmful, depending on the circumstances.

Soviet designers subscribed to the principle that the higher the level of nuclear command and control, the stricter the safeguards against unauthorized use.[65] The reasoning behind this principle was that while the unauthorized use of even a single weapon by low-level commanders certainly could have caused an unprecedented disaster, the consequence of illicit action at the top of the hierarchy could have been apocalyptic.

The Soviets embodied this principle in a "system for preventing the unsanctioned use [that] rules out the possibility of a one-man decision," in the words of a former SRF commander.[66] The checks and balances at the top of the system consisted mainly of the separation of rights and authority to form the three key nuclear commands discussed earlier. No individual or organizational entity could independently issue a fully valid permission or direct command, let alone both. Many senior officials—the president, defense minister, CGS, and military CINCs—had to participate actively and consensually. Stern organizational and technical measures also existed to ensure that the prescribed procedures for issuing the various nuclear commands were not violated by those in the key positions of trust. Certain environmental conditions—notably, detection of incoming missiles—were also doctrinal and organizational prerequisites for initiating the emergency release procedures.

There is obviously a limit to the effectiveness of safeguards when there is extensive collusion and malfeasance among persons in key positions. In the final analysis, nuclear safety depends on the competence, virtue, and rationality of the nation's leaders. The coup attempt in 1991 thus put a strain on the Soviet system. The coup plotters not only were acting unlawfully but were also exhausted, confused, sometimes intoxicated, and clearly susceptible to irrational behavior.[67]

Yet nuclear safeguards were never severely compromised during this political upheaval. The nuclear command system adapted to the situation in ways that ruled out any possibility of the coup plotters authorizing the use of strategic nuclear weapons. The main adjustment responsible for maintaining effective safeguards was a decision taken collectively by the three CINCs of the strategic forces to disobey any nuclear orders from the coup plotters and accordingly to ensure that the command system continued to function in the manual mode. The coup leaders could not have bypassed these senior commanders so long as the manual mode was in effect. The preliminary and direct commands necessary to launch nuclear forces could not have been transmitted to the firing units of the SRF, the navy, or the air force unless the respective CINCs of those services consented to and participated in their dissemination. The SRF commander took the additional precaution of forbidding anyone to assign equipment and people for the purpose of carrying out orders from the coup plotters. He also increased the security of "ammunition depots, missile positions, and alert duty."[68]

Would the situation have been different if the CINCs had been willing to follow orders? First, it should be noted that the coup plotters themselves made no attempts to change the status of nuclear forces. Second, the complicity of all three persons filling the key positions—acting president, minister of defense, and chief of the general staff—would have been required if they were to have had any chance of starting an attack. As noted earlier, at the time of the coup the system of safeguards at the top required the positive participation of all three under peacetime conditions. Third, the acting president, Gennadiy Yanayev, almost certainly did not acquire the technical wherewithal for nuclear release that President Gorbachev held before the coup. The coup plotters did effectively strip President Gorbachev of his nuclear authority by isolating him and taking away the equipment he and his military aide needed to give his approval to send a permission command. But Yanayev did not take over Gorbachev's nuclear role.[69]

There are several reasons to doubt that Yanayev could have done so and circumvented the safeguards that protected Gorbachev's prerogative to issue the presidential vote in favor of sending the permission command. First, Yanayev could not have operated the equipment taken from President Gorbachev, because any sensible safeguard would have arranged for Gorbachev to possess unique information necessary to activate the equipment.[70] Gorbachev's military aides also almost certainly possessed unique information needed to generate the presidential code and surely could at least have disabled the device in an emergency. Indeed, Gorbachev's nuclear suitcase was reportedly rendered inoperable when military aides, returning by plane from the Crimea, erased its magnetic memory before turning it over to general staff representatives in Moscow.[71] The football was in effect disabled much earlier. When communications with Gorbachev's vacation home were cut at the outset of the coup, the football immediately went dead. Simultaneously, the footballs assigned to the defense minister and CGS went dead because the control center that linked all three footballs shut down whenever the president's football was disconnected.

Second, the nuclear suitcases held in reserve for presidential successors—remember that Vice President Yanayev was actually second in line in the chain of presidential succession, followed by the chairman of the Soviet Supreme, another conspirator in the plot—were not put on-line. Gorbachev loyalists in the general staff responsible for giving successors access to the Kazbek system made sure that Yanayev remained disconnected and incapable of using a football.[72] Finally, it should not be forgotten that the footballs were designed to function only in the context of a surprise Western attack. They were not for starting a war.[73] Even if Yanayev had acquired a viable on-line football, he could not have issued a nuclear command out of the blue.

What confluence of conditions might have enabled the coup plotters to release strategic nuclear weapons? It appears this might have been possible if all three of the following conditions had existed: (1) Yanayev and both Defense Minister Yazov and Chief of the General Staff Moiseyev had taken up positions in their wartime command posts and collectively ordered the launch of strategic forces; (2) their immediate staffs obeyed their commands; and (3) one or more of the senior commanders of the strategic forces followed orders and allowed their portion of the preliminary and direct commands to be joined with the CGS's portion for dissemination down the chain of command. As an alternative to the last condition, the senior strategic commanders could have relinquished full control to the new leadership by allowing the nuclear command system to be switched over to the automatic mode. Any attack launched under these conditions would have been an example of nuclear inadvertence caused by the illicit circumvention of safeguards at the apex of government. The orders to launch would have seemed fully legitimate to their executors in the missile fields, submarines, or bombers.

Although the strategic CINCs, at least, were prepared to thwart any nuclear plot hatched by the conspirators, the Soviet nuclear command and control system was not paralyzed during the coup. The system did not lose its ability to retaliate. In the event of enemy nuclear attack the CGS and CINC SRF still had the capability to generate the requisite preliminary and direct codes. Together they could have disseminated the launch authorization and unlock codes. Alternatively, the command system might have switched over to the automatic mode of operation in the event of an enemy attack that had inflicted severe damage to the chain of command. Either the CGS or CINC SRF could then have bypassed subordinate echelons and exercised direct launch control over the individual strategic forces.

An open question is whether a military conspiracy involving the CGS and CINC SRF could in theory have triggered the unauthorized launch of strategic forces. Remember that the permission command from the president and defense minister gave the military leadership the right to disseminate the direct command to the individual weapons commanders. But what prevented the military from issuing the direct command without permission? The main safeguard seems to have been the fact that the crucial direct command was composed of two codes, each of which was controlled by a different military organization. If the CGS and the CINC SRF conspired to affect the launch of strategic forces, apparently they could have succeeded unless other unknown safeguards existed to stop them. For instance, a separate organization (like the KGB) might have resided at the CGS or CINC war rooms to ensure that a direct command was never issued unless permission from higher authorities had been granted. Alternatively, a valid permission command might have been technically required to activate the systems used by the military leadership to generate and disseminate direct codes. Such possibilities, alas, cannot be reliably ascertained on the basis of available evidence. But comments by Russian military sources familiar with the nuclear command system, suggest that any additional checks and balances were probably more organizational than technical.

The basic structure thus appeared to depend on the loyalty of the military. The president and defense minister together had the *right* to use nuclear weapons; the CGS and the relevant nuclear CINCs together had the *ability* to use them.

The current leadership faces some danger of another palace coup, a military revolt, or other severe ruptures of this sort. The politico-military coalition, headed by Boris Yeltsin, that exercises nuclear command authority appears to rest on personal loyalties. Its wider political legitimacy and institutional support in Russia are too shallow to make its nuclear authority secure. On the contrary, the authority is precarious. The situation is ripe for a sudden discontinuous shift of power that confuses the chain of nuclear command and allows the reins of nuclear control to be illicitly seized. The crisis of legitimacy at the top clearly needs to be resolved to ensure stable negative control. But in view of the summer 1991 coup, the chronic nature of many of the conditions that produced it, and the ongoing political struggle in Moscow, a collapse of responsible authority at the highest level cannot be dismissed.

Challenges from Ukraine, Belarus, and Kazakhstan

The command and control system also remains tangled up in the larger political struggle among the leaders of Russia, Ukraine, Belarus, and Kazakhstan, all of which are home to sizable numbers of strategic forces. The evolving nuclear command arrangements thus mirror the realignment of these broader power relationships. Nationalism also tugs hard on the domestic politics of these states, and in the case of Ukraine it is creating centrifugal strains on the strategic command and control system of the Commonwealth.

Although the likelihood is slight that the non-Russian states will wrest enough autonomous control over nuclear forces to split the unified chain of nuclear command and gain independent launch capability, Ukraine, in particular, seeks greater control over the strategic weapons on its soil. President Leonid Kravchuk signed a decree that places all such forces in the Ukrainian armed forces and created an administrative command and control center for these weapons in the Ukrainian defense ministry.[74] Ukraine claimed ownership of the strategic missiles, bombers, and nuclear warheads, and had not set a specific schedule for conveying these components to Russia. Sentiment was growing in the Ukrainian parliament to reject START, decline to join the Nuclear Non-Proliferation Treaty, and retain the strategic forces on its territory unless conditions were met. The government sought outside economic help in dismantling the forces and monetary compensation for its share of the value of the fissile material ultimately recovered from the strategic and tactical nuclear warheads formerly based on Ukrainian soil.[75] It also sought security assurances from the international community.

Ukraine's efforts to exercise administrative control included paying the salaries and controlling the promotions of personnel in SRF support units, and requiring them to swear allegiance to Ukraine. Ukraine also took charge of general supply and maintenance functions for the SRF support bases.[76] Although Ukraine sought direct access to nuclear weapons, the Russian military refused, and the Russian government continued to pay (in rubles) and presumably promote the SRF combat units—the launch crews and others with direct access to nuclear weapons.[77] Russia also retained responsibility for maintaining the missiles and their critical support equipment.[78] Moscow nonetheless undoubtedly depended heavily on Ukrainian support to operate the strategic forces. The well-being of all SRF personnel (and their families) depended substantially on the hospitality of the host government, and even critical combat functions presumably would not have been sustainable without Ukrainian support. For instance, the host government presumably supplied the electrical power for running the equipment in the missile silos and launch control centers. Had Ukraine shut off this energy supply, the SRF combat units probably would have been forced to rely on short-lived power sources such as diesel generators and batteries.

Besides these inroads that gave Ukraine a degree of indirect control over strategic nuclear forces, President Kravchuk apparently acquired a primitive capability to physically block the launch of the nuclear missiles based in Ukraine. Kravchuk had been clamoring for physical veto power since a meeting at Alma-Alta in late 1991 at which the Commonwealth's council of the heads of state asked Marshal Shaposhnikov to provide the necessary apparatus.[79] A workable mechanism was supposed to have been designed in 1992 and put in place as early as 1993.[80] Six months after the meeting, Shaposhnikov defended himself against charges of procrastination, saying, "All I promised was to study the problem and report the results."[81] He balked at giving Ukraine a physical veto on the grounds that such a link into the system of technical control of nuclear weapons would make it a nuclear state in the eyes of the world. He argued that the "hot lines" already established to permit an emergency teleconference among the leaders of Russia, Ukraine, Belarus, and Kazakhstan were "quite enough."[82] In principle, President Kravchuk would be consulted and his approval received before any orders to use nuclear weapons based in Ukraine would be issued. Despite this consultative obligation, Russia alone possessed the technical ability to unlock and authorize the employment of nuclear forces.

Marshal Shaposhnikov did suggest, however, establishing a special hot line between President Kravchuk "and the commander of the strategic forces in Ukraine so that the latter could also take part in making decisions on strategic armaments."[83] If the 43d SRF army commander at his headquarters in Vinnitsa, Ukraine, had been willing to obey orders from Kravchuk, or if troops loyal to Ukraine were positioned to disable communications serving the headquarters, the president's launch veto power would have been strengthened, because the installation was a key retransmission point of the Russian strategic command system.[84] This headquarters maintained direct contact with all 176 ICBM launch posts in Ukraine.[85] By controlling the major land-line switching centers, for example, the Ukraine leadership could have severed the normal primary link between Moscow and the missiles. Such an arrangement was evidently implemented in late 1992.[86] It did not provide an ironclad veto, however, because the Russian high command retained alternate links and the technical ability to bypass the key SRF installation, disseminating launch orders directly to the missile launch crews, or alternatively, firing the missiles using radio signals sent from Moscow directly to the silos. However, this switchover from the normal, manual mode to the automatic mode of strategic command-control that bypassed intermediate nodes might have been impeded or even prevented if launch crews broke ranks with Moscow and refused to implement the transitional procedures.

Suspicion about Ukraine's long-term nuclear aspirations, and to a lesser degree Kazakhstan's, persists despite the declared intentions of both to become nuclear-free states and abide by the seven-year START I schedule for removing all nuclear arms from their soil. Governments and minds can change in seven years. Furthermore, the short-term stratagem of these states seemingly was to plant seeds of doubt. Given its dire economic straits, Ukraine in particular hoped to capitalize on the world's desire to resolve the uncertainty with a firm commitment to denuclearize. In short, money was the heart of the matter.

Western offers of financial assistance to dismantle Ukraine's forces, notably the U.S. funds set aside for this purpose by legislation sponsored by Senators Richard Lugar and Sam Nunn, may be the cure for Ukraine's recalcitrance. On the other hand, the prospective disbursements under the Soviet Nuclear Threat Reduction Act of 1991 may have inadvertently encouraged nuclear gamemanship. The U.S. overtures were counter-productive insofar as they strengthened Ukraine's incentives to raise the ante in a game of nuclear poker.

Some Ukrainians doubtless drove a hard bargain out of a sincere conviction that their nation's security would be placed in jeopardy by surrendering the weapons. For them, an independent nuclear capability would help guarantee Ukrainian security against Russian nuclear hege-mony.[87] The benefits of nuclear independence outweighed the myriad potential costs—isolation as a pariah state, loss of foreign aid, trade and other economic sanctions, and the high costs of maintaining a nuclear infrastructure.

But this calculation assumed that Ukraine had the ability to create a nuclear deterrent vis-à-vis Russia by taking control of the missile instal-lations on its soil. The assumption was heroic. It defied technical con-straints because the strategic missiles were not designed for such a role. Ukraine's ability to train the modern SS-24 missiles on Russian targets appeared doubtful at best. Assuming a minimum range of 3,000 miles, the closest Russian targets that could be threatened were located in Siberia and points east. Moscow and central Russia could perhaps be targeted by the variable-range SS-19 missiles in Ukraine. To project a credible nuclear threat to Moscow, however, Ukraine would be better served by strategic bombers or tactical nuclear weapons.

But Moscow apparently concluded that missile retargeting could not be ruled out. Whether Ukraine has undertaken technical studies to define the targeting options, as seems likely, conservative Russian officials as-sumed that "a state like Ukraine is able to develop its own targeting system within a few years."[88] From Moscow's perspective, the strategic missiles in Ukraine would eventually pose a direct nuclear threat to Russia if the Ukrainian government inherited them.

The Russian military probably developed a contingency plan to deal with any attempt by an emboldened Ukraine or other state to seize control over strategic forces. With the troop strength of its army numbering hundreds of thousands, Ukraine could easily overrun many strategic installations on its soil. Significant steps have therefore already been taken to render the weapons inoperable in the event of such takeovers. As discussed later, strategic forces outside Russia have been taken off alert and other measures have been or could be taken to neutralize the weapons and their command and control equipment in an emergency. Steps short of emergency destruction of systems and warheads would at least buy time, but if Ukraine managed to take physical possession of intact strategic weapons, the state would eventually gain an independent nuclear capability. Russia would face the difficult choice of permanently relinquishing control or conducting a large-scale military assault to regain physical custody.

Nuclear Safeguards below the Top Leadership

The Soviet government instituted a wide range of technical and organizational measures to prevent the unsanctioned use of nuclear weapons by subordinate echelons of the chain of command. The main safeguards were (1) the division of the command and control structure into two distinct types of organizations with separate chains of command, one responsible for managing the technical state of nuclear forces and one for providing military direction to the combat units; (2) the standard practice of keeping nuclear warheads apart from their delivery units; (3) the application of a two-person rule; (4) the utilization of elaborate feedback loops that enable subordinate units to be closely monitored by higher echelons; (5) the extensive use of electronic systems that enable higher echelons to disable missile launchers quickly and to neutralize lower level command posts; and (6) the extensive use of blocking devices designed physically to impede the unauthorized use of weapons.

Since the breakup of the Soviet Union, these standard measures have been supplemented by such unusual steps as consolidating tactical nuclear weapons at central storage depots inside Russia and lowering alert rates and combat readiness for strategic nuclear forces.

Dual and Parallel Chains of Command

The earlier discussion of the alerting and release procedures identified a separation of rights and functions among the participating entities: the supreme high command, general staff, and nuclear CINCs. The division of responsibilities between the general staff and the CINCs extended down to the lowest echelon. While the general staff normally exercised control by regulating the technical disposition of the nuclear forces in the field, the nuclear CINCs normally exercised command by directing the combat activities of the forces. These two separate, though interchangeable, functions converged at the bottom. For instance, an SRF launch crew in a battalion command post had a main control panel divided into a technical part and a military part. In peacetime the launch crew worked with the technical part, which was concerned with the preparedness and functioning of missile equipment and warheads. The military part, used in conjunction with combat orders from the CINC SRF, was normally inactive. A coherent series of technical commands—notably, a preliminary command—approved by the general staff had to be disseminated to the rocket crews before they could gain access to and work with the military panel. The crews went back and forth between the panels as they performed the prelaunch and launch procedures. The technical panel, for example, was active in the processing of unlock codes normally issued by the general staff. Targeting instructions, launch times, and other critical military orders came from the CINC SRF through the military panel.

The scope of the general staff's involvement in the nuclear control process included many activities that Western observers had long believed were performed by the KGB. Although Western analysts credited the general staff with major responsibilities for planning and coordinating the operational activities of the armed forces and noted its pervasive if sometimes shadowy presence in the field,[89] many thought the KGB secretly pulled the strings on the nuclear control apparatus. Other organizations, with their own separate chains of command, were also believed to be involved in some aspects of nuclear operations—for instance, *zampolit* officers of the Main Political Administration (MPA) and special interior troops from the Ministry of Interior Affairs (MVD)[90]—but Western speculation usually centered on the KGB. Though technically subordinate to the Council of Ministers, it operated independently under the direction of the Politburo and seemed an obvious choice for the role of nuclear watchdog. KGB units, installations, and communications links, for example, appeared to become very active during emergency military operations and major exercises involving nuclear forces.[91] The KGB was considered an integral part of the custodial and combat operations throughout the nuclear command system. As recently as 1991, Alexander

Rutskoy, the Russian prime minister, reportedly asserted that the physical control of all nuclear weapons was in the hands of KGB special units.[92]

Custodial operations refer to the managing of nuclear warhead stockpiles during their storage or transportation when they are separate from the means of delivery. This separation was a standard safeguard for tactical (except sea-based) and some strategic nuclear forces. The KGB's alleged custodial responsibilities included the menial duties of guarding nuclear depots, transporting nuclear weapons, and turning them over to military units when necessary. For example, the nuclear warheads for the SCALEBOARD, SCUD, and FROG missiles as well as artillery guns were said to be controlled by local detachments of KGB troops.[93] Another longtime observer asserted that "Soviet nuclear storage sites are separate from the delivery systems and heavily guarded by KGB troops."[94] The KGB was also often assumed to provide the communications trunks and cryptographic services supporting these custodial tasks.[95] Western analysts have widely speculated that the units assigned these many and varied tasks were affiliated with either the Third or the Ninth Directorate of the KGB.[96]

Without doubt there existed some special custodial unit with its own chain of command that stood apart from the regular military. The former first deputy chief of the general staff (for general affairs) acknowledged this publicly in an interview about tactical weapons security: "Storage and maintenance of tactical nuclear ammunition is the concern of specialized bodies which have their own control and command structure. Transfer of tactical nuclear ammunition from maintenance and storage units to units designed to use them is affected by a special signal. It is impossible for troop commanders by themselves to decide on receiving, transferring or using these weapons."[97] However, the Defense Ministry and general staff, not the KGB, evidently played this role. A corp of elite volunteers assigned to the general staff, headed by a two-star army general, served as the custodians for tactical nuclear munitions.[98]

This special section of the general staff surely also managed the warheads for unarmed strategic forces. Sizable stockpiles were doubtless maintained near SSBN ports, airbases for long-range bombers, and ICBM fields. Since none of the bombers and only a small fraction of the SSBN forces were kept on alert in peacetime, the custodial units would have played an important logistical role in the event of a Soviet decision to place them on a war footing.[99] The same situation once existed for the ICBM, IRBM, and MRBM forces. Until the late 1960s the nuclear warheads for all such missile deployments were stored in peacetime at depots located tens of miles away from the launch pads. (The nuclear warheads sent to Cuba in 1962 were reportedly stored less than a mile from the SS-4 MRBM emplacements.)[100]

In this vein, remember the 1968 SRF alert discussed earlier, in which warheads were mated to SS-5 missiles. The defector who related this story said that special troops from outside the SRF installation arrived at the launch pads with nuclear warheads and loaded them onto the missiles. The affiliation of these special troops was not revealed, but it probably was not a KGB operation.[101] They probably took orders from the Defense Ministry through the general staff, which was responsible for the technical status of the missile forces. Consistent with that assignment, the special troops stood by at the launch pads to carry out any further instructions, which would have included, according to the defector, arming the nuclear warheads and setting their height of burst. Such wartime actions would have been coordinated at the scene with the SRF battery fire control officers who were responsible for launching the missiles on combat orders from the CINC SRF.

The suspected role of the KGB in controlling newer generations of nuclear forces on combat alert, with warheads attached, circulated for many years. William Scott considered it a logical assignment.[102] Others saw evidence for it. According to Stephen Meyer, "There are reports that KGB officers serve on all Soviet nuclear-weapons-carrying submarines as part of the command and control system."[103] Another report, said to be based on an authoritative source, claimed that each ICBM launch control center had a crew of four: two SRF and two KGB officers.[104] Another claimed the presence of KGB troops at regimental ICBM complexes who controlled the nuclear warheads for modern silo-based missiles.[105] The most authoritative source for the claim that KGB-affiliated special troops participated in firing modern ICBMs was a Western intelligence analyst who told me that two SRF officers, a political officer, and two KGB "special troops" performed launch duties in the ICBM launch centers. Regarding IRBM forces, Steven Zaloga identified the guard units and nuclear-use authorization teams assigned to the SS-20 missile forces (now defunct as a result of the INF Treaty) as KGB troops.[106] Finally, one interviewee believed that KGB counterintelligence personnel OOs from the Third Directorate were attached to SS-24 train-mobile ICBM regiments to control the nuclear warheads mated to these modern forces.[107]

These claims seem dubious. The best available evidence suggests that the KGB's presence in the nuclear combat units was nominal, and it performed no combat tasks. One source for this book has interviewed a number of Soviet émigrés and defectors who formerly served in Soviet nuclear units and has reached the same conclusion.[108] My interviews with many such persons, as well as with many military sources within Russia, affirmed the existence of some roles for political officers in some strategic and tactical nuclear units, but none for the KGB. The only other significant presence beyond the regular military personnel in the field was that of the special troops of the general staff who oversaw warheads in storage. It is of course possible, as one active-duty Russian general asserted in an interview, that a portion of the special troops were affiliated with the KGB.[109]

Regarding sea-based nuclear forces, a former Soviet naval officer who served in the central command post of a modern SSBN during the early 1980s said that a KGB officer was indeed assigned to his vessel. However, the KGB man had no combat portfolio. He merely "walked around and smiled," according to the Soviet naval officer. The political officer, on the other hand, was responsible for checking certain codes in a launch order to verify that they matched codes held in the vessel. A similar division of responsibilities existed on attack submarines (SSN) armed with nuclear torpedoes. In an interview a former Soviet naval officer who served aboard such a vessel revealed that a KGB officer sometimes accompanied it on a mission but that he had no combat duties whatsoever.[110] The activities of the KGB were unrelated to nuclear weapons control except that it apparently monitored crew discipline and political reliability. The SSN officer revealed that the ship's captain and political officer were solely responsible for verifying and carrying out nuclear release orders.

By some accounts, political officers also performed similar duties in ICBM command posts. One account came in an interview with a recent émigré who, shortly before he left the Soviet Union, attended an SRF training school to learn launch duties for a heavy ICBM launch control post. He identified the duties as those of a political officer. Recall also that the Western intelligence analyst who placed KGB troops in the ICBM launch control centers also claimed that each five-person launch team included a political officer with combat duties. Other Western sources also conceded that a combat role was possible for political officers in the strategic rocket forces. Meyer cited an article in *Pravda* as hinting at such a role.[111] But it is interesting to note that the SRF defector who described the nuclear alert in 1968 stated that the political officers were not even allowed into the battalion command post of his SS-5 unit. And in other interviews with Soviet officials and military officers familiar with modern ICBM operations, the existence of a combat role for political officers or, for that matter, KGB personnel was emphatically denied. (Since the breakup of the Soviet Union the MPA has been abolished, and political activities in the Soviet military have been banned.)

It also appears that the special custodians for ICBM warheads were withdrawn long ago as the Soviets deployed modern missiles fitted with warheads in peacetime. The manual control function once performed by these special custodians was clearly replaced by automated control systems, particularly the electronic blocking system.

Blocking Devices and Unlock Codes

The Soviet penchant for tight centralization gave rise to the extreme physical concentration of nuclear weapons control at the level of the general staff. This organization possessed the unlock codes for the blocking devices that physically prevented the illicit firing of strategic nuclear weapons. The incorporation of such locking devices in modern forces would go a long way to explain a diminishing presence of extra-military troops in firing units. Technical safeguards substantially replaced labor-intensive, procedural safeguards for the strategic forces in particular.

The top level of the general staff had responsibility for the safekeeping of the unlock codes. On the direction of the defense minister, who in turn received direction from the president, the general staff released the codes in conjunction with sending a direct command to the strategic units previously designated by the preliminary command.[112] For the tactical nuclear forces, custody of the unlock codes for the warheads or their containers lay in principle but not in practice with the CGS. The job was farmed out to lower echelons: CINC ground forces, theater (TVD) commanders, or military district commanders. General staff cells at these facilities were surely responsible for them, in keeping with the principle of maintaining strict separation between technical control and military command. Through general staff channels, the unlock codes were sent to the special warhead custodians in the field, who loaded warheads onto their means of delivery, while the regular military troops who fired the weapons stood by to receive the direct command that authorized use. Usually the regular troops also had to receive a different set of unlock codes to fire their weapons—for instance, two artillery troops each received separate codes that were inserted into the artillery piece to discharge the gun. This second set of codes came from higher authority in the direct military chain of command—for example, front or group-of-forces commanders—whereas the unlock codes for the nuclear warheads came, as mentioned, through the separate general staff channel.

There were several different types of such locks: mechanical, electro-mechanical, and electronic. As a rule the mechanical locks were used to secure containers for all types of warheads in storage or transportation. The electro-mechanical devices blocked the application means, such as the launchers for nuclear torpedoes and cruise missiles, or the hanger apparatus for bombs on aircraft. The electronic devices unblocked the warheads themselves. As the example given above illustrates, various combinations of these devices controlled variously by general staff and regular military channels could have been used. The precise configuration for each of the many tens of weapon types was uncertain. The Soviets released scant information on them, and other data are too flimsy to support firm conclusions.

LAND-BASED TACTICAL WEAPONS. Data on tactical weapons are the poorest, but enough information exists to provide tentative judgments. The Soviets claimed to have imposed stringent blocking devices on warheads for land-based systems, such as the artillery systems discussed earlier. One senior Soviet military source asserted that "in the army, warhead technical safety is ensured by a range of tough precautions against unauthorized use, including electronic code and mechanical blocking, to be lifted only by the supreme military-political leadership, namely the president as the supreme commander in chief."[113] This claim regarding the use of the locks on land-based tactical weapons was also made by Marshal Sergei Akhromeyev, the former CGS, in a private meeting with Western visitors in 1991.[114] Other Soviet military sources confirmed this claim in interviews with me.

Three major caveats, however, should be attached to such claims. First, the blocking devices often amounted to mechanical locks, such as padlocks on warhead containers. Second, the assertion that these blocks could be lifted only by the supreme leadership referred to rights, not capabilities. The unlock codes were not physically controlled by the president. Third, contingency plans for a crisis called for the warheads to be evacuated from depots, dispatched to the field, removed from their containers, and mated to the delivery systems. The technical safeguards could have been shed in the course of preparing for possible battle before a final decision on their use was made.

SEA-BASED TACTICAL WEAPONS. These seem to have had the weakest protection against unauthorized use. Not only were their warheads mated to their delivery means in peacetime, unlike the land-based warheads, but their technical safeguards appeared slipshod. Marshal Akhromeyev (who committed suicide shortly after the 1991 coup failed) testified before the U.S. Congress in 1990 that "we in the Soviet Union consider that the tactical naval nuclear weapons are less protected against nonsanctioned actions than nuclear weapons of other armed services because of unavoidable autonomous sea patrols of every ship carrying out training combat tasks."[115] Nuclear torpedoes, in particular, seemed to be subject to rudimentary safeguards. According to officers who served on an attack submarine and a ballistic missile submarine, each armed with nuclear torpedoes, the critical safeguard was an ignition device the size of a coffee cup that normally was stored in the captain's quarters.[116] Once screwed into the torpedo, the weapon was ready to be fired. The crew did not have the right to fire it—that was of course the exclusive prerogative of the supreme command—but it almost certainly had the capability to do so.[117]

BALLISTIC MISSILE SUBMARINES. Strategic nuclear forces, by contrast, were equipped with sophisticated blocking devices whose lifting appears to have depended physically on the joint actions taken by the general staff and CINCs on behalf of the top leadership. At a minimum, a direct command replete with unlock codes had normally to be received by the launch crews. The available evidence leaves room for debate, however, particularly in the case of ballistic missile submarines.

Marshal Akhromeyev's observation about the autonomy of naval forces raises the question whether SSBNs were restrained by stringent physical safeguards. Akhromeyev indeed told Western visitors in a private meeting that Soviet SSBNs were not equipped with blocking devices that required coded input from higher authority prior to launch.[118] General Batenin, a military adviser to the Russian Foreign Ministry, also claimed that SSBNs had physical autonomy and could technically have fired without authorization.[119] These contentions are supported by a Western news report that cited sources within the Bush administration as saying that Soviet nuclear-armed submarines did not have so-called permissive action links (the U.S. term for blocking devices).[120] Such autonomy raises the specter of a renegade crew taking matters into their own hands—the *Hunt for Red October* threat. This is precisely the alleged threat used to justify the U.S. deployment of limited missile defenses.

If the technical safeguards were in fact missing, negative control would have relied completely on crew reliability and procedural measures, as is true for U.S. SSBNs. The basic procedural safeguard could still have incorporated physical restraints—for example, locking launch keys inside the vessel's safes, whose combinations were known only to various crew members—the arrangement found on U.S. SSBNs.[121] Some evidence suggests the Soviets indeed took the same approach as the United States. In describing the U.S. method for lifting the blocking system on U.S. SSBNs by means of multiple keys, a Soviet general implied that a similar arrangement existed on Soviet strategic missile submarines.[122]

But Soviet SSBN safeguards were surely more stringent, in keeping with the Soviets' uncompromising stance on nuclear control. There is definite evidence that external input—information from outside the vessel—was needed to enable the crew to fire its missiles. Perhaps the strongest evidence came from a former Delta-II and Delta-III class SSBN crew member, whose version of the launch procedure alleged the existence of electronic blocking systems that needed to be lifted prior to launch.[123] Special unlock codes had to be received from higher authority and punched into the on-board weapon system computer to deactivate the blocking system that prevented unsanctioned launch.

A launch order (the direct command) came as a signals package sent jointly by the CGS and the CINC of the navy (or CINC SRF in special circumstances) through a communications network called *Volna*. This package was broken down into several parcels for verification by personnel and electronic devices. A designated officer (formerly the political officer), the executive officer, and the captain verified codes manually and ensured that the order was transmitted over the proper frequency, which the general staff periodically changed. The key verification required the insertion of certain codes into an electronic device called the decoding and interlocking system. If the codes failed to validate, this system would not have electronically activated the submarine's fire control and missile control systems, and the crew would have been deprived of the physical capability to launch its missiles. In addition, once the fire control system was turned on, the captain had to use a special key to operate it, and he had to insert a special code into the system before it would process launch procedures. That code, too, could have come from higher authority.[124]

Another Soviet military source familiar with SSBN launch procedures confirmed this account but added that the procedures varied with circumstances. Orders and procedures were different for preemptive and retaliatory launches. Sometimes a launch order received on one radio frequency had to be confirmed by an order sent over another channel. Sometimes a preliminary command was sent to the SSBNs, but it was not mandatory. A single direct command might have sufficed. Furthermore, this expert said, it was technically possible and permissible under certain special conditions for the SSBN crew to circumvent the blocking system and launch the missiles. Such procedures required a complex series of supplemental actions that military officials outside the submarine carried out in tandem with actions by the crew. The external-internal steps had to be taken in a certain sequence and in a certain amount of time. Different members of the SSBN crew established separate links to the outside, put separate codes together, and jointly performed procedures called preliminary unblocking. Upon another external command, the crew carried out the remaining launch procedures.

This description is intriguing, but it could be interpreted to mean that procedures existed to bypass the peacetime blocking system when primary communications faltered during war. The special conditions in question were probably nuclear detonations, which the SSBN is equipped to detect using on-board sensors. The emergency backup procedures might have ensured that the blocking devices on SSBNs did not interfere with the firing of missiles should an enemy attack destroy the general staff link used to disseminate codes for the blocking device. It should be stressed that the SSBN crew still did not operate independently in these circumstances, but instead acted in concert with unidentified outside entities who by some unknown means enabled a launch to occur. It is reasonable to surmise that the key outside entity was the CINC SRF, who held contingent authority over SSBNs in dire emergencies. According to the source of this story, the circumvention of the normal blocking devices in the manner described could not have significantly decreased the level of safeguards, because of the many additional requirements that had to be met prior to SLBM launch. This source added that sea-launched cruise missiles deployed on submarines (but not surface ships) were handled like SLBMs. In special circumstances their blocking devices could also be bypassed without the normal command.

The extreme stringency of Soviet SSBN safeguards indicated by these insider accounts squares with a recent evaluation by the U.S. director of

Central Intelligence. Robert Gates testified in January 1992 that Soviet SSBNs are "under the same strong control as the ICBMs."[125] Gates's assessment is perhaps too sanguine because the Soviet silo-based ICBM force surpassed every other weapon system in terms of negative control.

INTERCONTINENTAL BALLISTIC MISSILES. Blocking devices for modern Soviet ICBMs, like the SS-18, seemed more straightforward. Without exception, Soviet military sources say that the ICBM launch crews had to obtain unlock codes to be physically able to dispatch their rockets. The general staff normally transmitted these enabling codes over the Signal communications system to the battalion launch control centers.[126] Senior Soviet officers in the SRF presumably had this operation in mind when they emphasized that their launch pads were fail-safe and provided an absolute guarantee against unsanctioned actions.[127] On the other hand, missile launch crews in the SRF are reported to have been trained to handle situations such as "then somewhere in the distance an unauthorized missile launch has occurred."[128] If a launch crew issued improper commands to any of its missiles, indications automatically appeared on the monitors of the neighboring launch crews (one to the left and one to the right), who were supposed to cancel the commands.[129]

In private discussions Soviet military sources described the unlock system in some detail. They noted that after receiving the preliminary command, but before receiving the direct command, the launch crews gained access to the pertinent equipment and could try to guess the unlock codes. After three unsuccessful guesses of the multidigit code, all of which had to be tried in a matter of several seconds, the system locked out the user. Such mischief aside, the entry of the unlock codes sent by the general staff left little tolerance for human laxity or error. After the codes were successfully entered, the crew had only a short time to complete the remaining launch procedures before the blocking system was automatically reactivated.[130] Other features of the Soviet ICBM control system designed to strengthen safeguards included a capability for higher command posts to monitor and, if necessary, override by technical means the actions taken by crews. The missile launchers automatically reported their status to high-level command posts, which could take steps to neutralize the low-level rocket complexes. For instance, the higher centers could isolate rocket launch centers at the regiment level by remotely switching off the latter's communications. The higher centers could assign backup launch centers in the regiment to assume the control functions of the deviant unit.

Mobile ICBMs were nearly as tightly controlled as silo-based ICBMs. One significant difference mentioned by a Soviet military source was that a special command for canceling a launch order may have been less likely to be carried out. The reason was that the rules for validating a cancel launch command were more subjective. It involved more discretion on the part of a mobile ICBM crew than of a silo-based ICBM crew.

LONG-RANGE BOMBERS. Strategic aircraft were reasonably well safeguarded from a technical standpoint. The long-range bombers appear to have been equipped with blocking devices that were connected to the general staff and that had to be lifted for the bomber crews to use their nuclear payloads. More in the realm of speculation than fact, aircraft crews may also have had to follow an exact mission plan programmed on tape at the start of a mission. Failure to conform exactly to the mission profile might have prevented the on-board weapons system from arming. One variant of this process involved the activation of special ground beacons that automatically armed the weapons system if a nuclear attack was authorized and if the aircraft followed the proper course over a sequence of such radio beacons. A former U.S. government analyst claimed that such a remote arming system was apparently used for Soviet tactical nuclear aircraft during the 1960s. A similar system could also have been employed with strategic aircraft. The analyst also believed that Soviet long-range bombers flew in pairs and armed each other in flight as a precaution against an unauthorized nuclear attack by a single plane.

AIR-LAUNCHED CRUISE MISSILES. Interviews with a former SRF officer revealed there were no special circumstances that permitted the blocking devices for ALCMs on heavy bombers to be bypassed. This also applied to sea-launched cruise missiles on surface ships. It was noted, however, that these devices were integral to the bombers and ships rather than to the missiles themselves. The ALCM was an especially troublesome case, for in the event of its illicit seizure its possessor could have used it from any type of aircraft. Since the ALCM was the primary nuclear payload of the current strategic bomber fleet, this was a significant shortcoming. It may well be a major reason why the Soviets did not routinely keep bombers armed and poised for quick takeoff.

Weapons Consolidation and Lowered Combat Readiness

The Russians have been busily rounding up their far-flung nuclear arsenal and consolidating it inside Russian territory. This obviously alleviates the danger of weapons falling into the wrong hands. Previously, not only were the weapons too widely dispersed but large numbers were stored in depots that were not designed to deal with domestic threats. For many decades of authoritarian rule it was safely assumed that local populations posed no threat to the security of military installations. The main concern was to keep the location of warhead stocks hidden from Western detection in order to maximize their chances of survival during war. The Soviet forward-deployed sites thus blended into the surrounding environment and lacked the high-profile fences, flood lights, clearings, and other intense security systems that would be essential if domestic terrorism was the primary danger.[131] But in recent times the situation was reversed. The heirs to the Soviet Union began to worry less about Western targeting of nuclear sites and more about popular uprisings, terrorism, subnational and even national challenges, and other internal threats to nuclear installations. The consolidation of warhead stockpiles at central storage facilities inside Russia was the logical remedy.

All tactical nuclear warheads in Eastern Europe had been relocated to Soviet territory by about August 1991. As for tactical weapons stationed on the territory of the former Soviet republics other than Russia—an estimated 2,500 in Ukraine and a roughly equal number spread across at least eight other republics (including the three Baltic states) at the end of 1989—all had been relocated to central storage depots inside Russia by the summer of 1992.[132] This consolidation eliminated the problem of inter-republic conflict involving the use of tactical nuclear weapons, and greatly alleviated the danger of captured or stolen weapons falling into the hands of third countries. The small size and relative flexibility of use of tactical weapons made them a far greater threat than long-range strategic weapons, which are inherently more secure and less usable in regional conflicts.

As best one can tell from publicly available information, the unprecedented mass relocation of tactical nuclear weapons was not marred by any serious incidents. Extraordinary precautions were taken during the loading and shipping.[133] Prior to shipment to Russia, each warhead was mechanically disabled to preclude the possibility of a nuclear explosion, and no more than two warheads were carried in each rail car. When trucks were used, each vehicle was loaded with one warhead.[134] A convoy was heavily guarded using air cover and armored personnel carriers between each truck; public roads were closed when more than three warheads were transported.[135] By all accounts the general staff custodians

THE SOVIET COMMAND SYSTEM

who have supervised the transfer experienced no lapses of security and suffered no serious accidents.[136] The tactical weapons at greatest risk appear to be naval weapons such as nuclear torpedoes. Their safeguards were deficient enough to pose a potential danger until all tactical naval weapons had been removed from ships. This transfer was reportedly completed by the end of September 1992, as planned.[137]

A large quantity of strategic weapons remain in several of the former republics. Potential problems of control have been alleviated, however, by lowering their alert levels. The alert status of strategic forces cannot be precisely gauged, but apparently all 104 SS-18 missiles in Kazakhstan—a third of the first-line counterstrategic forces—have been taken off combat alert, along with the 130 SS-19 and 46 SS-24 missiles in Ukraine and the 81 SS-25 mobile missiles in Belarus.[138] In addition, the bomber nuclear payloads in Kazakhstan and Ukraine have been disabled or relocated. All such weapons in Kazakhstan were recently removed to central storage locations.[139] Last, the alert rate of SSBNs at sea appears to have dropped to one or two on combat alert, substantially lower than it was a year or so ago. Additional SSBNs remained on launch-ready alert in port.[140]

If the non-Russian states inherited the nuclear forces on their territory, could the forces be returned to combat ready status? The answer depends on the disposition of the constituent parts—the delivery systems, warheads, and launchers. The reconstitution of nuclear bomber capability depends far less critically on controlling the Bear H strategic aircraft than on getting hold of their armaments, notably the nuclear-armed air-launched cruise missiles. Possession of the armaments is key because they lack technical safeguards and hence could be released and detonated from virtually any aircraft.[141] Ukraine and Kazakhstan evidently did not have ready access to this ordnance, however. The payloads in Kazakhstan were inaccessible, because they had actually been removed to Russia. In Ukraine, the bomber weapons were more accessible inasmuch as they evidently resided in army storage facilities inside Ukraine, but the weapons had been disabled and remained under Russian custody.

The ability of the non-Russian states to reconstitute the strategic missile forces on their soil is a more complex issue. The combat potential of these forces varied according to location, missile type, and other factors. In Kazakhstan, a small number of SS-18 missiles have been removed from their silos,[142] while the remainder could probably be returned to full launch-ready status within a couple of days under normal SRF direction.[143] The measures taken to lower their combat readiness involved relatively minor changes in command and communications—for example, the deactivation of a key satellite link that connected the battalion launch control centers with the high-level command posts in the Moscow vicinity. In Belarus, the mobile SS-25s that were taken off alert and consolidated at their home garrisons could be regenerated in a matter of hours to days. In Ukraine, the SS-19 and SS-24 forces apparently have been thoroughly deactivated, though differing accounts were given by various Russian military officials. One source estimated that Russia would need about three months to regenerate all these missiles in Ukraine.[144] Another Russian officer reportedly said that 90 of the SS-19s in Ukraine had been "disarmed," leaving 40 SS-19s and 46 SS-24s in a more advanced state of readiness.[145] A third Russian general, recently retired from the SRF, suggested that the deactivation of the missiles involved "removing cables."[146] It is uncertain whether these assessments implied that nuclear warheads had been removed from a portion of the force, but another senior Russian officer reported that in Ukraine the warheads had been separated from the launchers to some extent.[147]

Although Marshal Shaposhnikov reported in mid-1992 that a concrete plan existed for detargeting the missiles, removing the warheads (replacing them temporarily with "non-nuclear equivalents") and transferring warheads and boosters to Russia by the end of 1993, the government of Ukraine rejected the plan except for its detargeting provision.[148] The proposal "to delete the flight maps from onboard computers" was not opposed, but the Ukrainian deputy defense minister, Ivan Bizhan, opposed Shaposhnikov's plans for repatriating the warheads and missiles any time soon.[149] It must therefore be assumed that the original deployments of nuclear-tipped strategic missiles in Ukraine remained in place. It is reasonable to suppose that none were immediately launch-ready and that the steps taken to deactivate the forces could not be quickly reversed.

These reductions in combat readiness may well have been intended to thwart any plot to seize control of usable strategic weapons outside Russia. The declining operating tempo of the forces may also be due in part to austere economic conditions, shortages of spare parts, and other maintenance problems.[150] In any case, the effect has been to alleviate potential problems of negative control.

What about the security of the thousands of nuclear weapons scattered around the territory of the Russian federation itself, which was hardly immune to sub-state and civil strife? Although the vast majority of strategic weapons were deployed in *oblast* and *kray* areas within Russia (administrative units with predominant Russian majorities), tactical nuclear weapons were probably distributed much more widely among republics and autonomous districts populated by non-Russian ethnic groups.[151]

The strategic bases at Yoshkar-Ola and Mozdok were the most exposed to civil unrest. A division of forty SS-13 and eighteen SS-25 strategic missiles was based near Yoshkar-Ola in the potentially unstable republic of Marii-El (Volga region),[152] which was also a candidate to receive SS-25 mobile ICBMs scheduled to be transferred from Belarus in 1993 and 1994. Far less stable than this region was the North Ossetian Soviet Socialist Republic in North Caucasus, where twenty-two Bear-H strategic bombers were stationed at Mozdok. A civil conflict raged only a few miles from this base. A blackjack bomber factory at Kazan' in the rebellious republic of Tatarstan (Volga region) also posed a potential problem.[153]

These dangers were mitigated by Russian plans to eliminate the SS-13 deployments at Yoshkar-Ola under START, to remove the nuclear cruise missile payloads for the Bear-H bombers to storage depots under the Gorbachev initiative of October 1991, and to halt production of Blackjack bombers in separatist-minded Tatarstan by decree of President Yeltsin in January 1992. The dismantling of SS-13s appears to have been completed. The removal of the bomber payloads from Mozdok to central storage in a more secure part of Russia may have occurred, but the Russian government had not disclosed the location of the storage sites. The cruise missiles may have remained in North Ossetia.

The even greater danger posed by the tactical nuclear warheads dispersed throughout the Russian federation received attention under the Gorbachev plan, which called for their consolidation and wholesale elimination. As of early 1992 the general staff's plan for removing tactical weapons to central and factory storage facilities set the following schedule: complete removal by 1995 of all nuclear warheads for tactical missiles, nuclear artillery shells and nuclear mines (elimination of mines to be completed in 1998, and all others in 2000); complete removal of nuclear weapons for ships and submarines by October 1992, and naval aviation payloads by 1996 (elimination of one-third of these inventories to be completed by 1996); complete removal of nuclear warheads for antiaircraft missiles by 1996 (elimination of one-half by 1997); and elimination of one-half the stockpile of nuclear munitions for tactical aviation (schedule unspecified).[154]

Under this plan, a total of about 14,000 tactical nuclear warheads would be consolidated at storage depots, and about 10,000 of these would be destroyed.[155] These figures could grow to about 16,000 and 12,000, respectively, if Gorbachev's other proposals requiring U.S. reciprocation were adopted. In addition, about 8,000 strategic warheads removed from forces decommissioned under the terms of START and the Bush-Yeltsin agreement could join the queue for dismantling.[156] A grand total of about 20,000 nuclear warheads would be slated for elimination during the next decade (1993–2003). Russia had previously been dismantling obsolete warheads since 1985; a total of 8,000 to 10,000 had been eliminated by early 1992.[157] According to one Russian estimate, warhead dismantling had been carried out at two facilities at a combined rate of 1,500 warheads per year; maximum capacity was double or triple this rate.[158] At twice the historical rate, it would take seven years to dismantle 20,000 warheads.

President Yeltsin announced in late 1992 that Russia had begun to dismantle nuclear warheads at three facilities.[159] The nuclear weapons repatriated from Ukraine and elsewhere were also sent to a central storage in Tomsk.[160] All these facilities, and most likely the handful of other central storage depots, were located in stable *oblasts* of the Russian federation. Security at these sites was probably compromised somewhat by the overflow of the bunkers caused by the influx of warheads from the non-Russian states. This saturation presumably delayed the removal of warheads from combat support depots dispersed throughout Russia itself. Thousands of tactical and strategic nuclear weapons doubtless remained in dispersed storage depots at upward of thirty locations around the country.[161]

Other Technical Safeguards

Three of the many other technical safeguards in the command and control system are noteworthy. First, certain weapons systems were rigged for automatic or manual disabling if security was violated. For instance, the unmanned ICBM launchers had sensors designed to detect a forced entry and trigger a disabling of the launch system.[162] Missile systems were also probably routinely rigged for emergency destruction using explosive charges, because of long-standing Soviet concern that Western forces might overrun and capture forward-based ICBMs during a large-scale conventional war.

Second, some delivery systems or their warheads had environmental sensing devices (ESDs) designed to ensure that specific conditions were met before a warhead was armed for detonation. A Soviet strategic missile warhead monitored its acceleration, the surrounding barometric pressure, and its deceleration to determine whether and when to arm itself for detonation. The necessary preconditions were next to impossible for anyone to simulate on the ground. An attempt to trigger a nuclear explosion by applying pressure, heat, electrical sources, and so forth would not have fooled the sensors. A normal flight was necessary. Many other types of weapons were not as immune to tampering, however. Nuclear land mines and artillery shells, for example, probably did not have ESDs.

Third, a sizable portion of the Soviet strategic missile force was rigged for self-destruction during flight if the missile strayed off course during the boost phase. On-board sensors took a three-star astral reading to determine whether the missile was following its proper trajectory. If the actual flight path fell out of the tolerable range, the deviation triggered an explosive charge that blew up the missile. This passive system, called system automatic destruction missile (SAPR is the Russian acronym), was unique to the Soviet force. It was extensively used in the SLBM arsenal and to a lesser but still considerable extent in the ICBM arsenal.[163] One former Soviet SRF officer asserted that these charges could be detonated while missiles were still in their silos.

Overall Assessment: The Efficacy of Safeguards in Historical Context

Although unforeseen loopholes lurk in any system, a long-standing and deep-seated obsession with controlling nuclear weapons led the Soviets to go to extraordinary lengths to ensure tight central control on nuclear weapons. Their safeguards were more stringent than those of any other nuclear power, including the United States.

SAFEGUARDS AND DOMESTIC CRISIS. Under present and in all likelihood future conditions, that system should be able to deal effectively with aberrant behavior within the chain of command and with threats stemming from social upheaval within the former Soviet Union. The outlook changes drastically for the worse if the social and political situation degenerates into civil war, an overthrow of the government, an all-

out effort by former republics to seize weapons by force, or other inter-
necine violence. The Soviet nuclear command system was not designed,
and could not be designed, to deal effectively with turbulence of such
magnitude. Although the system did prove remarkably resilient during
the 1991 coup and probably could weather far more social turmoil than
has occurred to date, the command and control system at root is a human
organization susceptible to the same degenerative processes that plague
the whole of society. There is a threshold at which the system would cease
to function as a coherent, effective organization.

At that moment of organizational collapse the technical safeguards
would also begin to lose effectiveness. In due time virtually any safeguard
can be bypassed. Since the risk increases with time, military organizations must be poised to react quickly to the temporary loss of control
over nuclear weapons. A stolen weapon that could not be recovered
would pose a special risk. Of greater concern is the specter of a national
social implosion that paralyzes the military establishment. Efforts to
bypass safeguards could then proceed with impunity and would thus
stand a greater chance of success. Indeed the complicity of military units
themselves is a distinct possibility in the context of social disintegration.

SAFEGUARDS AND INTERNATIONAL CRISIS. Below this threshold of
organizational dissolution the danger of nuclear inadvertence is contain-
able as long as the command system is not confronted with a threat of
attack by another country. Any confrontation serious enough to warrant
the dispersal of tactical weapons and strategic weapons, the elevation of
alert levels, and other emergency steps taken in anticipation of conflict
would increase the risk of nuclear inadvertence. Many of the safeguards
described in earlier sections would be abandoned or weakened during a
serious crisis.

The tension between negative and positive control that would emerge
in a nuclear crisis is aggravated by the commitment of the former Soviet
Union never to be the first to use nuclear weapons.[164] In keeping with
the policy adopted in the 1970s, the Russians plan to cede the nuclear
initiative to their potential adversaries, creating problems of control that
are readily imagined. Upon detecting signs of imminent enemy nuclear
attack, the command and control system would attempt to bring its nuclear posture to maximum combat readiness without making an irrevocable commitment to launch until after irrefutable evidence of the
launch of enemy delivery vehicles. During this apprehensive period safeguards on tactical weapons, in particular, would be compromised in order

to bring the weapons to peak readiness for combat—for instance, loading weapons onto delivery systems. In some cases these preparations require the prior dissemination of unlock codes, a cumbersome procedure for tactical forces that could not be delayed until the last minute. Similar steps would be taken to ready the strategic forces—for instance, loading bombers with ALCMs—though unlock codes for modern classes of strategic forces could be withheld until the last moment, because they can be disseminated rapidly through a streamlined command and control system. Under favorable conditions the Russian command and control system probably could wait for tactical warning before transmitting unlock codes and launch authorization codewords to the most modern classes of silo-based intercontinental rockets. An earlier start would be more essential to priming the rest of the strategic arsenal for rapid launch.

Yet the press of time and circumstances could incite the command and control system to bring all tactical and strategic forces to peak readiness— to distribute unlock codes, assign targets to weapons, and designate a contingent time of future launch—so that if the expected enemy attack did materialize, only a short direct codeword would be needed to trigger a coordinated retaliatory strike. Moreover, given the potentially acute vulnerability of the centralized command and control system (a proposition defended in the next chapter), pressure would mount to proliferate the authority to disseminate the direct command as a hedge against the threat of decapitation. By all indications the command system rejects such contingency planning, but the pressures exist nonetheless.

The pressure to predelegate nuclear authority was strongly felt about the time of the 1962 Cuban missile crisis. Since communications between Moscow and Cuba were tenuous, the general staff prepared an order giving the Soviet commander in Cuba the authority to employ Luna tactical nuclear missiles at his discretion provided they were needed to repulse an American invasion and the commander was unable to receive directives from Moscow. This order was allegedly signed by the Soviet defense minister and sent to Cuba just before the missile crisis began.[165] In reality, the order was neither signed nor sent. The actual orders sent to the senior Soviet commander in Cuba during the crisis explicitly prohibited the use of any tactical or strategic nuclear weapons without the explicit approval of Moscow. Moreover, the Soviet officer in charge of all nuclear warheads in Cuba did not take orders from the senior Soviet commander.[166] The Soviet tradition of strict centralized control over nuclear weapons employed was upheld in circumstances in which positive control could have been difficult to exercise. Safeguards took precedence, as usual, over the military purpose of the weapons.

Potential strains on safeguards at the moment of high suspense over the nuclear intentions of an adversary during a crisis were perhaps the basis for a statement made in 1982 by Defense Minister Dmitry F. Ustinov that the Soviets' unilateral renunciation of nuclear first use (formally pledged by Brezhnev on June 15, 1982,[167] but already in effect in military planning) meant "still more attention will now be given [by the Soviet armed forces] to preventing a military conflict from growing into a nuclear one," and to preventing the "unsanctioned launch of nuclear weapons, from tactical to strategic."[168] Presumably, these dangers were judged to have grown because of the heightened combat readiness required of the Soviet forces, and their increased reliance on launch on warning, when the adversary was given the advantage of initiative and surprise. Ustinov thus emphasized that "our pledge not to be the first to use nuclear weapons poses for us the objective requirement of continually improving the vigilance and combat readiness of the Soviet armed forces, systems for detecting nuclear weapons, and command and communications facilities and organs. . . . It is necessary to nullify the advantage of the element of surprise."[169] In sum, the cross-cutting military implications of no-first-use policy were (1) higher combat readiness in peacetime and the capability to move to full combat readiness on very short notice in a crisis to ensure an effective response to sudden attack; and (2) tighter restraints on forces put on higher combat readiness in peacetime or brought to maximum readiness in time of crisis to prevent unsanctioned or inadvertent actions.

Ustinov's pronouncements came at a time of souring relations between the nuclear superpowers, which alone could explain his call for an increase in Soviet vigilance and combat readiness. But the no-first-use policy provided additional strong justification. The increased vigilance advocated by Ustinov took the form of continuous satellite photoreconnaissance and satellite launch detection, both achieved by the Soviets for the first time in 1982–83, and a stepped-up KGB intelligence effort begun in late 1981 to uncover any secret Western plots to launch a surprise nuclear attack. (The special KGB activity was not halted until late 1991.)[170] Improvements in combat readiness and command and control were also made. Deployments of SS-22s in Eastern Europe may have been put on quick-launch alert for the first time in their history.[171] Intermediate high commands were established during the early to mid-1980s in the western, southwestern, and southern theaters facing NATO forces, a move that streamlined Soviet command over conventional and tactical nuclear forces. And the Soviets reorganized their strategic command system in the early 1980s to increase the coordination and decrease the reaction time of the strategic nuclear forces. The Kazbek system of nuclear footballs for rapidly disseminating political authority to launch the strategic forces became operational in the early 1980s. The command streamlining surfaced in exercises conducted in 1982, when the Soviets demonstrated for the first time a capability to launch their ICBM force on tactical warning.[172]

This shift to a retaliatory posture based on launch on warning created another set of concerns about inadvertent war: launch on false tactical indications of enemy attack. The problem of preserving effective negative control during a period of threat thus included errors in the early warning system as well as unauthorized actions by friendly nuclear units in the view of Soviet commentators. Regarding the matter of unauthorized use of nuclear weapons, the former Soviet defense minister Marshal Yazov reiterated the concern expressed previously by Ustinov. Yazov went further than Ustinov in emphasizing the difficulty of negative control during a period of a threat of war and the priority of preventing unauthorized actions in such circumstances. Writing in 1987, he stressed the "priority requirement in Soviet military programming, realized in practice in the training of staffs and the troops, and in the organization of strictest control designed to not permit unauthorized use of a nuclear weapon— from tactical to strategic, including at heightened readiness of the troops for repelling aggression."[173]

The bellicosity and extraordinary combat vigilance of the 1980s are of course ancient history. Recent trends in the political relationship and in the disposition of combat forces have worked to strengthen safeguards. That the safeguards could be weakened in a future crisis is a hypothetical, remote, and receding danger.

Yet the underlying theme—that a crisis would create irresolvable dilemmas of control—remains valid, and all the more so if any credence is given to scenarios in which acute domestic turmoil in the former Soviet Union degrades control over the nuclear arsenal, projects a global nuclear threat, and precipitates an international nuclear crisis.

Summary and Propositions: Soviet Operations

The Soviet command and control system was deeply fearful of a breakdown that could lead to the illicit use of nuclear weapons. Its obsession led to the imposition of tight central control and elaborate safeguards. This obsession also restrained impulses to generate forces quickly and comprehensively to full combat readiness in a crisis, out of fear that safeguards would be compromised. The system did not hesitate, however, to declare partial alerts at a relatively low threshold of nuclear tensions.

The extreme centralization of Soviet command served the goal of strategic flexibility but hampered the speed and efficiency of execution. The system appeared to be plodding and cumbersome in comparison with U.S. command. The chain of command eschewed initiative at subordinate echelons and suffered from immense inertia as a consequence. Yet this form of organization was appropriate because the politico-military leadership valued flexibility in the formulation of security objectives and strict forcewide compliance with implementing instructions. Implementation took longer but remained closely regulated. The Soviet command system maintained tight control over all aspects of nuclear operations to ensure alignment with the formulated intentions of the apex of government. The system was acutely sensitive to the trade-off between negative and positive control, and it strove to maintain stringent control even as it approached the brink of war.

Soviet targeting policy for intercontinental operations appeared to emphasize flexibility. The nuclear command and control system was expected to conform to the wishes of the supreme high command, which might demand a menu of options. High-ranking Soviet political officials often participated in nuclear exercises. In a real conflict they were expected to manage nuclear operations in a detailed way, not simply to endorse preexisting plans for all-out attack. In short, the Soviet command system was not rigid but flexible in developing a course of action, though it appeared quite rigid and ponderous in carrying out the plan. By contrast, the U.S. command system was agile in carrying out an intricate preestablished plan but appeared quite inflexible in supporting a novel course of action.

Although extreme centralization strengthened negative control, it also increased the potential vulnerability of the Soviet command system. The authority and ability to disseminate launch orders replete with unlock codes was concentrated in the top rung of the hierarchy. Control was far less dispersed than it was in the U.S. system. The Soviet system's sensitivity to developments that threatened its survival was thus acute. At the onset of a crisis the command system constantly monitored its own vital signs. The protection of the politico-military leadership, the large general staff infrastructure, and the control links down the chain of command took precedence. The perceived significance of force structure vulnerability paled by comparison. Target coverage would be a secondary or tertiary priority. Crisis operations concentrated less on meeting requirements for damage expectancy against U.S. targets than it did on detecting signs of an imminent decapitation strike and dispersing the leadership to foil the attacker's strategy.

The inadequacy of defensive precautions by themselves—the next chapter argues that the Soviet command system could not reliably withstand a well-designed and smoothly executed U.S. first strike—compelled the system to adopt a rapid reaction posture that, as its first priority, aspired to degrade a U.S. attack on the command system. Fearful of being decisively decapitated, the system would have promptly initiated an offensive campaign if U.S. nuclear strikes against the Soviet homeland had begun to materialize. This timing would have reflected not only the command system's own sense of vulnerability but also the perishable value of the most threatening U.S. targets.

Conclusion

Any deterioration of U.S.-Russian relations that increases nuclear tensions would undoubtedly be *sui generis*. Despite the idiosyncracies of the circumstances, however, the respective command systems possess traits acquired during the cold war and retained to this day that would systematically condition their operational behavior in a crisis. Centralization and negative control are the hallmarks of the former Soviet command and control system. Decentralization and target coverage are the hallmarks of U.S. command.

For all the dissimilarities in the command systems, and asymmetrical sensitivities, there exist two common denominators that have profoundly shaped the nuclear postures of both states: command vulnerability and launch on warning. The former drove both command systems to adopt the latter. Rapid reaction, or literal launch on warning, rendered the idea of strategic flexibility almost meaningless, while creating perhaps the greatest danger of nuclear inadvertence in a crisis. This evolution of the postures and the dangers that emerged from them are a legacy of the cold war that is not *sui generis*. It is a communicable legacy with a future in other nuclear rivalries.

CHAPTER FIVE

The Vulnerability of Soviet Command and Control in 1990

AN IMPORTANT lesson of the cold war is that when archenemies acquire the ability to deliver nuclear weapons, each will fear command and control decapitation. This chapter illustrates this phenomenon by analyzing the vulnerability of U.S. and Soviet nuclear command and control systems in 1990. Although the international situation has been transformed since 1990, it is necessary to examine mutual command and control vulnerability to gain historical perspective as well as to show the residual dangers that still lurk in the postures of the United States and the Commonwealth of Independent States. Also, the lessons of command and control vulnerability seem generally applicable to other nations with nuclear aspirations. They offer a cautionary tale for budding nuclear rivalries.

The assessment here challenges the long-standing belief that the Soviet command and control system could have weathered a nuclear barrage. Although U.S. planners were prudently conservative in crediting the Soviet system with a capacity to absorb even an all-out attack, an equally cautious Soviet planner had reason to be pessimistic. The survival of command and control, from a Soviet perspective, was far from guaranteed.

On the U.S. side, despite a surge of investment in command and control protection during the Reagan years, military planners still could not have counted on the system to withstand an attack. The cold war ended before ongoing improvements raised confidence to the level at which retaliation after ride-out would have been a viable option.

Building on an earlier assessment, this chapter concludes that while both sides had grounds to doubt their ability to decapitate the opponent, neither deserved to feel confident in the resilience of its own command system.[1]

Basic Problems

How was command and control vulnerability relevant to inadvertent nuclear war? Classical analysis links this vulnerability to advertent war. According to standard deterrence theory, command and control or force vulnerability, if severe enough, induces rationally calculating actors on the brink of war to launch a preemptive strike. Faced with the immediate prospect of a crippling attack by the enemy, a decisionmaker would succumb to pressures for "anticipatory retaliation" while effective command could still be exercised. Classical instability ensues because the payoff for initiating an attack, calculated either in terms of minimum losses or maximum gains, exceeds the payoff for inaction. In short, command and control vulnerability is a catalyst for advertent war according to standard deterrence theory.

This perspective is useful but inadequate inasmuch as it overlooks the ties between command and control vulnerability and inadvertent war. The fragility of command and control affects the operational stances of strategic organizations, and their stances create real perils of nuclear inadvertence. One peril is that their strong predisposition toward rapid reaction generates pressure on top policy officials to respond so rapidly to signs of enemy missile launches that the officials become susceptible to the effects of misinformation, misperception, and miscalculation. Another is that the organizations are themselves geared to react so rapidly to indications of attack that policymakers could have difficulty restraining them.

Asymmetrical perceptions aggravate these dangers. Planners become fixated on their own command vulnerability, leaving them oblivious to their counterpart's apprehension. Since both sides pose a far greater threat to each other's command system than they realize, neither is aware of the inherent volatility of a confrontation or of the dangers of escalating the tension. On the contrary, they seem wont to take the opposite view, which only further increases the danger: the opponent's command system is so resilient that steps designed to rattle confidence in it would moderate the opponent's behavior in a crisis.

Furthermore, overestimating the resilience of enemy command and control provides a dubious rationale for developing new anticommand targeting plans and weapons systems. The rationale is that they strengthen deterrence by providing a means for striking back at an aggressor's leadership, while from the adversary's point of view they constitute a growing threat of first-strike decapitation.

With respect to the nuclear superpowers in particular, command and control vulnerability also greatly complicates a task that is critically important to deterrence—analyzing the opponent's strategic forces and making judgments about the likely outcome of a nuclear exchange. The size, composition, and technical characteristics of the forces have been relatively transparent when analyzed in isolation from the command and control systems that direct them. They have been readily gauged by means of unilateral surveillance and disclosures during arms negotiations. Both the United States and the Soviet Union had standard measures and models at their disposal and could in principle replicate each other's strategic exchange calculations. Despite a large element of irreducible uncertainty and of sensitivity to assumptions, both sides could have a solid understanding of the first- and second-strike capacity of the respective arsenals.[2] As a result, most analysts could agree that, given the diversified portfolios and shielded configuration of the arsenals, no less than several thousand warheads would have survived an attack in the early 1990s regardless of the scenario. As far as forces alone were concerned, stable deterrence existed. Standard calculations performed on particular categories of forces also revealed to everyone the specific vulnerabilities plaguing each camp. Tutored in this knowledge, the adversaries could have fashioned crisis policies that reliably administered the intended dosage of reassurance and threat.[3]

But factoring in command and control performance would have made it much more difficult for the adversaries to appraise the overall strategic situation and the opponent's apprehensions or to distinguish prudent from provocative policies in a crisis. Command and control systems, particularly the opponent's, befuddled their examiners.

One reason is that the systems consist not only of physical infrastructure but also of constantly changing plans that have not been available for direct inspection: plans that assign forces to targets; plans that govern intelligence, logistics, decisionmaking, and communications operations;

and plans that direct the transition from peace to war. Even more opaque are the standard procedures, rules, traditions and ethos that lend coherence to military operations. This bewildering array of subjects frustrates and confounds analysis no matter how much access to privileged information is enjoyed.

Both sides have also kept each other guessing about such critical details as plans for delegating authority to employ nuclear weapons. Other missing pieces of the puzzle include the covert portions of the adversary's communications networks and command posts. An encyclopedic description of the respective command and control infrastructures comparable to the available information about numbers and characteristics of weapon systems is not at hand.

Even if the curtain of secrecy could be raised, an assessment of any system's wartime performance would founder on a reef of uncertainty. There are no widely accepted methods for calculating command and control performance under wartime conditions, and empirical validation of such an assessment cannot be done. Compared with the tight and tidy standard calculations of force vulnerability, any objective assessment of command and control systems would raise more questions than it answered. Rival planners can therefore be forgiven for discounting apparent deficiencies in the opposing system and dwelling on the more verifiable weaknesses of their own. Such conservatism is normal in military assessment.

On the face of it, the pervasive uncertainty would seem to be double-edged in crisis interactions. On the one hand, if each side believed it was futile to try to decapitate an adversary's command system, thereby neutralizing its strategic capability, the incentive to launch a preemptive attack during a deep crisis would be lessened. On the other hand, the doubtful resilience of one's own system stiffens the penalty for restraint if deterrence fails and an enemy attack occurs. These cross-cutting pressures alternately inhibit and reinforce the impulse to unleash the strategic forces at the brink of war.

Risk aversion sharpens both edges of the sword. Under the principle of conservative planning, uncertainty magnifies both the adversary's strengths and one's own weaknesses. Risk aversion dulls awareness of the threat projected at the adversary's command and control system while heightening sensitivity to threats, real and imagined, projected by the adversary. Each side grows more fearful of its own vulnerability to command decapitation, yet more oblivious to the other side's trepidation. This chasm was extremely wide during the cold war era.[4]

Crisis policy fashioned without taking into account the adversary's deepest apprehension runs a risk of inflaming rather than salving tensions, aggravating the danger of inadvertence. Mutual command and control vulnerability thus raises the specter of interactions that unwittingly accentuate threat and counteract gestures meant to reassure. This danger of inadvertent provocation, furthermore, accompanies the onset of tensions long before constructive policy positions can crystallize. This potential for abrupt deterioration of mutual confidence underscores the importance of crisis prevention as opposed to crisis management. Security hinges on *pre-crisis* diplomacy when nuclear postures rest on fragile command systems.

For rationally calculating actors, the certain horrible cost of nuclear war surely would vastly outweigh any hypothetical advantage of preemption in a crisis. Nevertheless, even if both sides resisted the urge to preempt in the face of command vulnerability, they would still be prone to react quickly to positive indications of enemy attack. This would remain a dangerous impulse. When strategic organizations fearing the imminent disintegration of their command and control, are primed to react quickly to such indications, the imperative of speed itself presents the main threat of nuclear inadvertence.

The U.S. and Soviet nuclear command and control systems lacked the resilience necessary to meet the classic textbook requirements of deterrence based on second-strike retaliation. This chapter pays particular attention to the Soviet system because the prevalent wisdom mistakenly credited it with a high degree of invulnerability. Within the Soviet system the command elements that Western analysts often cited as examples of invulnerable command fortifications are closely examined: deep underground command posts and super-hardened missile launch control centers. Contrary to common belief neither were invulnerable to attack by nuclear weapons in the U.S. arsenal. In 1990 Soviet planners could not by any means have taken for granted the survival of a functional system. Surgical decapitation strikes were a genuine concern for all layers of the Soviet system from the government leadership, which relied on deep underground structures for wartime protection, to the bottom rung of missile launch control that relied on super-hard underground bunkers.

Although analyses based on available evidence cannot prove conclusively that neither command system could have withstood a direct attack, they do lend considerable credence to this assessment. Moreover, this assessment survives scrutiny well enough to have justified using command and control vulnerability as a basic planning assumption in the shaping of each side's nuclear posture.

A key corollary to the argument made here about acute vulnerability is that each side perforce projected a potent threat to the other side's command and control system. Since this corollary appears to have been lost on the U.S. and Soviet planning communities, crisis interactions could have proved far more unstable than was generally realized at the time.

Soviet Command Infrastructure and U.S. Targeting

A cursory scan of the Soviet command and control system in 1990 reveals an impressive infrastructure. The Soviets, it would appear, spared no effort to ensure the survival of the national leadership as well as subordinate echelons of nuclear command and communications. Over the years the Soviets drilled innumerable shafts and tunnels to excavate underground shelters and escape routes for the top leadership; emplaced several dozen batteries of ballistic missile interceptors to defend the command bunkers in the Moscow vicinity; deployed trains, trucks, ships, helicopters, and planes to serve as alternate command posts and communications relays; proliferated land-line, satellite, and terrestrial radio communications networks to tie the command and control system together; configured a worldwide intelligence apparatus to provide strategic and tactical warning of enemy attack; and vigorously tested and exercised the command system under simulated conditions of enemy nuclear attack.

The motive underlying this massive investment was surely the "continuing concern with protecting national command [that] extends back well over four decades."[5] The claim that the Soviets "have steadily improved the protection" and the rejection of any suggestion that Soviet command and control had vulnerabilities comparable to its U.S. counterpart were both understandable in view of the Soviet's dogged efforts.[6] Historically the U.S. capital investment in command and control protection paled by comparison, and the redoubled infusion of funds into U.S. command modernization during the 1980s seemed a token compared with Soviet expenditures. No U.S. planner could seriously entertain trying to keep up with the Soviet Union. To follow suit by building, for example, a labyrinth of multistory command posts deep beneath the nation's capital and outlying suburbs would have drained this country's budget for defense construction.

The impression formed easily that the enormous Soviet effort conferred near invincibility on its command system. Even U.S. weapons targeteers privy to classified details of the system could not find an Achilles' heel. One participant deeply involved in strategic target planning noted the difficulty of identifying all the launch control centers in the missile fields. He and many others also emphasized the possible existence of major command and communications sites at higher levels that had escaped detection by Western intelligence.[7] Known facilities, particularly the deep underground command posts, could not be located with pinpoint precision within a sizable subterranean maze. Buried at depths of several hundred feet—in some cases up to one thousand feet[8]—many of these bunkers appeared to stand at least a decent chance of surviving a dedicated nuclear strike.[9] According to a National Intelligence officer in 1985, "deep underground facilities for the top national leadership might enable the top leadership to survive—a key objective of their wartime management plans."[10] These command posts, among others, were tied into numerous redundant channels of communications and untold numbers of individual radio sites, including a nationwide grid consisting of hundreds of buried antennas. The combination of hardness, redundancy, and mobility united many U.S. analysts in the conviction that "it seems highly likely that the Soviets could maintain overall continuity of command and control, although it would probably be degraded and they could experience difficulty in maintaining endurance after such attack."[11]

What is more, the operations plans that animated the entire command and control constellation remained puzzling. No Western planner knew the exact composition of the Soviet national command authorities empowered to authorize the use of nuclear weapons, or the exact contents of the enabling orders, or the precise procedures and channels used to disseminate authorization, or the exact method of launching the individual weapons. The Soviet concept of operations for prosecuting a strategic campaign was too obscure to design a realistic decapitation strike. U.S.

planners undoubtedly recognized that the war plans developed for this purpose rested on a foundation of bald assumptions about the physical and functional configuration of the Soviet command and control system.

U.S. strategic planners also discounted the threat to Soviet command and control posed by U.S. nuclear forces, because under the most likely attack scenarios the United States scrupulously avoided vital components of the Soviet system. The logic of these scenarios is clear. An initial nuclear salvo meant to uproot Soviet command and control in order to block retaliation ran a considerable risk of failing to prevent a counter-attack while foreclosing all opportunity to stop the war through negotiation. Furthermore, an attack on the command and control system once implemented would have removed a reputedly important source of negotiating leverage: the threat of command attack. From the standpoint of intrawar bargaining and coercion, this form of violence is instrumental only if suspended over, and not actually dropped on, the adversary's head.

U.S. plans had long been fastened to the idea of threatening Soviet command but not carrying out the threat so long as productive negotiations to end a strategic conflict remained alive. Since planners were unable to produce a foolproof strategy for decisive decapitation, the brief for initially holding back forces targeted on Soviet command carried substantial weight, and planners long ago devised a special "withhold" option for the U.S. strategic war plan.

This option sparing the Soviet leadership first appeared in the single integrated operational plan developed in the 1960s.[12] It was refined for the new war plan put into effect at the beginning of 1976. Fashioned in response to guidance issued by President Richard Nixon, the Joint Strategic Targeting Planning Staff built the plan, known as SIOP-5, during the period between 1973 and 1975. Like its predecessor, the plan grouped leadership targets into a separate category. SIOP-5 contained four major categories of targets—hereafter denoted nuclear forces, other military targets, leadership, and economic—which, like previous plans, were further subdivided to permit piecemeal release.[13] SIOP-5 allowed forces assigned to any of the four packages to be unwrapped and released in installments. U.S. command could, for example, order strikes against all Soviet nuclear forces except those located near urban areas, with a view to limiting collateral damage to the Soviet population. Similar suboptions were available within the other major target categories. The leadership option, for example, was split into political and military targets.

The Carter administration greatly expanded this option, adding more layers of the Soviet political hierarchy to the target list, which went down to the *rayon* level of the Communist party.[14] The number of people in this target set presumably totaled about 110,000, based on the CIA's 1978 assessment that the Soviet leadership, aside from the top national leaders, consisted of "5,000 party and government officials at the national and republic level; 63,000 party and government leaders at kray, oblast, city, and urban rayon level; 2,000 managers of key installations; and about 40,000 members of civil defense staffs."[15] The number of targets presumably equaled the number of shelters believed to have been built to house these officials and staffs (800 to 1,500) plus command posts for the top national politico-military authorities (approximately 20 to 30).[16]

Critics charged that Carter's so-called countervailing strategy valued this option less for its deterrent effect than for its military effect if deterrence failed. This criticism seems misplaced, because the Carter policy emphasized targeting a wider swath of the political bureaucracy, little of which overlapped the nuclear chain of command. It stretches the evidence to infer any intention to shorten the fuse on decapitation strikes. The Carter strategy apparently still regarded an attack on the Soviet leadership as the option of last resort. The administration thus continued along the path cleared by previous SIOPs. In so doing, it further clarified the trade-off between attacking command and control to reduce Soviet military capability and avoiding command and control to facilitate negotiations for a cease-fire. At the same time it honed options for command and control attack designed to dissuade Soviet leaders from initiating an attack or escalating a war that began with a limited exchange.

The Reagan administration affirmed this approach to deterrence. Some officials suggested that the importance of targeting Soviet leaders was growing, and even discerned a partial eclipse of the other target categories in the U.S. war plan.[17] But the long-standing requirement for blanket target coverage ensured that all four major classes of targets continued to receive high priority in strategic war planning.[18] Tradition also continued to ordain the order or sequence of strikes against the target sets. Whereas an attack on the Soviet leadership could not be made unless it was accompanied by a large-scale counterforce attack, an attack on Soviet leaders could have been withheld during a full-scale counterforce attack. The counter strategic mission was evidently an urgent and mandatory part of SIOP operations. By contrast, attacking the Soviet leadership was optional. The idea of deferring strikes against the very top echelon of Soviet command thus appeared to be firmly planted in U.S. nuclear weapons employment policy.

U.S. strategic planners could reasonably expect U.S. decisionmakers to at least spare the upper echelon of Soviet command, leaving the Soviet Union with a relatively intact system with which to coordinate nuclear strikes during the initial and perhaps subsequent exchanges. This restriction not only would have dashed any hope of decisive decapitation of the Soviet command system, but would have saddled the U.S. planner with a secondary handicap, because coordinated Soviet strikes could have been made against the U.S. command and control system. The U.S. system's ability to mount an attack against the Soviet system would have been degraded should the United States have eventually resorted to this option.[19]

The bane of any would-be U.S. planner of schemes to decapitate the Soviets in wartime was of course the prevalent view that the United States would never initiate a strategic exchange. Deterrence was based on the threat of retaliation, which made impossible the attack timing required to impede the Soviets' opening salvo. Although the unpredictability of crisis interactions left ajar the door to preemptive U.S. attack, U.S. military planners expected their civilian masters to balk at the brink, eliminating any chance of neutralizing Soviet command and control before Soviet firing commenced. The military utility of the decapitation option, as opposed to its deterrent-compellent value, depended almost completely on going first.

Soviet Perceptions of U.S. Threat to Command and Control

U.S. strategic planning was nonetheless scant comfort to Soviet planners. Prudence compelled them to entertain with deadly seriousness the prospect of a sudden first strike against the entire Soviet target base, including the nuclear command and control system, at the outset of a nuclear war. The Soviets' long-standing concern with protecting their command and control system indeed suggests an obsession with this very contingency. Command survival was paramount, and the Soviets' ability to coordinate a retaliatory strike in the wake of a U.S. attack on their command system was probably the central question of mainstream threat assessment.[20] The high priority of an attack on the command and control system in war was deemed axiomatic, and it was only natural to ascribe such predilections to the United States.[21]

Through this perceptual filter U.S. nuclear guidance, emphasizing leadership targeting during the Carter and Reagan administrations, together with other developments discussed below, surely concentrated the Soviet mind on its command problem perhaps as never before.[22] Citing the leaked documents, one notable Soviet military commentator maintained that leadership targeting took absolute priority in U.S. nuclear strategy, that it was "deemed necessary above all to decapitate the structure of military-political power in the USSR."[23]

This almost innate Soviet suspicion received ample reinforcement from authoritative U.S. statements indicating that the SIOP pegged at least a portion of the Soviet nuclear command system for early destruction. The open testimony of General Larry D. Welch, for example, referred to "Soviet hardened ICBM launch control facilities that we have to deal with, and that is clearly a class of target that requires a prompt hard target kill capability."[24] Soviet planners would have been naive to believe that ICBM launch control facilities were the only vital components of their nuclear command system likely to be struck during an attack "restricted" to their nuclear forces. They would have been prudent to expect strikes against the full array of nuclear command, control, and communications nodes below the level of the main headquarters of the Soviet strategic rocket forces (SRF), navy, air defense, ground forces, and air force headquarters, even when the United States exempted the Soviet top leadership from immediate direct assault. Although the United States has never revealed where it draws the line between leadership targets (arguably the least time-urgent) and command targets associated with Soviet nuclear forces (undoubtedly the target set marked for attack at the outset), most elements in the Soviet nuclear command and control system probably fell within the latter category. Thus if the U.S. exercised its "limited" option aimed at Soviet nuclear forces, the Soviet command and control system (including warning and radar installations that needed to be suppressed to ensure bomber penetration) would have been severely degraded.

Soviet planners' conditioning over the years disposed them to seize upon the real or imaginable threat to command and control posed by virtually every new U.S. weapon to appear on the scene or on the horizon. A prime example was the Pershing II intermediate missile, whose deployment provoked one of the most vitriolic reactions in memory. With its short flight time from launch sites in West Germany, this missile, which was originally slated to carry earth-penetrating warheads,[25] was meant, according to the Soviets, to deliver a sudden paralyzing strike on the Soviet command and control system.[26] Although the United States dismissed the charges as propagandistic, the Soviets' fears were hardly baseless.[27]

The ground-launched cruise missile was indicted on the same charges, as were assorted other U.S. weapons projects, particularly the newer generations of strategic nuclear forces with pinpoint accuracy and large theoretical lethality. U.S. weapons entering the inventory carried the potential to obliterate all stationary targets save perhaps the dozen or so subterranean sanctuaries at depths beyond their reach. (As argued later, even U.S. weapons already in the inventory had considerable capability to threaten these deep underground command posts.) And Soviet planners surely foresaw the advent of burrowing warheads dooming these last havens to obsolescence. The United States certainly intended to use earth-penetrating warheads successfully tested for the first time in late 1988[28] as the tools for decapitation.[29] The means of delivering them were sure to include ballistic missiles, whose release could occur early or late in a war, notwithstanding arguments against premature attack on Soviet command.[30]

Everything from the B-2 stealth bomber to third-generation nuclear weapons seemed part of a U.S. commitment to expose the Soviets' entire command system to rapid suppression in wartime. The former, touted by the U.S. Air Force as a superb platform for bombing Soviet command bunkers, portended sneak flights deep into Soviet territory, where they would deliver a surprise, lethal blow to key command posts as a precursor thrust to a large missile attack. (As discussed later, this scenario featuring B-52 precursor attacks on Soviet strategic command and control during the transition from a conventional to nuclear phase of conflict was the theme of a large-scale Soviet exercise in 1984.) The next generation of U.S. nuclear weapons was thoroughly implicated as well by dint of their electronic countermeasures applications. Specially designed weapons could generate intense pulses of electromagnetic energy over wide areas, causing widespread disruption of Soviet command and communications networks until a follow-on wave of ballistic missiles aimed at the full array of targets arrived to complete the mission.[31]

That the Soviets worried about future threats to their command and control system is not to imply that they were comfortable with the existing situation. Although they made brave statements about the futility of any Western nuclear aggression, the Soviets' operational posture configured for launch on warning betrayed doubt about their command and control system's ability to ride out an attack.

Soviet Strategic Nuclear Exercises

Soviet nuclear exercises also betrayed doubt, albeit mixed with some optimism, about the resilience of their command and control system. Soviet nuclear command and control often suffered massive disruption from the fictional blows administered by Western nuclear forces. Two especially large and noteworthy exercises simulating strategic nuclear exchanges, one in 1984 and another in 1988, illustrate the point. These exercises also offer a frame of reference for testing the central thesis of this chapter.

The 1984 Exercise

The Soviet nuclear exercise in 1984 assumed a large-scale conventional war lasting ten days before the West stoked the conflict with nuclear weapons.[32] This escalation took the form of a U.S. precursor strike employing nuclear-armed bombers against critical nodes in the Soviet command and control network. A wave of U.S. strategic bombers immediately rolled in, followed soon by U.S. land- and sea-based ballistic missiles. Because of the dense concentration of aircraft from both alliances flying in the European theater at the moment of escalation and because of the extensive outages that the aircraft early-warning sensors along the Soviet border suffered during the conventional phase of the war, the transiting nuclear bombers blended into the background noise of the air battle and flew undetected to their targets deep inside Soviet territory.[33]

By exploiting the blind spots in the Soviet warning network, the United States stunned the Soviet command and control system with its initial blow and nearly crippled it with the follow-on massive SIOP strike. The Soviets did manage to launch an SS-17 ICBM carrying a communications package just before the impact of the SIOP forces (their national early-warning sensors for detecting U.S. SIOP missile lift-off were assumed to be functional at this stage) in an apparent last-ditch effort to disseminate authorization to retaliate at once. Sent on a lofted trajectory above Soviet territory, this ECRS missile broadcast a launch order for fifty-five minutes, but only a small fraction of Soviet forces apparently copied it successfully. As a result, Soviet retaliation during this phase of the exercise was ragged. Its scope was limited to a small contingent of ICBMs, SLBMs, and theater nuclear forces.[34]

Soviet command spent the next twenty-four hours tallying the damage, reconstituting command and control, and revising the main strike plan. An airborne command post attached to the SRF headquarters or a subordinate army headquarters flew to the distant missile complexes to poll the field commands—divisions and regiments—on the status of its forces and then relayed these reports back to the SRF's command post, an underground facility in the Moscow area. Command of the SRF apparently passed to this center (presumably the large alternate facility south of Moscow after the simulated demise of the main headquarters at another location near Moscow). With the aid of a large computer center linked to the underground headquarters, the Soviet's main strategic strike was replanned. Intercontinental ballistic missiles of the SRF and long-range aviation of the Moscow-based Thirty-sixth Air Army finally carried out the main retaliatory strike several days after the opening salvo by U.S. forces.

The 1988 Exercise

The 1988 exercise featured a demonstration of launch on warning and also shed light on the Soviet position on preemption, topics discussed in the next chapter. It is also important because of the severe command disruption written into the script.

In the exercise the opposing camps had been waging a conventional war for about thirty days when the Soviet Union received early warning of a ballistic missile attack launched by a Western submarine plying the waters of the Norwegian Sea. Although the Soviet general staff had been forewarned of the attack several hours before it began, presumably by intercepting the launch order, the decision to retaliate was made only after early-warning systems detected the missiles in flight. The general staff then immediately disseminated orders to respond in kind. Such a prompt response might reflect the ample time available to draw up a contingency plan and get the national command authorities to approve it in advance, a process presumably made easier by the identification of the attacking submarine as a British vessel with a theater mission. The contingency plan evidently called for a proportionate reply to Great Britain by lobbing back a small number of ballistic missiles onboard Delta I–class submarines stationed on patrol in the home waters of the Northern Fleet.

Orders authorizing this response began to be transmitted over the Northern Fleet broadcast network, which used land-based radio towers operating on very low frequencies (VLF) and high frequencies (HF). From their normal peacetime war room, located in an underground command center in Moscow (previously at 19 Ulitza Frunze but recently moved to modern facilities near the former Lenin Library not far from Red Square), the general staff operations directorate could seize the keying of the remotely sited Northern Fleet transmitters and by this means send messages directly to the ballistic missile submarines. This centrally automated broadcast network overrode lower priority navy traffic, keyed at the navy main headquarters in Moscow or perhaps at fleet command headquarters near Murmansk, and allowed for delivery of emergency war orders directly to the individual submarines from the general staff in seven minutes or less, depending on the mode of transmission and the type and contents of the message.[35]

During the exercise the Soviet submarines apparently did not receive a complete message before the broadcast network was knocked out by the British submarine missile approximately eight minutes after breakwater.[36] By the time of this interruption the Soviet plan had already been overtaken by events,[37] yet its implementation proceeded apace as backup communications links kicked into operation (the switchover taking about twelve minutes). Consisting of Bear-J communications relay aircraft with long trailing wire antennas and an extremely low frequency (ELF) terrestrial radio grid in the Kola Peninsula—both designed to transmit signals that can penetrate seawater to reach submerged submarines— these backup links successfully delivered the launch message. Since the data rate of the Bear-J VLF transmitter should be comparable to that of the VLF fleet broadcast network, it may be presumed that the two Delta I submarines with European targets received message elements over a span of seven minutes. In the exercise, after copying a complete launch message, one Delta I boat fired seventeen minutes later, and the second took an additional ten minutes.[38] In sum, forty-four minutes after the West fired the first shot via a submarine missile, the Soviets sent off their reply, which by then had become a sideshow to the main event. Twenty-three minutes earlier in the exercise the Soviets simulated a massive Soviet strategic strike launched on tactical warning of a massive U.S. first strike.

Following the script for the main event, Soviet command emptied groups of land-based missiles from their silos nine minutes before the silo-busting U.S. forces completed their thirty-minute polar journey. Soviet submarines with intercontinental missions, however, faced a communications outage and hence had to wait longer than land-based missiles to receive the order to fire. The British precursor attack had severed the primary communications links to all submarines, and the backup channels were servicing the initial plan of theater response-in-kind, using the Delta I submarines discussed above.

Contact with Soviet submarines became even more difficult when the U.S. land-based missiles began bombarding the Soviet command and force structure thirty minutes into the nuclear phase of the war. This bombardment destroyed the primary command center of the general staff and political leadership and shut down all strategic communications for the next two hours. (During the exercise satellite communications were used exclusively for real-world control of submarine operations; everything else went silent to simulate a complete outage of communications.) With the loss of the primary facility, central command and control evidently devolved to an alternate underground facility. Launch authorization apparently sent by this Moscow-area facility reached a navy airborne command post attached to the Soviet navy main headquarters and normally based at a Moscow airport. About two and one-half hours after the U.S. SIOP wrecked havoc on the Soviet's command and control system, this navy aircraft began transmitting a series of two messages over HF radio to waiting submarines committed to combat by the Soviet war plan (Delta III–class boats in the exercise, and presumably in the real-world plan as well).[39] Twenty-eight minutes later, a Delta III submarine on patrol near the Soviet coast fired its complement of missiles.

The two war games outlined reveal basic features of the Soviet command and control system and clarify the Soviet perspective on the major forms of command degradation that could materialize under wartime conditions. They are flimsy grounds, however, on which to base an assessment of Soviet command and control vulnerability in war. The main purpose of exercises was after all to practice operations under various artificial conditions—some favorable, some adverse—not to validate those conditions. The games ignored many factors that affect command

and control performance and manipulated the rest in a stylized fashion to craft the desired training theme. The games are nonetheless a useful reference and departure point.

High-Level Strategic Command

The rest of this chapter examines the ability of Soviet command to function in the wake of a U.S. strike, that is, retaliation after ride-out. This section assesses the vulnerability of the bunker and mobile system of the high command; the next section the vulnerability of low-level command posts. The ability of the Soviet command system to perform other missions enacted in the exercises, particularly the prompt launch of forces on tactical warning, is evaluated in the next chapter.

Nuclear Netherland: Deep Bunkers of the Top Leadership

An assessment of the vulnerability of Soviet strategic command and control requires an analysis of the labyrinth of underground bunkers in the Moscow vicinity. A small subset of this network functioned as major command posts whose survival was crucial to directing the Soviet strategic forces. Contrary to widespread belief, a frontal assault on these critical nodes might have crippled and perhaps neutralized them. From a conservative Soviet perspective direct attack could have meant catastrophic failure of nuclear command and control. Decapitation was a genuine threat.

Both nuclear exercises support the contention that a few key bunkers played a vital role in Soviet nuclear command and control. Each followed a script in which command devolved to major alternate underground facilities after the simulated destruction of the primary facilities. The crucial role played by the alternates appears to be commensurate with their actual wartime responsibilities. These centers apparently became the hub of planning and decisionmaking as well as the source of attack orders sent to all three branches of the Soviet intercontinental nuclear forces.

The contention that the alternate centers were vulnerable is contradicted by the exercises, however. The centers smoothly took charge and coordinated retaliatory strikes despite the onslaught by U.S. strategic forces. But this smooth transition was an artifact of the exercises. Prudent

Soviet planners had grounds to doubt whether it corresponded to realistic conditions.

Putting aside the question of vulnerability for the moment, the extraordinary importance of the alternate centers in the Moscow vicinity deserves further comment. It is certainly debatable whether these centers were essential linchpins whose destruction would have unhinged the Soviet command and control system. After all, a multitude of hardened command posts and buried shelters were scattered around the country. Not counting 150 ICBM launch control centers and 400 other hardened military command posts,[40] the U.S. defense department estimated there were 1,500 to 2,000 hardened facilities for the Soviet leadership.[41] The National Intelligence Council offered a figure of "at least 800, perhaps as many as 1,500, relocation facilities for leaders at the national and regional levels."[42] In addition, there was an array of mobile command and control elements and an unknown number of other nodes. The military and political hierarchy could thus have scattered if not disappeared into a vast physical infrastructure. And to complicate matters, prudent U.S. planners attributed powers of regeneration to the command system—that is, contingency plans for transferring the authority to employ nuclear weapons upon the loss of key nodes.

However, core principles of Soviet military organization dictated otherwise. The philosophy of command attached overriding importance to centralization, especially placing the nuclear forces under the direct operational control of the highest politico-military organ of the state. Soviet-style centralization meant micromanagement. The supreme high commander (in the person of the Soviet general secretary or president), defense minister, general staff, and nuclear commanders in chief (CINCs) would have orchestrated the actions of nuclear forces in nearly exhaustive detail. Not only did the leaders score the music and lead the band, but they sometimes played the instruments themselves.

A burgeoning top-heavy infrastructure sprung from this predilection for central control. Authority, intelligence, and operational control functionally depended on an elaborate physical infrastructure based in the Moscow area.[43] This hub carried such a heavy load in the conduct of nuclear operations that it was not practical to disassemble and disperse it to remote, covert, austere facilities throughout the country. Dispersal would have increased its chances of survival but at the expense of its effectiveness. Although the high command—time permitting—would undoubtedly have dispatched representatives to subordinate formations in the field to enforce compliance with high-level instructions and in some instances to direct the operations—its brain almost certainly would have burrowed itself into the catacombs of the greater Moscow area, protected by concrete and earth, defended by antiballistic missile deployments, and backed up by a few redundant alternates in and around the city.

Besides, the Soviet high command could not assume that it would have time for an orderly dispersal of leaders. It in fact expected to receive almost no advance warning. U.S. plans for Pershing II deployment in Europe, coupled with other apparent signs that the United States was adopting a strategy to decapitate the Soviet command system, had made an indelible impression on the Soviet leadership during the late 1970s and the 1980s. They invested heavily in systems designed to thwart the worst-case threat of surprise decapitation. In the late 1970s the Soviets apparently began to develop the portable *Kazbek* system (so-called nuclear footballs), designed to give the top leaders the ability to rapidly authorize nuclear retaliation in the event of an attack that caught them by surprise. They also started furiously excavating deep underground command posts beneath the Kremlin and other workplaces so that top leaders could descend quickly to safety in the few minutes of warning that would be available in the event of a surprise U.S. strike.

In general terms the contention that the bunkers in the Moscow vicinity constituted the core command and control capability dovetails with official U.S. estimates. The Joint Chiefs of Staff asserted in 1977 that while hardened command headquarters had been dispersed throughout the Soviet Union, Eastern Europe, and Mongolia, "the first echelon command-control-communications centers of the Soviet Government and Armed Forces at a national level are dispersed and hardened within an 80-mile radius of Moscow."[44] More recently the Defense Department described Soviet preparations for leadership protection as "most intensive around Moscow because of its critical role in wartime management."[45] It disclosed the existence of deep underground facilities beneath the city interconnected by secret subway lines that also tie into nearby underground complexes outside Moscow.[46]

According to the estimate, in these complexes the Soviet wartime leadership "plan to survive nuclear strikes and to direct the war effort." A deep underground installation at Sharapovo, located about sixty kilometers south of the Kremlin, is identified as one such "wartime relocation center for the Soviet National Command Authority."[47] This site was doubtless one of the terminuses associated with "tunnels from Moscow 60 km in two directions to give underground access to the High Level Command Posts."[48] At Chekhov, just across the highway going west from Sharapovo, lay another cavernous installation for the general staff. A short distance away was a subterranean alternate headquarters for the SRF.[49] These exurban deep underground command posts were connected to the deep underground post at the Kremlin by a special subway line. Two other special subway lines branched out from the Kremlin. One wound through the Ramenki area deep underground command post southwest of Moscow State University and on to exurban deep posts farther to the southwest of the city. The other ran twenty-five kilometers east to a deep underground complex housing the national air defense headquarters.[50]

The exurban fortifications, joined by train tunnels to bunkers in Moscow, rounded out a hydra-headed labyrinth to which Soviet leaders would repair for safety in an emergency. The installations in Moscow offered the added attraction of close proximity to the normal workplaces of top officials. Shelters existed on the premises where key political and government bodies conducted daily business. Built perhaps by KGB or general staff construction teams,[51] such shelters were hardened against nuclear effects.[52] Numerous military headquarters and alternates in Moscow were similarly fortified. All together, there were, even before the redoubling of the construction effort that started in the late 1970s, reportedly seventy-five underground command posts for the civil-military leadership within the Moscow beltway.[53] The largest of these installations could accommodate hundreds to thousands of people, and the most heavily fortified allegedly could withstand blast overpressures as high as several thousand pounds per square inch.[54] Others were shallow and quite vulnerable. Some were relatively shallow but heavily protected, such as the buried facility beneath the KGB "old building" in downtown Moscow, which had been observed undergoing concrete reinforcement.[55]

Some sites were special meeting places that were neither primary nor true alternate command posts and offered minimal protection. Vnukovo airport, seventeen miles from the Kremlin, was the site of one such meeting place.[56] During a nuclear exercise in the late 1970s the top political leaders, who happened to be traveling in limousines at the time, were notified by car telephone to meet at Vnukovo because warning sensors had detected the onset of a Western nuclear attack.[57] A small group of top officials, including the general secretary, a senior KGB official, and two defense officials (presumably the defense minister and chief of the general staff), converged on the hardened bunker at Vnu-kovo, where they presumably convened an emergency session of the supreme high command to weigh options for retaliation. Using links installed by the KGB, or general staff, their instructions could be sent to the key primary and alternate command posts in the Moscow vicinity.[58] They could also have taken secret subway lines from Vnukovo to these command posts or boarded aircraft and flown to remote relocation facilities.[59]

Other special meeting places similar to Vnukovo doubtless existed at convenient locations in and out of Moscow to expedite the rendezvous of key leaders, the transmittal of their initial decisions, and their subsequent removal to more suitable redoubts, when emergency circumstances found them away from their assigned wartime posts. Among the various high-level command posts just outside Moscow was one at the presidential dacha at Kuntsevo, a short distance west of the capital.

The combat readiness of the various main and alternate centers apparently varied in peacetime. The primary centers, such as the war rooms of the general staff's main operations directorate and the strategic rocket forces near Moscow, doubtless kept a constant vigil, while the alternate centers, such as the underground facilities near Chekhov, south of Moscow (which apparently assumed control after the simulated destruction of the primary nodes in the exercises), probably maintained lower combat readiness but should have been able to perform such basic critical tasks as disseminating a *direct* command (a launch order) on short notice.

Within the confines of Moscow the most logical location for the wartime post of the supreme command was inside a very deep underground command center beneath the Kremlin. The completion of this facility and one like it beneath the headquarters of the Central Committee in the early 1980s earned a Lenin prize for former general secretary Chernenko. The largest underground complex built during the period was situated at Ramenki at an estimated depth of 650–1,000 feet. It could accommodate an estimated 10,000 people.[60]

These key installations needed to be linked to the central command post of the Soviet military intelligence directorate (GRU) of the general staff. The GRU post, located at the Moscow central airfield—Khodinka—was the operational watch office for the chief of the GRU, responsible for keeping tabs on enemy military preparations.[61] It could pass along its interpretation of the latest hostile indicators, together with tactical warning indicators received from the air defense forces (PVO) (particularly from the Soviet counterpart to U.S. NORAD, known as the Center for Analysis of Space and Missile Situation, or CASMS) directly to the denizens of the national command post beneath the Kremlin and elsewhere.[62] Representatives of the general staff's main operations directorate would have correlated the GRU's and PVO's early warning with KGB reports on the political situation, and hurriedly routed the product to its consumer—the supreme high command. Such integration of intelligence was important in supporting a posture of rapid reaction. To support launch on warning, however, the Soviets linked the CASMS directly to the CGS and the defense minister (also the CINC SRF) either of whom could have contacted the president to discuss the attack warning and the Soviet response.

Assessing the Vulnerability of Soviet Leadership Bunkers

A CIA study completed in 1978 found that "all fixed leadership shelters which have been identified are vulnerable to direct attack."[63] Subsequent Soviet investment in leadership protection, particularly the construction of deep command posts that began in the late 1970s, reversed the earlier judgment. Among U.S. planners the prevailing assessment during the 1980s was that new U.S. weapons were needed to attack the underground facilities effectively.

Soviet planners might have begged to differ with the revised assessment. The survivability of their vaunted underground facilities was certainly debatable. Using a standard reference for calculating the effects of nuclear weapons on deeply buried structures,[64] one can show that deep underground command posts were theoretically vulnerable to weapons in the then-current U.S. inventory if those weapons were accurately delivered to their targets. The survival of the bunkers depended less on their depth than on the inability of U.S. forces to pinpoint their location below the surface. The general locations of the underground complexes were difficult to hide, but the exact spot beneath the earth where a bunker was situated proved difficult to determine using satellite reconnaissance. This uncertainty, unless resolved through espionage, rendered an attacker's weapons inaccurate. The attacker could compensate, however, by barraging the area. Barrage attack stood a strong chance of destroying, or severely damaging, the subterranean installations.

Recently the U.S. Department of Defense reviewed the pertinent historical evidence gathered during nuclear tests and developed new models of the vulnerability of underground structures to nuclear explosions. These calculations differed substantially from those derived from earlier models. For example, the dimensions of a crater produced by a nuclear explosion were estimated to be considerably smaller than previously thought. To give a specific comparison, the radius of a crater produced by a one-megaton nuclear explosion on the surface of wet soil would be 651 feet according to the old formula,[65] whereas the new formula estimated the radius to be 394 feet.[66] The revised crater dimension is about 40 percent smaller than previously estimated. Comparable differentials typically hold across the spectrum of weapons yields and soil varieties.

Under the revised formulas weapons in the 1990 U.S. arsenal were no longer credited with the potential to deliver a lethal blow to the deepest of the buried Soviet command posts (estimated to be as much as a thousand feet below ground). In consequence, U.S. planners were forced to allocate a very large number of weapons to the deepest targets to meet requirements for damage expectancy, pending the deployment of earth-penetrating weapons. Despite its gross inefficiency, this allocation was upheld upon review by political authorities after a skeptical SAC officer questioned its wisdom.[67]

There is no reason to believe that Soviet planners applied the same formulas. If they erred on the side of caution in their assessments, they might well have applied the standard formulas that produce more worrisome results. In any case the Soviets appreciated the extreme variation produced by different models.[68] No model had been verified experimentally and proved accurate. For the sake of illustration and argument, suppose that a plausible range of estimates were bounded at one end by using the standard formula and at the other end by using the newer revised formula. Suppose further that conservative Soviet planners gauging the vulnerability of their command bunkers used the high-end estimates of the cratering effects of nuclear weapons, while U.S. planners assessing the lethality of weapons aimed at the Soviet bunkers used the low-end estimates. One of the effects of the different estimates is striking. U.S. planners, compensating for what they believed was the marginal effectiveness of each individual weapon, would have projected a threat of overkill proportions in the eyes of Soviet planners.

Soviet planners, using the old formula from the standard authoritative U.S. reference (Glasstone and Dolan), would have concluded that a Minuteman II missile armed with a one-megaton warhead (the largest yield available on any U.S. missile in 1990) posed a severe threat to their deepest facilities (1,000 feet down).[69] In theory this U.S. missile could have destroyed a structure buried as deep as 977 feet in wet soft rock (or wet soil) if the warhead was delivered accurately to the target. The same weapon would have caused systems destruction (incapacitating damage to equipment and occupants as opposed to structural destruction) down to a depth of 1,628 feet. In short, the United States in 1990 projected a potent and prompt threat to the deepest leadership sanctuaries known to U.S. intelligence.

By comparison, U.S. planners, using the new formula, would have concluded that the same weapon could destroy a structure buried as deep as 590 feet in wet soil (somewhat atypical for the Moscow basin) or 344 in wet soft rock (more typical for the area). The same weapon would have caused systems destruction down to a depth of 983 feet (wet soil) or 573 feet (wet soft rock). In short, the United States did not project a prompt lethal threat to the deepest Soviet bunkers.

A Soviet planner must have also factored U.S. strategic bombers into the assessment. Although weapons delivered by aircraft take longer to arrive on target than weapons delivered by missiles, the transit time for bombers loitering at their forward orbits outside Soviet territory (the so-called positive control turnaround points) was only two or three hours to the Moscow area. Moreover, Soviet exercises indicated a fear that U.S. strategic bombers could blend into the noise of a European theater conflict and covertly slip into Soviet territory to attack the key command posts. (Stealthy air-launched nuclear cruise missiles aggravated this headache.) Heavy bombers could also carry gravity bombs with very high explosive yields and deliver them with pinpoint accuracy to the target. (This accuracy was actually better than MX missile accuracy.)

Under the old formula a heavy U.S. bomber armed with a B-53 gravity bomb with a nine-megaton yield would have destroyed an underground facility buried as deep as 1,889 feet in wet soil or wet soft rock.[70] By comparison, the new formula produces a less lethal threat, though still a substantial one in absolute terms. A nine-megaton bomb would have created a crater radius of 590 feet in wet soil, which converts to a lethal depth of 886 feet; in wet soft rock, the crater radius would have been 394 feet, which converts to a lethal depth of 590 feet. Structural destruction was therefore not expected. System destruction would have theoretically occurred, however, unless the target depth exceeded 1,475 feet in wet soil, or 985 feet in wet soft rock. Despite the large variance in the computations, both formulas cast strong doubt on the resilience of deep Soviet underground command posts. Soviet planners certainly had cause for genuine concern regardless of the formula used.

Remote redoubts outside the Moscow basin could have been better protected by harder geological insulation. The famous spy Oleg Penkovskiy disclosed in the mid-1960s that an underground headquarters had been built beneath the rugged tundra in the Ural Mountain range for the wartime use of the Communist party's Central Committee CPSU, the Ministry of Defense, and all other vital government agencies.[71] Another such installation was more recently reported to exist beneath the rocky terrain near Kuybishev in the central part of the Russian republic, where the Soviet government retreated during World War II.[72] Under the new formula the pertinent calculations for this location's geological composition (dry soft rock, according to U.S. analysts) indicate a crater radius of only 180 feet for a one-megaton weapon, or 262 feet for a nine-megaton weapon. For structural damage this converts to a lethal depth of 270 and 393 feet, respectively; for systems destruction the lethal depths are 450 and 655 feet. Calculations based on the old formula would have been even more disturbing to the Soviets. The crater radius would have been 485 and 937 feet for one- and nine-megaton weapons, which converts to structural destruction down to a depth of 728 and 1,406 feet. Systems damage could have occurred at much greater depths.

The Vulnerability of Bunker Communications

Underground command posts could have sustained additional damage from the effects of blast overpressure, ground shock, and electromagnetic pulse.[73] Communications cables and surface or near-surface radio antennas also suffered damage from these nuclear effects. Furthermore, radio communications across the spectrum of frequencies used by Soviet deep command centers would have been degraded by the effects of nuclear explosions on the atmosphere.

Normal links connecting the static command posts of the supreme high command and the general staff with the Soviet strategic forces were not nearly as survivable as the buried-antenna grid. Satellite dishes used to communicate with the modern generations of submarines and strategic rocket forces were exposed and fragile. (Older submarines and land missile units had not been equipped with satellite receivers.) Nuclear explosions were also likely to degrade satellite signals severely. Terrestrial links, including most buried cable networks, could have been readily severed. Low-frequency (LF) and VLF communications associated with fixed command centers for the most part employed large "soft" radio antennas. Most such transmitters connecting high-level headquarters with naval and land-based rocket forces were active in peacetime, and most of them undoubtedly had been identified. These fixed LF and VLF sites were relatively few in number—a few dozen—and were fragile. On the other hand, LF transmitters associated with wartime command bunkers provided a semisurvivable communications link with ICBM launch control centers and perhaps naval forces. Such transmitters as well as the receivers could have been covertly buried at shallow depths to avoid direct targeting. Buried transmitters would not have performed as well as above-ground antenna farms, however, and their signals in any case were susceptible to nuclear effects.

The Soviets relied heavily on standard HF radio transmitters to communicate over long distances with all branches of their strategic forces. These transmitters were exposed on or near the surface and could not survive a direct attack. It was unlikely, however, that all communications from a surviving bunker would have been permanently suppressed. The Soviets were careful to ensure a correct disposition of radio transmitters, which involved running underground cables to transmitting antennas located many miles away from the deep command center. By proliferating and concealing remote antennas, the Soviets made the exact location of the stationary center harder to pinpoint and enhanced the survivability of communications. The Soviet command bunker at Zossen near Berlin, which housed the headquarters of Soviet forces in Germany and was one of ten large hardened bunkers devoted to Warsaw Pact wartime management, illustrated the configuration of communications at large static command posts. The communications for this command bunker were housed in a ring of bunkers about seven miles away from the main command facility.[74] The Soviets reportedly also used increasing numbers of underground antenna networks with transmitting aerials that telescope up after a nuclear attack.[75]

Although such redundancy probably ensured the survival of adequate numbers of HF transmitters and receivers, it by no means ensured effective HF communications. An acute weakness of standard HF radio is that the transmitters have to bounce signals off the ionosphere to communicate over long distances. These sky-wave signals are very susceptible to disruption from nuclear effects on the ionosphere. Even if the transmitters were not destroyed, a communications blackout affecting virtually the entire Soviet landmass could have lasted for many hours or days after a nuclear attack. Since an attack might have been prolonged, the restoration of HF communications might have been delayed indefinitely.

On the other side of the ledger, the Soviets had deployed HF and other radio networks designed expressly for surviving the blast effects of nuclear attack and communicating reliably in a nuclear environment. The backbone of Soviet survivable links for communicating with its strategic forces, particularly its SRF, was a nationwide grid of several hundred buried antennas built in the 1960s and later expanded and updated. These so-called garden plot antenna farms employed radio frequencies that were tested during Soviet and Chinese atmospheric nuclear testing and proved resistant to nuclear effects.[76] The Soviets pioneered the design of buried antenna communications and have published the seminal technical studies of the subject.[77] Nevertheless, the exact specifications and capabilities of their operational buried radio network were not well understood because it was rarely activated in peacetime. The locations of antennas were therefore also partially protected from detection, though an extensive, countrywide grid had been spotted.[78] Although their nuclear blast resistance was uncertain, U.S. versions of the system could withstand blast overpressures in excess of 1,000 pounds per square inch.[79] Assuming that the Soviet version was hardened to comparable levels, the United States could have destroyed those at known locations if U.S. planners had been willing to expend several hundred of the more lethal counterforce weapons in the strategic arsenal.

The Operations and Vulnerability of Top-Level Mobile Command Posts

The secret Voroshilov course materials reveal that the supreme high command could have used, as auxiliary and alternate command posts, specially prepared command posts of military district forces, groups of forces, and fleets. This network of alternates consisted of various types of vehicles, helicopters, aircraft, and ships. According to the U.S. Defense Department, "higher commands have multiple mobile alternate command posts available for their use, including land vehicles, trains, aircraft, and ships."[80] Such mobile systems seriously complicated U.S. targeting and increased Soviet confidence in the resilience of the command and control system. Indeed, such mobile command posts and communications centers played a crucial role in reconstituting Soviet strategic capability in some of the exercises described earlier. Aircraft in particular played a key role. Trains were also important in managing strategic operations (though apparently not in these exercises). Little significance was attached to land vehicles and ships, however.

Ships were heavily downgraded as high command posts after their poor performance during the 1967 Arab-Israeli conflict. The admiral of the Soviet fleet, Admiral Sergey Gorshkov, tried unsuccessfully to manage Soviet naval operations from a shipborne command post in the Mediterranean Sea instead of from his command post at navy main headquarters in Moscow. The Soviets later equipped selected cruisers and submarines for communicating with fleet and navy main headquarters,[81] but these primarily supported theater naval operations.[82] By all indications, particularly exercises, the combat operations of individual Soviet navy units and above all strategic nuclear units were centrally managed from the Moscow headquarters with little or no intervention by intermediate commands.[83]

The first factor to be weighed in analyzing the vulnerability of the major mobile command posts used in strategic control—aircraft and trains—is their operating tempo, which was very slow in peacetime. Usually dormant, the mobile command posts became active mainly during exercises that assumed a superpower crisis. In the exercises discussed earlier, it had been assumed that conventional hostilities had been under way for weeks, enabling the Soviet command and control system to bring itself and the strategic forces to a high state of readiness before the nuclear cauldron boiled over.

The airborne command posts of the navy and SRF sat idle in peacetime. The command post aircraft flown during the exercises—the airborne command posts of the navy main headquarters and of the SRF headquarters—and indeed the vast majority of planes reserved for top-level nuclear command, were normally consigned to inactive status at a single airport in the Moscow vicinity. (These aircraft typically carried Aeroflot markings.) The airborne command posts attached to the widely dispersed army headquarters of the SRF, and those attached to the Northern and Pacific fleet commanders, were also off alert in peacetime. Most, if not all, these planes were old Coot turboprops, which were austerely equipped.[84] They functioned less as true command posts than as transport vehicles for relocating top leaders, communications aircraft for relaying orders, and centers for assessing the status of friendly forces and delivering status reports to the underground command posts. For instance, the SRF airborne command post flew to the missile fields to poll launch control units and then relayed the status reports back to a high-level SRF underground command post. This airborne post carried representatives from each of the six SRF armies as part of the battle staff, each with its own communications links to its particular army.[85]

The fleet of Bear-J communications relay aircraft, outfitted with VLF antennas—wires several miles long that had to be reeled out behind the plane to communicate with submerged ballistic missile submarines—consisted of six aircraft divided equally between the Northern and Pacific fleets,[86] all of which normally sat idle in peacetime at a single airbase in each of the two theaters.[87]

Trainborne command posts for the minister of defense, the supreme high commander, and particularly the general staff were somewhat active in peacetime—for example, the train command post of the general staff regularly transited back and forth between Moscow and the Ural Mountains, stopping periodically at presurveyed sites to set up and plug into communications outlets. The train for the supreme commander apparently was deactivated permanently in the 1980s. (It was Leonid Brezhnev's train.) The Soviets also allotted a train command post to the CINC of the Far Eastern TVD, whose static wartime headquarters was at Ulan-Ude.[88]

As a rule, virtually all the mobile backup components of the Soviet nuclear command and control system were kept on a low level of alert and required many hours to get ready. In consequence, they were vulnerable to destruction in a surprise attack. To avoid this acute vulnerability, the Soviets needed to mobilize the many backup elements and disperse them from their normal static locations. This process required enormous effort on the part of the general staff, which maintained a large special signals organization responsible for establishing resilient wartime communications.[89]

The generation of reserve command systems would have mitigated their peacetime vulnerability. The additional redundancy established during a crisis would certainly have lowered U.S. confidence in the effectiveness of strikes against the Soviet leadership and military command system. Whether it really boosted Soviet confidence in the command and control system's wartime performance is harder to say. Although Soviet command and communications aircraft played critical roles in the strategic war games, their pre-takeoff vulnerability, even while they were poised on runway alert, was very great. An attack by U.S. submarine-launched nuclear ballistic or cruise missiles could have theoretically caught them on the ground because of the short or nonexistent tactical warning that Soviet sensors could have provided. The Soviet fleet of command aircraft was too small and outmoded to support a continuous airborne alert. Hence their exposure to attack on the ground was substantial. The U.S. SIOP targeted primary airfields and secondary dispersal bases, and U.S. strategic bombers planned to conduct follow-on operations against them by flying search and destroy missions to the austere airstrips and other possible addresses at which the Soviet planes might have been found. Similar missions would have been flown against the trainborne command posts. U.S. SIOP bombers planned to check known presurveyed sites used by the trains and attack them if found.

Other hazards of airborne and trainborne operations in a nuclear environment, such as the adverse effects of electromagnetic pulse on their radio equipment, added to the uncertainty. These mobile command posts also relied heavily on standard HF radio for communications with one another and with dispersed submarine, bomber, and land-based ballistic missile forces. Nuclear effects and jamming could have severely degraded this crucial means of control. Satellite links augmented HF radio on some mobile command posts. Moreover, the Soviets had demonstrated a capability to replenish satellites using ground mobile launchers. In an exercise an SS-20 mobile missile launched a satellite into orbit, suggesting a capability to reconstitute satellite communications.[90] This role could have been assumed by SS-25 mobile ICBMs. Nevertheless, satellite links would have lacked robustness in the face of jamming and nuclear effects.

Overall Assessment of the Vulnerability of
Top-Level Command and Control

The cumulative effect of these many potential hazards was incalculable, but it surely eroded Soviet confidence. Cautious Soviet assessment warranted a gloomy prognosis for the survival and endurance of mobile backup command assets deployed in 1990. The deep underground command centers, though far from offering total safety, probably appeared to be the Soviets' bulwark. For survivable communications, hardened LF transmitters associated with the deep bunkers offered perhaps the highest confidence. The Soviet emergency rocket communications system, though deployed at fixed sites and therefore subject to direct attack, could have constituted a reliable backup if ERCS missiles had been deployed in sufficient numbers or covertly enough to escape drawing concentrated fire. (To ensure that one ERCS missile survived a two-on-one attack by U.S. MX forces, the Soviets would have to have fielded at least ten ERCS missiles in silos hardened to withstand six thousand pounds per square inch.)

The uncertainties were a source of major Soviet discomfort. The flip side of this uncertainty should also be acknowledged, however. In 1990 U.S. planners had reasonable doubts they could inflict decisive damage to Soviet fixed or relocatable command targets.

Low-Level Strategic Command and Control Systems

Low peacetime readiness applied to a substantial fraction of Soviet strategic nuclear forces. The Soviet intercontinental bombers that participated in the exercises were neither armed with nuclear weapons nor ready for takeoff in peacetime. The Moscow-based Thirty-seventh Air Army, which used to manage all Soviet strategic bombers with intercontinental missions (a responsibility that was at least partially transferred to the Forty-sixth and Thirtieth Air Armies), maintained its fleet of planes at a very low level of combat readiness. Most SSBNs were also maintained at a low state of readiness, with few at sea on combat patrol at any given time. Similarly, a small number of mobile ICBMs maintained a dispersed alert posture in peacetime. The notable exception appeared to be the silo-based ICBM force, although the normal alert rate and combat readiness of this leg of the Soviet force structure were debatable because of intelligence uncertainties.

The Operations and Vulnerability of ICBM Command and Control

The chain of command for alerting and releasing Soviet ICBMs in silos normally ran from the supreme high command through general staff channels to units of the SRF via the Signal communications network. Within the SRF, orders nominally flowed down several echelons of command in the following order: SRF headquarters, armies, divisions, regiments, battalions, and batteries. When operating the command and control system in the automatic mode, the general staff was able to bypass the upper and intermediate echelons, issuing orders directly to the launch crews in the field. These crews resided at regimental, battalion, and battery command posts, depending on the type of missile involved.[91] Under certain special circumstances the general staff could have also bypassed the crews at the bottom and used special equipment to put the firing of the missiles under their remote control. But the general staff itself could have been bypassed in favor of a direct channel from the supreme high command to the CINC SRF. This option meant that the SRF headquarters could have served as an alternate to the general staff's main operations directorate.

Within the SRF were reportedly six armies of various sizes and shapes (the largest was the Twenty-seventh Army).[92] An SRF army corresponded roughly to a U.S. Minuteman wing. There were six Minuteman wings in the SAC in 1990. Each SRF army commanded a number of divisions. There were approximately sixteen silo-based and twelve mobile ICBM divisions in the SRF.[93] An SRF division corresponded roughly to a squadron of Minuteman missiles. There were twenty Minuteman squadrons in the SAC ICBM force, each consisting of fifty silo-based missiles and five underground launch control centers. A Soviet SRF division of silo-based ICBMs varied much more widely, but an "average" division consisted of sixty batteries (that is, sixty missiles) and six underground launch control centers.[94] A typical division of mobile ICBMs consisted of three regiments, nine battalions, and twenty-seven batteries.[95]

Silo-based launchers were organized in groups of six or ten.[96] For fourth- and fifth-generation fixed ICBMs, each group was under the local control of a primary battalion launch control center, which could remotely launch the six or ten missiles under its command.[97] In a typical formation three battalions were interwoven to provide launch redundancy for the eighteen to thirty missiles in the formation (the three battalions made up a regimental formation).[98] For older silo-based Soviet ICBMs (SS-11 and SS-13 units) and for mobile ICBMs, a regimental command post was the main launch control center. For silo-based forces a regimental complex controlled ten missiles. For mobile ICBMs a regiment controlled nine transport-erector launchers.

These control arrangements lend themselves to quantitative assessment of the effectiveness of a U.S. attack on the command and control system associated with silo-based forces. The modeling produces startling results. A few tens of U.S. missiles in the 1990 inventory of day-to-day alert forces could do a great deal to suppress retaliation by Soviet silo-based ICBMs. A small-scale attack aimed exclusively at the low-level launch control posts—namely, the battalion and regimental launch control centers—would have neutralized the local launch facilities for a large part of the Soviet ICBM force deployed in fixed silos if—and these are important conditions—the Soviets elected or were forced to absorb the brunt of the U.S. attack and backup launch methods, such as the remote-fire link between Moscow command posts and ICBM silos, failed to work.

If it is further assumed that had the United States directly attacked the silos as well, which meant the unleashing of the lion's share of the U.S. strategic arsenal on day-to-day alert, the combination of silo and launch center attrition would have been extreme. The number of silo-based Soviet ICBMs that survived and remained linked to a surviving launch control center would have been a very small fraction of the total peacetime force.[99]

The surviving static ICBM forces with intact launch control centers, and any mobile ICBMs that dispersed out of their vulnerable garrisons before the U.S. attack, faced the additional difficulty of establishing contact with higher authorities. Some portion of this surviving force might have found itself isolated from higher authority. A judiciously aimed attack might have severely degraded their communications links with superiors. Moreover, the higher-level command posts themselves— SRF division, army, SRF main headquarters, as well as the command centers of the supreme high command—might not have survived a comprehensive decapitation strike. Soviet planners surely feared that the command and control system, notwithstanding ERCS and other capabilities for launching isolated forces by remote control, would have been unable to reconstitute launch control.

The analysis and calculations that follow provide empirical support for the general assessment.

SILO-BASED ICBM OPERATIONS AND COMMAND VULNERABILITY. As of September 1990, the inventory of Soviet silo-based ICBMs totaled 1,109, spread over approximately sixteen divisions. Older, third-generation missiles accounted for fully one-third of the total force (375 out of 1,109).[100] Newer, SS-18 forces with lethal countersilo capability formed the backbone of the Soviet intercontinental strike force (308 missiles). This force was supplemented by 70 SS-17s (several, perhaps as many as 10, carried communications packages rather than nuclear warheads, as part of the Soviet emergency rocket communications system), 56 SS-24s, and 300

SS-19s. The SS-19 force included a contingent of 120 variable-range missiles divided equally between two divisions in the Ukraine. They along with many of the older SS-11s deployed in the Far East along the Chinese border were believed to support regional nuclear options.[101]

The U.S. Department of Defense indicated that the Soviet ICBM force was maintained at a high level of combat readiness in 1990.[102] The Soviets had been credited with high readiness for at least a decade. In 1981, for instance, a spokesman for the intelligence community testified that "Soviet ICBMs, like US ICBMs, are fully manned and on a normal readiness condition on a routine basis. Most, if not all, Soviet ICBMs could be launched within minutes of a valid launch order."[103] A U.S. specialist on Soviet SRF forces, Stephen Meyer, similarly asserted in 1987 that more than 80 percent of the Soviet ICBM force stood ready to be launched in minutes from their day-to-day alert status. He cited published Soviet sources which indicated that a complete launch sequence, including the release of final safety catches, took no longer than three minutes to perform.[104]

The exercise data presented earlier revealed a similar timeline for firing the forces, though the background context for the simulated SRF strike was a crisis that provided warning time to bring the ICBM force to full combat readiness. Additional confirmation of these estimates comes from an analyst who equated SRF ICBM readiness with U.S. Minuteman readiness.[105] Since nearly 90 percent of the U.S. Minuteman force could be launched within three minutes after receipt of an order, the bulk of the Soviet ICBM force was judged to be ready for combat at a moment's notice.[106]

Such judgments are not easily reconciled with testimony from the late 1970s, when the Soviet silo-based ICBM force consisted essentially of the same missile types deployed a decade later. The testimony attributed "much lower readiness levels than U.S. levels" to the Soviet ICBM arsenal.[107] Although it is clear that the Soviets emphasized the importance of raising the combat readiness of the SRF during the period of strained superpower relations in the early to mid 1980s, the public record does not show any substantial change in actual SRF alert levels. Many informed analysts interviewed for this study believed that SRF readiness had been and continued to be considerably lower than advertised. Most of the spectrum of opinion clustered around a 50 to 60 percent figure for the portion of the silo-based ICBM force that could be launched within minutes from a day-to-day posture. This estimate is consistent with the fact that the SS-11s were difficult to keep on high combat readiness and required hours to get ready for launch from a lower state of readiness. Maintaining the SS-17 on launch-ready alert was also problematic. The SS-13 was considered a lemon. The SS-18 was universally acknowledged to be the workhorse of the day-to-day alert force, but it constituted only 28 percent of the arsenal.

According to some analysts interviewed, the portion of the SRF at high combat readiness in peacetime was low. On the basis of communications traffic between field units and higher authority, they estimated the fraction on combat alert to be 10 to 15 percent.[108] A large portion of the remainder, they alleged, were not even manned and required many hours to bring up to full combat readiness.

Most of the analysts cautioned that all these estimates involve a fair amount of guesswork. As an analyst from the Defense Intelligence Agency put it in testimony confirming that the portion of Soviet ICBMs kept at peak readiness in the late 1970s was less than the analogous U.S. figure, "We cannot prove it one way or the other."[109] Conservative assumptions as much as hard evidence appears to have driven the intelligence estimates of readiness.

Orders to launch these SRF units would have normally been issued jointly by the general staff and the CINC SRF at the behest of the supreme high command. The primary links for disseminating authorization to launch (*direct* command)—either on command or at a designated time in the future—were land-line, satellite, or HF radio. A portion of the SRF had not been outfitted for satellite reception and hence relied on the other media. Buried LF receivers at the battalion launch control centers and the silos themselves provided a more survivable one-way link from the supreme high command to fourth-generation ICBM forces.

Assuming an intact communications network, orders to the newer units like the SS-18 force would have been simulcast over multiple links, including satellite and terrestrial (cable-microwave) Signal network channels, to the battalion launch control centers. Their Signal video monitors probably displayed some or all of the following critical information: targeting instructions, arming and unlock codes, launch hour, and launch authorization codeword. This information could have been sent in parcels in a series of messages, or it could have been packed into one message (a so-called doublet composed of a preliminary and a direct command.)[110] The messages could have directed an immediate launch on command or a launch at a designated time (LDT) in the future.

In the event of enemy strikes that disrupted normal communications to the battalions or that destroyed all three battalions in a given regiment, the Soviets had additional redundant means of fire control. The buried garden plot HF antennas discussed earlier were concentrated in areas of SRF deployments and would have been activated as a backup channel from the high-level commanders to the launch crews. The airborne command posts and other alternate systems would also have become active.[111] KGB and civil communications networks might have augmented the general staff and SRF networks. SRF divisional headquarters would have flown helicopters, and SRF regiments would have dispatched ground mobile control centers to roam the local missile fields. Although the capabilities of the regiment's vans were uncertain, it is believed that some were equipped for satellite reception and that they could have deployed to individual silos to fire isolated missiles as a last resort.[112] Lastly, there were the links between the top command centers and the ICBMs that were designed for unattended launches by remote electronic command.

The doubtful performance of such backup systems in an environment as forbidding as nuclear attack hardly needs elaboration. Ground mobile command centers, for example, would have been forced to operate in the immediate vicinity of massive nuclear detonations. In all likelihood they would have been severely stressed by the direct and collateral effects of nuclear weapons. At any rate, Soviet planners ought to have heavily discounted their contribution to retaliatory launch control. It is reasonable to suppose that retaliation by silo-based ICBMs depended critically on the survival of the underground battalion launch control centers.

If that is so, then the United States projected a potent threat to the Soviet ICBM force because it could have destroyed the vast majority of the launch control centers (LCCs). Despite their extreme hardness— estimated conservatively to be about 6,000 pounds per square inch (psi) resistance to blast overpressure for SS-17, SS-18, SS-19, and SS-24 LCCs—and redundancy (three redundant LCCs per regiment for the above-mentioned missile types), the hardest LCCs were vulnerable to attack by U.S. MX ICBM and D-5 SLBM weapons. Other LCCs for older forces were less redundant (one LCC per group of ten missiles) and less protected (2,000 psi for SS-13s and 1,000 psi for SS-11s).

One set of calculations using plausible assumptions for late-1990 forces on day-to-day alert projects the virtual obliteration of the Soviet ICBM force in three phases of attack.[113] In the first phase the United States focused a judiciously targeted assault on the Soviet LCCs. The leverage produced was enormous. The United States expended only 222 missile warheads to deprive many entire regiments of normal ground launch control. Out of 1,098 ICBMs armed with 6,420 warheads, only 244 ICBMs armed with 1,330 warheads remained connected to a surviving launch control center. The remainder—about 854 ICBMs with 5,090 warheads—were deprived of launch control and thus neutralized. The force exchange ratio was extremely favorable to the attacker: 23 warheads destroyed for 1 attacking warhead. The overall damage expectancy against all Soviet silo-based ICBMs in this initial attack by a mere 222 U.S. strategic nuclear warheads was 78 percent against the launchers and 79 percent against the warheads.

In the second phase, which occurred almost simultaneously with the first, the United States attacked all the individual Soviet silos (hardened to 6,000 psi in most cases). The number of U.S. warheads committed to this attack was 1,969. The number of Soviet silo launchers destroyed was 787. The number of Soviet warheads destroyed was 4,747. The exchange ratio was again favorable to the United States—more than 2 warheads destroyed for every 1 attacking warhead. The overall damage expectancy against all Soviet silo-based ICBMs in this phase of the attack was 72 percent against the launchers and 74 percent against the warheads.

The combined overall damage expectancy from this two-pronged U.S. assault that targeted both the LCCs and the individual silos was even higher. The reason is that the regiments with surviving launch control centers had lost most of their weapons. The total number of U.S. warheads committed to the attack was 2,191 (222 plus 1,969). The number of Soviet silo launchers that survived and remained under the control of an LCC in the regiment was only 68. These 68 launchers carried 336 warheads. The exchange ratio was 1:2.8 in favor of the attacker, who achieved an amazing damage expectancy of 94 and 95 percent against the ICBM launchers and warheads, respectively.

In the third and final phase of the hypothetical attack the United States sent bomber forces to attack individual Soviet LCCs and silos that survived the ballistic missile laydown. Assuming that forces in the day-to-day alert inventory were used, and that the crews had a reliably effective capability to perform bomb damage assessment on the scene, perhaps aided by satellite sensors on the global positioning system designed to detect and report the location of nuclear explosions, the U.S. bomber force obliterated the residual Soviet force—the 306 silos and the handful of LCCs that had survived the initial attack. This third phase began a few hours after the start of the missile assault and lasted for about ten hours. The calculations assume, not unreasonably, that the Soviet command and control system was unable to reconstitute itself during this brief pause in the U.S. strategic offensive.

MOBILE ICBM OPERATIONS AND COMMAND AND CONTROL VULNERABIL-ITY. Using an assessment like the one presented above would have given the Soviets a rationale for putting their silo-based force on full alert during a crisis and for acting quickly to unleash the forces upon detecting the mass launch of U.S. missile forces. Such an assessment may also have been the impetus behind the Soviet mobile ICBM program.

It is reasonable to suppose that the basic arrangements for exercising positive and negative control over Soviet mobile forces were virtually identical to those used to manage silo-based ICBMs. The mobile units themselves appeared to be survivable if a timely decision was made either to put them on full combat readiness in their peacetime garrisons, enabling them to be launched on tactical warning, or to disperse them out of garrison. If they were dispersed and if higher authority survived and could establish contact with the mobile units in the field, these mobile forces would have constituted a substantial survivable capability: 300 intercontinental missiles armed with 570 nuclear warheads.

Strategic exercises indicate that mobile SS-25 ICBMs were assigned a reserve role along with Delta IV and Typhoon SSBNs and long-range strategic aviation.[114] The Soviets had been rapidly expanding the SS-25 force, which numbered about 270 batteries as of September 1990. It was a truck-based mobile system similar to the intermediate-range SS-20 weapon system, and it was being deployed mainly at the former bases of SS-20 regiments.[115] In garrison each SS-25 resided in a garage with a sliding roof that could be retracted for quick launch of the missile, which carried a single warhead.[116] In peacetime the combat readiness of some portion of the forces in garrison was probably high enough to exercise launch on warning.[117] In all likelihood the alert level of the remainder needed to be raised to get them ready to be launched within minutes of an order. In peacetime a very small number of SS-25s probably operated out of garrisons in the field. A plausible estimate is roughly 15 to 20 percent. The vast majority were confined to a small plot of land in peacetime.

A typical SS-25 base (a division) consisted of three regiments, each with three battalions; each battalion consisted of three single-warhead missiles (batteries). A representative SS-25 base thus consisted of twenty-seven missiles, each housed in a garage.[118] The procedures for dispersing the full contingent of 270 SS-25s out of garrison were doubtless similar to the SS-20 procedures described by a defense intelligence analyst: "The procedure that is used by the Soviets is primarily a scatter-on warning system whereby they are primarily based within a secure complex, in a period of crisis or period of warning they will move out to the surrounding country, and fire from predesignated launch positions."[119] In their road-mobile configuration the SS-25s appeared to roam as far as sixty miles or so from home base, although the START agreement declared their field deployment areas to be much larger. Most likely the SS-25s could have roamed more than 100 miles in any direction from home base.[120]

Like the SS-20s, which in exercises dispersed to some locations where they hid for up to six hours before moving to another location to hide or to a presurveyed launch site, the SS-25s presumably would have scrambled to hide upon receipt of a preliminary command and moved to pre-surveyed launch points when instructed to fire by a direct command. The units presumably received their targeting instructions, unlock codes, and launch codeword over HF radio, satellite links, or land-lines with outlets at some of the locations where they hid. The regimental and battalion commanders and the battery fire control officers must have coordinated their actions to effect the launch. If the reaction time of the SS-25 was comparable to the SS-20, the launch crews were able to complete the setup and launch procedures in about an hour.[121]

The SS-24 mobile ICBM force deployed on trains operated out of two or three home bases in 1990. According to press accounts, SS-24 trains had been spotted at two operational bases for fixed ICBMs—Kastroma in the northwestern Soviet Union and Gladkaya in Siberia—as well as the missile test facility at Plesetsk.[122] Gladkaya, but not the two other bases, was identified by the Defense Department as the location of a mobile ICBM site.[123] The 1991 START agreement identifies three locations: Kostroma, Bershet', and Krasnoyarsk.[124]

Each SS-24 train carried three launchers (batteries) and therefore constituted a battalion.[125] The battalion train also included a fire control car headed by the battalion commander. Three separate battalion trains formed a regiment. This regiment of three trains (with a total of nine launchers) was serviced at a fixed installation called a missile servicing position, a garrison of sorts where nuclear warheads were mated to missiles (ten warheads per missile) and final checkout occurred prior to deployment on the rail system. The railroad troops of the Ministry of

Defense operated the trains themselves, but of course the SRF troops controlled the nine missile batteries spread over the three trains in the regiment. These trains probably did not travel much beyond a radius of about sixty miles from the main servicing position, though thousands of additional miles of track was available if operational security warranted wider dispersal. Their travel routes, time of movement, hide and fire locations, and other operational details were undoubtedly prespecified by high-level authorities. It is estimated that an SS-24 train needed forty-five to ninety minutes to set up for launch and another ten to fifteen minutes to perform the firing procedures.[126]

Launch orders could have been sent over HF radio, satellite links, airborne command post radio relay, and meteor burst communications. There were also wire-lines running parallel to the track, allowing trains to plug into land-lines at certain prearranged locations. This network would have been useful for disseminating orders to move to the final firing location. As a last resort, communications used by the railroad troops, as opposed to the dedicated SRF channels, could have provided a channel to the mobile platforms.[127]

According to the START agreement, the Soviets had deployed 33 SS-24 rail-mobile ICBMs by mid-1991. That number converts to between 3 and 4 operational regiments, each having 3 trains (battalions) and 9 missiles. Specifically, the Soviets had fielded 11 trains. The SS-24 rail-mobile force thus consisted of 33 missiles and 330 warheads. Further deployment to an expected maximum of 12 trains was curtailed as part of the Gorbachev initiative of October 1991.[128]

The Operations and Vulnerability of SSBN Command

The Soviet ballistic missile submarine force consisted of sixty-one boats operating out of six major bases in 1990.[129] Thirty-seven SSBNs belonged to the Northern Fleet, whose headquarters was at Severo-morsk.[130] The other twenty-four SSBNs belonged to the Pacific Fleet, based at Vladivostok.[131] The Soviets habitually kept these forces on a short leash. Under normal peacetime conditions three-fourths of them were anchored in port, and the lion's share of the remainder plied waters near to home ports.[132]

Some analysts attributed this low tempo of operations at sea to the high priority of strict nuclear command and control in Soviet operational philosophy.[133] A shortage of trained SSBN crews partly explained the low at-sea alert rate, though this observation begs the question why more crews were not trained.[134] Others argued that the low tempo reflected a Soviet readiness philosophy in which the maintenance and surge potential of SSBNs took precedence over at-sea operations.[135] Also the Soviets developed capabilities and procedures for rapid SLBM launch from submarines in port and grew to rely heavily on a pierside alert posture. A former SSBN crew member who served eight years on modern SSBNs from the late 1970s through the mid-1980s reported that he went on a total of five seventy-eight-day combat patrols at sea during his period of service.[136] In addition, he spent three to four months a year on combat alert at dockside. In sum, most of his alert time was spent at pierside and not at sea.[137] This trend continued through the time of this writing (fall 1992). Fewer and fewer SSBNs were going to sea on combat patrol. As few as one or two SSBNs were reportedly on combat patrol at any given time during the early months of 1992.[138]

The alert disposition of Soviet SSBNs was governed by the highest level of the nuclear command and control system. The fleet headquarters and the immediately subordinate organizations, known as flotillas, which had jurisdiction over the SSBN contingent in their area—for example, a flotilla based at Petropavlovsk, which supported the SSBNs in the Pacific Fleet and the larger Northern Fleet Flotilla at Polyarnyy near Murmansk—provided only administrative, logistical, and training support for the strategic submarine mission. For that matter, the senior naval commander of the entire Soviet fleet, whose headquarters was based near Moscow, performed a largely administrative function. His wartime functions were not, however, "purely administrative," as one observer claims.[139] Although the supreme high command managed the SSBN (as well as SRF and intercontinental bomber) forces through the main operations directorate of the general staff, the navy CINC participated in the forming and disseminating of the launch orders. Contingency procedures existed to allow the chief of the General Staff (CGS) to bypass the navy CINC, but the standard mode of execution involved both organizations. Nuclear release normally required coded inputs from the CGS and navy CINC, which were combined and disseminated as a direct command to the submarine crews via the *Volna* communications network.

In the case of SSBNs on combat alert in port, directives from Moscow could have been sent and received almost instantly over land-line or radio communications.[140] If ordered to surge out to sea, an SSBN left port on the surface, usually escorted by surface tenders and SSN attack submarines.[141] The maximum time required to surge out of port was fifteen hours, according to a former SSBN crew member.[142] The tender's use of radar for navigating safely to sea from port inlets provided a detectable signature for Western antisubmarine operations.[143] Approximately twenty to fifty miles out of port the Soviet submarines would dive to depth and proceed to alert patrol areas. A patrol zone (*the box*) was reserved for a single SSBN and any friendly attack submarines assigned to protect it.[144] The box within which a submarine operated (typically a square area of 100 × 100 nautical miles) was situated in the open seas. The Northern Fleet was in the Barents, Kara (behind Novaya Zemlya), North Greenland, and Norwegian seas and the north Atlantic Ocean; the Pacific Fleet was in the Sea of Okhotsk. During the 1980s the launch stations also encompassed arctic ice edges and close-in territorial waters such as fjords in the White Sea, Murmansk coast, and northern Sea of Okhotsk. The Delta SSBN hulls were designed to break a meter of ice (a thickness found at the edges of the ice pack), and they also carried a conventional torpedo for breaking ice.[145]

Hiding in fjords or other areas close to shore, SSBNs could sit motionless for prolonged periods instead of patrolling within a box. To illustrate, the first duty patrol of the newest SSBN class, the Typhoon, consisted of spending one month submerged and anchored in 350 meters of water near Novaya Zemlya. The Typhoon listened for launch orders through a buoy it floated near the surface.[146] In such stationary deployments close to land it was also feasible to plug into underwater cables connected with higher authority. Land lines could have been strung from Moscow to the coast of Murmansk, for example, and extended underwater for many miles using undersea cable. Acoustic devices attached to the cables could also have been used to relay messages via sonar transmissions to nearby submarines, which themselves could have checked the devices for stored messages using acoustic communications. Messages could have also been prerecorded in pods and dropped into the ocean from aircraft for later acoustic retransmission. Finally, acoustic communications between SSBNs and escort SSNs (and surface escorts) were overheard, suggesting another method of indirect communications with higher authority.[147] In all likelihood such interaction would have been rare for SSBNs on full combat alert, as opposed to modified alert.

If SSBNs had been surged out of port on an emergency basis and been ill prepared for a combat mission as a consequence, they might have sallied to offshore holding areas, dived to depth, and stayed put awaiting further instructions instead of proceeding to their normal launch stations.[148] Sitting on the bottom of the continental shelf near their home ports, they could have periodically floated a tethered whip antenna to the surface to receive HF or LF radio transmissions. By this means they might have been instructed, for example, to move to a different launch station, wait for antisubmarine warfare (ASW) protective escorts, or rendezvous with missile tenders.[149]

At sea Soviet SSBNs on combat patrol at their launch stations were required to listen continuously or at regular intervals for instructions sent by higher authority. During routine patrols in peacetime they deployed antennas four times a day (every six hours) for ten to fifteen minutes to monitor prescheduled broadcasts. If a danger of war was declared, they were required to listen eight times a day (every three hours) or continuously.[150] Such declarations would have been issued by the supreme high command through the general staff, or through the naval main headquarters over prescheduled broadcasts from the Soviet fleet network. (Again, the central headquarters of the naval main staff near Moscow often keyed the transmitters at the behest of higher authorities.)

This network consisted primarily of VLF and LF radio stations scattered across the country.[151] The Soviets had dozens of such transmitters, though they appeared to rely on a handful of high-power VLF stations for long-distance communications with submerged submarines that trailed a long wire or buoy just below the ocean's surface.[152] Six VLF stations provided the yeoman service for the worldwide control of SSBNs.[153] The maximum range was about six thousand miles under ideal conditions, but atmospheric anomalies, poor sea conditions, ice, and other factors substantially reduced the effective range.[154] These problems were especially acute in the polar region and at northern latitudes in general. Backup transmitters using LF and HF radio (the latter requiring an antenna on the water's surface) were located with the major Soviet VLF stations to compensate, though signal propagation from these stations also suffered similar degradation from the same effects. (The range of LF was also far less than VLF.)

For under-ice operations Soviet SSBNs, particularly the Typhoon and Delta IV class submarines built for this purpose, trailed an underwater antenna that received ELF signals from an ELF transmitter on the Kola Peninsula.[155] This system penetrated ice effectively and penetrated seawater to much greater depths than VLF signals. Reception down to several hundred feet, compared with fifteen or twenty feet for VLF, was possible using ELF. Its data rate was too low to convey detailed information on a timely basis, but it served well as a "bell-ringer." ELF could contact SSBNs that were otherwise isolated because of their speed, depth, or inability to deploy VLF antennas because of physical interference from ice formations. ELF could also notify them to come to shallow water and deploy antennas to receive instructions from higher authorities.[156] This was especially useful for Typhoon and Delta IV patrols in the arctic region. These SSBNs appeared to constitute a strategic reserve force that would be withheld during an initial strategic salvo. The Typhoon, for example, reportedly never fired its missiles simultaneously with land-based strategic rocket forces during the initial salvos in exercises. It normally received launch orders from the Bear-J communications relay aircraft a long time after an initial exchange.[157] ELF bell-ringing or the sudden cessation of ELF transmissions would have explicitly or implicitly signaled the Typhoon SSBNs to deploy a VLF antenna to listen for messages relayed by the Bear-J aircraft.

According to Western sources, a Soviet SSBN on patrol regularly transmitted back to higher authority. Twice a day it would come to shallow water, position a transmitting antenna on the surface, and communicate with the general staff or naval main staff in Moscow. These transmissions to Moscow occurred at intervals planned ahead of time to facilitate contact using only very brief "burst" radio communications. Unscheduled radio contact with higher authority was immediately required if the SSBN lost and could not regain normal radio reception.[158] In either case the SSBN broke radio silence to report status and acknowledge receipt of earlier messages from Moscow. The usual practice was to use HF radio to make contact. Several different constellations of satellites also provided links: spacecraft in geosynchronous and Molniya elliptical orbits carried VHF-UHF transponders for communicating with Moscow, and store-dump low-altitude satellites permitted covert (low probability of intercept), though delayed (by as much as twenty minutes), tactical communications with fleet headquarters.[159] A lengthy exchange with Moscow sometimes occurred when an SSBN experienced mechanical or other difficulties that seriously undermined its ability to carry out its combat mission. According to interview material, Soviet SSBNs could avoid blame if they dutifully reported performance problems to Moscow authorities, who then held the administrative commanders accountable for failing to prepare the boats properly for combat duty.

Frequent overt contact with Moscow obviously increased the risk that an SSBN's location would be compromised. According to a former SSBN crew member, such interaction was forbidden for this reason. Both the Western and Soviet accounts of the procedures seem credible if contradictory. Perhaps the two-way interaction involved SSBNs on modified as opposed to full combat alert. Periodic two-way contact with Moscow would have at least been consistent with the Soviet's penchant for strict central control of the strategic forces. That it would have strengthened control at the expense of submarine exposure to detection and attack was a trade-off the Soviets were more prone than the United States to accept.[160]

Soviet SSBNs surfaced periodically to fix their location. Approximately every six days a sub exposed a satellite cone used for navigation. An operational leeway of one-half mile of position location uncertainty was allowed. This meant that Soviet SLBMs were inaccurate at best. The scope for guidance error was such that all SLBMs, including the solid fuel types, were equipped with a self-destruct explosive charge designed to blow up the missile during its boost phase if, after taking a three-star astral reading, the missile determined that it was straying substantially off course.[161] A former SSBN crew member said he had heard of several incidents in which missiles destroyed themselves in flight during operational tests.

SOVIET SSBN LAUNCH PROCEDURES. Although the procedures for launching missiles from SSBNs have not been fully revealed, there were apparently two basic forms of the orders: LDT (up to twelve hours in the future if exercises are any indication), or launch on command (fire immediately). The former, which probably required the dissemination of a series of orders rather than a single message, would have been the preferred approach if time and circumstances permitted, in order to coordinate SSBN strikes with other strategic nuclear operations according to Soviet combined-arms operational concepts.[162] The former SSBN crew member downplayed the significance of LDT, however, stressing that all training emphasized the launch of missiles in the shortest possible time after receiving the command to fire, though in special circumstances the fire control system was unblocked early in preparation for a subsequent launch order. This emphasis on immediate launch was of course especially pertinent to SSBNs on combat alert at dockside. Because of their high combat readiness and reliable communications it was not vital for them to receive prior notification in the form of an LDT.

SSBN alert and launch orders had to be verified and implemented by a minimum of three key officers: the ship's captain, executive officer, and a third person (the political officer until that position was recently abolished). These orders included codes for missile unlocking, targeting, and friend or foe identification, the latter being a code that changed every few hours. The codes underwent both human and electronic validation. The radio officer and cipher officer were the first to recognize the launch order and provide it to the executive officer and third crew member. The executive officer verified that the proper frequencies had been employed, and using internal communications (*Kashtym*) reported to the captain in the central command post that the "set of frequencies have been verified." The third person used documents on board to check a short code in the message, and using internal communications reported to the captain that the "coding was done properly." The officers in the communications room (called the Third Department) inserted the codes into a decoding and interlocking device (called *Commanda* equipment in the older Delta submarines and *Kamin* equipment in the newer ones), which electronically validated the launch order codes. If the computer check was positive, the device automatically displayed the relevant information in the central post and issued a signal to the fire control system (called *Diana* in the older Delta submarines, or *Atoll* in the newer ones) and the missile control system (tubes, missiles, and so on).[163]

Once activated, the fire control system began an automatic process of launch preparations—trajectory calculations, astro-correcting system, and so forth. Then the four officers—radio, cipher, executive, and formerly political officer—joined the captain in the central post and delivered a hard copy of the launch order. The captain checked the order and retrieved several items from his safe: a special key to be inserted into the fire control console; a six-digit combination from an envelope, probably determined in part by information in the launch order, which was also an input to the fire control system; and the correct perforated tape. In a combat situation the captain inserted the key, ordered the operator of the fire control console to insert the six-digit combination and the current Greenwich mean time, and handed one of the several perforated tapes in the safe to an operator responsible for feeding it into a separate piece of equipment in the central post. The six-digit combination established the target set, height of burst, and distribution of decoys for each missile.[164] The perforated tape, selected on the basis of the launch order, performed a targeting function and had to correlate properly with the six-digit combination.[165] On orders from the captain the chief missile control officer then inserted his own key into the missile control console of the fourth compartment and turned it to the launch position. The

missiles were then automatically launched after the submarine maneu-
vered into the proper launch position. This maneuvering was largely an
automatic process that took about four minutes to achieve proper pitch,
yaw, depth, velocity, and course change. If these conditions could not be
maintained during the launch sequence, either an emergency shutdown
occurred or the missile self-destruct mechanism activated, after breakwater. Because of the extensive automation of the prelaunch and launch
sequence, only 15 crew members out of the entire crew of 120 men were
vitally involved.[166]

For a modern Soviet SSBN on combat patrol the time between the
receipt of final launch orders and first missile breaking water was about
seventeen minutes according to exercise data collected by the United
States. An SSBN crew member who served on Delta II and Delta III
SSBNs observed launch sequences that ranged from nine minutes to
fifteen minutes. Twelve minutes was typical: six for prelaunch procedures, including message validation, and six more for final launch preparations, which were largely automated. Missiles were then automatically
fired from each tube, one at a time, zigzagging from one end of the boat
to the other. There was a four- to twelve-second interval between each
missile launch.

For older SSBNs with severe shortcomings in inertial navigation, such
as the Yankee-class boats,[167] the firing process probably depended on
such external aids as moored undersea navigation buoys that could have
been checked for information with acoustic communications from a distance of about half a mile. (A prior alert order would presumably have
signaled the SSBN to get within range of such aids.) Several missiles
might have been fired during each pass of the navigation buoy, requiring
continuing communications with the necessary buoy to ensure the proper
orientation of the firing platform at the moment of release. Older Yankee
SSBNs *wet-launched* their missiles (tubes flooded, hatches opened manually, missiles fueled and released for buoyant ascent to surface where
motors then fired) from a depth of some 150 feet, traveling at a speed of
three knots with a three-degree bow elevation angle.[168]

Contrary to often heard claims, the Yankee-class subs could not have
been fired from dockside.[169] By contrast, Delta-class SSBNs and probably
the Typhoon submarines could have fired their missiles while submerged
or surfaced. This capability to fire from dockside was frequently tested.

SOVIET SSBN VULNERABILITY. How effective Western forces were in
exploiting the pattern of Soviet SSBN operations just outlined is an open

question with many facets. One key factor, antisubmarine warfare against the boats themselves, lies beyond the scope of this study. Suffice it to say that Soviet planners surely worried about the timeliness of a supreme command decision to surge the SSBNs from port, where the vast majority of their force resided in peacetime; about the ability of Western forces to detect and engage those SSBNs sent to sea in time of hostilities; and about the timeliness of a direct command to launch SLBMs from vulnerable SSBNs on alert at dockside.

The vulnerability of the command and control channels that directed Soviet SSBNs was also likely to have been cause for concern to Soviet planners. The extreme centralization of control over SSBN operations carried the risk that effective decapitation strikes against the Soviet politico-military leadership or strikes that severed communications could have neutralized the sea-based strategic arsenal. Individual weapons commanders would have been physically unable to launch missiles on their own if special unlock codes were needed to fire them and if these codes had not been disseminated before the enemy assault. If such codes had been distributed in advance, perhaps as part of an order with an LDT, the SSBNs could have fired their missiles in the wake of a communications blackout at the predesignated time. But negative control would have been severely compromised in technical respects, and the option of canceling the launch would have been more difficult to exercise reliably.

One can imagine circumstances in which higher authority would have wished to revoke launch orders even if an enemy attack materialized. There are circumstances in which the top leadership would not have relished the idea that a communications outage, which might not have been caused by deliberate enemy action, would have constituted the decisive precondition for SSBN missile salvos. Such a specter encouraged the supreme command to withhold unlock codes and launch authorization until the last possible moment. Yet this hesitation would have increased the difficulties of positive release if the adversary had mounted a sudden attack on Soviet command and control channels. These difficulties were apparently addressed in part by the procedures described in chapter 4 that enabled the SSBN crew to circumvent to blocking devices through actions coordinated with outside entities. In the event of a Western attack that severed the main channels of SSBN command and control, the CINC SRF may have been chiefly responsible for coordinating these emergency backup launch procedures.

The Soviets recognized that SSBNs presented thorny dilemmas of control. The especially stark trade-off between positive and negative control was well appreciated. Soviet commentators frequently voiced their concern that the United States, by virtue of dispensing with unlock devices on nuclear weapons at sea, had tipped the balance too far in the direction of positive control at the expense of safeguards. The Soviets took the opposite tack and imposed strict central control over SSBNs, an approach that created additional burdens on their system of positive release. The Soviet SSBN patrol areas were drawn closer to home waters within easier communication range of central commanders. Elaborate redundancies in communications were developed to ensure reliable signals for employing SSBN forces. As summed up in general terms by the recent authoritative survey edited by Admiral Gorshkov: "This very important moment of submarine control can require many complex measures and actions aimed at improving reliability of the signal's passage: accelerated launch of additional communications satellites; deployment of additional control and relay means at sea, beneath the water, and in the air; deployment of command ships; involvement of civil radio communications centers; and reduction of time intervals for submarines to rise to near the surface for radio communications."[170]

Few if any of the redundant means developed for this purpose—specifically, ground-based ELF, VLF, LF, and HF radio stations; satellites; national and naval airborne command posts; command cruisers; Bear-J VLF communications relay aircraft; and undersea cable and hydroacoustic communications—could have withstood a direct, intense nuclear attack. Their resilience was sufficient to have a powerful deterrent effect on U.S. decisionmakers, but it was not sufficient to remove doubt from Soviet assessment.

The Operations and Vulnerability of Strategic Bomber Command

The Soviet strategic intercontinental bomber force consisted of 159 Bear and 21 Blackjack aircraft in 1990.[171] About 85 Bear aircraft were obsolete bomb- and missile-carrying planes that were being retired. The new Bear-H16 bombers, each of which carried up to sixteen AS-15 air-launched cruise missiles, had become the backbone of the inventory. They numbered about 75 and were being produced in quantity as replacements for the older planes. A modern fleet of tankers was also in production to improve in-flight refueling support of the bombers. With tanker support or by staging from bases in the Arctic region, Bear-H bombers were able to put their 1,800-mile-range cruise missiles within reach of any target in North America.[172]

The strategic bomber force designated for intercontinental strikes had traditionally been managed by the Thirty-seventh Air Army based in Moscow (often mistakenly identified as the Thirty-sixth Air Army), one of the five Soviet strategic air armies under the direct control of the supreme high command. The 700 heavy and medium bombers in the five air armies combined were spread across about twenty-eight main operating bases in the Soviet Union,[173] including about seven Backfire bases. The heavy intercontinental bombers—the Bear and Blackjack aircraft— apparently operated out of about five main bases scattered around the country.[174] The Thirty-seventh also had an Arctic control group that operated five staging bases for the forward deployment of heavy bombers.[175] The new Bear-H heavy bombers, armed with AS-15 cruise missiles, regularly operated at the forward Kola bases.[176]

More recently, heavy bomber operations were reportedly taken over by the Forty-sixth and Thirtieth Strategic Air Armies, headquartered at Smolensk in the west and Irkutsk in the east, respectively. In 1990 heavy bombers participated in most of the ten major strategic nuclear force exercises conducted that year. In those exercises the Thirtieth army bombers and the Delta IV and Typhoon submarines constituted strategic reserve forces. The Forty-sixth army bombers were committed along with mobile ICBMs and Delta III submarines to strikes against North America after an initial strike by silo-based ICBMs. Bomber attacks involved a staggered laydown of weapons over a simulated flight path running north to south and west to east (for example, across Alaska, down to Cold Bay, Canada, and down to the United States for a laydown from the west to the east coast).[177]

The air force commander or air army commanders apparently exercised direct operational command over the heavy bombers during the period before their release. While nuclear exchanges involving other strategic forces were taking place, the heavy bombers played the role of airborne reserve forces. In an unusual display of decentralized control over strategic forces the air army commanders apparently assumed responsibility for the bomber fleet's survival and reconstitution. The commanders eventually relinquished control to the general staff. At a certain point, the bomber force "chopped" (that is, command and control was transferred) to the general staff, and only then was tanker support provided to the fleet. Such a transfer of control to the supreme high command was probably scheduled by the general staff to coincide with a designated time of launch issued to the other reserve forces, particularly the Delta IV and Typhoon SSBNs and the mobile ICBMs.[178]

The day-to-day alert status of heavy bombers was low. None were combat ready. Recall also that by all accounts bomber aircraft were not even loaded with nuclear armaments under normal circumstances. A dated but apparently still accurate assessment by the U.S. intelligence agencies states that "Soviet Air Force strategic bombers do not maintain an airborne alert or continuous ground alert (that is, with a reaction time of 15 minutes or less). Soviet Air Force bombers would assume higher stages of readiness during periods of international crisis."[179] Bomber readiness may have been slightly increased for a while in the 1980s. The annual report *Soviet Military Power,* issued by the U.S. Defense Department, noted in the 1983 and 1984 editions that the bombers had alert procedures and were assigned dispersal airfields.[180] Since no mention was made of alert procedures in subsequent editions and since the period 1983–84 was one of very strained U.S.-Soviet relations, it is imaginable that some Soviet heavy bombers had assumed a posture of increased combat readiness.[181] Analysts interviewed for this study indeed confirmed this. For about a year and one-half between 1983 and 1985, the Thirty-seventh Air Army regularly operated one or two Bear-H heavy bombers on ground or airborne combat patrol. It apparently was not known whether the AS-15 cruise missiles carried by these bombers were armed with nuclear weapons.[182] If they had been nuclear-armed, it would have been yet another indication that the superpowers were edging closer to a nuclear crisis than was generally appreciated in the West at the time.

The main communications network for transmitting the direct command to the bomber force was called *Wing.* This release channel between higher authorities and the bombers probably depended heavily on HF and VHF radio links as well as land-lines. Satellites might have been in limited use. It is reasonable to conclude that communications with heavy bombers, especially aircraft operating out of far-flung bases, would have been tenuous in a nuclear environment in which the aircraft were expected to operate as withheld reserve forces for a considerable amount of time. The vulnerability of the aircraft on the ground, the vulnerability of their basing infrastructure and tanker support, and inherent communications weaknesses cast doubt on the viability of this force and its approximately 1,150 nuclear weapons.

Conclusion

For nearly four decades the nuclear superpowers had proliferated strategic weapons in large numbers in the name of deterrence, which was premised on a credible threat of retaliation. But the deterrence logic on which the prevention of nuclear war was presumed to hinge unfortunately suffered in the translation from theory to practice. The burden of retaliation fell on complex strategic organizations whose basic coherence was severely threatened by opposing nuclear forces. Command and control systems remained vulnerable despite huge investments to protect them. In the U.S. and Soviet cases their functions could have been severely disrupted by the effects of a few hundred weapons at most. On available evidence, analyzed theoretically according to conservative principles, either superpower could have mounted a well-designed first strike using 1990 forces that threatened to demolish the opponent's command centers and communications tentacles, voiding the retribution so necessary to standard deterrence policy.

The Soviets clearly worried about threats to their command and control system despite brave declarations to the contrary. While the ability of the system to rebound from a decapitation strike appeared to be sufficiently uncertain to discourage a Western war planner, the flip side of this uncertainty eroded Soviet confidence in its resilience. The Soviet system could not have reliably protected the top leadership and preserved strict operational control over strategic forces.

The U.S. command and control system was equally exposed to nuclear attack. Soviet strategic targeting attached high priority to the destruction of U.S. nuclear command and control, and scant evidence exists to suggest that an attack would have been restrained at war's outset in order to facilitate negotiations to end it. Although Soviet planners surely could not reckon that an attack on U.S. command and control would have neutralized its retaliatory capability, U.S. planners expected severe disruption from the attempt. Notwithstanding unprecedented investment in its protection during the 1980s, the U.S. command apparatus could not have withstood a direct attack well enough to provide coherent direction to dispersed strategic forces, even if it received timely unambiguous warning and braced itself for an impending Soviet strike.

Retaliation after ride-out was an abstract idea in the theory of stability, but not a viable option in the real world. Irremediable command and control vulnerability was a constant in the equation of cold war nuclear confrontation, and there is every reason to suppose it was the general rule that makes no exceptions for other nuclear rivals.

The command system's consequent bias against basing deterrence on a posture of retaliation was compounded, moreover, by mission commitments the two military establishments had developed. Each strategic organization aspired to attack its opponent's strategic forces despite its inability to do so decisively. Each side's commitment contradicted the principle of retaliation, because an attack on the opponent's strategic weapons made little sense unless it was preemptive. A second-strike strategy made some sense if one side attached significant value to destroying the opponent's empty missile silos (especially cold-launch Soviet silos that might be reloaded) or that portion of the silos with missiles still in them by design (withheld reserve missiles) or chance (launch aborts). Such an attack against the residual systems of the opponent nevertheless could not have been effective unless it was mounted before absorbing the opponent's initial attack and thereby violating the strict definition of retaliation.[183] Under no circumstances could either strategic organization have accomplished its wartime goals if a massive attack had to be ridden out before retaliation. As a practical matter, the susceptibility of command and control systems to disruption, the mutual vulnerability of each side's most threatening silo-based counterforce weapons (MX and SS-18 missiles), and the commitment to strategic weapons targeting created a strong bias for extremely rapid reaction to evidence of impending attack, in effect a launch-on-warning posture for both sides.

The other mission commitments imposed on the U.S. strategic organization and to a lesser extent on the Soviet organization strengthened this bias. To provide systematic coverage of the long list of other military targets, leadership, and war-supporting industry, as well as nuclear forces, the full inventory of U.S. strategic weapons had to be generated to high alert status in a crisis. If the U.S. command and control system had attempted to ride out an attack before retaliating, it would have suffered such degradation that its coverage of these relatively vulnerable targets would have fallen far short of the demanding requirements levied on it. Thus the system considered it vital to bring the full weight of its strategic arsenal into play before an exchange began and to react rapidly to evidence of enemy attack.

It is reasonable to suppose that the postures of other nuclear archenemies would evolve along similar lines. They are no more able than the nuclear superpowers to resist pressures to adopt a rapid reaction posture to compensate for vulnerable command and control systems.

CHAPTER SIX

Launch on Warning

Any Soviet planner in his right mind could not advise his decision maker that we are going to ride out a nuclear attack.

General Charles A. Gabriel, Air Force Chief of Staff[1]

A MAJOR source of nuclear inadvertence grew out of what could be called the characteristic timing of nuclear release built into the command and control systems of the United States and Soviet Union. In broad outline, any one of the following three timing plans or options could be embedded in the operational stance of a nuclear power: preemption, launch on warning, or retaliation after ride-out.

Contrary to widespread belief, the postures of the nuclear superpowers evolved toward launch on warning. Although official policy was ambiguous, by the early 1980s the respective strategic command and control systems were geared to disseminating launch authorization after enemy forces launched but before they had landed. The Joint Chiefs of Staff (JCS) used the term launch under attack, which they defined as "execution by National Command Authorities of Single Integrated Operational Plan forces subsequent to tactical warning of strategic nuclear attack against the United States and *prior to first impact* [emphasis added]."[2]

Launch on warning meant that tactical warning systems played a critical role: early warning sensors designed to observe the launching and transit of strategic delivery vehicles provided tactical information that would have been the triggering condition for disseminating launch orders. This reliance on sensors to make decisions during the short flight times of ballistic missiles—fifteen to thirty minutes—increased the danger of inadvertent war. Such a stance risked premature release on false warning,

168

miscalculation, or confusion. This chapter examines the evolution toward rapid reaction and considers the grave dangers that emerged from it. The next chapter presents a simple quantitative model that shows the inherent difficulty of the tactical warning problem.

Rapid reaction or launch on warning is controversial. U.S. officials acknowledged that this option existed as a capability, but they never conceded and often strenuously denied that it had become the cornerstone of U.S. operational plans. U.S. declarations of strategic policy similarly dismissed or at least heavily discounted the role of strategic preemption.[3] Officials conveyed the distinct impression that retaliation after the impact of a Soviet first strike was the principal U.S. strategic option.

This impression dovetailed with an article of faith that had guided U.S. strategic weapons procurement for thirty years. To safeguard deterrence, the United States needed a force structure capable of riding out a massive nuclear attack without warning. According to the underlying theory, deterrence depended on a threat of retaliation that a sudden enemy attack could not remove. U.S. nuclear security was therefore commonly understood to require the ability of the United States to destroy the Soviet Union as a functioning state not only after absorbing a massive attack but also after absorbing one that was greater than expected and that came as a total surprise.

As for the Soviet Union, official U.S. publications throughout the cold war credited the Soviets with ample capacity to exercise any and all of the three options—preemption, launch on warning, and retaliation after ride-out—although Western observers usually argued that the Soviets intended to preempt. This argument was based partly on the vestige of long-discarded Soviet doctrine. It also stemmed partly from a logical deduction: since the United States supposedly did not intend to strike first, a strategic exchange would have to begin with a Soviet strike. The argument also emerged from the habit of imputing aggressive tendencies to the Soviet Union.

In arguing that both sides actually organized their operational postures around launch on warning, this chapter marshals evidence pertaining to the timing bias of the command and control systems. The argument does not presume that the postures would have invariably forced leaders to render a quick decision to launch. Without minimizing the discretionary authority of leaders and the uncertainty of their decisions, one can reasonably suppose, nevertheless, that the dominant mode of command

system operation would have exerted strong influence on their deliberations and decisions. Release timing would have been heavily biased toward the assumptions, expectations, and preferences embedded in established operational plans drawn up by military organizations.

The Lack of Alternatives

Launch on warning owed its de facto adoption to the acute disadvan-
tages of the alternatives. It represented a compromise between the ex-
tremes of preemption and retaliation after ride-out that skirted their
political and technical drawbacks. It perched precariously between them,
however, inasmuch as the difference in release timing among all three
was measured in minutes. Slightly earlier timing than launch on warning
amounted to preemption. Launching slightly later amounted to retaliation after ride-out.

Basic Drawbacks of Preemption and Retaliation after Ride-Out

For both sides, command and control vulnerability was the main drawback of retaliation after ride-out. The vulnerabilities of each side differed
in form and severity because of dissimilarities in the configuration of the
two command and control systems. But the result was the same: the
option of retaliation after ride-out was not technically viable. In consequence, the U.S. system could not have expected to meet its damage
expectancy requirements if it absorbed an attack before retaliating. And
the Soviet system likewise would have expected to forfeit its wartime
objectives if it waited too long to strike. Retaliation after ride-out thus
could not have been a sound basis for strategic planning on either side.

In theory, preemption—attacking when the other side's launch appeared imminent[4]—could have compensated for the vulnerability of command and control. This option may have seemed superficially attractive,
particularly to U.S. planners. It would have taken advantage of the technical capacity of the United States to rapidly unleash a massive barrage
with little advance preparation. It would also have exploited the relatively
sluggish process by which Soviet command and control generated forces
to full combat readiness in preparation for launch. On paper the United
States could in some circumstances during the 1960s and 1970s have ceded
the attack initiative to the Soviet Union and, assuming expeditious pro-

cessing of intelligence and political approval, still could have got its forces off the ground first, possibly in time to catch a sizable portion of Soviet forces in their silos just before their scheduled lift-off.

However, the Soviets' efforts to streamline their nuclear command and control system during the 1970s and 1980s succeeded in establishing a credible option of launch on warning for most of their land missile forces and for some SSBNs on pierside alert. This diminished substantially, if it did not negate, the advantage of preemptive timing in U.S. strategy. Other drawbacks of preemption were surely equally dismaying to U.S. planners. Preemption required a correct estimate of Soviet intent, yet political intelligence was notoriously faulty. The option also required timely strategic warning of Soviet launch preparations, yet it would have been foolhardy to count on unambiguous warning under all Soviet attack scenarios.

In the last analysis the interpretation of intelligence is so subjective that the potential for a terrible miscalculation cannot be eliminated. It is highly unlikely that the United States would have been able to justify a decision to launch preemptively, because the United States probably could not have been sufficiently confident of its ability to detect an irreversible launch decision by the Soviet Union. Moreover, no sensible military planner would have designed a posture that counted on getting approval from U.S. political leaders to preempt on strategic warning. On the contrary, a wise planner expected authorization to be withheld no matter how compelling the indications were of impending Soviet attack. The planning community was well aware that U.S. political leaders had all but renounced preemption. In sum, the preemptive option withered on the vine of U.S. nuclear planning. By the beginning of the 1990s, its role in nuclear strategy was considered marginal.

Preemption also underwent radical devaluation in Soviet policy. In Soviet usage preemptive action as a response to an imminent and irrevocable enemy decision to attack was referred to as *kontrpodgotovka*, literally *counterpreparation*. It connoted an attempt to seize the initiative at the last minute and get in the first blow to forestall, disrupt, and weaken the enemy's nuclear offensive. It did not connote a surprise first strike against an unsuspecting, innocent adversary. Soviet doctrine eschewed the notion of mounting a nuclear attack in the absence of an imminent and irrevocable threat of enemy attack.

The Soviet military had first developed this concept of a forestalling attack in the mid-1950s but had abandoned it as a cornerstone for plan-

ning by the late 1960s. Although its residual influence on strategic intercontinental and theater nuclear planning remained significant throughout
the 1970s, the thrust of Soviet policy during the past two decades emphasized launch on warning. During this period the Soviets pursued a
strategy that decoupled nuclear and conventional operations, the former
assuming a well-nigh exclusive role as a reserve force to be withheld as a
deterrent to Western nuclear escalation. At one time a tripwire for Soviet
escalation to strategic nuclear attack, conventional conflict gradually became a firebreak or threshold whose crossing with nuclear weapons was
left to the West to agonize over. This policy thrust was embodied in an
extensive new Soviet command and control infrastructure fielded in the
1980s for prosecuting a protracted conventional war on several fronts and
theaters simultaneously. The nuclear backdrop to this policy included a
pledge of no first use backed up by operational changes, the modernization of nuclear deterrent forces, and, above all, the incorporation of
launch on warning into the Soviet nuclear posture.

Several additional facts worked against pursuing preemption as a major objective of Soviet planning. First, U.S. strategic readiness became
so high even in peacetime that reliable indicators of impending U.S.
attack were not available. To an unparalleled degree the U.S. strategic
posture had been designed to cope with a surprise attack, so a large
fraction of its arsenal always stood ready to strike on the shortest notice.
Once final approval was granted, only a few minutes would have elapsed
before missiles lifted off on a short flight to Soviet territory.

Second, this permanent condition of war readiness meant that Soviet
intelligence had to concentrate on the intentions of American policymakers. Such political intelligence was inherently unreliable if for no
other reason than that leaders could change their minds at the last minute. To muddy the waters further, the United States vested its nuclear
commanders at all echelons with substantial discretionary authority to
alert, disperse, maneuver, and otherwise change the disposition of their
forces without the explicit approval of political leaders. Soviet intelligence
thus could not have easily inferred American political intent by monitoring the activity of U.S. forces.

Third, the Soviets' highly centralized command and control system,
its lower state of combat readiness, and the relatively low readiness of
Soviet nuclear forces meant the Soviet system took longer than its counterpart to prepare for war. As plodding marathoners up against agile
sprinters, they ought not to have expected to gain any preemptory ad-

vantage during a nuclear crisis. Undertaking alerting preparations risked triggering a quick global counteralert if not a preemptive lunge by a fast, decentralized U.S. system. When they did alert the strategic forces, the Soviets did it selectively and covertly. Nuclear alerts were never used to send political signals.

Last, the Soviets surely recognized that successful preemption would have had a negligible payoff should the United States have launched on tactical warning in response to positive indications of a Soviet missile salvo. The United States had doubtless conveyed the clear message that it was prepared and disposed to respond in such a fashion.

The Resort to Launch on Warning

Both retaliation after ride-out and preemption were therefore ruled out, the former for technical reasons, the latter for political, intelligence, and other reasons. Caught in this bind, the planners in both camps seized on launch on warning. The U.S. strategic posture gravitated to this option between the late 1960s and early 1970s. It became entrenched after the United States deployed a constellation of early warning satellites in the early 1970s. The eroding capacity of the U.S. land-based missile force to ride out a Soviet attack boosted its putative utility during the 1980s.

The Soviet posture followed the same path, though at a slower pace. Lagging behind the United States in the technical development of the requisite warning, communications, and command systems, the Soviets took ten years longer to achieve a comparable posture of rapid reaction for the full spectrum of threats, particularly surprise attack. Launch on warning, called a meeting strike (*vstrechnyy udar*) in the Russian vernacular, became technically feasible in the early 1980s. The Soviets then began to demonstrate in exercises their ability to launch strategic missiles on tactical warning in under thirty minutes, the nominal flight time of land-based missiles launched from the United States.

This parallel evolution toward launch on warning carried mixed implications for deterring advertent war. Its theoretical contribution to deterrence was considerable. It stripped preemption of what remained of its original rationale, because launch on warning thwarts a potential aggressor's plans to exploit the vulnerabilities in the opponent's force and command and control structure. By the same token it diminished the penalty for ceding the attack initiative to the adversary, because an attack did not need to be ridden out. In classical theoretical terms, symmetrical launch on warning thus lends stability to crisis interactions between rationally calculating actors.[5]

Launch on warning was nevertheless a thin reed to lean on, for a host of practical reasons: (1) it was intolerant of error and delay in information processing, decisionmaking, and plan execution; (2) an unforeseen stratagem might have defeated it; (3) much of the physical infrastructure—warning, command, and communications elements—could have been damaged deliberately or incidentally during a conventional phase of war, thereby degrading the capability for rapid reaction; (4) stealth-equipped weapons entering the inventories posed new problems of in-flight detection; cruise missiles, in particular, were able to fly undetected to their targets, including critical nodes in the adversary's command network; (5) time and information constraints would have put decisionmakers under enormous pressure and strained rational deliberation to the limit; and (6) the same constraints compromised hallowed values and ingrained attitudes in the political culture of nuclear decisionmaking, particularly on the Soviet side—collective, centralized, and conservative (risk-averse) sanctioning of the use of nuclear forces.

All these practical factors, among others, called into question not only the efficacy of rapid reaction in deterring advertent nuclear attack but also its wisdom from the standpoint of inadvertent war. Safety was indisputably compromised. The analogy to the accidental discharge of a gun with a hair trigger was generally appreciated. Two related hazards stood out. One concerned the potential for tactical warning to be misleading or false, a problem that ambiguous strategic warning could have exacerbated. In certain circumstances information provided by the strategic intelligence network could have been the dominant input triggering the dissemination of launch authorization. The command system, though ostensibly operating in a launch-on-warning mode, could have slipped subtly into a preemptive mode. The conceptual model presented in chapter 7 shows how combinations of false or ambiguous strategic and tactical warning can conspire to produce either an inadvertent preemptive attack or inadvertent launch on warning.

The second major danger that emerged was that reliance on launch on warning created additional pressure to predelegate nuclear release authority down the chain of command to cover contingencies in which the normal chain of command was severed. Although such arrangements facilitated rapid reaction under very adverse conditions and thereby buttressed deterrence of advertent attack, they increased the scope for nuclear operations to elude direction from the top and culminate in an inadvertent war. The Soviets do not seem to have embraced predelegation to the same extent as the United States.

Launch on Warning and the U.S. Strategic Posture

The epigraph to this chapter and other uncensored comments by senior U.S. officials sent a clear signal that the United States was ready to launch its strategic forces before Soviet missiles reached North America. Whatever impact it had on attentive Soviet audiences, however, the message generally made most Western observers wary. In the popular view U.S. strategy was geared for retaliation after absorbing a Soviet attack. Statements to the contrary as well as the capacity for extremely rapid reaction were unassimilated or interpreted as ruses meant to confuse Soviet planners. Launch on warning's supposed purpose was to gird deterrence with additional uncertainty about the timing of any U.S. response to acts of aggression.

This popular view was wrong. Retaliation after ride-out was an abstraction remote from operational predilections. From that standpoint it qualified as one of the great myths of the nuclear age. And though launch on warning did complicate Soviet attack planning, its role in the posture was central—the command and control system's preferred and best prepared mode of wartime operation.

The Fable of Assured Destruction

The neglect of launch on warning in spite of its operational importance was in no small measure due to the big embrace of *assured destruction* during the 1960s. Trumpeted by Secretary of Defense Robert S. McNamara, assured destruction became a canon of U.S. strategic policy during his tenure and framed all future debate on nuclear deterrence and force acquisition. Under this conservative planning principle, the United States, to satisfy the basic requirements of deterrence, would maintain the capacity to destroy a large fraction of the Soviet population and economic base in retaliation against Soviet nuclear attack even after the worst attack the adversary could conceivably mount.

The original idea behind assured destruction was that it would provide rational and compelling criteria of nuclear sufficiency for curbing the military's voracious appetite for strategic forces. Outsiders misinterpreted this narrow bureaucratic objective, however, and imbued it with grander meaning and purpose. As assured destruction attracted endorsements across the spectrum of opinion, its adherents inflated it from a procurement norm to a norm for wartime mission planning.

Public debate over strategic policy took as its basic premise the dubious notion that the United States planned to absorb a massive attack before unleashing its surviving strategic forces to ravage the urban-industrial base of the Soviet Union. Assured destruction became widely, though mistakenly, viewed as synonymous with the presumed targeting priorities of the single integrated operational plan. During the 1960s policy discourse became clearly detached from the mundane realm of operational planning.

But strategic orthodoxy did not for long abide the myth that U.S. targeting was exclusively countervalue (urban-industrial). Thanks to an arduous, fitful process of disclosure and scholarly investigation, attentive audiences learned during the 1970s and 1980s that most aimpoints in the U.S. attack plans were Soviet military targets rather than cities. The folklore of countervalue targeting was discredited.[6]

Research and debate nevertheless perpetuated a serious misconception about the timing of nuclear release. A strategy of deterrence based on second-strike retaliation had become so vital a pillar of policy consensus and so much a part of the lore of strategic policy that it enjoyed virtual immunity from scrutiny, obscuring the importance of launch on warning. Although rapid reaction was a built-in bias of the SIOP, it was still widely believed that retaliation after ride-out was the cornerstone principle and the basic operational modality of the U.S. wartime posture.

The battle waged over the fate of U.S. land-based missiles was symptomatic of this gulf between operational reality and popular belief. The controversy, which raged until the end of the cold war, boiled down to an undeclared contest between opposite operational premises, one inspired by the ideals of assured destruction, and the other impelled by the pragmatic necessity of operational planning. Launch on warning was the safety valve in the high pressure face-off with the Soviet arsenal of theoretically lethal counterforce weapons. U.S. military planners, though wont to deny it, expected to protect the silo-based forces by launching them out from under an attack during the fifteen to thirty minute interval between the lift-off and arrival of Soviet missiles. The willingness of planners to deploy new missiles in vulnerable fixed silos in lieu of mobile-basing schemes reflected their considerable confidence in the operational feasibility of a rapid reaction strategic posture and their strong faith in its deterrent effect. In their view, congressional skeptics and their other sparring partners in the political arena had blown the issue of vulnerable land missile installations all out of proportion. U.S. planners recoiled in dismay at the idea of retaliation after ride-out, because of its problematic implications for operations, target coverage, and deterrence.

By contrast, most other parties to the debate over strategic moderni-zation paid homage to the principle of survivability. It was considered the sine qua non of the U.S. posture and essential to stability. They recoiled in horror at the idea of disseminating authorization to launch before definitive evidence of nuclear detonations on U.S. soil, and hence dis-counted the potential contribution of launch on warning to force surviv-ability. In their view, it was dangerous folly to house land-based missiles in fixed silos that could not withstand a massive missile barrage. They conceded that ICBMs could be deployed in a manner that permitted launch on warning in order to bolster deterrence, but not in a manner that depended on this option. The premium placed on mobility, in par-ticular, reflected an unstinting devotion to the hallowed idea of basing deterrence on second-strike retaliation.[7]

Regardless of the merits of this position, it was naive. It failed to plumb the depth of the U.S. command system's reliance on rapid reac-tion. From the perspective of a military planner, invulnerable forces were desirable not for riding out an attack but mainly as a hedge against the possibility that the United States would fail to execute its principal option of launch on warning. Invulnerability also protected the strategic forces, especially SSBNs, from attrition during conventional hostilities. The pre-vailing mission commitment of blanket target coverage virtually de-manded the prompt launch of a large portion of all three legs of the Triad—whether vulnerable like the ICBM leg or invulnerable like the alert SLBM leg—as part of any initial SIOP response to large-scale Soviet attack. It was equally likely that future U.S. force deployments, no matter how invulnerable, would have been assigned missions that required a large portion of them to be committed to the opening salvo of a major attack. Mobile ICBMs, for instance, would most likely have maintained a quick reaction posture whether in garrison or dispersed and would have been launched in large numbers as part of any initial U.S. response to a large Soviet ICBM attack.

Thus the parties to the debate over basing schemes for ICBMs and over strategic policy in general held views that could not be bridged. Consensus foundered because their underlying premises did not mesh and because launch on warning was too controversial to advocate openly. During congressional hearings with senior military witnesses, the discussions were typically circuitous and seldom got beyond stating that "our policy is not to have a policy."[8]

The Folly of Preemption

Although either preemption or launch on warning could have fulfilled the ambitious damage expectancy requirements of the U.S. command and control system, various factors favored launch on warning. The main virtue of launch on warning was that it corresponded more closely to most widely accepted versions of deterrence policy. The standard version imposed an expectation on strategic organizations that the timing of nuclear release would conform as closely as possible to the principle of retaliation. Preemption was a more flagrant departure from this norm.

Preemption also carried the liability mentioned earlier: it presupposed prior warning of Soviet preparations as well as intention to initiate an attack, but such activities and proclivities might not have been discovered or acted on in time to avoid the effects of surprise attack. It had therefore been a long-standing tenet of U.S. nuclear policy that U.S. nuclear forces should not depend on strategic warning for their survival. Planners sought to create a force and command structure that could respond effectively to a sudden massive attack, a "bolt-from-the-blue." In the words of Secretary of Defense Harold Brown, in presenting his department's budget ten years ago: defense planners are "obliged to make the contingency of a Soviet surprise attack on our strategic forces the fundamental test of the adequacy of those forces and the main basis for our strategic nuclear planning."[9]

It is worth reflecting on the motivation behind this cardinal obligation to hedge against surprise attack.[10] Throughout the twentieth century, with only rare exceptions, the intelligence services of the major powers had been able to offer strategic warning—defined as the prediction of incipient or imminent attack on the basis of any and all sources of intelligence, such as the detection of ominous troop movements, intercepted messages, peculiar leadership behavior, and so forth. Yet two of the century's most devastating attacks, the bombing of Pearl Harbor and the Nazi invasion of Russia, caught their victims by surprise even though Washington and Moscow had acquired ominous evidence that war could be at hand.

Intelligence gathering improved tremendously in technical respects after World War II, but throughout the cold war there was no discernible improvement in the human ability to assess political intelligence and convert it to reliable strategic warning. This art may even have regressed, because the ideological and cultural distance between the cold war contenders was far larger than that which separated many of the enemies of past wars. Deep-seated and rational preconceptions may prevent an entire intelligence community from uncovering an adversary's intent, especially if that adversary is engaging in skillful deception.[11]

Compounding the difficulty of inferring political intention was the unprecedented circumstance of two adversaries with vast forces confronting each other for decades on end. Both stood ready to launch large portions of the arsenals on the shortest notices (a few minutes). The time required to monitor and assess changes in the disposition of opposing forces preparing for war and then act on this strategic warning was interminable compared with the time needed to order, launch, and deliver a ballistic missile attack consisting of thousands of nuclear warheads. In sum, the fear of surprise attack produced postures capable of such rapid action that strategic warning became even more doubtful. The fear became a self-fulfilling prophecy.

Another reason for hedging against surprise attack concerned the uncertain reaction of political leaders to strategic warning. Would political decisionmakers raise the alert readiness of forces, much less launch them, on the basis of these strategic indicators?

UNRELIABLE STRATEGIC WARNING OF SOVIET NUCLEAR ANOMALIES. The historical record illustrates some of these difficulties in detecting, interpreting, and counteracting Soviet nuclear activities that deviated from normal peacetime routine. As mentioned in chapter 2, Soviet nuclear alerting activity in 1960, 1962, 1968, and 1973 apparently went unnoticed by Western intelligence. For example, the Soviet nuclear alert undertaken just before the 1968 invasion of Czechoslovakia apparently went undetected by the United States.[12] This alert was plainly consistent with a plan of Soviet nuclear attack on NATO forces in the event of

Western military intervention to foil the Soviet invasion. The alert was potentially provocative because it involved the assembly and transportation of nuclear weapons to launch pads of the SRF, where the warheads were joined to ballistic missiles aimed at Western Europe.

A countrywide stand-down of the Soviet air force during the 1969 border dispute with China also illustrates the ambiguity of strategic warning. Although this low-level alert was detected at the time, according to a British analyst familiar with the intelligence collection, the nuclear intentions of the Soviet leadership remained unclear to outside observers.[13] The alert involved dual-capable aircraft, but whether nuclear contingency plans were being drawn up could not be ascertained.[14] Although the strategic indicators were ambiguous, the United States may have reacted by raising the alert level of its strategic forces in early October 1969.[15] The Soviets detected the U.S. October alert but were apparently unsure of its purpose.[16]

Another case of perplexing strategic indicators was the Soviet nuclear activity noticed by U.S. intelligence at the time of the Soviet invasion of Afghanistan in late 1979. In conjunction with the ground assault, the Soviets surged SSBNs from the port at Petropavlosk in the Far East, and signs of nuclear activity near the Afghan border were also detected.[17]

Other more recent illustrations raise doubt about the timeliness of strategic warning and underscore the technical plausibility of surprise attack. In 1982, for instance, the Soviets conducted a major exercise involving multiple launches of various types of offensive and defensive missiles. The scope, speed, and coordination of the operation evidently came as a surprise to Western intelligence. By all print and interview accounts, the first indication of Soviet firing plans and capabilities, which greatly surpassed previously known capabilities, came from a U.S. early-warning satellite. In short, the operation became transparent only after the weapons began to fly.[18] On other occasions Soviet exercises involved missile launches whose timing could not be accurately predicted. A Soviet submarine might disappear for a relatively long time, only to reappear suddenly and fire a missile, leaving Western analysts mystified in its wake. In some instances even the source of the launch orders (which were normally transmitted by radio direct from the Soviet general staff) remained uncertain.[19]

Another illustration with lessons for both sides concerns an episode in November 1983. The Soviets were suspected by some analysts to have increased the alert readiness of some unspecified portion of their nuclear command system and forces in response to a NATO nuclear exercise called Able Archer. Although the details of the incident have not been officially disclosed, a KGB colonel named Oleg Gordievskiy, who was spying for the West at the time, has revealed that the Soviets misinterpreted the nuclear release procedures being exercised by NATO and grew alarmed that NATO tactical nuclear forces were preparing for an actual attack.[20] Strategic indicators of Western attack sounded a false alarm; in this respect Soviet strategic warning was a failure.[21] Western strategic warning failed for the opposite reason. Although precautionary Soviet defensive measures, perhaps involving some Soviet nuclear units, were apparently instituted on an emergency basis, these responses were evidently not detected at the time.[22] Western intelligence analysts apparently discovered these steps after the fact as a result of close retrospective analysis of the events surrounding the NATO exercise.[23]

An additional illustration of the difficulties of detecting increases in alert levels concerns Soviet tactical nuclear forces in Eastern Europe. In early 1984 a special national intelligence estimate that evaluated U.S.-Soviet tension from 1983 to 1984 indicated a possible increase in Soviet nuclear combat readiness. Whether or not related to the NATO exercise cited above, this nuclear activity was not definitively established. As a summary of the intelligence estimate said, "The Soviets *may*, for the first time during peacetime, be keeping a portion of their nuclear forces in Eastern Europe on quick-alert status, using sites for their SS-22 brigades in East Germany and Czechoslovakia" (emphasis added).[24] In March 1984 the Soviets conducted an unprecedented civil defense exercise at Omsk in which nearly one thousand people walked fifty kilometers.[25]

The ambiguity of strategic warning, as well as the questionable propensity to act on it without hesitation, was suggested by an operation conducted by the Soviets in the late 1970s. Virtually all seaworthy Soviet ballistic missile submarines surged out of port and disappeared for many days. The scale of the surge, the unusual pattern of operations (the subs did not communicate back to higher authority and they dispersed to unexpected locations), and the sudden departures without full crews in some cases caused concern within the U.S. intelligence community that the Soviets were acting as though a real emergency existed. U.S. analysts worked around the clock to interpret the activity, and some considered notifying the president that a threat of attack possibly existed.[26] Apparently no such notice was sent. A similar surge in the early 1980s did receive high-level attention, owing perhaps to the context of the Polish crisis and the tense state of relations between the nuclear superpowers. At any rate, both of these large-scale operations posed a difficult problem of interpretation, as have many other exercises that involved Soviet nuclear forces.

Although in nuclear exercises and genuine alerts in crisis situations the Soviets apparently never activated their entire strategic arsenal, there was nothing to prevent that from occurring. The Soviets undoubtedly possessed the capacity to manage a simultaneous operation involving the top political leadership, the general staff, the navy main staff and SSBNs, all six SRF missile armies, the strategic aviation armies, and the entire strategic command infrastructure. Distinguishing such exercises from preparations for a real attack would have been no trivial feat of intelligence. On the contrary, a strategic attack of large proportions could have been mounted under the guise of an exercise, and the U.S. ability to rule out the possibility seemed limited. As the cases discussed earlier illustrate, the detection of preparations and the deciphering of intentions were problematic. Western understanding of the Soviet command and control system for nuclear release was too rudimentary for analysts to have dismissed the possibility of surprise Soviet attack on technical grounds. To hope for unambiguous strategic warning would have been a leap of faith, if for no other reason than that a massive Soviet ICBM attack, in principle, could simply have been launched from a peacetime posture. Although the Soviets kept their strategic forces at a lower state of readiness than the United States did, their capacity for rapid attack at least approached that of the United States by the early to mid-1980s.[27]

Another motivation for avoiding reliance on strategic warning and preemption was to eliminate the advantage of surprise and hence remove the opponent's incentive to perfect any such scheme. In a world of weapons that did not depend on strategic warning for their survival, surprise attack would not have given the attacker a decisive advantage. Paradoxically, if an aggressor gained no advantage by concealing its preparations for attack, those preparations were more likely to be overt and detectable by the victim. The corollary is that deception by the aggressor would assume importance if the victim depended on strategic warning. If one side counted on getting strategic warning and based its strategic posture on the assumption that it would not be surprised, it would have strengthened the other side's incentive to devise a plan that achieved surprise. The end of the cold war obviously relieved the burden on strategic intelligence analysts. The background presumption of possible surprise attack evaporated, and the Western interpreter's task was further eased by a substantial decline in Soviet nuclear and conventional exercise activity.[28]

A SCENARIO FOR RELIABLE STRATEGIC WARNING. One cold war scenario posed the distinct possibility that an irrevocable Soviet decision to launch a nuclear attack would have been discovered by Western intelligence in time; that U.S. decisionmakers would have been convinced of the validity of such strategic warning; and that a preemptive U.S. strike would have been ordered. The scenario was a full-fledged conventional war in Europe that triggered a Soviet nuclear assault on Western forces. (This was viewed as a serious threat only before the Soviet withdrawal from Eastern Europe, the dissolution of the Warsaw Pact, and the end of the cold war.) Scenarios for nuclear war in what the Soviets called the continental theater of operations (a TVD) called for Soviet nuclear preparations and release procedures that could have been transparent to Western intelligence. These activities would have been far more extensive and carried Soviet forces to a far more advanced stage of combat readiness than the Soviet alert activities described earlier had ever gone.

The Western theater of operations, encompassing the NATO European region, was the traditional focus of Soviet strategic nuclear planning during the cold war.[29] According to the Voroshilov lectures, the decisive action in a continental theater in nuclear war was the initial nuclear strikes involving "several thousand nuclear rounds" expended in a coordinated attack by the strategic rocket forces (SRF), long-range aviation, nuclear submarines, and the nuclear delivery means of the fronts and fleets.[30] Such operations were said to be the most difficult and complex form of strategic action by the armed forces, requiring detailed preparation in all aspects.[31] The general staff conducted planning for the use of the strategic nuclear forces, and the staffs of fronts and the navy conducted planning for the use of operational-tactical nuclear weapons on the basis of instructions from the general staff.[32] The planners aspired to "narrow the time gap (to the maximum) between the initial salvo of strategic nuclear rockets and nuclear strikes by front and fleet nuclear delivery means,"[33] as well as to ensure close coordination between nuclear and conventional actions according to a unified plan of operations.[34]

The potential transparency of such an operation stemmed from its scale and, more important, from the fact that a coordinated strike by weapons systems of such different operating characteristics required very elaborate and time-consuming preparations after the decision to employ them had been made. Thousands of operational-tactical weapons needed to be dispersed from storage depots, positioned, and armed before the designated employment time, and most nuclear rounds delivered by submarines and bombers also required extensive preparation. In a rapidly deteriorating situation that called for the immediate employment of nuclear weapons before preparations were complete across the board, strategic rocket forces could have been fired quickly on command.[35] But the Soviets would have strived to set up the entire arsenal for a coordinated salvo, a process that would have meant issuing detailed instructions down the chain of command well ahead of the designated time of launch. Even the SRF, according to the secret lectures, would have been instructed well in advance on their specific assignments.

The directives in the form of *preliminary* commands, discussed in chapter 4, would have specified the targets to be destroyed during the initial nuclear strike; the yield and number of nuclear warheads to be used against each type of target; and the type of burst (surface or air), time of readiness for fire, and time of delivery of nuclear and conventional warheads. Front commanders (or TVD commanders) would have received similar instructions.[36] The illustrative instructions presented to students at the Voroshilov Academy indicate the kind of guidance that would have been issued to the submarine and bomber forces as well as to other formations participating in the initial nuclear strikes.[37] In the case of ballistic missile submarines assigned to strike theater targets (in recent exercises, such missions were carried out by Yankee and Delta I and II SSBNs), the lead time to prepare for launch could have been as long as twelve hours.[38]

Additional information such as unlock codes had to be disseminated to some forces, particularly operational-tactical forces, well in advance of the designated launch time. Initial strike missions might also have been reconfirmed by the supreme high command prior to launch. Message traffic down and up the chain of command would thus have been profuse. Communications patterns would have detectably changed—for example, *burst communications* would have become prevalent. The quantity of nuclear orders would have been prodigious, and their content might have been correctly inferred, if not literally deciphered, by intelligence means.

Western analysts interviewed for this book held mixed opinions on the transparency of such Soviet nuclear preparations to strike. An initial Soviet nuclear strike in the continental (or intercontinental) theater of operations might or might not have been reliably forewarned. Officials of the U.S. agencies whose mission included real-time eavesdropping on Soviet communications were portrayed as exuding considerable confidence in this regard, while officials of other organizations, such as the Defense Intelligence Agency, reportedly emphasized the difficulty of providing unambiguous warning. The difficulty in collecting and interpreting launch orders disseminated via cable networks as opposed to radio communications was one of the grounds for skepticism. But no one categorically ruled out the prospect of gathering persuasive evidence of impending attack in time to parry it. Within the range of possibilities lay a reasonably good chance of getting about an hour of advance warning. That was enough time, in principle, to launch a massive preemptive strike. That was also enough time to initiate urgent diplomatic steps to dissuade the adversary from issuing the final confirmation of its attack orders.

It is evident that Western surveillance of launch preparations, the interception of nuclear deliberations among the top authorities—notably, the general secretary (later president), defense minister, chief of the general staff, and nuclear CINCs—and especially the interception of launch orders issued to the senior commanders or individual units, even if revocable, would have greatly alarmed Western decisionmakers. No one can say whether Western restraint would have given way to preemptive attack. But even in such a scenario the cumulative liabilities of preemption that accrued from the inherent unreliability of strategic warning were onerous. Even during the height of the cold war, the specter of Soviet nuclear attack was so remote as to cast doubt on the likelihood that indications of imminent attack would produce enough certitude to trigger U.S. preemption. U.S. military planners harbored no illusions that U.S. national command authorities would under any circumstances authorize a preemptive strategic attack against the Soviet Union on the basis of strategic warning alone.

Launch on warning—that is tactical as opposed to strategic warning—thus inexorably emerged as the apparent logical solution to the operational dilemmas of the cold war.

The Evolution of Midnight Express

The U.S. strategic posture gravitated to the launch-on-warning option—Midnight Express became the colloquial Strategic Air Command (SAC) term for it—between the late 1960s and early 1970s. Its feasibility under many Soviet attack scenarios grew after the United States deployed a constellation of early-warning satellites in the early 1970s. The U.S. command and control system gained fifteen minutes more tactical warning time in addition to the fifteen minute warning already provided by ground radar systems (for ICBM attacks) and achieved a vital capability for dual-sensor detection (satellite infrared and ground radar) which helped screen out the false alarms that periodically afflicted a single sensor.

Further efforts to refine the option were made toward the end of the 1970s. By this time the Soviets projected a theoretically potent threat against Minuteman land-based installations. The acute vulnerability of U.S. command and control systems became more generally appreciated as a result of a series of classified studies completed in the late 1970s. What could be described as a cognitive switch occurred in the planning arena, producing an explicit recognition of the crucial importance of "prompt launch" to the achievement of U.S. strategic war aims. Among the steps taken as a consequence, ordered by Secretary of Defense Harold Brown, was the construction of a new SIOP option designed explicitly for effecting a successful quick launch of the Minuteman forces.[39] This option, designated launch under attack (LUA) by SAC,[40] originally fell into the category of *selective attack options* and provided for the selective release of Minuteman forces to prevent their destruction on the ground.

Under this SIOP option, all SLBMs and strategic bombers could have been withheld, although the bombers would have been sent aloft to wait for further instructions. As Brown testified in 1977, launch under attack boiled down to the question "Would you launch land-based missiles before explosion of nuclear weapons on the United States?"[41] He said there was no reason to launch SLBMs before Soviet missiles landed, because they were going to survive for an extended period after the attack, because "there will always be a National Command Authority and it would decide what to do with the submarine-launched missiles later," and because launching them on warning throws away their principle advantages—"they might just as well be ICBMs in that case."[42]

The LUA option was later expanded, however, to include large numbers of strategic bombers and sea-based ballistic missiles, placing the LUA option in the category of *major attack options*. This expansion acknowledged the fact that the protective launch of Minuteman forces was too narrow an objective and that an attack which threatened a large portion of the Minuteman force would be massive. A major attack option, involving all legs of the Triad, was deemed a more appropriate response under these circumstances. Prompt retaliation by a single leg of the triad was taken off the SIOP menu.

Related steps were taken to facilitate launch on warning, including the provision of pre-positioned National Command Authorities (NCA) replete with the requisite authenticating and unlock codes (see chapter 3). This arrangement emphasized a rapid and orderly devolution of nuclear command in the event of a rupture in the normal chain of command. Contingent predelegation helped ensure that SIOP firing orders could be rapidly disseminated on the authority of senior military commanders (wearing their pre-positioned NCA hats). Such a response would have taken only slightly longer than the usual reaction time of launch on warning.

Although the devolution plan was based on an expectation that launch orders would be withheld until the onset of nuclear detonations, the pre-positioned authorities were not expected to wait until definitive evidence of massive damage from Soviet forces had accumulated, nor were their choices of SIOP response options constrained in any way. They were given complete discretionary authority over the scale and character of U.S. retaliation. The arrangements also specified a sequence of succession so that a single authority could assume responsibility for giving common instructions—a targeting plan, a coordinating reference time, authorization, and unlock codes—to all SIOP forces. As a practical matter, this centralization could not be established and preserved in all circumstances. In cases of severe disruption of command channels, the system of rolling authority may not have found its provisional resting point, or center of gravity. Authority could have become dispersed so widely that overall attack coordination would have been lost.

STRESS ON WARNING SYSTEMS. Tactical warning sensors obviously played a critical role in a rapid reaction or literal launch-on-warning posture, and the growing reliance on this option put pressure on the North American Aerospace Defense Command (NORAD) to speed up its collection and assessment of tactical information. This organization continued to perform the same basic tasks, but it took it upon itself to make some subtle changes in the way sensor reports were interpreted and validated, in order to expedite NORAD assessment. These changes of procedure lowered its standards of evidence, a relative laxity that improved the feasibility of launch on warning under conditions of actual attack but that also made NORAD more prone to infer an attack when none existed. The priority of the wartime mission commitment to prompt launch grew during the 1970s and 1980s at the expense of negative control. Protection against false tactical information declined. In typical fashion, this major shift in the balance between positive and negative control was the result of diffuse modifications of decision rules made deep within the bowels of an organization. The shift was basically consistent with evolving national policy, however.

NORAD's basic tasks were to detect the launch and transit of opposing strategic missiles; establish a telecommunications conference with the Pentagon (National Military Command Center), Ft. Richie (Alternate National Military Command Center), and the SAC headquarters in Omaha, Nebraska; determine whether North America was under missile attack; upgrade the conference to a more urgent exchange of information among higher-ranking officials if attack indications were positive; and report the findings to the senior military and civilian command authorities.

The expected normal sequence of assessment began with the observation of missile launches by infrared satellites in geosynchronous orbit over the eastern and western hemispheres. The booster rocket signatures of ICBMs launched from Soviet territory would have been observed by the eastern satellite and immediately relayed to a ground station at Nurrungar, Australia, while SLBMs fired from locations near the U.S. coasts would have been observed by the Western satellites linked to a ground station in Colorado. Initial satellite detection should have occurred within half a minute after missile lift-off. The sensor data would have been immediately transmitted to the ground station for computer processing. The on-site personnel then had to decide, usually within about fifteen seconds, whether to forward the tactical information to the missile warning centers at NORAD, SAC, the Pentagon, and the alternate national command post near Camp David, Maryland. The duty officers at those centers would thus have been notified of a missile event about one minute after an apparent launch.[43]

A conference was to have been immediately established, and the command director on duty at NORAD would have been allowed three minutes to evaluate the validity of the satellite warning indications and report his confidence level to the war rooms at the Pentagon and SAC headquarters. The director's verbal report would have been *no, medium,* or *high confidence* that a missile attack on North America was under way. That judgment was to have been informed by telephone conversations with the ground station operators in the field whom NORAD planned to call within thirty to forty-five seconds after receiving its initial event report. The field operators would have been asked to reverify the detection and confirm that it could not have been due to any equipment malfunction. During the three-minute assessment period the NORAD director would also have received a report from the in-house strategic warning branch. On the basis of strategic warning indicators—intelligence from all sources on the disposition of Soviet forces gathered over the course of days and weeks prior to the event of immediate concern—this branch would have informed the director of its confidence that a missile attack was being launched. (The branch had to choose one of the alternative confidence levels identified above.) Using all this and additional information, the director was supposed to reach a conclusion and report it by telephone to the interested parties.[44]

In peacetime this procedure was exercised routinely because there were typically several events each day, such as missile test launches, that generated *missile event conferences* requiring a threat assessment from the NORAD director. In 1984, 580 missile launches, 488 of which were Soviet launches, occurred, each of which required NORAD to call a conference and declare its confidence.[45] Sensor anomalies also frequently required an assessment from the director.[46] On rare occasions a false alarm generated by false data, defective computer chips, or other malfunctions persisted long enough to produce a nuclear alert. The last incident to be publicly disclosed occurred in 1980, when NORAD received indications of a massive Soviet missile attack.[47]

According to an informed former official, no nuclear alerts caused by warning system malfunction occurred after that 1980 incident. However, it is likely that the background presumption of peace deserved as much credit as the warning system itself, because there were serious malfunctions after 1980. In one instance, to cite an official document, false reports from an infrared satellite "could have resulted in unacceptable posturing of SAC forces," a situation that required urgent remedial action, including the repositioning of satellites.[48] Such false reports would have been more dangerous during a crisis against a background of possible attack. The likelihood of false warning would have been greater if the adversary's forces had presented unusual deployment patterns that warning networks had never before encountered, and there would have been less time and opportunity to implement remedial measures.[49]

If the NORAD director issued a medium- or high-confidence assessment during the conference, the National Military Command Center at the Pentagon (or its alternate at Ft. Richie, depending on circumstances) was to contact the JCS chairman, who in turn would have notified the secretary of defense. Depending on the outcome of their consultation, a missile attack conference involving the president, defense secretary, JCS chairman, and all twelve nuclear commanders in chief might have been convened. If time and circumstances permitted, the senior commanders (as opposed to their deputies or other substitutes) from all major nuclear commands would have participated. The key participants, however, were the NORAD commander, the SAC commander, the JCS chairman, and the National Command Authorities (the president, or the defense secretary, or in extreme circumstances other designees, including the pre-positioned national authorities discussed above). As described by Defense Secretary Brown in 1977, the agenda of this conference would have been "examining the warning, discussing it, deciding what option to carry out and deciding indeed whether one should not wait until nuclear weapons have exploded in the United States before launching."[50]

The NORAD commander would have led off the missile attack conference with an assessment of the missile threat, a critical input to SIOP decisionmaking. By this time about eight to ten minutes would have probably elapsed since the initial observation of Soviet missile launches, and the NORAD commander would have received additional information from ground radar sensors if the attack scenario involved SLBMs fired from ocean areas near the U.S. coasts. Four Pave Paws coastal radar sensors were designed to detect these missiles several minutes after breakwater and report through site operators the positive indications to NORAD, SAC, the Pentagon, and Ft. Richie.

If the attack scenario involved only the launch of ICBMs from Soviet territory (with SLBM launches delayed or withheld), the NORAD commander might or might not have received confirmation of the launch from ground radar sensors (ballistic missile early warnings, or BMEWs, radar stations in Greenland, Alaska, and England). These radars monitoring the polar missile corridors would normally have picked up the incoming vehicles about nine minutes after lift-off. Under some circumstances this confirmation of the earlier satellite observations would have been forwarded to NORAD (unlike Pave Paws warning of SLBM attack, BMEWs warning of ICBM attack was reported directly only to NORAD, which in turn relayed processed summary reports to SAC, the Pentagon, and Ft. Richie) in time to inform the president and others participating in the missile attack conference.

At the conclusion of NORAD's threat briefing, less than twenty minutes would have remained before the first impact of Soviet ICBMs on U.S. territory, assuming a total flight time of thirty minutes. (ICBMs based in the northern region of the Soviet Union could have reached the northern part of the United States in about twenty-five minutes.) Almost no time remained before the impact of SLBMs, whose nominal flight times from patrol areas off the U.S. coasts (800 to 1,000 miles away) ranged between ten and twelve minutes. (Soviet SSBNs ceased routine patrols in these areas several years ago.) If the attack scenario involved the simultaneous launch of ICBMs and SLBMs, then the SLBMs would pose a severe threat to the decision process. Of particular concern was the threat from SLBMs detonated at high altitude during the upward portion of their trajectory, a tactic that theoretically could have shaved minutes from an already short flight time. The U.S. intelligence community estimated that the Soviets planned to exploit the LDT procedure using twenty-four SLBMs to generate electromagnetic pulse effects that theoretically could have blacked out critical U.S. communications links.[51] The missile attack conference could have been abruptly interrupted at any moment, forcing the U.S. command and control system to fall back on contingency plans that delegated authority to disseminate launch orders down the chain of command.

Had the attack scenario involved only ICBMs, then the remaining time before initial impacts—just under twenty minutes—would have allowed the participants to spend about ten minutes in deliberations if the basic mission commitments of the U.S. strategic organization were to be accomplished. These commitments depended on a prompt launch of U.S. strategic forces before the command and control system and land-based missiles sustained damage. And successful launch on warning depended on a prompt decision. The decision would have had to have been made at least five minutes, and optimally ten minutes, before the arrival of opposing missiles to allow two minutes for transmitting launch orders, three minutes for the firing of Minuteman missiles, and several more minutes for the missiles to fly a safe distance away from their home bases, which would quite possibly have been the primary destination of incoming Soviet missiles.[52] This irreducible processing time thus compressed decision time for the missile attack conference to about ten minutes. During this short time, the JCS chairman and the SAC commander would have briefed the president on his SIOP response options and offered recommendations about which categories of targets to strike.

THE PREEMPTIVE CHARACTER OF LAUNCH ON WARNING. The de facto adoption of launch on warning changed the rules for evaluating threats so that NORAD could reach and report high confidence at an earlier stage.[53] Although tactical warning assumed great importance in this posture, the role of strategic warning also grew. In fact, strategic indicators of imminent attack became so critical in threat evaluation that launch on warning became practically synonymous with preemption. The two options became almost indistinguishable in operational terms under some conditions.

This blurring of options resulted from several rule modifications introduced by NORAD in the early to mid-1980s. First, NORAD downgraded the importance of nuclear detonations. Previously NORAD high confidence had depended on the definitive evidence of nuclear explosions in bolt-from-the-blue scenarios. Under normal peacetime conditions, positive indications of the launch and transit of Soviet missiles supplied by U.S. spaceborne sensors, ground-based radar, or both, would have been considered highly suspect. Definitive confirmation of the opponent's surprise attack depended on actual nuclear detonations in North America. But since this evidence came too late into the attack scenario to meet the time constraints of launch on warning, NORAD dropped the requirement. High confidence no longer depended at all on the presence of nuclear detonations, even in circumstances of surprise attack.

NORAD also revised its rules for threat evaluation during crises. Previously NORAD high confidence depended on a combination of positive strategic warning (pre-attack indications of possible imminent hostilities) and positive attack information from at least two different tactical warning sensors. If crisis alert procedures had been initiated and nuclear tensions ran high, whereupon two different tactical warning systems detected the launch or transit of the same strategic delivery vehicles, then the sensor information would have been treated as conclusive evidence of attack. By the mid-1980s, however, NORAD applied a new rule which required a positive indication from only one tactical sensor system. In response to pressures for rapid threat assessment, NORAD considered that strategic warning indicators provided evidence equivalent to the output of any single tactical sensor. NORAD in effect assigned equal weight to infrared satellite sensors, ground radar sensors, and strategic intelligence. Positive indications from any two of these sources were sufficient to justify a high-confidence assessment. This formula posed a danger that heightened nuclear tensions (strategic warning) could have combined with a false alarm from a tactical sensor to convince NORAD that a Soviet attack was under way. The formula allowed relatively ambiguous strategic indicators to be substituted for the more valid and reliable information supplied by tactical sensors.[54]

Moreover, NORAD procedures institutionalized during the mid-1980s allowed the loss of a tactical sensor to presumed hostile action to be treated as a positive tactical indication of strategic attack. It thus became distinctly possible that a NORAD high-confidence judgment would have been based on a combination of positive strategic warning and a tactical sensor outage. Given the inherent ambiguity of strategic intelligence, the susceptibility of sensor systems and their rearward communications to interruption from nonhostile causes, and the fact that even deliberate attack on the sensors might not have been part of a larger strategic nuclear attack, NORAD's assessment procedures presented an even greater danger of fatal misinterpretation. Consider the danger posed by accidental electronic interference during a crisis. If the interference had been attributed to deliberate Soviet jamming, NORAD could have grown alarmed that a missile attack had been initiated.[55]

NORAD's assessment formula appeared to rely so heavily on strategic warning in these situations that it carried all the liabilities of a strategy of preemption. It is indeed fair to say that U.S. employment policy in certain circumstances was preemptive even though it was understood by the strategic command and control system to be launch on warning.[56]

The compromises NORAD made to support launch on warning can be explained on a host of technical grounds. The U.S. nuclear command system could not always wait for nuclear detonations, because the delay could have been fatal for it and land-based missiles, and it relied heavily on strategic warning in lieu of tactical warning because of the many deficiencies that plagued the tactical warning system. Among the main technical difficulties, the early-warning satellites were frequently put out of commission for hours by the effects of sun glare, and ground radar sensors were frequently and severely degraded by adverse atmospheric conditions produced, for example, by unusual solar activity. During a typical day, one or the other tactical sensor was not functional for about two hours. Several times a year both sensors were down at the same time for several minutes.

Compounding the problems of sensor reliability were the inherent limitations on sensor coverage, such as range limitations. Tactical sensors were especially deficient in their capacity to detect low-flying cruise mis-

siles fired from bomber aircraft or Soviet vessels near U.S. coasts and
SLBMs fired from Soviet submarines stationed in Arctic waters. The
latter threat was especially troublesome because the primary U.S. early-
warning satellites were parked in geosynchronous orbit above the equator
and simply could not reliably observe launches from the northern ocean
areas where Soviet submarines routinely patrolled. The Soviet rockets
were over the horizon and out of the satellites' line of sight.[57] Last, the
sensors and rearward communications were acutely vulnerable even to
sabotage. NORAD had become worried that an inexplicable outage of a
tactical sensor might actually be the handiwork of saboteurs. This threat
(and jamming) was considered serious enough to justify treating an outage as a positive indication of attack in the context of a nuclear crisis.

NORAD's ability to perform the requisite tasks reliably in the case of
actual attack is not known, for obvious reasons. Perhaps the most relevant
experience on which to grade NORAD's performance was a well-publi-
cized and investigated incident in 1980 in which a false alarm was generated and a missile event conference was declared,[58] the last serious
false alarm in NORAD's history that has been publicly acknowledged.
Note that this incident occurred before NORAD modified its rules of
threat evaluation to support launch on warning. In 1980 it applied stricter
rules with higher standards of evidence than it did a few years later.

According to interview material gathered for this study, the NORAD
director was presented with positive attack indications from dual-detection sensors. But on-site operators at the radar installations and satellite
ground stations reported no such observations were being made by the
equipment. Also, the strategic intelligence branch at NORAD headquarters informed the director within the requisite three minutes that it
had no confidence an attack was under way. In the ensuing confusion the
director failed to give an assessment at the required time (three minutes
after the initial event alarm, or E + 3). He finally issued a no confidence
report to the conference participants at E + 8 minutes. The NORAD
commander, who was not on duty at the time, fired the director the next
day. Thereafter only flag officers (general officers) were allowed to serve
as command directors at NORAD. (The fired officer was a colonel.)

NORAD was of course not the only component of the command and
control system that would have had difficulty carrying out the expectations imposed by the deepening commitment to a rapid reaction posture.
Comparable pressures affected the entire system. Launch on warning
compelled authorities to decide whether to retaliate and against which

targets within a very short time and without a clear picture of the provocation. NORAD could not have accurately determined the number of
incoming nuclear warheads, their specific targets, the objectives of the
attack, the yield and height of bursts, or the resultant civil and military
damage. Nor could NORAD, or anyone else, have distinguished a deliberate attack from an unauthorized one. Even if all the crucial information
had been available, people could not have easily comprehended it and
reacted sensibly in the fleeting time allowed by launch on warning. And
if the crucial information had been missing or distorted, a nuclear war
could have plausibly begun in error.

Launch on Warning and the Soviet Strategic Posture

A lengthy quotation from the Voroshilov course materials outlines
Soviet policy toward this option in the mid-1970s. This position remained
in effect throughout the rest of the cold war. Like the United States, the
Soviet Union evolved a rapid reaction posture:

> All levels of control, including the Supreme High Command, will have
> limited time to assess the situation, to make decisions, and to assign mis-
> sions to the troops. If in World War II the "efficiency" of control was
> measured and explained in terms of days, in nuclear-rocket warfare the
> "efficiency" is measured in terms of minutes. It is quite obvious that any
> information about the launching of an enemy's intercontinental rocket will
> lose significance after, for example, 20–25 minutes of the actual launch,
> and for Polaris and Poseidon rockets, after 5–10 minutes.
>   Needless to say, delays in making a timely decision on the employment
> of nuclear strikes, and in conveying the missions to the executing elements,
> will have disastrous consequences for the fate of the nation. Only through
> reliance on the most modern technical means of reconnaissance and com-
> mand can we make a logical decision, and send the command to the nuclear
> rocket forces.
>   In case the enemy initiates a nuclear attack, the preestablished warning
> system must disclose the launching of enemy missiles and should inform
> the Supreme High Command, within three to four minutes, so that it can
> make a decision on committing friendly Armed Forces into action.[59]

Soviet planning for quick launch evolved along the same lines as U.S.
policy and for the same basic reasons. Retaliation after ride-out suffered
from the technical difficulties of protecting Soviet command from a decapitation strike and to a lesser extent from the vulnerability of Soviet
strategic forces. The preemptive option suffered from the liabilities as-

sociated with strategic warning—notably the difficulty of ensuring timely and unambiguous warning of imminent U.S. strategic attack and of ensuring decisive political reaction to ominous strategic indicators.

Soviet Doctrine and Alert Posture in the 1950s and 1960s

Soviet strategic policy at one time did embrace a strategy of preemption.[60] In 1955 the Soviet military concluded that a surprise U.S. nuclear attack could cripple Soviet retaliatory capability and thus deny the Soviets the ability to prevent a U.S. victory in nuclear war. Before this time the Soviets assumed that nuclear surprise conferred only a temporary advantage that would not decisively affect either the course or the outcome of war. This view reflected Stalin's low opinion of the significance of surprise. It was deemed a "temporarily operating factor," whereas the "permanently operating factors"—the inventory of arms, the coherence of the rear, the size and quality of army divisions, troop morale, and organizing potential of the top army staff and command system—were credited with having the decisive impact on the course and outcome of war.[61] The advent of nuclear weapons and their initial deployment did not change this 1942 formulation until after Stalin's death. The Soviets planned to cope with surprise nuclear attack by relying on a strategy of launch on warning (in Soviet terminology, *vstrechnyy udar*, a *meeting strike*, which means a response to enemy launch of forces before their arrival), a strategy aided by the relatively lengthy period of tactical warning associated with the strategic delivery systems available to the West: slow-flying bombers.[62]

The publication of an important article in the confidential military-theoretical journal of the general staff, *Military Thought*, in February 1955 marked a sharp departure from previous doctrine.[63] The new thesis, endorsed by Marshall Zhukov, held that surprise could well be decisive if the victim of the attack failed to take measures to prevent its success.[64] The thrust of the argument, subsequently elaborated in the journal and elsewhere, was that Soviet security depended on its ability to avoid being surprised by the West. The Soviets did not believe they could win a nuclear war by a surprise first strike of their own against an unsuspecting Western adversary. The emphasis was laid upon seizing the initiative from an enemy already preparing for and committed to launching a surprise attack against the Soviet Union. The Soviet strategists merely acknowledged that they could be defeated in war if they failed to anticipate an imminent Western attack and respond quickly to indications that the enemy had made an irrevocable decision to strike.

Accordingly, the Soviet Union aspired to acquire the capability to launch its nuclear forces before they could be destroyed by the United States and preferably to seize the initiative in time to inflict damage on U.S. forces that were still being prepared for imminent employment. The optimum contingent response to signs of an irrevocable U.S. decision to strike was to launch a strike before the U.S. plan could be implemented, that is, to preempt. (In Soviet terminology *kontrapodgotovka*, a *counter-preparation strike*, means a defensive action designed to disrupt the enemy's first strike.)

Soviet doctrine continued to emphasize the avoidance of surprise during the early 1960s but apparently began to shift the main method of avoiding it from preemption back to launch on warning.[65] This shift almost certainly stemmed from the increasing capability of U.S. strategic forces to launch on very short notice missiles with very short intercontinental flight times. By 1963 the United States had begun a massive deployment of Minuteman missiles that could be maintained on a continuously high level of combat readiness and fired immediately upon receipt of launch orders. The Soviets credited Minuteman with a combat readiness time—"the interval of time from the moment the launch signal is received to the moment the carrier leaves the launcher"—of extremely short duration ("on the order of one minute").[66] The missiles meant that Soviet planners could not count on advance warning, depriving them of the opportunity to launch a preemptive strike. Moreover, even if the Soviets anticipated an attack and preempted, the short reaction times of Minuteman ballistic missiles reduced the effectiveness of Soviet preemption because theoretically U.S. missiles could be launched on tactical warning before Soviet weapons arrived.

On the other hand, the bulk of the U.S. strategic arsenal remained concentrated in the bomber leg, whose maximum preparation for combat required considerable time and involved overt measures such as dispersal to second-tier bases and augmentation of overseas forward bases. In all likelihood a U.S. first strike would have involved the virtually simultaneous launch of land-based ballistic missiles, a fully generated bomber force (up from the normal peacetime level of 50 percent on combat alert), and sea-based missiles carried by a fully generated strategic submarine force, according to the attack sequence established by the SIOP. And preparations for such a strike would have been sufficiently visible to

Soviet intelligence to allow a defensive preemptive reaction to be plausibly undertaken. Still, the preparations would not necessarily have revealed an irrevocable U.S. decision to attack. Such preparations could have occurred as a decentralized precautionary response to the possibility of a Soviet first strike. For the Soviets to launch first upon the detection of such steps would have been reckless.

The Soviets evidently believed that while strategic intelligence could not reliably disclose an enemy decision to attack, it would register the possibility of imminent attack in time to bring their strategic nuclear forces to a high level of combat readiness, a posture from which the Soviets could have launched quickly on tactical warning if and when the expected U.S. attack materialized. Shifting from preemption to launch on warning thus alleviated, but did not eliminate, the need for advance notification of Western nuclear attack. Some prior notice was indeed crucial because the day-to-day alert readiness of the Soviets' nuclear forces was very low at the time. Their forces required many hours if not days to get ready for launch. Until the late 1960s the nuclear warheads for their strategic as well as tactical delivery systems were kept at storage depots located a considerable distance from missile launch pads and other staging points. Technical constraints as well as inadequate safeguards apparently precluded the maintenance of Soviet strategic nuclear forces at a level of combat readiness comparable to U.S. alert levels.

The pendulum swung further away from preemption and toward launch on warning during the late 1960s. By this time the United States had deployed a very large arsenal of land- and sea-based ballistic missiles that could be launched on almost an instant's notice. Soviet strategists for the first time credited strategic nuclear weapons launched in the initial mass strike with the capacity to have a decisive influence on the course and outcome of a war and credited Western nuclear forces with unprecedented ability to achieve surprise in launching such a strike. The Voroshilov lectures thus emphasized the "enemy's capability to initiate general nuclear war without passing through an intermediate phase of mobilization."[67]

According to the lectures:

New means and modern methods of action have been introduced to ensure the surprise initiation of war . . . more than 1,000 intercontinental ballistic rockets, up to 500 strategic bomber aircraft, and 41 nuclear armed submarines with a total of 656 rockets can fire a total of more than 4,000

nuclear rounds against the Soviet Union in a short time. . . . Strategic
rockets of the Titan and Minuteman type are always kept at a level of
combat readiness requiring one to two minutes to bring them to action.
Submarines on combat patrol are maintained at a level of combat readiness
requiring 15 minutes to initiate combat actions, while the rest of the submarines are at a level of combat readiness requiring 1–2 days to initiate
combat actions. Forty percent of strategic bombers are maintained at a
level of combat readiness that enables them to commence combat flights
on notice of 15 minutes, while this time is 6 hours for the rest of such
aircraft. The pilots are continually conducting practice flights with aircraft
loaded with nuclear bombs. . . . The duration of flight of intercontinental
rockets from their bases in America to their targets in the Soviet Union is
25–30 minutes; for Polaris rockets based on nuclear submarines and ships
deployed in the North Sea, Mediterranean Sea, and the Norwegian Sea it
is 10–12 minutes; and for operational-tactical rockets it is 3–5 minutes.
Enemy strategic aircraft can launch attacks from their forward bases, as
can aircraft carriers in the Atlantic Ocean and North Sea, within two to
three hours. Tactical aircraft can launch their attacks on targets in the
USSR within 30–35 minutes. . . . Therefore . . . the possibilities of surprise attack by the enemy have increased significantly . . . by the presence
of such large numbers of nuclear weapons, . . . *the enemy can launch an
invasion without announcing mobilization, and without having to concentrate and deploy large groupings of forces beforehand* [emphasis added].[68]

The emergence of these conditions of potential threat during the latter
half of the 1960s invalidated an already weakened assumption of advance
warning of U.S. strategic nuclear attack. Moreover, the Soviets assessed
the regional nuclear threat in the European theater of operations as being
comparable in terms of the potential for surprise attack.[69]

One of the main effects of this growing concern over the surprise
initiation of Western nuclear attack was to increase the day-to-day readiness of Soviet nuclear forces, especially the command and control system.
According to the Voroshilov lectures, circumstances "necessitate a constantly combat-ready system of control of the Armed Forces to effectively
cope with the surprise initiation of nuclear war. This requires that the
structure and system of control of the Armed Forces be established and
organized in peacetime in a way that will require little change at the
beginning of war."[70] Particular attention was also paid to the combat
readiness of strategic nuclear forces. The Soviets mated the nuclear
charges to their modern land-based missiles—the SS-11s during the late
1960s—and initiated regular combat patrols by their modern submarines—the Yankee-class SSBNs. The command and control system, in-

cluding the tactical warning sensors, was improved with a view to establishing a rapid reaction posture for the strategic rocket forces in particular.

The substitution of launch on warning for preemption in Soviet strategy proceeded apace. Authoritative discussions of this option appeared in Marshal Sokolovskiy's second edition of *Soviet Military Strategy* and in an article in the confidential general staff journal written by the commander of the Strategic Rocket Forces. Sokolovskiy wrote, "Modern means of detection and warning permit intersecting the launch of ballistic missiles, primarily strategic missiles, and transmitting signals concerning such launchings to the corresponding command posts . . . during this time . . . a counter salvo of rockets can be launched in answer to the imperialist aggression."[71] Marshall Krylov wrote, "With the presence in the armament [of the Soviet armed forces] of launchers and missiles completely ready for action, as well as systems for detecting enemy missile launches and other types of reconnaissance, an aggressor is no longer able suddenly to destroy the missiles on the territory of the country subjected to aggression prior to their launching. They will have time during the flight of the missiles of the aggressor to leave their launchers and inflict a retaliatory strike against the enemy."[72] These revelations were confirmed by the Voroshilov lectures, in which it was stated that "the notification by alert (*opoveshchenie po trevoge*), given to bring the strategic nuclear forces to the level of full combat readiness, is only some minutes. . . . The Strategic Rocket Forces are ready [in peacetime] to begin action on the signal given to them by the Supreme High Command."[73]

It nevertheless appears that these bald assertions about the state of combat readiness of Soviet nuclear forces during the late 1960s and early 1970s were exaggerated. The statements are better understood as goals than capabilities. The SS-11 missile force was not nearly as combat ready as the statements suggested. Most likely a portion of these silo-based missiles did not have warheads attached in peacetime,[74] and the armed missiles needed to be warmed up for several hours before launch. Some of the missiles could have been armed and warmed up on a rotating basis, but further time-consuming preparations were necessary before carrying out their launch. In particular, this generation of missiles was equipped with unlock devices (since a normal configuration of alert missiles would have nuclear warheads attached) requiring the insertion of special codes prior to launch. This unlock procedure probably involved the transmission of the combinations from SRF army level headquarters to field units in a labor-intensive and cumbersome manner. Unlock codes, perhaps held by special custodians from the general staff at the six SRF army headquarters, would have been disseminated to regimental command posts in the missile fields via land-lines or radio communications in many cases. In sum, most likely only a small fraction of the ICBM force was armed, warmed up, and ready for launch on short notice in the event of a surprise U.S. attack. Soviet release exercises indicated even greater difficulties in preparing the rest for launch.[75]

An even more severe limitation on rapid reaction was the poor performance of the Soviet tactical warning system. It almost certainly did not provide warning timely enough to support a strategy of launch on warning. The Soviets' primary system during the mid- to late 1960s consisted of a couple of so-called Hen House radars deployed northwest of Moscow. By 1970 there were about seven such radars deployed or under construction near Moscow, on the Kola Peninsula, the Baltic coast, near the Black Sea, and in the southern part of the country. According to a Soviet chief designer interviewed for this book, the ballistic missile radars became operational as an early-warning system replete with links to decisionmakers for the first time in 1971. The U.S. defense secretary reported in 1970 that these radars provided fair coverage of U.S. ICBM attack corridors and of SLBM corridors from most ocean areas.[76] However, large gaps existed in this coverage.

More important, the warning time provided by these sensors was too short to effect a prompt retaliatory launch before incoming U.S. warheads reached their targets in the Soviet Union. Designed for line-of-sight surveillance, the radars could not have detected missiles until they came within direct view above the horizon. (A Soviet effort to develop radars that looked over the horizon is discussed later.) By that time the missiles would have nearly reached the halfway point in their journey. Even if the primitive Soviet sites had possessed the range of the more advanced U.S. BMEWs radar systems (about three thousand nautical miles), a doubtful assumption, they could have provided a maximum of only seventeen minutes tactical warning of U.S. ICBM attack under optimum conditions, and far less against U.S. SLBMs fired from forward patrol areas near Soviet territory.[77]

That seventeen minutes advance warning was too little to permit launch on warning was acknowledged, albeit elliptically, in the confidential general staff journal in 1969. Writing in *Military Thought* on the capabilities of the U.S. BMEWs ground radar warning system deployed in the early 1960s, A. B. Krasnov noted that the system provided only fifteen to seventeen minutes of warning time. He went on to say that "in the opinion of the Americans it is exceptionally difficult to advise the necessary officials, put one's forces into combat readiness and initiate combat operations within such a short time."[78]

The Soviets doubtless held the same opinion of the difficulties of Soviet launch on warning, particularly in light of the relative inferiority of their ground radar system and the lower combat readiness of their strategic nuclear forces. The secret course materials of the Voroshilov academy program of the mid-1970s disclosed that contemporary Soviet ground radars could detect the flight of intercontinental ballistic rockets within only twelve to fifteen minutes before their arrival on target (and could detect low-flying aircraft within only three to five minutes before they passed over intercontinental boundaries) and that "obviously, such times are not sufficient for the organization of countermeasures."[79] As strategic exercises demonstrated in later years, after vast improvements in command and force readiness, the Soviets required approximately twenty-one minutes of advance warning to launch on warning.[80]

Doctrine and Posture in the 1970s and 1980s

Soviet military strategists and other commentators continued to emphasize launch on warning as the main method of avoiding surprise throughout the 1970s. The most authoritative affirmation of this reliance appeared in the confidential journal *Military Thought*, in an article written by the head of the department of strategy at the General Staff Academy, who said, "A decision on dealing a retaliatory strike on the aggressor must be taken in the limited minutes after detection of his launch of the ballistic missiles. That fact in turn requires maintaining the whole system of command-control in a constant high combat readiness."[81] Efforts to establish the requisite combat readiness, command arrangements, and tactical warning performance were redoubled during the 1970s and early 1980s. The Soviets intensively pursued the development of new sensors that would extend the amount of tactical warning time by an additional fifteen minutes (from fifteen to thirty minutes), streamlined the nuclear command system, and fielded fourth-generation missiles capable of being unlocked and fired on very short notice.

During this period of growing reliance on launch on warning, the Soviets further downgraded the importance of preemption. Through 1973 arguments against its abandonment were still voiced. For instance, Colonel Ye. Rybkin, writing in a Soviet military journal in 1973, contended that "it would be premature to declare the exclusion of the possibility of use of nuclear weapons in case of the unleashing of a [conventional] war by aggressors."[82] But Raymond Garthoff found evidence that such arguments were silenced sometime in 1973–74 by a secret directive issued in the name of the party's Central Committee. The committee instructed Soviet planners not to assume that the Soviet Union would be the first to use nuclear weapons. Garthoff found a reference to this directive in the confidential general staff journal under the name of the same Colonel Rybkin in 1975.[83] The colonel's previous brief against a no-first-use declaration had apparently been rejected.[84]

Although the final step toward renouncing the first use of nuclear weapons was not taken until early 1981, leading to a unilateral public pledge by Leonid Brezhnev in June 1982, Soviet nuclear exercises reportedly ceased to practice the preemptive use of nuclear weapons in 1977, with one possible exception in a 1978 exercise.[85] The secret directive of 1973–74 thus seems to have been incorporated into Soviet nuclear strategy and operations not long after its issuance.

But if that is an accurate account of the historical period, the Soviet Union, by rejecting nuclear first use, painted itself into a corner. The Soviets replaced preemption with launch on warning before the latter option became viable. It was not yet viable because of the slow reaction time of the Soviet command and control system. The chief deficiency was the inability of Soviet warning sensors to provide the requisite warning time. The crash programs undertaken during the 1960s and 1970s to extend tactical warning time had so far been unfruitful. Another deficiency was the cumbersome procedure used by the supreme high command to authorize the release of nuclear weapons. The crash program undertaken during the late 1970s to develop the *Kazbek* system of nuclear suitcases also had not come to fruition. The Kazbek system was to enable the general secretary, defense minister, and chief of the general staff to rapidly convey the permission command to the nuclear CINCs even under conditions of surprise attack that might have caught these officials away from their wartime posts. To further complicate matters, NATO was preparing to deploy Pershing II missiles, whose short flight times threatened to make launch on warning totally infeasible.

Major technical accomplishments in tactical warning were not realized until 1982, the year Brezhnev stood before the U.N. General Assembly at the Special Session on Disarmament to declare his country's categorical rejection of nuclear first use. Meanwhile the feasibility of launch on warning was questionable at best. Soviet military leaders surely took issue with their political instructions, denying them the option to initiate the use of nuclear weapons when Western nuclear attack appeared imminent. The level of anxiety must have been especially high in the early 1980s, when U.S.-Soviet tension ran high and the Soviets saw an increasing danger of war.[86] The defense minister himself questioned the wisdom of no-first-use during this period of confrontation. He emphasized its problematic implications for command and control, but alluded to launch on warning as the key to deterring enemy attack.[87]

Soviet efforts to lengthen the warning time of enemy ballistic missile attack had been following two separate technological tracks, over-the-horizon (OTH) Backscatter radar and satellite infrared sensors. With the policy renunciation of no-first-use and the de facto adoption of launch on warning, these programs assumed great importance.

BACKSCATTER RADAR DEBACLE. During the 1970s the Soviets pinned their hopes for a rapid reaction posture on OTH radar. The several OTH installations built during the decade were the only operational sensors theoretically able to detect U.S. ICBMs early enough in their flight (the powered boost phase, which lasts several minutes after lift-off) to provide the requisite minimum of twenty-one minutes of tactical early warning. In theory, the signals beamed from radar stations on Soviet territory could travel to North America by bouncing between the ionosphere and the earth and reflect back to the Soviet Union if they encountered missiles.[88] With almost instantaneous transmission and reflection over great distances, the OTH technology promised to give Soviet commanders the launch detection capability they sorely needed. Soviet claims for acquiring a credible option of quick launch during the late 1960s and early 1970s were probably based on the expectation that this technology would soon be fully operational and reliably effective.

An experimental OTH backscatter radar went into operation in 1971, and a few years later the Soviets were operating two such radar stations that reportedly could observe missiles launched from Cape Kennedy. By 1979 three newer OTH-B radar installations were operational, two of which monitored U.S. ICBM launches and one of which watched Chinese missiles.[89] As Soviet scientists had feared, however, all performed very

poorly.[90] The natural instability of the ionosphere, especially in the northern auroral zone (the polar zone through which the northerly pointed
OTH stations aimed at North America must have transmitted and received signals), strongly attenuated and distorted signal propagation and
hence severely hampered the detection of missile launches. Soviet scientists also appreciated the inaccuracy of the system, its low resistance
to jamming, and its susceptibility to severe disruption by the effects of
nuclear explosions on the ionosphere.[91]

   One of the more optimistic scientific assessments predicted that new
computer-assisted means of adapting to ionospheric disturbances could
be devised to enable OTH radars reliably to determine the approximate
character and launch origin of an attacking missile force.[92] An assessment
in the secret lecture materials of the general staff academy is representative of prevailing judgment in the mid-1970s: "Land-based, over-the-
horizon, backscatter radar stations can detect enemy ballistic rockets in
their launch phase at a distance of 10,000–12,000 km, but it should be
noted that such radar stations have less power to allow them to accurately
and sufficiently determine the location of the launch sites of these ballistic
rockets. Practically speaking, with the aid of such stations, only the
launch action and the location of the launch can be determined."[93] But
even this qualified assessment, which provided some basis for claiming
at least a limited operational capability for launch on warning, touted
the OTH system far more highly than it deserved.

   A Soviet newspaper recently published a scathing indictment of the
OTH system by a former head of the Soviet antiballistic missile program.
This account by an insider privy to confidential data indicates that the
OTH system was a bigger flop than almost anyone knew. As translated
and paraphrased by a Western journal, the interview with Gigoriy Kisunko revealed that the performance of the OTH radars was so poor "that
operators stooped to deception to hide their shortcomings from national
leaders. Military and civilian officials connected with the radars would
determine, through published reports or through KGB contacts, when a
scheduled NASA space launch would take place. Then on the appropriate
day, the radar sites would announce they had tracked the launch. Unfortunately this ruse proved transparent on more than one occasion when
the NASA launch was scrubbed or delayed due to weather."

   According to Kisunko, the radars were still considered under "experimental operation" even though they had been functioning for nearly two
decades. Developers of the radar system attempted to deflect this criti-

cism with the line of argument that it could detect a mass salvo of ICBMs even if it could not reliably detect individual launches.[94] And for better or worse, OTH radar was integrated into the operational warning system and was relied on to confirm missiles detected by satellites.[95]

SPACEBORNE LAUNCH DETECTION AND SOVIET POSTURE. The shift from preemption to launch on warning in Soviet strategy during the 1970s also outpaced the development of space-based warning technology.[96] Inaugurated in 1972, the satellite program for missile launch detection experienced severe growing pains that lasted more than ten years. Major technical obstacles included getting a constellation of long-lasting satellites into proper orbit and outfitting the spacecraft with reliably effective infrared sensors. One of the greatest frustrations stemmed from the need to keep at least one satellite in continuous view of both the U.S. missile fields and the ground readout stations on Soviet territory. This was necessary in order to monitor the central and western part of the United States while communicating launch indications directly to ground stations in the Soviet Union. To meet both requirements, Soviet early-warning spacecraft had to fly in highly elliptical orbits, which limited the observation window of each satellite to several hours. When this dwell time expired, the satellite left the vicinity and lost its prime vantage point. This surveillance slot then had to be filled by another satellite, which in turn performed several hours of monitoring before being relieved by the next satellite in the constellation. Since each stint lasted only a few hours, a total of nine satellites were needed for the clockwork rotation that ensured continuous coverage of the U.S. land-based missile fields.

After a test program that ran from 1972 through 1975, the Soviets began the deployment of operational surveillance spacecraft in late 1976. The rate of launch averaged two per year from 1976 to 1979 and then rose to six and five launches in 1980 and 1981, respectively. Twelve of these twenty-five spacecraft failed to reach proper orbit or had broken up by the end of 1981, however. Furthermore, the infrared sensors on board the satellites proved ineffective.[97] According to an analyst interviewed for this study, before 1982 the absence of downlink transmissions from the satellites during U.S. test launches of ballistic missiles fired from California may have been the clearest empirical indication of severe deficiencies in the detection technology.

Only two of the spacecraft launched through 1981 were still operational at the end of 1982, but five successful launches in 1982 brought the number of slots filled by operational satellites to seven. Two of the nine slots apparently were occupied by inoperative satellites, but in spite of these voids the spacecraft apparently provided nearly uninterrupted coverage of the area of interest. Furthermore, the on-board sensors were finally working well enough to detect the launch of U.S. missiles reliably.

This breakthrough coupled with the expansion of the satellite fleet to seven operational slots marked a watershed in the program. Notwithstanding the intermittent gaps in coverage totaling several hours each day, the Soviets had moved very close to achieving their goal by the end of 1982. As a result, the Soviet option of launch on warning had become quite credible from the standpoint of tactical warning. This capability was acknowledged in 1984 by the U.S. Defense Department: "The current Soviet launch detection satellite network is capable of providing about 30 minutes warning of any US ICBM launch, and of determining the area from which it originated."[98] A special national intelligence estimate completed in mid-1984 said the Soviets in 1983 had achieved a continuous launch detection capability from space.

Despite setbacks in 1983, when two of the three replacement spacecraft launched that year either failed to reach proper orbit or broke up on station soon after launch, the Soviets quickly recovered the lost ground. A herculean effort in 1984 replaced virtually the entire fleet with new spacecraft—seven satellites were sent up—though one or perhaps two slots were missing operative satellites by the end of the year. The short lifespan of these new spacecraft—all but two failed within a year after launch—forced the Soviets to replace them at a high rate in 1985 (seven more launches that year). As a result of this replenishment, all but one of the nine slots in the constellation were restored to active status by year's end. This concerted effort continued the next year. As the longevity of Soviet spacecraft steadily increased, the satellite early-warning program achieved full deployment in all nine slots by the middle of 1987.

The maturity of this program, combined with progress in satellite warning from geosynchronous orbits,[99] enhanced the credibility of launch on warning, as noted in a section entitled "Launch on Warning" of a report written by the U.S. Defense Department in 1988: "In the event the Soviets fail to execute their preemptive option, they will depend on their early warning networks to provide them with sufficient response time. This network comprises launch detection satellites and over-the-horizon radars that can ascertain the general direction of an attack and provide up to 30 minutes warning. . . . Once notified, the SRF would have to launch its missiles before enemy warheads hit. To ensure that it can do so, the SRF exercises the procedures involved in such a response."[100]

At the same time the Soviets publicly claimed to have an efficient missile attack warning system composed in part of space-based assets. A senior Soviet general elaborated: "From space it is possible to keep track of missile launches and issue a timely early warning of a possible attack. . . . It is necessary to 'watch' continuously, every minute. For this it is necessary to have several special satellites and to replace them as their operating life comes to an end."[101] The average lifespan of their "special" satellites grew to about two years, allowing the Soviets to maintain the nine-member constellation with a launch rate of two a year. The operators of these infra-red satellites reportedly could get a fix on the U.S. missile "about 20 seconds after launch."[102]

Soviet Exercises of Launch on Warning

Given these background developments, it comes as no surprise that launch on warning was the theme of the 1982 training year for the Soviet SRF.[103] The major exercise in this regard occurred over seven hours on June 18, 1982.[104] A wide array of offensive and defensive missiles were fired during the exercise, and at a certain stage a multitude of missiles were launched within about thirteen minutes.[105] The Soviets demonstrated very rapid reaction to warning by means of a streamlined, highly automated command and control system that allowed the general staff to communicate directly with the regimental command posts of the SRF.[106]

The 1984 exercise described in chapter 4 practiced the rapid launch of the Soviet emergency rocket communications system (ERCS), which apparently used missiles capable of being loaded with launch orders and fired directly by the top leaders from command bunkers in the Moscow vicinity. Few details have been disclosed, but the fifty-five-minute retransmissions of the fire orders by the ERCS missile during its flight triggered a minimal immediate response by the far-flung strategic and theater nuclear forces.[107] As discussed previously, the context for this exercise was a sneak U.S. nuclear bomber attack in the midst of conventional conflict. The U.S. attack promptly and gravely degraded Soviet command and control. Except for a small contingent of Soviet forces that successfully received the fire codes, the main retaliatory strike was delayed for days while Soviet strategic capability was reconstituted. According to interviews, Soviet links used to send the arming-unlock codes to forces in the field suffered severe disruption; this simulated degradation was most acute in the southwestern theater of operations. Forces therefore could not be comprehensively launched on warning.

The timeline of response for Soviet strategic forces released on tactical warning of U.S. attack was clarified by a general staff exercise conducted in 1988. This major exercise began with the launch of a submarine ballistic missile, followed five minutes later by the simulated Soviet detection of the lift-off of large numbers of ICBMs from U.S. missile bases. Soviet spaceborne infrared sensors doubtless provided the initial simulated positive indications of U.S. SIOP attack, which triggered a Soviet decision nine minutes later (presumably after receiving attack confirmation from ground radar sites, because missile detection by two tactical sensors [dual phenomenology] was mandatory in the release procedures). The decision was to launch a massive salvo of land-based strategic rockets. The permission command from the Soviet supreme high command thus occurred fourteen minutes after the initial lift-off of U.S. Minuteman forces from silos in the central and western parts of the country.

During a large naval nuclear exercise later in 1988, the Soviets simulated a Western SLBM strike that took four minutes to detect. The Soviet command authorities decided to launch only one minute later, but this abbreviated decision period was surely an artifact of the exercise that bore scant resemblance to an actual decisionmaking process. A former SRF officer told me that Soviet strategic exercises often demonstrated the supreme command's ability to make a decision in two to four minutes in order to impress the West with the Soviets' capacity for launch on warning. The Soviets tried to ensure that Western intelligence registered this short decision time. This might have been accomplished by conducting the emergency deliberations among the general secretary, defense minister, and chief of the general staff over insecure telecommunications links that could have been readily intercepted by the West. At any rate, in the exercise two minutes elapsed while the Soviet supreme command disseminated its launch permission to the general staff (and presumably the CINC SRF, too), who in turn used between two and three minutes to transmit the fire orders to the battalion launch control centers in the field. Upon receipt of this direct command from the general staff (normally also requiring CINC SRF input to form a valid command), the battalion launch crews completed the launch sequence in three minutes.

Thus a total of about twenty-one or twenty-two minutes elapsed between the time of the simulated U.S. ICBM lift-off and Soviet ICBM lift-off in the exercise. Assuming a flight time of thirty minutes for U.S.

forces, the Soviet missiles left their silos eight or nine minutes before the arrival of U.S. missiles. Since Soviet missiles needed to put considerable distance between themselves and their silos to avoid damage from ground-level explosions during the boost phase of launch, a minute or so of these eight or nine minutes was needed to fly a safe distance away.[108] The margin of safety for the launch of ICBMs in this exercise was therefore about seven minutes. This was of course not much time to spare, but if the procedures could have been implemented in wartime as smoothly as they were in this exercise, the Soviets could have succeeded in launching on warning.

As best as one can judge from open sources, the procedures for warning the Soviet leadership in the event of an actual attack involved several different organizations. The Soviet counterpart of the U.S. NORAD headquarters would have provided the initial tactical warning. This organization, the air defense forces (PVO), and its main facility, the Center for Analysis of Space and Missile Situation, received and processed early-warning intelligence from ground- and space-based sensors.[109] The PVO central command post in Moscow and its alternate just outside Moscow (reportedly at Kalinin) were apparently the conduits for the initial data collected by the radio-technical troops who operated the dispersed sensors.[110] From these installations tactical warning would have been disseminated to the general staff war room near the Kremlin and other key command centers, especially those of the defense minister and CINC SRF. Important central posts such as the general staff's war room (the command center of the main operations directorate), the supreme command facilities such as the deep underground command post beneath the Kremlin, and the command posts of the CINC SRF might have received tactical warning data directly from certain PVO sensors, as is the U.S. custom.[111]

Certain key command facilities would have also received strategic warning information about imminent attack from the GRU command post at Khodinka and from the KGB.[112] The KGB had its own specialized reporting channels that ran directly to the political leadership, but it was also tasked to collect signals and other intelligence relating to Western operations and plans and to report such critical information to the GRU command post. Military signals and other intelligence gathered by the GRU itself were also funneled into the GRU command post. The GRU then would have forwarded the information to the general staff war room, though some critical information could have been simultaneously conveyed directly to the political leadership.

Whatever the mix of tactical and strategic warning, the chief of the general staff (backed up by the CINC SRF) might have been the key person normally responsible for notifying the defense minister and general secretary immediately if an enemy nuclear attack was deemed under way. Such an arrangement would have been similar to U.S. procedures for notifying the National Command Authorities (defense secretary and president) through the Pentagon war room (the J-3 operations branch) and the JCS adviser (the chairman or an alternate).

Both U.S. and Soviet procedures were streamlined during the early to mid-1980s to iron out the wrinkles of notification, consultation, and release authorization in support of launch on warning. Of particular interest on the Soviet side was the introduction of procedures that allowed the chief of the general staff and the nuclear CINCs to rapidly disseminate a preliminary command to the individual nuclear units immediately after receiving attack indications from satellite sensors. This initiated prelaunch procedures while the top leaders waited for confirmation of the attack from a second set of sensors, notably the ground radar stations on the periphery of Soviet territory. If the attack was confirmed, the Kazbek system nuclear suitcases would have been switched to a combat mode to enable the supreme command authorities to transmit their portions of the codes that formed a permission command. Then the newly automated network of communications systems used by the chief of the general staff and the nuclear CINCs to disseminate a direct command releasing nuclear weapons would have triggered the final launch procedures in the field.

Various Soviet exercises, at any rate, clearly demonstrated that extremely rapid reaction was feasible at least under favorable conditions. U.S. planners conceded the point and credited the Soviets with a viable option for launch on warning. Whether it was deemed viable by Soviet planners is a harder question.

Drawbacks of Launch on Warning in the Soviet Posture

For at least four reasons launch on warning was a rather weak reed for the Soviets to lean on. First, its technological infrastructure was inadequate. Although the warning, communications, and command technologies appeared adequate by the early 1980s for basic scenarios that featured Western ICBM attack, they could not have dealt with some more exotic variants of attack, particularly any that involved precursor strikes by submarine-launched ballistic missiles. Warning systems were unable to reliably detect SLBMs inside certain attack corridors. In any case the flight time of SLBMs fired from forward patrol stations was much shorter than the cycle time of Soviet launch on warning. The ground-based radars had holes in their coverage and the space-based early-warning sensors provided only very limited coverage of the ocean areas patrolled by U.S. strategic submarines.

In recent years the U.S. Defense Department predicted that the Soviets would deploy geosynchronous early-warning satellites that would vastly expand the ocean area under surveillance, but the improvement in coverage remained unclear. The new large phased-array radars (LPARs) deployed during the 1980s to augment the Soviets' older Hen House radar sites did not plug the holes. They still left gaps in SLBM coverage and still gave too little warning time to implement a launch-on-warning option. Although Soviet exercises indicated confidence in the command and control system's ability to withstand the effects of strikes by older SLBMs,[113] that confidence was surely perishable in the face of the imminent U.S. deployment of D-5 SLBMs. These highly lethal counterforce weapons posed a much greater threat to hard targets ranging from Soviet command posts to missile silos. Their potential for suppressing Soviet strategic capability within twenty minutes called into serious question an option that required twenty-one minutes to carry out. Furthermore, other U.S. weapons innovations posed an equivalent threat, especially long-range cruise missiles that could have eluded Soviet detection while striking key links in the networks supporting Soviet ICBM launch on warning.

The breakup of the former Soviet Union aggravated these problems because at least eight of the ground radar installations that provided missile attack early warning were situated outside Russia.[114] Local environmental protests in Ukraine halted construction of a new, important large phased-array radar, at Mukachevo, slated to replace a site described as "obsolete and performing limited tasks,"[115] and another in Latvia was to be the subject of negotiations with Moscow. The LPAR under construction in Krasnoyarsk, which had promised to fill a large gap in SLBM coverage for Trident SSBNs patrolling the Pacific Ocean, had to be dismantled because its location violated the ABM Treaty. The government of Azerbijan took control over the Lyaki radar. The result is a system with many gaps in coverage.

Holes in the outer perimeter of the air defense network also appeared after the Soviet Union disintegrated. The breakdown of defense cooperation between Russia and the outlying republics, now sovereign states, produced gaps through which enemy aircraft could fly undetected to targets inside Russia.

Second, launch on warning was also problematic because conventional or theater nuclear hostilities might have worn down the Soviet strategic warning, tactical warning, communications, and command system. The infrastructure that supported a rapid reaction strategic posture might not have been intact when it was most needed, the moment hostilities escalated to the level of a strategic intercontinental attack. Soviet planners had to contend with the prospect that prior degradation of this infrastructure would deny them the option of launch on warning.

Third, a moment's reflection casts doubt on the acceptability in Soviet (or anyone else's) eyes of any option that permitted decisionmakers so little time to decide whether to order the launch of strategic forces. In the 1988 general staff exercise the top leadership reached the fateful decision nine minutes after the U.S. ICBM attack was initially detected. Attack confirmation and assessment presumably consumed a significant portion of this brief period, leaving only a few minutes for deciding whether and how to respond. Time permitted only an essentially automatic response, not any deep deliberations on the military, much less the political or moral repercussions, of alternatives. This constraint was especially incompatible with the Soviets' deep-seated aversion to risk-taking and the related commitment to tight central control over war aims and force execution. As Benjamin S. Lambeth argued in 1984:

> The Soviet leadership has recently taken the position that it can no longer "rule out" launching its own missiles upon unambiguous warning of an incoming attack. . . . Nevertheless, launch on warning runs diametrically against the grain of Soviet doctrine's emphasis on retaining operational control over the war process at all times. Indeed, its entire logic rests on the abandonment of any semblance of control in favor of blind reliance on a mindless gamble. . . . Accordingly, whatever the Soviet leaders may say on this score, it taxes credulity to suggest that they would easily give in to such a dire resort in the heat of a crisis.[116]

The chief liabilities of a rapid reaction posture were that it stood in stark opposition to what Karl Spielmann identified as two long-held tenets of Soviet strategic thinking, "an emphasis on the dangers of accidental war and a concern for the control problems associated with high readiness of the strategic forces."[117] During the Gorbachev period these concerns, which can be traced back to the late 1950s and early 1960s, were ascendant. One need only recall former defense minister Yazov's view, previously voiced by Ustinov in the early 1980s, that the unauthorized use of Soviet nuclear weapons during periods of heightened alert remained a serious concern that should continue to receive high priority.

Raymond Garthoff's study of new developments in Soviet security policy and military doctrine found that the danger of nuclear inadvertence was recently given more political weight and had a new impact on military doctrine.[118] Soviet analysts elucidated the categories of factors that had long been identified as the sources of unintended war: "political (miscalculation and misperception of a threat), psychological (decisionmaking under crisis and time pressures), and technical (computer malfunction)."[119] Launch on warning and the high level of combat readiness that attends it were seen as particular dangers, in part because of the increased role of automation in the launch decision.[120] Two respected Soviet generals writing in the late 1980s warned that military-technical factors had eroded political control over the launch process and increased the risk of accidental war. Major General Valentin Larionov wrote, "In general today placing the armed forces at a high alert level of combat readiness presupposes automation of systems for issuance, transmission and receipt of commands for firing, in which the participation of men is extremely limited. For deliberation, consideration and decision the human brain has literally only minutes. And this all greatly increases the risk of accidental outbreak of war."[121] He cited errors in early-warning systems and technical malfunctions in weapons systems as two of the main contemporary causes of inadvertent nuclear war.

Recent disclosures by military officers confirmed these sources of danger. A retired Soviet general told how he once witnessed signals from space-based sensors warning of the launch of U.S. Minuteman missiles against the Soviet Union. A "competent operator," the general recalled with relief, determined that the supposed missile exhaust plumes were in fact merely "patches of sunlight."[122] Another general, the chief of staff of the SRF, disclosed during a recent interview that "once there was a case when, in the course of regulation work, a missile without its nose cone dismantled, 'left' the launcher of its own accord and fell not far from the launch pad."[123]

Major General Yu. Kirshin also seemed to allude to the central role of launch on warning in military strategy and to the danger that such a rapid reaction posture weakened political control over the launch decision:

> Military strategy has always influenced policy. But in the nuclear age under the impact of military-technical factors this influence has so increased that

the relative independence of military strategy has grown by an order of magnitude, and the sphere of political decision can narrow, especially in relation to the unleashing of war. Under contemporary conditions military strategy, always occupying a subordinate position [to policy], may to a great extent slip out from under political control. It seems strange but in the nuclear age war can begin even without the intervention of the political leadership. . . . The independence of strategy can manifest itself in such a way that the accidental initiation of nuclear war is not excluded.[124]

The Soviets sought to minimize the risk of nuclear inadvertence posed by launch on warning by making dual-sensor tactical warning a precondition for unleashing the Soviet strategic forces. Attack indications from a single sensor would have triggered only a preliminary command; confirmation from a second sensor was required to issue the permission and direct commands authorizing retaliation.[125] But the technical and operational deficiencies mentioned earlier made this mandatory requirement difficult to satisfy. The Soviets could have lowered their standards of evidence and changed the rules of warning interpretation, but their deep-seated aversion to risk argued against it. Unlike the United States, which tolerated greater warning ambiguity in its rapid reaction posture, the Soviet Union maintained a strict requirement for dual phenomenology. As a result, positive control was compromised for the sake of negative control. Nevertheless, the danger of inadvertence was inherent in the heavy Soviet reliance on launch on warning.

The ascendant concern over nuclear inadvertence was accompanied by a new interest in problems of conflict termination. This interest became manifest in an exercise during the 1980s, according to one account.[126] The context was a conventional war that had pushed NATO forces back to the Rhine. The United States then resorted to battlefield nuclear weapons for the next four days. At that point, according to this account, the SRF headquarters sent a message to the Soviet supreme high command urgently requesting it to force the United States to capitulate before the U.S. launched a massive strategic attack.

Fourth, launch on warning argues for vesting ultimate launch authority in a single individual; by the same token it militates against collective decisionmaking at the apex of command. But such arrangements rubbed against the grain of Soviet political culture. Lambeth noted, "Soviet decisionmaking is largely a product of consensus politics. It is therefore not unreasonable to wonder whether launch under attack (if not preemption, for that matter) is not fundamentally incompatible with a collective leadership system."[127]

Launch on warning was presumably regarded by the Soviets as aggravating a problem that had long been troublesome—devising national command arrangements that were politically acceptable in peacetime but also met wartime requirements quickly and effectively. More specifically, in Spielmann's words, "It has been difficult for the Soviets to reconcile collective political leadership with the principle of one-man command at the NCA level, which is desired by the Soviet military."[128] Spielmann's conclusion, drawn from historical evidence through the Brezhnev regime, doubtless remained germane through later phases of the cold war. For example, in 1990 the chief of the general staff chastised Soviet legislators for failing to expand the powers of the Soviet presidency to include "in the event of enemy nuclear attack, the right to personally make the decision and issue the authority to use nuclear weapons as a retaliatory measure."[129] In view of this long-standing aversion to one-man command, it seems even less likely that provisions were ever made to allow launch authority to devolve automatically to any single predesignated successor as a hedge against decapitation. Such arrangements were militarily desirable—they would have ameliorated the effects of command disruption on response time and facilitated launch on warning under such dire circumstances—but politically questionable in peacetime. Predelegation could have eroded the effective power of the existing political regime and implied political succession rights during interregnums.[130]

For all these reasons launch on warning was not as technically and politically robust an option for the Soviet command system as it was for the United States. Nevertheless, the alternatives were no better in Soviet eyes and probably seemed worse. Garthoff cites evidence that the Soviets in recent years sought ways to reduce reliance on launch on warning in favor of a policy of retaliation after attack in order to strengthen political control and lessen the risk of inadvertent war.[131] Garthoff agrees, however, that as the cold war wound down launch on warning appeared to still be the principal option in Soviet strategy for intercontinental nuclear war.

Conclusion

Although the command and control systems of the superpowers had evolved sophisticated weapons designs and operational procedures to preserve effective control with widespread dispersal of weapons, they could be severely disrupted with very few nuclear weapons. This situation produced tension between the peacetime and wartime functions of the systems and made the transitions between positive and negative control difficult.

Fearful of the disruptive effects of initial damage, both the U.S. and Soviet command and control systems strained to detect an attack. Both were also strongly disposed to give the launch orders, unlock codes, and targeting instructions before definitive evidence of massive damage had accumulated. This commitment to disseminate launch authorization irreversibly in response to evidence of an attack required the warning and decisionmaking processes to perform amazing feats. The entire process was compressed into no more than about twenty minutes. The danger of inadvertent war that stemmed from this stance was greater than has generally been recognized.

The danger was compounded by two features of the U.S. system. First, the U.S. posture depended on a warning system that, although technically superior to its Soviet counterpart, was more prone to infer an enemy attack from ambiguous evidence. Second, U.S. contingency plans rapidly and irreversibly dispersed discretionary authority to order SIOP implementation in the event of initial disruption to the normal chain of command. Numerous military units and officers held all the codes needed to implement the nuclear war plans, and many were delegated the authority to execute the plans in the event of a communications outage or other adverse circumstance that could impede the prompt release of the strategic forces. This too was a greater danger than has generally been recognized. The speed with which fateful decisions had to be rendered was a serious problem, and this predelegated release authority increased the complexity of the transition from negative to positive control while diminishing the effective control of the political leadership. A significant danger existed that in a serious crisis, particularly one that involved a degraded command system, the shift of priorities from peace to war would have occurred as a decentralized, spontaneous reaction of the system. Such arrangements partly compensated for vulnerabilities in command and control and force structure, bolstering deterrence of premeditated attack. But they also increased the chance for military operations to overrun the intentions of the political leadership and cause the unpremeditated use of nuclear weapons. Positive control was thus strengthened at the expense of negative control.

The Soviet command and control system attached greater relative importance to unambiguous warning and central political control. The system nonetheless relied heavily on rapid reaction and hence posed a comparable threat of launching an attack inadvertently.

It seems unlikely that other nuclear archenemies could avoid this danger. It appears to be intrinsic to nuclear postures evolving in an atmosphere of confrontation akin to the cold war, and lends further importance to the prevention of nuclear proliferation.

CHAPTER SEVEN

A Model of the Effects of Warning on Stability

THE FACT that the U.S. and Soviet strategic organizations were committed to the dissemination of launch orders in response to evidence of an attack in progress made crisis interaction turn on the process of warning and imposed severe requirements on that process.[1] Several feats of intelligence had to be accomplished without any major error and without the benefit of accumulating experience. The spaceborne infra-red and ground radar sensors that constituted the tactical warning network had to be sensitive enough to detect signs of transiting weapons, yet discriminating enough to screen out spurious signals that only mimicked an attack. Tactical information had to be distilled from the raw sensor data and evaluated at processing centers according to unassailable rules of evidence. Decisionmakers had to assimilate the results of this interpretation without introducing their own errors of judgment. The entire process had to operate in no more than about twenty minutes.

For practical reasons these were daunting feats of questionable feasibility, as discussed throughout the earlier chapters. To appreciate the problems posed and explore them in a rigorously systematic fashion, it is useful to consider a simple model. The model removes all the emotional turbulence that would attend the event and reduces the warning and decision process to realistic rational calculations. That perspective produces difficulty enough without a consideration of what extreme fear and intense recrimination might add.

Description of the Model

In this simple model the warning system operates as a process of inference that uses the information derived from tactical warning sensors to make an overall judgment of the probability that an attack is occurring. The process recognizes the traditional types of statistical error, type I and type II. Type I error is the rate at which the warning sensors fail to detect the actual launch or transit of enemy delivery vehicles. Such sensor blindness threatens positive control. Type II error is the rate at which sensors produce false alarms, which threaten negative control.

The model assigns some probability to each of these errors, and with these taken into account changes the overall assessment in reaction to warning sensor outputs according to logical rules.[2] Sensor output is sampled at periodic intervals that determine the cycle of judgments for the warning process as a whole. Before they disseminate authorization for retaliation the command and control systems are assumed to require a very high (say, greater than 99 percent) probability of attack calculated by this process.

The main effect of this simple model is to shift analytic perspective from outside the warning process (the system designer's perspective) to inside it (the operator's perspective). The discussion of the warning process to date has been predominantly from the designer's perspective. Designers have been instructed, of course, to develop tactical warning systems with extremely low rates of type I and type II error. Once rapid reaction postures became the linchpin of the nuclear postures, ensuring the virtual immunity of the sensor systems to these errors became critical. And as best as can be judged from the public record, the designers have succeeded. The warning process never seems to have approached any point of catastrophe in which strategic operations might have been dictated by a false inference.

To a degree rarely appreciated, however, or at least rarely mentioned, the designer's perspective and the assurances that emanated from it were a result of peacetime experience. Since the advent of modern tactical warning systems and the configuration of the postures for prompt launch, neither the U.S. nor the Soviet strategic organization ever seriously began the process of preparing for an immediate attack on the other. Warning systems had the opportunity to test their immunity to type II errors only in the context of an overriding presumption that no attack was imminent. A serious crisis in which one or both of the main strategic organizations were undertaking the final preparations for attack would have triggered alert procedures that significantly altered normal operational patterns and disrupted the peacetime inferences within the opposing warning systems. That would probably have changed the real error rates of the system and would even more likely have changed the perceived error rates. It would also have changed the underlying presumption on which the overall assessment heavily depended. To explore this uncharted territory, it is useful to adopt the operator's perspective.

Operators—notably, political decisionmakers and military commanders—who carry the burden of controlling strategic forces inevitably depend on their presumptions. Unlike warning system designers, operators must consider all the practicalities that intervene, and they cannot mechanically tie their actions to any sensor system, however highly touted it might be. They are aware of the inevitable errors that human operators introduce into even the most "flawless" physical systems, and experience has told them no physical system really operates flawlessly. What they think of any sensor report is inevitably and appropriately weighed by the background information they bring to it that attunes them to the inherent possibilities of war and the potential adversary's intentions. Whereas the system designer is charged with making sure both types of error occur rarely and have a negligible effect, the operator must consider these errors practical possibilities that have extreme significance should they occur. To the operator a sensor alarm does not automatically mean an attack is in fact in progress, and the absence of such an alarm does not automatically prove it is not. An integrating judgment is necessary, and prior evidence must be brought to bear on the situation.[3]

The application of logic provides an account of how the required judgment from within a warning system might be made in a disciplined, responsible manner. The process begins with an initial estimate of the probability of attack.[4] This baseline estimate is a parameter in the model; its value, or setting, varies according to the operator's perception of threat. The initial subjective expectation of attack depends on the mindset of the operator and the outputs of the strategic warning system. In the model, low settings represent low expectations of attack, as might be usual in peacetime. Higher settings would be considered a response to strategic warning indicators during a crisis. However, the settings used in the model simply illustrate the importance of initial subjective expectations.

This initial expectation is then exposed to confirmatory or contradictory warning reports and is revised using a logical rule that takes into consideration the assumed type I and type II error rates of the warning system.[5] Successive readings over time thus produce a stream of sequentially revised calculations of the expectation of enemy attack. Positive warning reports strengthen the decisionmaker's belief that an attack is occurring; negative warning reports (or the absence of positive reports indicating attack) weaken it. The magnitude of the effect of the reports on the decisionmaker's belief of course depends on his confidence in the warning system, which ideally should correspond to the system's inherent type I and type II error rates.

All these calculated expectations of attack are strictly subjective; they exist in the minds of individuals. Data supplied by warning sensors do not objectively validate the probabilities but merely enable existing opinion to be revised logically by the successive application of rules of inference. The rules permit decisionmakers to assimilate evidence acquired by space- and ground-based surveillance in a manner that ensures coherence and consistency in the evolution of expectations.

There is an important sense in which the mental probabilities can be considered objective, however. As more sensor data become available over time, the probabilities in the minds of individuals will converge, even though they began with disparate probabilities. The weight of initial opinion declines and eventually dissipates completely as it is combined with the accumulating data outputs of the tactical warning network.[6]

The inductive reasoning performed by the model is of course not necessarily the way real-world operators would have analyzed the warning output of tactical sensors. Since it assumes an idealized system that functioned as though ruled strictly by logical reasoning, the model projects the maximum performance the system could have attained. The judgments of operators who inhabited the actual system undoubtedly would have fallen short of such logical perfection. Psychological studies of human perception and information processing raise strong doubt that an operator's expectation of attack would have undergone a strictly logical revision on the basis of incoming tactical warning information.

This literature portrays the expectations or preexisting beliefs of individuals as often rigid and sometimes virtually impervious to change. Decisionmakers tend to mold new information to fit their preconceptions instead of modifying those preconceptions to accommodate new data. Psychological analysis of decisions made in foreign relations show that cognitive consistency rather than rational-analytic logic operates on new information. The result is that preestablished beliefs resist alteration when exposed to information that does not conform to those beliefs.[7] For example, a deep suspicion that an adversary is bent on aggression ossifies over time into a stereotype etched into the psyche that tends to deflect rather than assimilate contrary evidence. Similarly, a strong faith in the military restraint of an adversary makes a decisionmaker discount the accumulating signs of hostile intent. In either case rigid preconceptions distort reality and court disaster of one form or another. The specific implication for warning system operation is that the output of tactical sensors may be ignored or distorted. In theory, the illogical assimilation of new information to preexisting beliefs would be normal.

Although the model here also shows that the interpretation of fresh intelligence can be excessively influenced by the prior expectation of war, the political science literature jumps too quickly to the conclusion that foreign policy decisions have commonly been the result of closed-mindedness. Its central argument that cognitive consistency inhibits the logical absorption of new information stems from a misunderstanding of the logic of inductive reasoning. It neglects the crucial effects of the accuracy of the information on the decisionmakers' assimilation of it. Many of the 'illogical' decisions in international politics cited to support the argument seem logical if only decisionmakers were credited with having made plausible assumptions about the rate of type I and type II errors in the intelligence they received. A valid test of a decision's soundness must take into account the error rates of the intelligence system that produces the new information. The prevailing theories of cognitive bias rarely consider such rates.[8]

The model used here measures the relative contributions of initial expectations and the two varieties of error rates to the iterative estimation of attack probabilities. The factors are logically connected according to a powerful general theorem known as the rule of Bayes. Bayesian analysis is a rigorous treatment of cognitive consistency that often draws counterintuitive conclusions from the data inputs. Patterns of thought that may seem intuitively illogical often prove to be perfectly logical (though not necessarily objectively accurate) upon closer scrutiny using the model. Although it is not my purpose to establish the models utility in empirical assessment, Bayesian logic may help explain, indeed justify, some of the foreign policy decisions classified as illogical by other theories.

The warning process nonetheless posed a threat of inadvertent war even when operating with logical infallibility. The root cause of this danger was the requirement of the rapid reaction posture to make a launch decision before sufficient tactical information became available.

Reassuring Illustrations

For the sake of illustration, assume a tactical warning system has a constant error rate of 5 percent for each type of error. Suppose the initial warning from an early-warning satellite indicates an attack is being launched. The alarm is very credible from a non-Bayesian perspective that ignores context, particularly the subjective state of the command and control system, and focuses exclusively on design specifications of the tactical warning system. It is credible because the system is unlikely (only a 5 percent chance) to sound an alarm when an attack is not occurring. Suppose the system uses ground radar to take a second look at the environment, and radar confirms the earlier satellite report. According to designer logic, an attack is definitely under way because the tactical warning system is extremely unlikely to sound two false alarms in a row. The likelihood of that happening is 5 percent × 5 percent, or one-fourth of 1 percent, or 0.0025. This unimpeachable calculation suggests that two positive readings would warrant a high-confidence assessment by NORAD (North American Aerospace Defense Command) and would strongly justify the dissemination of authorization to retaliate.

But a reasonable commander would take a broader view of the situation and would not rely on warning reports to the exclusion of prior information or opinion. The commander combines the reports with prior expectations of attack to produce his revised expectation.[9] The same warning reports from the identical system can lead this person to a different, even opposite, conclusion.

Table 7-1 illustrates this point. The first column displays a range of degrees of belief in the imminent prospect of enemy attack that a command system might have before receiving attack information. The columns to the right of it show how these initial expectations would be altered according to Bayes's formula after the command system receives one or more positive reports of attack from the tactical warning system, knowing the inherent error rate of the system (assumed to be a constant error rate of 5 percent for type I and type II errors). As the table clearly

Table 7-1. *Initial and Revised Expectations of Attack (Given Attack Warning) Assuming a Warning System with 5 Percent Types I and II Error Rates*

Initial estimate[a]	Revised estimate given attack warning					
	Number of positive warning reports:					
	1	2	3	4	5	6
0.0001	0.002	0.035	0.407	0.929	0.996	1.000
0.001	0.019	0.265	0.873	0.992	1.000	
0.01	0.161	0.785	0.986	0.999	1.000	
0.05	0.500	0.950	0.999	1.000		
0.10	0.679	0.976	0.999	1.000		
0.20	0.826	0.989	0.999	1.000		
0.30	0.891	0.994	1.000			
0.40	0.927	0.996	1.000			
0.50	0.950	0.997	1.000			
0.60	0.966	0.998	1.000			
0.70	0.978	0.999	1.000			
0.80	0.987	0.999	1.000			
0.90	0.994	1.000				
0.95	0.997	1.000				
0.99	0.999	1.000				
0.999	1.000					
0.9999	1.000					

a. Degree of belief in the hypothesis "an attack is under way."

suggests, the effect of tactical warning information depends on the expectations of the commanders receiving it.

Suppose the initial subjective expectation of attack was 0.001, a very low prior probability consistent with normal peacetime tensions. After receiving the first attack warning from the sensor network, a rationally calculating commander upon applying Bayes's rule of inductive inference would revise his personal subjective probability from 0.001 to 0.019. Although the commander's degree of belief in the proposition that an attack is under way would increase nearly twentyfold, the revised probability remains very low in absolute terms. After taking a second reading of the warning system that confirms the earlier positive indication of attack, the commander would undergo another change of opinion, revising his probability from 0.019 to 0.265. He would thus remain highly skeptical that an attack was under way in spite of two back-to-back reports of attack. His implicit subjective estimate that both alarms are false is about 73 percent, 1.000 minus 0.265. This calculation stands in stark contrast to the earlier non-Bayesian calculation that yielded a probability of only one-fourth of 1 percent. The Bayesian calculation, unlike the non-Bayesian estimate, would strongly argue against a decision to launch. Additional evidence of enemy attack is necessary to tip the scales in favor of the launch. To be precise, a third positive alarm would raise the probability to 0.873, and a fourth would push it to 0.992, which crosses the presumed threshold for ordering retaliation.

The Feasibility of Quick Launch and the Danger of False Alarms

In the illustration just discussed, the feasibility of launch on warning is questionable, because four cycles of judgment are needed to establish a strong belief that an attack is under way. With dual-sensor (satellite infrared and ground radar) technology, ballistic missiles with short flight times over intercontinental range allow for at most two cycles. Under the assumptions of this illustration, NORAD could not have reached high confidence that North America was under enemy missile attack before the incoming missiles arrived and exploded. The assessment rules adopted by NORAD in the 1980s (as discussed in chapter 6) to facilitate reaching high confidence on the basis of dual-sensor reports under conditions of surprise attack were imprudent in Bayesian terms. In bolt-out-of-the-blue scenarios, NORAD should have had to wait for nuclear detonations.

Launch on warning is feasible in crisis circumstances, however, when the initial expectation of attack is stronger and the necessary cycles of judgment are therefore fewer. Bayesian commanders whose initial expectations of attack exceed 20 percent will approach the certainty ($p >$ 0.990) that presumably would be demanded to trigger retaliation after two cycles of judgment. As table 7-1 shows, two attack alarms in succession, which correspond to the dual-detection technology of missile warning systems, are sufficient data to infer that the enemy has indeed launched an attack. Lower in the columns the table shows, moreover, that if the commander enters the sequence of warning system readings with a very high expectation of attack ($p > 0.840$), a solitary alarm will drive it over the threshold ($p > 0.990$) in a single cycle of judgment. The table thus confirms the feasibility of launch on warning in situations in which the command and control system is already apprehensive about an enemy attack when the attack alarm goes off. These are of course crisis situations, not normal peacetime conditions. NORAD's assessment rules for crisis circumstances, as modified in the 1980s to allow high confidence to arise from a combination of strategic warning and one or two tactical sensor reports, ensured NORAD's support for launch on warning.

Initial apprehension is a double-edged sword, however. While it renders launch on warning a feasible and rational response to positive indications of attack, it also renders the command and control system more susceptible to the effects of false positive indications of attack. In the last-mentioned illustration, a solitary alarm sends an apprehensive commander over the edge in a single cycle; a prior expectation of 0.84 goes to 0.99 upon receipt of one report. The commander's personal subjective estimate that the alarm is false is only 1 percent (1.000 minus 0.990), yet according to design specifications the false alarm error rate is five times higher because the type II (falsely detected attack) error rate is assumed to be 5 percent. An anxious command and control system is thus prone to overreaction to preliminary indications of attack. It should wait for the second report, since the indications are likely (95 percent) to be negative if no attack is actually occurring, in which case the commander's subjective expectation will revert back to 0.84 and his impulse to disseminate authorization to retaliate will be checked. NORAD's rules allowing high confidence to be based on a single tactical sensor in the context of positive strategic indicators thus created a danger of launching on false warning.

Table 7-2 illustrates the effects of negative warning reports on prior subjective expectations. The first column shows a range of degrees of belief in the prospect of enemy attack that a command and control system might have before receiving attack information. The columns to the right of it show how these initial expectations would be altered according to Bayes's formula after the command and control system receives one or more negative reports of attack from the tactical warning system, knowing the inherent error rate of the system (assumed to be a constant error rate of 5 percent for type I and type II errors).

The table clearly suggests that the effect of warning system information depends on the expectations of the commanders receiving it and that Bayesian commanders whose initial expectations of attack are very high will remain very apprehensive after one cycle of judgment with negative indication of attack; for instance, 0.990 goes to 0.839. After two cycles of judgment, each with negative indication of attack, their fears will abate considerably; for instance, 0.990 goes to 0.215 after two iterations. Apprehension thus lasts for a while when commanders enter the sequence of warning system readings with very high subjective expectations of attack. Negative reports do not totally discredit their belief that an attack

Table 7-2. *Initial and Revised Expectations of Attack (Given No Attack Warning) Assuming a Warning System with 5 Percent Types I and II Error Rates*

Initial estimate[a]	Revised estimate given no attack warning					
	Number of negative warning reports:					
	1	2	3	4	5	6
0.0001	0.000					
0.001	0.000					
0.01	0.001	0.000				
0.05	0.003	0.000				
0.10	0.006	0.000				
0.20	0.013	0.001	0.000			
0.30	0.022	0.001	0.000			
0.40	0.034	0.002	0.000			
0.50	0.050	0.003	0.000			
0.60	0.073	0.004	0.000			
0.70	0.109	0.006	0.000			
0.80	0.174	0.011	0.001	0.000		
0.90	0.320	0.024	0.001	0.000		
0.95	0.500	0.050	0.003	0.000		
0.99	0.839	0.215	0.014	0.001		
0.999	0.981	0.735	0.127	0.008	0.000	
0.9999	0.998	0.965	0.593	0.071	0.004	0.000

a. Degree of belief in the hypothesis "an attack is under way."

is under way, even though the assumed type I (undetected attack) error rate is only 5 percent. The design specifications of the tactical warning system suggest there is a 5 percent chance that the system's initial report will provide negative attack indications when an attack is actually occurring, and a 0.25 percent chance that it will file two such erroneous reports in a row. But a Bayesian commander implicitly estimates the chances at 84 percent and 22 percent, respectively, if that person entered the sequence of readings with an initial expectation of attack of 99 percent.

The overall performance reflected in tables 7-1 and 7-2 suggests that a warning system with a constant error rate of 5 percent for type I and type II errors would have been serviceable, though just barely, for supporting the rapid reaction or launch-on-warning postures of the U.S. and Soviet strategic establishments. Dual-sensor technology allowed for two cycles of judgment before launch on warning was authorized, which was both necessary and sufficient to limit the scope for gross misjudgment in the decision process within the most plausible range of circumstances. A warning system so configured would have adequately served the basic aims of the command and control system: positive and negative control. NORAD, alas, was configured in such a way that negative control was compromised.

Regarding positive control, launch on warning was a feasible option in the event of enemy attack except in the implausible circumstance of a surprise attack in peacetime, when commanders least expected an attack and hence required more than two readings from the tactical warning system to become convinced. Two readings were sufficient for the more plausible circumstances of a superpower crisis, when commanders would have become attuned to the possibility of war and grown more apprehensive as the situation deteriorated. As table 7-1 indicates, an initial subjective expectation of 20 percent would be revised to almost 99 percent (0.989 to be precise) after two cycles of judgment, each with positive indication of attack. It seems reasonable to suppose that commanders' initial expectations in the midst of an intense confrontation would have approached or surpassed the 20 percent level.[10]

Regarding negative control, two cycles of judgment that each had negative attack indications would, as table 7-2 shows, have produced a sharp downward moderation of apprehension if commanders had entered the sequence of warning readings with a very high expectation of attack. Dual-sensor technology thus helped ensure that the preconceptions of commanders were exposed to sufficient tactical warning evidence to correct their biases. A strong predisposition to authorize attack in anticipation of imminent enemy attack would have slackened enormously after two successive negative reports had been received from the warning system. Since the command and control system, under many circumstances of attack, could have afforded to wait for two such assessments before committing to its reaction, the scope for miscalculation was greatly reduced in principle. The dangers associated with launch on warning were only partially mitigated in practice, however, because NORAD did not require two sensor reports in all circumstances.

A secondary drawback of the warning system outlined here is that one cannot safely assume that two successive alarms would have sounded in the event of attack or that two successive negative reports would have been issued in the event of no attack. There was a small chance that the tactical warning system would have filed a different combination of reports, given its 5 percent rate of type I and type II errors. The probability that it would have given a positive reading twice in a row in the event of attack was 95 percent × 95 percent, or approximately 90 percent. In consequence, there was a 10 percent chance that it would fail to provide the two successive positive attack indications necessary to facilitate launch on warning under the range of prior expectations that seem most plausible under crisis circumstances. Similarly, the probability that the system would have given a negative reading twice in a row in the event of no attack was also 95 percent × 95 percent, or 90 percent. In consequence, there was a significant chance (10 percent) that a very high expectation of attack would not have declined as steeply as the benign state of nature warranted.

The Effects of Reduced Tactical Error Rates on Warning Performance

These apparent liabilities would have been smaller if, as many system designers believed, the deployed warning system was less error prone than this analysis assumes. Typical estimates of the inherent error rates of the U.S. tactical warning network were so minuscule as to be negligible. The type II (false alarm) rate, in particular, was generally deemed to be almost nonexistent. The MITRE Corporation, for example, which played an important role in designing the U.S. tactical warning system, noted in a memorandum that a 5 percent false alarm rate corresponded to 5 false alarms per 8-hour duty shift in the operational system, based on an average false alarm duration of 300 seconds. In the words of the authors of the memorandum, "In the fairy tale, the little boy who called 'wolf' too often got eaten; here his sensor system would never have been bought in the first place."[11] The authors assumed the system produced only ten false alarms a year, each with a duration of 300 seconds, which corresponded to a type II error rate of about 0.0001. They did not choose to contest the assumption of a type I (undetected attack) error rate of 5 percent. This assumption is defensible for two reasons: the blindness of some U.S. sensors to missiles launched from certain areas of the Arctic Ocean, and the frequent downtime experienced by operational sensors because of equipment malfunction, routine maintenance, and periodic modernization efforts.

For the sake of illustration let us accept the MITRE assumptions to show the effect of warning system information on the expectations of commanders. Let us assume a tactical warning system with a constant error rate of 5 percent for type I (undetected attack) and 0.01 percent (0.0001) for type II (falsely detected attack) errors. Column 1 of table 7-3 shows a range of prior subjective estimates, and the columns to the

Table 7-3. *Initial and Revised Expectations of Attack (Given Attack Warning) Assuming a Warning System with 5 Percent Type I and 0.01 Percent Type II Error Rates*

	Revised estimate given attack warning	
	Number of positive warning reports:	
Initial estimate[a]	1	2
0.0001	0.487	1.000
0.001	0.905	1.000
0.01	0.990	1.000
0.05	0.998	1.000
0.10	0.997	1.000
0.20	1.000	
0.30	1.000	
0.40	1.000	
0.50	1.000	
0.60	1.000	
0.70	1.000	
0.80	1.000	
0.90	1.000	
0.95	1.000	
0.99	1.000	
0.999	1.000	

a. Degree of belief in the hypothesis "an attack is under way."

right show the revised estimates after one or more readings of the warning system are taken. The table clearly suggests that the effects of tactical warning on commanders' expectations are dramatic. Initial beliefs carry little weight in the calculation. Tactical warning evidence carries overwhelming weight, swamping the influence of prior subjective opinion on subsequent belief in a single cycle of judgment.

These calculations imply that rapid reaction, even when triggered solely by tactical sensors, is feasible and safe under all conditions, including surprise attack in peacetime. Even when the initial expectation of attack is extremely low, positive indication of attack would produce a sharp upward adjustment in a single cycle of judgment. Still, there is a small chance (5 percent) that the tactical warning system would not detect an attack on the first scan. Furthermore, if command and control system procedures require two successive alarms before authorizing retaliation, as prudence would dictate, then the type I (undetected attack) error rate has two opportunities to manifest itself. The probability that the warning system would give a positive reading twice in a row in the event of attack is 95 percent × 95 percent, or approximately 90 percent. In consequence,

Table 7-4. *Initial and Revised Expectations of Attack (Given No Attack Warning) Assuming a Warning System with 5 Percent Type I and 0.01 Percent Type II Error Rates*

Initial estimate[a]	Revised estimate given no attack warning				
	Number of negative warning reports:				
	1	2	3	4	5
0.001	0.000				
0.01	0.000				
0.10	0.001	0.000			
0.20	0.012	0.001	0.000		
0.30	0.021	0.001	0.000		
0.40	0.032	0.002	0.000		
0.50	0.048	0.002	0.000		
0.60	0.070	0.004	0.000		
0.70	0.104	0.006	0.000		
0.80	0.167	0.010	0.000		
0.90	0.310	0.022	0.001	0.000	
0.99	0.832	0.198	0.012	0.001	0.000
0.999	0.980	0.714	0.111	0.006	0.000

a. Degree of belief in the hypothesis "an attack is under way."

there is a small but significant chance (10 percent) that it would fail to provide the two successive positive alarms.

On the other hand, if the criterion for authorizing launch is simply that virtual certitude ($p > 0.99$) exists after two readings of the tactical warning system are taken, then both readings need not be positive in most circumstances. It can be determined from tables 7-3 and 7-4 that one positive reading would suffice when commanders enter the sequence with an expectation of 20 percent or higher, as well they might in crisis circumstances. If either the first or second report provides positive indication of attack, the commander's subsequent probability would exceed 99 percent despite exposure to a negative report during one of the cycles of judgment. A solitary negative report, whether it preceded or followed a solitary positive alarm, would not drive his expectation below the triggering threshold. High confidence would result unless both reports are negative. The probability of this happening under conditions of actual attack is remote (5 percent × 5 percent, or 0.25 percent). In light of these calculations, it all the more understandable that NORAD modified its procedures in the 1980s so that attack indications from a single sensor produced high confidence in the context of a nuclear crisis.

Not only do the MITRE assumptions inspire confidence in the feasibility of a rapid reaction posture under a wider range of circumstances, but they also allay concern about the susceptibility of the command and control system to miscalculation stemming from false alarms. The type II (falsely detected attack) error rate is extremely small (0.0001). Although an apprehensive commander with an initial expectation of 20 percent or higher would be driven above the triggering threshold by a single false alarm received during either cycle of judgment, the chances of this happening are remote. The probability that the warning system would not issue a false alarm on either scan is 99.99 percent × 99.99 percent, or 99.98 percent. Thus the probability that it would mistakenly issue the fateful report is only 0.02 percent (0.0002).

Overall Evaluation of Warning System Performance during the Cold War

These calculations help explain the prevailing confidence during the cold war in the stability of an international security arrangement based on opposing strategic forces operationally committed to rapid reaction in response to direct evidence of immediate attack. The historical record seems to reinforce this theoretical confidence in the viability and safety of operational practices that at first blush strike many observers as too tenuous to underwrite deterrence and too catalytic to avoid fatal mistakes. Although a small theoretical chance existed that launch on warning could not have been exercised successfully in a real attack, both military establishments prudently credited the adversary with the capability and expressed cautious optimism about their own capability. They could have also cited the historical record to contest the view that launch on warning put the nuclear postures on a dangerous hair trigger. Dual-sensor technology arguably reduced the theoretical odds of accidental war to negligible proportions. The fact that false alarms produced by the operational warning systems had never even resulted in the notification of the top leaders of either side, let alone induced nuclear release deliberations, provides empirical substantiation of the theoretical claim.[12]

Reasons for Doubt

Closer investigation of the difficulty of the tactical warning problem, however, using the Bayesian model as the main tool of analysis, reveals serious grounds for doubting the prevailing confidence in the viability and safety of the operational stances during the cold war, especially the stances adopted during a nuclear crisis. Doubts begin with the elementary observation that the frequency of false alarms is a relative measure that varies with the amount of time one allows for them to appear. The incidence of false alarms thus rises as the duration of a crisis increases. A type II error rate of 0.0001 per 300-second interval (the nominal duration of a warning report period), for instance, means that a false alarm rarely occurs in any given 5-minute period but that one will occur with statistical regularity every 35 days. A false alarm is thus virtually bound to arise during a month-long crisis. A crisis that lasted for 1 week would stand a 20 percent chance of suffering a warning failure of the second type.

Another elementary observation is that the nuclear decision process involved a group of people. A launch-on-warning decision would not have stemmed from the inductive inference of any single person. The decision would have been collective, and it presupposed a consensus among key military and civilian actors on whether an enemy attack had been launched.

This need for intersubjective agreement presented a special difficulty. Because the actors occupied different positions within the warning network and command and control system, they were unlikely to hold uniform subjective expectations of attack before receiving tactical warning information; moreover, their disparate initial beliefs were exposed to different levels of tactical information at different times and rates.

To illustrate the difficulties of synchronizing a process of collective judgment, consider the relationship between NORAD and the president. The former entered the sequence of tactical warning readings with initial expectations of attack that at times surely differed from those of the president, given their dissimilar perceptual filters and accesses to strategic warning, political intelligence, and special sources of assessment.

The differences were presumably small in peacetime. A bolt-from-the-blue attack would have surprised everyone, a psychological reaction implying that a very low expectation of attack permeated the command and control system. Subjective expectations were likely to diverge in crisis circumstances, however. It is characteristic of crises that ambiguity surrounds the intentions of an adversary and that cleavages of perception develop within the command and control system. The adversary's behavior supports a range of alternative explanations and threat estimates. This diversity gives rise to disparate opinions within a command and control system on the likelihood that the crisis will lead to enemy attack. Achieving internal consensus to mesh the beliefs at the apex of government with the projections of the military establishment is one of the chief dramas of crisis management. Mutually consistent expectations among the many political and military actors in the command and control system may prove difficult to establish and maintain during a crisis.[13]

Decentralized processing of tactical information further hampers the convergence of collective judgment. The NORAD organization, for example, would have received tactical warning information and begun processing the data before the president was even notified. It could have completed two cycles of judgment before the national level received its initial notification. Although NORAD might have converged on a clear judgment after multiple exposures to tactical information, national commanders might have treated NORAD's summary interpretation as a single positive alarm to be processed in a single cycle of judgment. Convergence on clear judgment was thus likely to proceed more slowly at the national level. Several parallel processes of Bayesian adjustment, each converging on independent judgments at a different pace, would have to have been reconciled in a very short time. Consensus might have emerged but not as readily as it would have if the various actors had shared the same initial expectations and simultaneously processed the identical tactical warning information.

Although Bayesian calculations will eventually overcome disparate beliefs and converge in clear consensual judgment, given sufficient cycles of judgment and reasonably accurate tactical sensors, the fact that launch on warning restricts the number of judgment cycles to two at most means that initial subjective expectations often strongly determine judgment at the point of its forced truncation. The problem of intersubjective agreement aside, it is evident that accurate prior estimates facilitate convergence within the small number of cycles that rapid reaction times allow.

Strategic Ambiguity and Preemptive Launch on Warning

But it is also evident that the initial predictions of commanders rest on very imprecise indicators of enemy intent. Strategic warning is a notoriously dubious source of knowledge about the future. This then is another characteristic of a crisis. During a cold war crisis subjective expectations of attack would have undergone significant change under the influence of low-grade strategic warning. It is also troubling that the exposure of these suspect expectations to clarifying tactical warning evidence was too limited under the time constraints of the cold war postures to wash out their biasing effect on subsequent opinion.

The truncation of Bayesian learning after only one or two cycles of judgment in effect transferred a large part of the burden of proof from tactical to strategic warning systems. Although tactical warning would have offered or withheld the increment of certainty needed to carry commanders across the threshold for authorizing retaliation, initial belief and the marginal certainty derived from tactical information were additive. Both were often responsible for driving certainty to the release flashpoint. In this sense the accuracy of initial belief is crucial to the outcome. The overall quality of Bayesian inference in these cases cannot be better than the quality of one of its essential constituent parts, initial belief. It constitutes the weakest link in the Bayesian train of logic because of its relative unreliability and because of the short learning time allowed by launch on warning.[14]

A hypothetical case in point is a situation in which an initial expectation of 50 percent jumps to 99 percent after positive attack indications are received from the tactical warning system. If the two tactical alarms are false (from table 7-5, the risk of this happening is 1 percent), then the inaccurate initial expectation is no less responsible than the tactical warning system for producing the mistaken conclusion that an enemy attack is under way. Had the prior belief been less apprehensive (more accurate in its correspondence with the true state of nature), the certainty that induces nuclear response would not have been reached. For instance, a prior expectation of 1 percent goes to 45 percent after two positive indications are received in succession. This comparison shows that initial expectation based on strategic warning can be a decisive factor.

Rapid reaction or literal launch on warning in such cases is no less susceptible to the effects of strategic misjudgment than preemption is. Contrary to prevalent opinion, launch on warning, though triggered by tactical indications, does not avoid the problem of unreliable strategic warning usually associated with preemption. The option cannot divorce itself from this problem unless the error rates of the tactical warning system are almost nil, in which case initial expectations carry negligible weight in Bayesian computations over one or two cycles of judgment. The problem was further compounded in the 1980s, when NORAD changed its procedures (discussed in chapter 6) to allow strategic warning indicators to be substituted for tactical warning information in reaching a "high" level of confidence that an enemy missile attack is under way.

Advertised versus True Error Rates

The standard assumption that error rates would be constant and low for all situations is dubious. That error rates attributed to operational tactical warning systems reflect performance in peacetime operations raises the question whether the rates in a crisis might be substantially worse. No one knows the answer. The systems have never been tested in the crucible of a real attack situation.

There are grounds nonetheless for believing that one of the effects of a superpower crisis might well have been a degradation of both type I and type II error rates. The potential rate of unusual observations would have increased as strategic systems under surveillance began to change their peacetime routines. The adversary's dispersal of strategic forces over wider geographic areas in increasing variety and numbers—for example, the alerting of cruise missiles on aircraft and submarines—would have represented an unusual deployment pattern that tactical warning networks had never before encountered. The normal rate of observational error might well have increased as the scale and the scope of observations expanded, and the interpretive logic used would have been forced to depart from accustomed routine. The distinct possibility also existed that an enemy's opening salvo might have been timed to exploit the sensor degradation that occurred naturally at certain times of the day. Thus the error rates assumed in tables 7-1 and 7-2 (5 percent rates of type I and type II error) and tables 7-5 through 7-8 (10 or 25 percent rate of type I, and 10 or 25 percent rate of type II error), while undoubtedly too high for peacetime operations, might well have been more realistic for crisis circumstances. It is in any case difficult to prove the contrary.

In fact, one distinguishing feature of a crisis is its murkiness. By definition, the type I and type II error rates of the intelligence and warning systems rapidly degrade. A crisis not only ushers in the proverbial fog of crisis symptomatic of error-prone strategic warning but also ushers in a fog of battle arising from an analogous deterioration of tactical warning. Again a simple explanation underlies this effect. Warning systems that have been calibrated for peacetime surveillance and seldom exercised in crisis circumstances have not evolved, through trial and error, a proved effective repertory of observational routines to deal with those unusual circumstances.

Deeper Reflections

With these doubts in mind it is useful to develop a more rigorous conception of the discontinuous deterioration of intelligence that plagues the transition from peacetime to crisis environments. In stable peacetime environments an intelligence system learns through trial and error to monitor and interpret the adversary's strategic disposition. The system experiments with alternative configurations of technologies and procedures, focusing on selected critical variables of the adversary's operations, and gradually achieves partial successes in keeping the variables within proper limits. It then retains the successful trial designs while improving what is still unsatisfactory. The stable environment permits use to be made of partial adaptation, and further experimentation produces yet more successes, driving down the error rates for the environment to which the warning network is adapting, namely a peacetime environment.

To illustrate the process, suppose that the peacetime operation of a single sensor system involves four independent components: sensor, communications, computer analysis, and human operators, each with a type II error rate of 10 percent for every 300-second report period. Through trial and error the system evolves a repertory of responses to positive attack indications that ensures that an attack alarm will never be sounded unless all four components are mutually consistent and self-confirmatory. Cross-checking and other diagnostic procedures ensure that no positive attack report is issued if the readings from any of the four components are negative during a report interval. Furthermore, at the end of a given 300-second report period all four components are reset for the next cycle of readings, so that no previous attack indications, positive or negative, spill over into subsequent periods. In this case of continuous recycling, the probability of a systemic type II error—defined as a simultaneous type II error in all four components in the same report period—is only 0.0001, which corresponds to one false alarm every 833.33 hours (about once every 35 days). This false alarm rate for a single sensor system (infrared or radar) is identical to the MITRE Corporation's assumption and is consistent with factual knowledge of peacetime performance.[15]

Suppose, however, that one of the effects of crisis is the lowering of the adaptive capacity of the warning system's repertory. Human fatigue, changes in surveillance configuration, an increase in the potential rate and scope of observation, the departure of interpretive logic from accustomed routine, and other unusual factors present a unique situation to which the command and control system has not adapted through the standard learning process. The result is a slower accumulation of trial successes and a stronger retention of trial errors. A system that proved nimble in its usual environment suddenly becomes clumsy in an unfamiliar situation.

The frequency and duration of both types of error increase and might even take a quantum jump. The incidence of systemic type II errors could be dramatically higher if component type II errors—for example, the misreading of warning output by human operators—were carried over from one report period to the next. A simple calculation shows that the temporary retention of component type II error could produce a systemic false alarm approximately every 50 minutes on average instead of every 35 days. In other words, the false alarm rate of the tactical warning system changes from 0.0001 per 5-minute report period to 0.1 per period, a degradation of 3 orders of magnitude.[16]

The error rates of the warning systems might deteriorate still more if the crisis erupts into war and the networks sustain damage before or during the release of strategic forces.

Effects of Dynamic Error Rates on Warning Interpretation

The prospect of sudden nonlinear degradation of warning performance caused by rapid environmental change has systematic implications for Bayesian inference and hence for the rapid reaction posture of current strategic forces. A nonlinear change in error rates either severely impedes Bayesian convergence on clear judgment or causes expectations to converge too rapidly, depending on whether the error rate change actually registers with the operators in the command system.

If there is a corresponding degradation of internal confidence in warning performance—for example, case 1, in which an increase in warning system error leads to a corresponding correction of the error rate assumptions used in the commanders' calculations—the result of error rate change is a dramatic diminution of the impact of tactical warning information on expectations of attack. Initial subjective expectations are

Table 7-5. *Initial and Revised Expectations of Attack (Given Attack Warning) Assuming a Warning System with 10 Percent Types I and II Error Rates*

Initial estimate[a]	Revised estimate given attack warning							
	Number of positive warning reports:							
	1	2	3	4	5	6	7	8
0.0001	0.001	0.008	0.068	0.396	0.855	0.982	0.998	1.000
0.001	0.009	0.075	0.422	0.868	0.983	0.998	1.000	
0.01	0.083	0.450	0.880	0.985	0.998	1.000		
0.05	0.321	0.810	0.975	0.997	1.000			
0.10	0.500	0.900	0.988	0.999	1.000			
0.20	0.692	0.953	0.995	0.999	1.000			
0.30	0.794	0.972	0.997	1.000				
0.40	0.857	0.982	0.998	1.000				
0.50	0.900	0.988	0.999	1.000				
0.60	0.931	0.992	0.999					
0.70	0.955	0.995	0.999					
0.80	0.973	0.997						
0.90	0.998	0.999						
0.95	0.994	0.999						
0.99	0.999	1.000						
0.999	1.000							
0.9999	1.000							

a. Degree of belief in the hypothesis "an attack is under way."

slower to change after exposure to this information. Successive readings of warning system output do not readily converge on a clear judgment.

If there is no corresponding degradation of confidence—for example, case 2, in which commanders continue to use the peacetime error rates in their calculations despite an actual degradation in warning system error rates—the effect is to accelerate convergence on a judgment that credits tactical warning information with more validity than it deserves. In this circumstance subjective expectations of attack are overdetermined by tactical information.

CASE 1

Tables 7-5 and 7-6 illustrate case 1, when the error rate assumptions used in commanders' calculations have been changed to 10 percent for types I and II errors. Tables 7-7 and 7-8 assume an even greater decline in confidence in warning performance, owing perhaps to damage suffered by the warning networks: the actual and assumed error rates are 25 percent. The format of the presentation is the same as in the previous tables.

Table 7-6. *Initial and Revised Expectations of Attack (Given No Attack Warning) Assuming a Warning System with 10 Percent Types I and II Error Rates*

Initial estimate[a]	Revised estimate given no attack warning						
	Number of negative warning reports:						
	1	2	3	4	5	6	7
0.0001	0.000						
0.001	0.000						
0.01	0.001	0.000					
0.05	0.006	0.001					
0.10	0.012	0.001					
0.20	0.027	0.003					
0.30	0.045	0.005	0.001				
0.40	0.069	0.008	0.001				
0.50	0.100	0.012	0.001				
0.60	0.143	0.018	0.002				
0.70	0.206	0.028	0.003				
0.80	0.308	0.047	0.005	0.001			
0.90	0.500	0.100	0.012	0.001			
0.95	0.679	0.190	0.025	0.003			
0.99	0.917	0.550	0.120	0.015	0.002		
0.999	0.991	0.925	0.578	0.132	0.017	0.002	
0.9999	0.999	0.992	0.932	0.604	0.145	0.018	0.002

a. Degree of belief in the hypothesis "an attack is under way."

These data demonstrate that reduced performance of the system (matched by reduced subjective confidence vested in the system) increases the number of cycles required for the Bayesian commander to adjust the initial expectation. Tables 7-5 and 7-7 show that many cycles of judgment, each having positive indication of attack, are necessary before judgment becomes clear enough to support the decision to retaliate or not. Since U.S. and Soviet strategic postures permitted only two readings before a decision had to be rendered, launch on warning was virtually infeasible in circumstances reflected in table 7-7 and feasible only in a narrow band of circumstances reflected in table 7-5 (when commanders enter the sequence of tactical warning readings with a high $[p > 0.590]$ initial expectation of attack). This limited feasibility is further reduced by the risk of the tactical warning system issuing a negative report in circumstances of actual attack. Given an assumed type I error rate of 10 percent, detecting an attack on each of two successive scans of the environment is not assured. The likelihood of this is in fact 81 percent (90 percent × 90 percent). For the warning system reflected in table

Table 7-7. *Initial and Revised Expectations of Attack (Given Attack Warning) Assuming a Warning System with 25 Percent Types I and II Error Rates*

| | Revised estimate given attack warning | | | | | | | | | | | | | | | |
| | Number of positive warning reports: | | | | | | | | | | | | | | | |
Initial estimate[a]	1	2	3	4	5	6	7	8	9	10	11	12	13	14	15	16
0.0001	0.000+	0.001	0.003	0.008	0.024	0.068	0.179	0.396	0.663	0.855	0.947	0.982	0.994	0.998	0.999	1.000
0.001	0.003	0.009	0.026	0.075	0.196	0.422	0.686	0.868	0.952	0.983	0.994	0.998	0.999			
0.01	0.029	0.083	0.214	0.450	0.711	0.880	0.957	0.985	0.995	0.998	0.999					
0.05	0.136	0.321	0.587	0.810	0.927	0.975	0.991	0.997	0.999	1.000						
0.10	0.250	0.500	0.750	0.900	0.964	0.988	0.996	0.999								
0.20	0.429	0.692	0.871	0.953	0.984	0.995	0.998	0.999								
0.30	0.563	0.794	0.920	0.972	0.990	0.997	0.999									
0.40	0.667	0.857	0.947	0.982	0.994	0.998	0.999									
0.50	0.750	0.900	0.964	0.988	0.996	0.998										
0.60	0.818	0.931	0.976	0.992	0.997	0.999										
0.70	0.875	0.955	0.984	0.995	0.998	0.999										
0.80	0.923	0.973	0.991	0.997	0.999											
0.90	0.964	0.988	0.996	0.999												
0.95	0.983	0.994	0.998	0.999												
0.99	0.997	0.999														
0.999	1.000															

a. Degree of belief in the hypothesis "an attack is under way."

7-7, which assumes a type I error rate of 25 percent, the likelihood of getting two positive attack indications in a row is only 56 percent (75 percent × 75 percent), though the point is moot, since two cycles of judgment that each have positive indications are insufficient to reach a conclusive judgment.

It is useful to note a significant difference between strategic delivery systems in the type of burden they imposed on warning systems during the cold war. Ballistic missiles with a 30-minute flight time over intercontinental range allowed for only two cycles of judgment, yet a mass attack by ballistic missiles would have given relatively unambiguous warning to satellite infrared sensors and thus produced fairly rapid convergence of judgment. For this reason a type II error under crisis conditions would have been very dangerous even though a single false alarm would not have driven attack expectations all the way across the triggering threshold for launch on warning. The error would have inadvertently brought commanders perilously close to the level of certainty presumably required to authorize retaliation. Table 7-5, for example, shows that an initial expectation of 40 percent would have jumped to 86 percent (0.857) on the basis of a single positive indication of attack, while the assumed type II error rate (10 percent) would have generated this indication by mistake once every 10 readings (once every 50 minutes).

In contrast, piloted aircraft and to a lesser extent cruise missiles gave more ambiguous warning information that was more difficult to interpret even if it was reliably received. As partial compensation, the relatively slow speeds of these systems allowed more decision time and thus more cycles of judgment than ballistic missiles did. But as suggested by tables 7-7 and 7-8, that allowance could have presented problems of a different sort. If stealthy aerodynamic threats in effect increased the error rate of the warning system—error rates of perhaps 25 percent compared with 10 percent for ballistic missiles, recognizing the less ambiguous warning associated with missiles—then the result was a sluggish convergence of judgment. This sluggishness was due not only to Bayesian logic, which revises judgment in smaller increments as the error rates increase, but also to the greater incidence of negative readings mixing in with positive readings to muddy the picture. (The effect of negative reports on prior expectations is shown in table 7-8 for a warning system with assumed error rates of 25 percent and in table 7-6 for error rates of 10 percent.) A sequence of positive and negative readings might have trapped the decision process in a cycle of estimates that remained in the mid-ranges

Table 7-8. Initial and Revised Expectations of Attack (Given No Attack Warning) Assuming a Warning System with 25 Percent Types I and II Error Rates

Initial estimate[a]	Revised estimate given no attack warning													
	Number of negative warning reports:													
	1	2	3	4	5	6	7	8	9	10	11	12	13	14
0.0001	0.000													
0.001	0.000													
0.01	0.003	0.001	0.000											
0.05	0.017	0.006	0.002	0.001	0.000									
0.10	0.036	0.012	0.004	0.001	0.000									
0.20	0.077	0.027	0.009	0.003	0.001	0.000								
0.30	0.125	0.045	0.016	0.005	0.002	0.001								
0.40	0.182	0.069	0.024	0.008	0.003	0.001								
0.50	0.250	0.100	0.036	0.012	0.004	0.001								
0.60	0.333	0.143	0.053	0.018	0.006	0.002	0.001							
0.70	0.438	0.206	0.080	0.028	0.010	0.003	0.001							
0.80	0.571	0.308	0.129	0.047	0.016	0.005	0.002	0.001						
0.90	0.750	0.500	0.250	0.100	0.036	0.012	0.004	0.001						
0.95	0.864	0.679	0.413	0.190	0.073	0.025	0.009	0.003	0.001					
0.99	0.971	0.917	0.786	0.550	0.289	0.120	0.043	0.015	0.005	0.002	0.001			
0.999	0.997	0.991	0.974	0.925	0.804	0.578	0.314	0.132	0.048	0.017	0.006	0.002	0.001	
0.9999	0.999	0.997	0.992	0.976	0.932	0.821	0.604	0.337	0.145	0.053	0.016	0.006	0.002	0.001

a. Degree of belief in the hypothesis "an attack is under way."

of subjective probability. The process would not have readily converged on any judgment clear enough to support a decision on retaliation.

At the same time, the process did not allow for a rapid downward adjustment of expectations when an attack was not under way. There were ample opportunities for false alarms to appear, given a type II error rate of 25 percent and substantial scope for repetitive false indications. Although the decision process would usually have become trapped in the mid-ranges of subjective probability, there was a significant risk of successive false alarms that drove expectations to dangerous levels, though still below the triggering threshold for launch on warning. Table 7-7 for example, shows that an initial expectation of 40 percent would jump to 67 percent (0.667) in one cycle with positive indication and to 86 percent (0.857) in two cycles that each have positive indications. Given the assumed type II error rate of 25 percent, the repetitive false positives that elevate expectations to 86 percent have a significant chance of appearing. This likelihood is 6 percent (25 percent × 25 percent). By comparison, recall that expectations rise from 40 percent to 86 percent on the basis of a single false positive when the assumed type II error rate is 10 percent (table 7-5).

The difficulty of Bayesian convergence is also exacerbated in an attack sequence that does not begin massively and that includes partial damage to sensors. At the onset of the attack an intact warning system might provide a strong indication of attack, particularly ballistic missile attack, but only weak, preliminary indications of its size and objective. With the onset of damage to sensors the system might be unable to confirm the initial strong indication, assess the character of the initial salvo, or detect follow-on raids by other forces.[17] These circumstances could initially produce the rapidly converging judgment characteristic of a good (low error rate) warning system, followed by the slowly converging or nonconverging process characteristic of a poorer (high error rate) system after the sensors are damaged. If the command and control system is not prepared to take damage to warning sensors as decisive evidence of a full-scale strategic attack, then its internal decision process would be in considerable difficulty. If it does react decisively on that evidence alone, it would make itself prone to type II errors. In striving to support launch on warning during the 1980s, NORAD opted to run the latter risk.[18]

CASE 2

If subjective confidence vested in the tactical warning system is not lowered, despite an actual degradation in the system's error rates, then

Figure 7-1. Initial and Revised Expectations of Attack Given Attack Warning

A. Initial Estimate = 0.01′

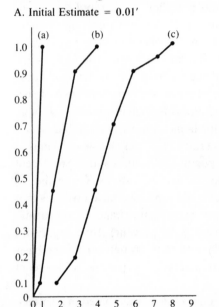

B. Initial Estimate = 0.20′

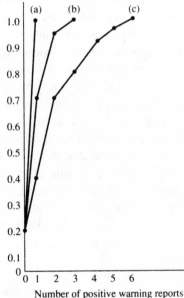

Number of positive warning reports

Degree of belief in the hypothesis "an attack is under way";
    (a) assuming a warning system with 5 percent type I and 0.01 percent type II error rates;
    (b) assuming a warning system with 10 percent types I and II error rates;
    (c) assuming a warning system with 25 percent types I and II error rates.

the expectations of attack are overdetermined by tactical information. Commanders reach conclusions faster than is warranted. The consequences of these excessive adjustments depend on whether an attack actually has been launched.

Figure 7-1 shows that this overdetermined process works to the advantage of a rapid reaction posture under conditions of actual enemy attack. The graph displays several curves, one of which (curve *a*) represents the changes in expectations caused by positive attack indications when the subjective confidence vested in the warning system corresponds to peacetime error rates rather than to the actual wartime rates (0.1 to 0.25). The other curves (*b* and *c*) represent the revision of expectations when subjective confidence vested in the system is reduced to the true level (alternatively 0.1 and 0.25). They clearly indicate that overrating the performance level of tactical warning systems (curve *a*) facilitates rapid convergence on the correct judgment in the circumstance of actual attack. The overrating fortuitously bolsters the feasibility of executing, for example, a classic launch-on-warning response, even when initial expectations of attack are low.

The effects of overrating the system are the opposite of fortuitous, however, if an attack is not under way. A single false positive alarm (whose actual probability would be 10 or 25 percent) catapults expectations of attack to near certitude, as curve *a* of figure 7-1 shows, instead of raising it to the lower levels displayed in curves *b* and *c*. Gross misinterpretation of tactical information thus results from vesting unwarranted confidence in the performance of the warning system. NORAD compounded this danger in the 1980s by adopting procedures that allowed sensor degradation itself to be interpreted as a positive attack indication in the context of a crisis.

The Role of Luck

Because rapid operational reactions of strategic forces sharply limited the amount of tactical data available for use in testing the hypothesis "an attack is under way," the randomness inherent in the frequency distributions associated with type I and type II errors had an opportunity to play a dangerously mischievous role in Bayesian inference. Probabilities stabilize as sample size increases, as every statistician knows. A small sample of trials, whether readings from a warning system or flips of a coin, invites a run of bad luck. Flip a fair coin a hundred times, and the result is a pretty even distribution of heads and tails. Flip it a couple of times, and the result may easily be all heads or all tails.

Similarly, the types I and II error rates of the tactical warning system tend over the short run to deviate from their long-run rates. A system with a type I error rate of 10 percent, for instance, detects an attack about 90 percent of the time when tested over a large number of trials, the expected value of the theoretical distribution. But the distribution over a small number of trials tends to be more scattered. A detection failure on the first or second reading, or both readings, of the tactical warning output would defy the odds but would not violate stochastic sense.

Monte Carlo simulation techniques can be applied to explore the possibilities for unusual distributions to manifest themselves on a given trial run. In this technique a random number generator determines whether an attack indication is present (+) or absent (−). This determination is made for each of two scenarios: a scenario of attack (case A) and a scenario of no attack (case B). For each scenario the random number generator in effect blindly selects a symbol from an imaginary urn containing + and − symbols. For the attack scenario (case A), the proportion of + and − symbols in the urn corresponds to the assumed type I (detection failure) error rate of the tactical warning system. If the type I error rate is assumed to be 10 percent, for example, the ratio of + to − symbols in the urn is 9:1. The random number generator is thus likely to pluck a + (attack indication) from the urn, but it might pluck a − (no attack indication) instead. This pick would be unlucky in that scenario (attack). For the no attack scenario (case B) the proportion of symbols in the urn corresponds to the assumed type II (falsely detected attack) error rate. If the type II error rate is assumed to be 10 percent, for example, then the ratio of + to − symbols in the urn is 1:9. The random number generator is thus likely to pluck a − (no attack indication) from the urn, but it might pluck a + (attack indication) instead. This pick would be unlucky in that scenario (no attack).

One can then apply the Bayesian inference model to the randomly selected events. When a + is picked from the urn the model selects the subsequent probability associated with the presence of attack warning. When a − is picked it selects the subsequent probability associated with the absence of attack warning. In either event the model replaces the original prior probability with the appropriate subsequent one, which becomes the new prior probability for a second cycle of readings and judgments. This cyclic process continues under both hypothetical scenarios until Bayesian computations converge on the proper judgment, that is, until the subsequent expectation of attack rises to 100 percent for the attack scenario and drops to 0 percent for the no attack scenario. A single trial run of the model is displayed as repetitive calculations of the subjective expectation of attack for each of the separate cases.

Figure 7-2 is an example of a trial run when the model parameters assumed a prior probability of 50 percent and a type I and type II error rate of 25 percent. Despite the high error rate of the tactical warning system, the iterative revision of expectations, using Bayes's theorem, gradually but inexorably converges on the correct final judgment in both cases. The number of judgment cycles needed to get there is quite large, far exceeding the small number of readings of tactical warning output allowed by the current rapid reaction posture of strategic forces.

Figure 7-2. Bayesian Updating of Attack Expectations, One Typical Trial Run

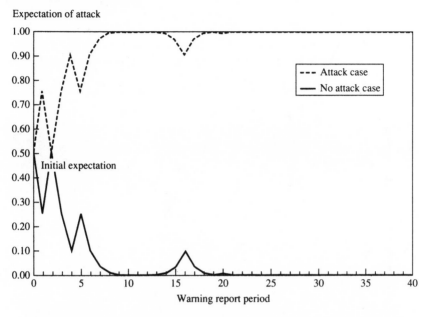

Expectation of attack

Warning report period

With the same parameters the model produced the results displayed in figure 7-3 on another trial run. Compared with other trial runs using these settings, the results are atypical. (Figure 7-2 is a typical set of results.) They are nonetheless illuminating for showing the short-run instabilities of a stochastic process. The early odds-defying readings from the tactical warning system brought Bayesian commanders to the brink of fatal misjudgment before the process settled down. A subjectively rational process of logical inference temporarily suffered from erratic warning performance. A streak of bad luck afflicted the warning system, which in turn fed incorrect data into the hopper of Bayesian logic. This pattern substantiates the point that subjectively and objectively warranted degrees of belief do not necessarily coincide.

The model ran many times using the same parameters, and for each trial it recorded the serial adjustments of subsequent probabilities as they gravitated toward 0 or 100 percent. It then computed the average subsequent expectation across all the trial runs each time the model received a warning report and revised expectations. Put differently, the subsequent

**Figure 7-3. Bayesian Updating of Attack Expectations,
One Atypical Trial Run**

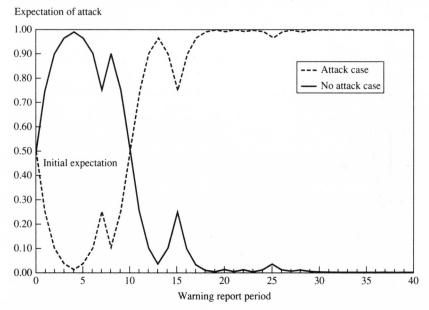

Expectation of attack

Warning report period

expectation after the first cycle of judgment in all the trials was averaged
and plotted on a single graph. In like fashion the average for the second
cycle of judgment in all the trials was computed and plotted, and so forth.
The total number of trial runs was large enough (forty) to warrant statistical confidence that the computed averages along the curves shown in
figure 7-4 conform to the expected values of the theoretical distribution,
though not exactly because the effects of random chance are still present.

The model repeated the trials using the same error rate parameters
but varying the degree of initial expectation of attack. For each different
prior probability, the model executed forty trial runs. It then varied the
error rate parameters and executed forty trial runs for each of the prior
probabilities. As an excursion the model also ran a series in which the
command and control system assumed error rates that were lower than
those actually achieved by the warning system.

Some of the results are summarized in table 7-9, which shows that a
command and control system attuned to the prospect of attack is less
likely to miss an attack but is also more susceptible to believing an attack
is under way when it is not. As table 7-10 shows, too much confidence in

**Figure 7-4. Bayesian Updating of Attack Expectations,
Average over Forty Trial Runs**

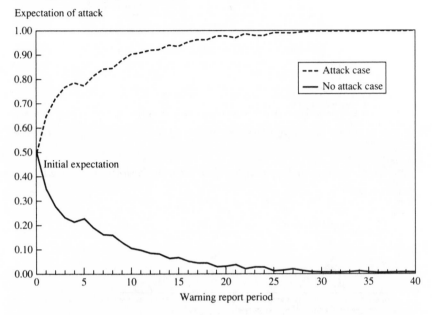

Expectation of attack

the tactical warning system aggravates this trade-off. The command and control system becomes less prone to miss an attack, but it pays for this improvement by a greater propensity to detect an attack falsely.

The results are not egregiously alarming, but neither are they comfortably reassuring. They suggest, which is all they can do, that catastrophe was not inevitable during the cold war, even at the appreciable error rates assumed, but that it was distinctly possible. The chances of it happening did not build continuously over time, for it was associated with crisis conditions—that is, a sharp departure from normal peacetime circumstances to which the respective strategic forces had become stably adapted.

So What?

The main implication that emerges from the Bayesian model is that conclusions drawn in a perfectly logical manner from incoming tactical information may be wrong even when the warning system performs to

Table 7-9. *Judgment Errors after Two Warning Periods*[a]

Initial estimate[b]	Undetected attack[c]	Falsely detected attack[d]
0.001	40	0
0.1	7	0
0.4	8	1
0.7	5	2
0.9	0	5

a. Assumes a warning system with 5 percent types I and II error rates.
b. Degree of belief in the hypothesis "an attack is under way."
c. Number of times out of 40 trial runs that the final expectation of attack failed to reach 90 percent when an attack in fact occurred.
d. Number of times out of 40 trial runs that the final expectation of attack reached 90 percent when an attack in fact did not occur.

Table 7-10. *Judgment Errors after Two Warning Periods (Unrevised Assumptions)*[a]

Initial estimate[b]	Undetected attack[c]	Falsely detected attack[d]
0.001	10	0
0.1	0	7
0.4	3	10
0.8	0	8

a. Assumes a warning system with 10 percent actual types I and II error rates, but the command system assumes 5 percent type I and 0.01 percent type II error rates.
b. Degree of belief in the hypothesis "an attack is under way."
c. Number of times out of 40 trial runs that the final expectation of attack failed to reach 95 percent when an attack in fact occurred.
d. Number of times out of 40 trial runs that the final expectation of attack reached 95 percent when an attack in fact did not occur.

high standards. A well-designed warning system cannot save commanders from misjudging the situation under the constraints of time and information imposed by a posture of launch on warning. Such a posture truncates the decision process too early for iterative estimates to converge on reality. Rapid reaction is inherently unstable because it cuts short the learning time needed to match perception with reality. Such a posture runs inherent risks of reinforcing incorrect beliefs. The result may be a positive control failure (due to underconfidence that an attack is under way) or a negative control failure (due to overconfidence).

The truncation of the learning curve also works to blur the distinction between launch on warning and preemption. Premature closure of information processing boosts the influence of initial expectations on the concluding judgment. If decisionmakers' preconceptions hold sway over tactical information, preconception plays a role in launch on warning comparable to its role in preemption. To the extent that preliminary strategic intelligence reinforces initial bias, moreover, the decision process becomes anchored to the less valid and reliable sources of attack detection—strategic intelligence—and detached from the more dependable error-correcting sources of attack detection—tactical intelligence. In sum, strategic information can supplant tactical information as the dominant triggering condition under a posture of launch on warning. When this happens, the decision process in effect reverts to a preemptive mode and assumes all the risks of inadvertent war associated with it.

Among other significant implications of the model for inadvertent war is the extent to which judgment is impaired by damage to warning systems (degradation produced in some cases by unintended collateral damage) and by ambiguous tactical information emitted by stealth-equipped delivery vehicles such as piloted aircraft and cruise missiles. Such factors can cloud, misguide, confuse, or suspend the judgment of decisionmakers even if the situation allows more time for interpretation than would normally be allowed by launch on warning.

Since the empirical validity of the Bayesian inference model cannot be established for the crisis conditions to which it is most sensitive, the analysis that emerges from it poses a larger question of perspective and presumption; namely, where should the burden of proof lie? In the normal practice of science there is a simple, well-established answer to that question. Any theoretical argument carries the burden of demonstrating its validity; if a theory cannot be empirically tested, the theory is contemptuously dismissed. In terms of security policy, however, that is not an acceptable standard. Because of the destructive capabilities of strategic forces some judgment must be made about the stability of unexperienced crisis conditions and some theory must be used in making the judgment. Security requires that any serious flaws in the utilized theory be discovered before they are proved by decisive experience. Given that situation, there is a good reason to impose the burden of proof on anyone who would deny the more somber implications of the Bayesian model, namely, that strategic force deployments in their cold war operational configuration were a fatal accident waiting to happen. Launch on warning was inherently risky and, moreover, NORAD adopted rules of threat evaluation that increased the danger of inadvertent war.

As a practical matter, of course, the normal scientific standard holds for reasons that go well beyond the priorities of science. There is a natural, understandable predilection to believe that at least one's own strategic forces were safely managed and that ultimate wisdom prevailed in the disposition of such annihilating power. Quite apart from the question of scientific proof, there is considerable psychological and political resistance to any perspective that encourages doubt about one's own actions as distinct from doubt about the opponent's. That was part of the subtle danger that modern strategic forces imposed during the cold war. Self-doubt, often the crucible of new insight and illuminating perspective, was powerfully discouraged.

For those, however, who are willing to contemplate the possibility that neither U.S. nor Soviet strategic security policy captured complete and final wisdom, some practical implications of the Bayesian inference model are worth pondering. We can suppose that a future crisis between the nuclear superpowers is not very likely, but the harder truth is we simply do not know. The demise of the cold war nonetheless presents an opportunity to remove the latent dangers of rapid reaction from the nuclear postures. If it is admitted that reasonable requirements of deterrence are today easily satisfied and certainly do not depend on rapidly accomplished destruction, and that ensuring the fail-safe operation of warning, command, and other nuclear systems is a higher priority of security policy, then some useful implications for U.S. and Russian security policy emerge. These implications are the subject of the next chapter.

For those who believe nuclear proliferation poses an even graver threat to international security, the model and the analysis in chapter 6 are useful in illuminating the underlying dangers. In brief, the emerging nuclear rivals cannot avoid the pressure to adopt postures of rapid reaction that heavily depend on strategic and tactical warning, but they lack the resources and experience needed to create dependable warning systems. By contrast, the United States and Soviet Union, two wealthy and technologically advanced nations, each spent many billions every year on the infrastructure of intelligence and warning. And still they did not fully satisfy the severe operational demands imposed on the warning process. The proliferating states are bound to cut corners in their pursuit of warning, introducing high rates of error and leaving themselves and the world vulnerable to inevitable intelligence failures. The operational postures of these nuclear rivals are virtually certain to become accidents waiting to happen.

CHAPTER EIGHT

Responsible Nuclear Custodianship

THE command and control systems of the nuclear superpowers are adapting in characteristic fashion to the decline of the cold war and the rising threat of nuclear proliferation—widely considered "the chief security threat we face in the post-Soviet era."[1] Each system's core values have been provoked by sudden, unanticipated shocks. A targeting culture permeates the U.S. system; targeting continues to receive top priority in nuclear security policy. A control culture permeates the Russian system; preserving strict central control over nuclear weapons remains its dominant goal and critical challenge. Energized by the recent upheavals in the international situation, each system has responded vigorously, if predictably.

Continuity and Change in U.S. Command and Control

The planning apparatus of the U.S. command system has so far interpreted the political revolution in the former Soviet bloc, as well as arms reductions, defense budget cuts, and the curtailment of modernization programs for nuclear offensive weapons, mainly in terms of their implications for targeting. This orientation is deeply engrained in the U.S. strategic culture and thus permeates the analysis of nuclear security conducted within and outside government. Strongly affected by the sweeping changes in international affairs, this narrow perspective on the environment spawned a stream of academic policy studies seeking to determine the numbers and types of targets in Russia and elsewhere that will need to be covered by U.S. nuclear forces.[2] Similarly, the U.S. government undertook a series of important targeting reviews and revisions of operational plans. Even though National Security Decision Directive (NSDD) 13, issued in 1981, had not been replaced (through 1992) by any new political direction from the president to guide the process through the transition from the cold war to the post–cold war, the decentralized strategic planning system operating under general guidance from the secretary of defense rapidly adapted to the new environment by altering target sets and requirements.[3]

The most conspicuous change was a steady decline in the size of the strategic target base. As dramatic events unfolded—the collapse of the Warsaw Pact, the withdrawal of Soviet forces from central and eastern Europe, the disintegration of the Soviet Union, and the breakthroughs in U.S.-Russian arms control—the aggregate number of targets dropped sharply.[4] Other more subtle and politically sensitive changes were also made. For instance, the view of the influential Strategic Deterrence Study Group, chaired by Thomas C. Reed, on the nature of leadership targeting has probably been reflected in operational planning. According to that group, leadership targeting should be restricted to the *nomenklatura* who directly control nuclear weapons in the former Soviet Union.[5] By this logic, the more numerous government and police entities previously included would be eliminated from the target list. Another example of changing targeting precepts in the wake of Soviet disintegration is the supposed new requirement to get presidential approval before putting nonstrategic targets in the former Soviet republics other than Russia on the target list.[6]

The U.S. strategic culture, with its targeting orientation, simultaneously cast a wider net to deal with the proliferation of weapons of mass destruction. Within this culture, the first questions raised about third-world proliferators of weapons of mass destruction concerned the role of U.S. nuclear weapons—their value as instruments of coercion or deterrence vis-à-vis rationally calculating tyrants or their military utility in neutralizing irrational despots. The 1991 Reed report thus advocated a "Nuclear Expeditionary Force," primarily for use against China or third-world targets.[7] Citing the example of Saddam Hussein, the report argued that "no despotic leaders should be allowed to believe that they can embark on major aggression against the United States, its deployed forces, or its allies and friends, while enjoying personal sanctuary from American weapons, including nuclear weapons."[8] The report also flirts with the provocative notion of reinstating China as a target priority for the single integrated operational plan.

The targeteers thus dove headlong into the uncharted realm of the post–cold war and global proliferation. The idea of deterrence and coercive diplomacy continues to frame the issues, even though any premeditated use of nuclear weapons by either nuclear superpower now seems implausible. The targeteers also seized upon the old framework to handle the emerging problem of proliferation. The United States lacks a comprehensive foreign policy to deal with the spread of nuclear weapons within the former Soviet Union and in the third world, but it is formulating a coherent targeting policy to deal with them.

Despite these habits of mind and organization, U.S. nuclear security policy is slipping out of its cold war moorings. Strengthening control over nuclear weapons to prevent their unpremeditated use—accidental, unauthorized, or inadvertent—is now an important item on the security agenda. Even though strong resistance to radical departures continues, a sea change in outlook is occurring and new priorities are emerging. At the heart of the new policy agenda is the drastic reduction in the size of the nuclear inventories and in their level of combat readiness, a strengthening of safeguards to ensure ironclad control over nuclear operations, and a joint U.S.-CIS endeavor to facilitate the safe dismantlement of Russian nuclear weapons. A comprehensive nonproliferation policy is also likely to become an integral component of the agenda.

In broad outline, this agenda will deal with the inertia of cold war commitments by adjusting the balance of positive and negative control embodied in the strategic command systems of the nuclear superpowers. Operational procedures that undermine safeguards against nuclear inadvertence will receive more attention. Preserving the cohesion of nuclear command and control systems will take precedence over projecting draconian threats of rapid destruction. By eliminating the hasty time lines and operational shortcuts adopted to impart a convincing performance of the wartime mission, the United States and Russia can not only improve negative control while maintaining sufficient deterrence but also set an example of responsible custodianship of nuclear weapons for the rest of the world. And this effort can draw the world's attention to the specific operational dilemmas that accompanied the cold war and that pose analogous threats of operational instability among emerging nuclear rivals.

New presidential guidance is sorely needed to underscore these ascendant priorities and shift the emphasis away from targeting. Nuclear targeting ought not to be the main strand of U.S. nuclear security policy in the post–cold war era. The thrust of the new guidance should be to diminish the importance of nuclear weapons.[9]

Continuity and Change in Russian Command and Control

If targeting is the hallmark of the U.S. system, preserving central control is the overarching priority of the Russian nuclear command and control system. Adapting to the disintegration of the former Soviet bloc has been the central preoccupation of the system. Long before the West perceived a danger of nuclear anarchy in the former Soviet bloc, the Soviet command system was repatriating tactical nuclear weapons from eastern and central Europe and several of the unstable republics. While busily rounding up these warheads and removing them to storage depots in more stable and secure regions of the country, the system took steps to reduce the risk of usable strategic weapons coming under the operational control of non-Russian states in the Commonwealth.

Although the full scope of this intense activity is unknown, it would be uncharacteristic if the Russian command system has not prepared contingency plans for the emergency disabling and recovery of strategic nuclear weapons to foil any attempt by an emboldened state like Ukraine to seize them by force. It would be characteristic of the system to anticipate threats to Russian control and move with determination to stave off the danger of Ukrainian nuclear independence. This adaptive behavior is the essence of the Russian system. Its dedication to the control function hardly needs Western reinforcement in principle, though Russian solicitation of outside help in pressuring Ukraine to adhere to its non-nuclear commitments and in otherwise strengthening nuclear weapons security is consistent with this ethic. The high priority of control is further evident in a variety of ongoing programs, including efforts to increase the wartime protection of top leaders. At a time of acute housing shortages for Russian military officers, crack military construction teams are building deep underground command posts in the Urals region.[10]

Russia's obsession with control and its effective efforts to ensure weapons security invalidate the claim that there is a growing danger of accidental or unauthorized use of Russian nuclear weapons, or of a serious leakage of nuclear weapons, component technology, and expertise to third-world proliferators. The pessimism prevalent in the West stems largely from understandable apprehension over the palpable distrust and political tension between Russia and Ukraine, the latter's creeping administrative control over the nuclear weapons on its soil, the significant nationalist sentiment in Ukraine to inherit those weapons in the full sense of the word, successionist movements and civil strife in some parts of the Russian federation on whose territory nuclear weapons reside, and the protracted timetable for implementing arms control agreements.

These uncertainties justify Western anxiety, but they do not establish any actual drift toward nuclear anarchy. The alarmist rhetoric has curiously grown louder during the past year or two in spite of the effective steps taken by the Russian command system to preserve strict control. Many analysts seemed hardly impressed by the consolidation of all tactical nuclear weapons within Russia during 1990–92 and the lowering of combat readiness of strategic forces outside Russia (including SSBNs at sea), even though such measures substantially alleviated the immediate operational dangers. Ukraine acquired no positive operational control, and nuclear weapons inside Russia, even those near areas of civil turmoil, appeared very secure.

No hard evidence exists of any deterioration of strict operational control over Russian nuclear weapons. Nor does hard evidence exist of any significant diversion of nuclear technology or expertise to illicit purposes such as third-world proliferation. To the contrary, safeguards generally were strengthened in technical and organizational respects during the first year of the Russian federation. In my estimation, the regime of existing safeguards, combined with the command system's adaptive capacity, should inspire confidence in the system's ability to endure acute domestic turmoil probably on a scale far exceeding anything witnessed to date and to contain the effects of aberrant behavior within the nuclear chain of command and throughout the life of the nuclear weapons.

This does not mean the safeguards are ironclad. They fall far short of that standard. Russia especially needs to ensure the security of fissile materials, given that the illicit diversion of even small amounts could result in the spread of nuclear weapons around the world. Further remedial steps could be taken to reduce a multitude of other dangers: the false-alarm hazard caused by the high combat-alert level of ICBMs, coupled with a predisposition to launch on warning in a crisis; the lack of locking devices on certain classes of warheads; the technical inability to neutralize nuclear forces by radio command after their accidental or unauthorized launch; the difficulties of maintaining nuclear safety and surety in the face of shortages in matériel and demoralization within the ranks; the backlog of nuclear weapons slated for dismantlement; and the exposure of strategic ICBM forces in Ukraine, Kazakhstan, and Belarus, and strategic bomber warheads in Ukraine, to the turbulent political currents within and among those states and Russia.

These dangers are overshadowed by a weakness inherent in any nuclear command system but one of particular concern in the Russian system at this juncture: the potential unreliability of the apex of nuclear command. No command and control system can stand apart from the foibles and mischief of persons who hold, or seize, the top positions of leadership. The system reflects their virtues or lack thereof; and its effectiveness depends on their legitimacy, loyalty, and competence. These are the guardians of the nuclear arsenal. The malevolence, corruption, or greed of a few of them could sweep aside a regime of safeguards.

The loyalty and discipline of nuclear custodians below the top level are also matters of concern. Worsening economic and other hardships could severely test the perseverance and integrity of the entire hierarchy of Russian nuclear control. The military custodians of nuclear weapons pose a smaller security risk than the custodians in charge of safekeeping plutonium and highly enriched uranium (HEU).

The threat posed by Ukrainian nuclear gamesmanship pales by comparison with the endemic threats to the basic fabric of the Russian command and control system. From the standpoint of U.S. policy, little can be done about these endemic weaknesses beyond efforts to enhance the legitimacy and power of reform-minded democratic leaders in Russia. Economic assistance would help reduce the incentive to sell nuclear weapons to bolster the ailing Russian economy. A generous Western aid policy for improving the economic performance and general welfare of the populations of Russia and the other former Soviet states would serve the security interests of the United States.

An Agenda for Responsible Nuclear Custodianship

The twenty policy options that follow mainly address the problem of nuclear inadvertence.[11] They are directed at alleviating problems arising from interaction between U.S. and Russian nuclear postures, as well as from domestic threats to Russian nuclear safeguards, and at setting an example of responsible custodianship. The wide-ranging proposals would affect the configuration of the nuclear arsenals and the command and control systems that regulate force operations. They admittedly do not constitute a strategy of denuclearization that promises to marginalize the role of nuclear arsenals. They are stop-gap remedies in the absence of a global regime based on cooperative security—a concept that eliminates the legitimacy of nuclear weapons through sweeping multilateral, reciprocal measures.

Nonproliferation Policy for Belarus, Kazakhstan, and Ukraine

Although the non-Russian states with nuclear weapons on their territory have so far not acquired any positive launch control, many Western officials fear that Ukraine in particular might emerge as an independent nuclear state. A recent national intelligence estimate, for example, reportedly reflects "a broad consensus among government analysts that Ukraine is now as likely to keep the nuclear weapons as it is to give them up."[12]

This prediction is debatable and probably wrong. The Ukrainian government—the executive branch and the vast majority of the legislators—still subscribes to its early and bold declaration of intent to become a non-nuclear state. Except for the majority view of the military, virtually all signs indicate a desire only for negative control—the ability to prevent the employment of weapons in the absence of Ukrainian permission. In the unlikely event that Ukraine (or Belarus or Kazakhstan) tries to gain independent positive control over ICBMs, the chances of success would be slim, given inevitable Russian counteraction. The security of bomber warheads in Ukraine is more precarious. Although they are disabled, their immediate removal to Russia should be a high priority.

The cooperation of Belarus, Kazakhstan, and Ukraine on nuclear issues is nonetheless vital in light of their pivotal role in the implementation of START I and START II. START II hinges on START I, and the latter's implementation depends on a complex of preconditions. First, Belarus, Kazakhstan, and Ukraine must accede to the Nuclear Non-Proliferation Treaty and ratify the START I agreement before Russian ratification (November 1992) goes into effect. At the end of 1992, only Kazakhstan had ratified START I; its parliament's approval of the NPT was also imminent. Second, START I ratification by Belarus and Ukraine depends on their ability to reach an agreement with Russia satisfying the terms of article 2 of the Lisbon protocol—the schedule of implementation, verification provisions, and allocation of costs. (Kazakhstan is also a party to this negotiation.) Money, particularly Ukrainian compensation for the market value of fissile material contained in the weapons on (or previously removed from) its territory, for the costs of dismantling the strategic forces, and for cleaning up the mess afterward, has become a serious problem in this negotiation. Ukrainian officials have bandied about figures ranging from $1.5 billion for "first-stage disarmament" to $5.0 billion in total.[13] Third, Ukraine seeks additional support in exchange for its consent to the ratification of START I. It understandably wants security assurances from Russia and the United States that remove the threats of nuclear attack or invasion. This demand raises thorny territorial issues, such as the Ukrainian-Russian disputes over Crimea and Sevastopol. Last, Ukraine demands assurances that the nuclear materials from dismantled weapons will not be recycled into new ones.

The United States has been slow to develop a coherent nonproliferation policy that effectively promotes the denuclearization of the non-Russian states that host Russian strategic weapons on their territory.[14] Although the many liabilities of nuclear independence outweigh the benefits in any case, the West, led by the United States, could clarify this calculus by offering economic support and security assurances and tying them to these states' accession to the Nuclear Non-Proliferation Treaty and strict adherence to their START protocol obligations.

The Nunn-Lugar legislation providing direct assistance for denuclearization in the former Soviet Union is an integral part of overall U.S. policy. Senator Richard Lugar argues that the release of any funds to Ukraine should depend on Ukraine's affirmation of its START and NPT commitments.[15] The linkage could be even stricter, with aid released to the non-Russian states in installments tied to the withdrawal of warheads to Russia, the completion of safeguard agreements with the International Atomic Energy Agency (IAEA), and the establishment of effective mechanisms to control nuclear exports.[16]

It is important that a policy of linkage be pursued in a spirit of respect for the statehoods of Belarus, Kazakhstan, and Ukraine. American haranguing on this issue sends the wrong signals. Vitriol would prove tactically counterproductive in the short run, and strategically harmful to U.S. relations over the long run. Although the prevailing view in the West is that time is the enemy in this case, the main obstacle has been the lack of a coherent policy with incentives. Such a policy, along with patient and sensitive diplomacy, could break the impasse and allow START implementation to proceed.

Overall U.S. policy also should be crafted with a keener appreciation of the limitations of the Nunn-Lugar legislation and fund. Apart from the fact that this largesse has been only symbolic so far—the tangible assistance actually rendered has been minuscule—the aid does not begin to resolve the deeper issues that underlie Ukraine's nuclear gamesmanship. It neither satisfies Ukraine's hunger for international recognition of its statehood and importance on the world stage nor relieves its severe economic distress. The Nunn-Lugar fund will help underwrite technical projects that denuclearize Ukraine, but it will scarcely confer the status or provide the economic rejuvenation that Ukraine desperately seeks.[17]

The United States thus needs to engage the larger issues of sovereignty and security, both economic and military, as well as the narrower technical aspects of the denuclearization of Belarus, Kazakhstan, and Ukraine. The issue of security assurances from both Russia and the United States appeared close to resolution at the beginning of 1993, although a permanent solution depends on bolder reciprocal steps toward nuclear disarmament by Russia, the United States, and the other nuclear powers. Still unresolved was the issue of Western assistance for Ukraine's ailing economy.

U.S. Technical Assistance for Denuclearization[18]

The denuclearization of the former Soviet Union has so far proceeded without significant U.S. technical or financial assistance. The $800 million fund allocated by Congress under the Nunn-Lugar initiative has scarcely been tapped. In early 1993 about three-fourths of the money still had not been earmarked for projects, and little of the remainder had been put to actual use in the former Soviet Union.

The United States should redouble its efforts to get the Nunn-Lugar and other related projects under way. The most important projects are devoted to facilitating the dismantlement of warheads and the disposal of fissile materials, and to strengthening export controls and safeguarding fissile materials against theft and sale on the black market.[19] Current plans and schedules for major projects are as follows:

—Provide Russia armor blankets to protect nuclear weapons. A $5 million program for the production and delivery of blankets is planned for completion in 1993.

—Provide Russia, Belarus, Kazakhstan, and Ukraine accident response equipment for use in diagnosing any damaged weapons, stabilizing and packaging damaged weapons, and assessing radioactivity in the vicinity of a nuclear accident. Deliveries of equipment to Russia are scheduled to begin in early 1993.

—Provide Russia storage containers for nuclear fissile material, meeting IAEA standards for impact, crush, and burn. At a total cost not to exceed $50 million, the United States will produce at least 10,000 containers for delivery within several years. Prototype testing is nearing completion, and full production is expected to begin in late 1993.

—Provide Russia kits that upgrade the safety and security of railcars used for transporting nuclear weapons and material. Using a Russian cargo railcar for developing the kits, the United States plans to deliver the kits for 100 Russian railcars beginning in late 1993 and ending in April 1994. The cost is $20 million.

—Provide Russia technical assistance in designing a Russian storage facility for fissile material. Administered jointly by the U.S. Department of Energy and U.S. Army Corps of Engineers, at a cost of $15 million, the design phase will be complete by September 1993. The United States may assist in the construction of the facility scheduled for completion by late 1996.

—Provide Russia, Kazakhstan, and Ukraine assistance in developing internal accounting and physical protection against the theft or diversion of nuclear-related materials and equipment.

—Buy from Russia highly enriched uranium and plutonium from dismantled nuclear weapons. The Russians have 100 metric tons currently available as a result of weapons dismantled under the Intermediate-Range Nuclear Forces Treaty and expect to extract a total of 500 metric tons of HEU (valued at about $5 billion) from the overall dismantlement activity. The U.S. Department of Energy agreed to purchase 500 metric tons of HEU from Russia, some of which might be reprocessed by Russia into low enriched uranium suitable for use as fuel in commercial nuclear power plants. Russia expects to extract and process the fissile material at a rate of about 30 metric tons a year. The final purchase agreement has not been signed, however, because Russia has not reached an agreement with Belarus, Kazakhstan, and Ukraine on the distribution of profits from the sale.

—Provide Russia, Belarus, Kazakhstan, and Ukraine assistance in establishing an effective export control system. This effort is multilateral, with representatives from the United States, United Kingdom, France, Germany, Japan, Australia, Italy, and Canada. Their agenda, conducted under the Nunn-Lugar umbrella, covers licensing procedures, enforcement, international nonproliferation obligations, and other topics related to preventing the flow of nuclear materials, technology, equipment and delivery vehicles. The United States is considering providing personal training and system infrastructure.

—Support science centers in Russia and Ukraine to engage weapon scientists in nonweapons activities to inhibit any leakage of nuclear expertise to the third world. The United States has committed $25 million and another $50 million has been pledged by other founding members.

—Provide Russia, Kazakhstan, and Ukraine assistance in dismantling ballistic missiles. Denuclearization of the non-Russian states involves providing a means for the safe storage and disposal of enormous quantities of toxic liquid fuel for missiles.

—Establish government-to-government communication links with Belarus, Kazakhstan, and Ukraine.

Antiballistic Missile Deployments

Some proponents of missile defenses argue that an extensive deployment exceeding the limits of the Antiballistic Missile (ABM) Treaty is needed to protect the United States against nondeterrable attacks. Such scenarios include small-scale strikes by Russian ballistic missiles fired by accident or without proper authority. Other scenarios project threats that might materialize in the early part of the next century: intentional strikes by third-world countries that acquire long-range ballistic missiles armed with conventional or nuclear warheads. These two supposedly nondeterrable threats provide the basic rationale for deploying a fairly extensive antiballistic missile system capable of defending the U.S. population. An effective system is likely to take a form that would violate the existing provisions of the ABM Treaty, and hence the renegotiation of its terms would be necessary.

The alleged Russian threat does not rest on credible evidence. The possibility cannot be ruled out categorically, but the magnitude of the danger is less than commonly portrayed. No one has advanced a plausible scenario that could result in such an attack. While reliable information on Russian missile safeguards is incomplete, and while measures that strengthen such safeguards should be pursued, the available evidence supports the conclusion that the safeguards are effective enough to prevent the accidental or unauthorized firing of Russian missiles.

With respect to the Russian threat, two basic scenarios are driving the missile defense program. For an accidental launch, the nominal threat consists of a single SS-18 land-based missile carrying 10 warheads or a single SS-N-20 sea-based missile carrying 10 warheads. For an unauthorized launch, the threat consists of a group of 10 SS-18 missiles carrying a total of 100 warheads, or a boatload of 20 SS-N-20 missiles carrying a total of 200 warheads. The worst-case threat is therefore either a 100-warhead ICBM attack or a 200-warhead SSBN attack.

The SS-18 scenario assumes an unauthorized launch by the two-man combat crew that normally controls the missiles. The safeguards that stand in the way of such an act were described earlier. The Russian silo-based ICBM force, particularly modern forces like the SS-18s, are under an extremely strict regime of technical safeguards from the top to the bottom of the nuclear chain of command. The scenario is fanciful, and moreover the SS-18 force, along with the rest of the multiple-warhead ICBMs in the Russian strategic arsenal, are slated for elimination under START II. This nominal threat is thus likely to be replaced by a different system—notably, a group of single-warhead ICBMs in fixed silos, or a single mobile ICBM carrying one warhead. Of all the scenarios for an unauthorized or accidental ICBM launch involving currently deployed forces, an incident involving Ukrainian-based SS-19s seems the least implausible if control lapses because of disputes over custody. The safeguards for this force are nonetheless stringent. The missiles there have also been taken off alert, and they will very likely be eliminated under START II before effective U.S. missile defenses could realistically be fielded. The next least implausible scenario involving current ICBM forces is an accidental or unauthorized launch of a single SS-25 mobile ICBM. This threat is too small to warrant deploying missile defense, however.

The current SSBN force also presents a negligible threat of unauthorized attack, certainly one too small to warrant deploying missile defenses.

The Russian strategic forces with the least impressive safeguards are the long-range cruise missiles, but they are not mated to their delivery vehicles in peacetime and thus present no immediate threat. At any rate, ballistic missile defenses provide no protection against cruise missiles. Ironically, the United States put pressure on Russia to abandon the weapons system with the strongest safeguards—silo-based missiles like the SS-18—because of their first-strike potential, and to rely more on the weapons with weaker safeguards—cruise missiles and other mobile strategic forces.

Regarding the threat to the United States posed by the third world, a nuclear-armed ICBM threat is too far off to warrant early deployment of U.S. missile defenses. The United States should acquire operational theater missile defenses for possible use in a regional conflict, but intercontinental defenses are not currently required. A prudent U.S. policy would be to stand ready to deploy such defenses on a schedule that beats the threat if it ever actually materialized.

The deployment of extensive missile defenses not only is unnecessary at the present time but also would inhibit further reductions of the very forces presumed to pose the hypothetical threats of accidental, unauthorized, *or* deliberate nuclear attack. Deployment on the dubious grounds that protection is needed against errant missiles is unwise enough, but the mistake is compounded if it slows progress in reducing offensive arms. The ABM Treaty in its existing form is compatible with the logical next phase of arms control—lowering the future ceiling on strategic forces to 1,000 or fewer warheads. Extensive missile defenses are much less compatible with this goal.

Size of the Deterrent Force and Future Nuclear Guidance

Although deterrence remains a relevant principle for defining the future role of nuclear forces, the requirements of deterrence have become far less demanding. Reducing the deterrent arsenals has the serendipitous effect of alleviating (though by no means removing) the risks of their illicit, accidental, or inadvertent use. When it comes to defining the floor for further reductions, however, no definitive wisdom exists. The criteria to be used in evaluating alternative force structures are value-laden matters of choice. Besides deterrence, criteria worthy of consideration include crisis stability, economic cost, safety, nonproliferation, verification, environmental impact, nuclear materials production, and morality. To be taken into account as never before are the internal politics of the former Soviet Union, the nuclear arsenals of the other nuclear powers (Britain, France, China, Israel, and others), the proliferation of nuclear weapons, the role of strategic missile defenses, the future of tactical nuclear forces, the technological revolution in conventional weaponry, and the enormous task of nuclear weapons disposal and environmental cleanup.

One reasonable perspective on the future requirements of strategic deterrence sets a ceiling, a maximum deployment, of 1,000 strategic warheads on each side. This limit depends on several key assumptions: that the parties negotiate an additional further reduction of nonstrategic nuclear weapons down to several hundred (400 at most) on each side; that nuclear warheads slated for elimination but not yet destroyed are declared, tagged, and verified pending their destruction; that no significant expansion of the nuclear arsenals (combined strategic and nonstrategic) of Great Britain, France, or China takes place; that the parties continue to abide by the terms of the ABM Treaty and protocol that permits a limited deployment of defense interceptors at a single site, or, alternatively, that the parties jointly conduct efforts in the strategic defense field on a cooperative basis; that confidence-building measures and verification regimes are sufficiently strengthened to preclude any realistic chance of a breakout of either strategic offensive or defensive arms; and that the further expansion of nuclear arsenals by the emerging nuclear powers is contained.[20]

An appropriately structured force consisting of 1,000 strategic warheads would satisfy the major and many minor criteria of nuclear sufficiency. Among the minor and admittedly arbitrary requirements that are satisfied is the common desire for rough numerical parity between the United States and Russia and for substantial numerical superiority over the other world nuclear powers. These aims were stipulated in the Reed report, commissioned by Air Force General George L. Butler, head of the Strategic Command and the director of strategic targeting. This high-level study proposed that, in principle, it would be best if the U.S. nuclear inventory equaled the combined inventories of all but Russia's.[21] The proposal, allowing for a 1,000 strategic and a 400 tactical warhead nuclear force, would meet this condition in rough terms, since the combined inventory of Britain, France, and China is expected to level out at about 1,000 (200, 500, and 300 nuclear warheads, respectively).[22]

The much more important criterion is the ability of the 1,000 strategic warhead force to provide a nuclear insurance policy, that is, to meet reasonable requirements of deterrence across a wide spectrum of possible circumstances, including a serious deterioration in U.S.-Russian relations. This classical aim means that the arsenals must be able to reliably project a threat of retaliation destructive enough and credible enough to override any calculation of benefit. From this overarching aim flows the requirement that the forces be sufficiently survivable and flexible to retaliate with a devastating blow against a broad spectrum of high-value economic-industrial and military targets.

For a force of the size proposed here, this deterrent capability should be more than adequate if one-half the total inventory of weapons can be assured of surviving a first strike and reaching their assigned targets. A total of 500 deliverable U.S. retaliatory warheads, for instance, could destroy "most [Russian] petrochemical, electrical, metallurgical, and heavy-machinery industry; all major [CIS] storage sites for ammunition, fuel, and other military supplies; all major tactical airfields; some troop concentrations; and all major [Russian] transportation nodes and choke points en route to the European and Far Eastern theaters"; all garrisons for mobile strategic missiles; all primary strategic bomber bases and submarine pens; most strategic bomber dispersal bases; and most major fixed and mobile command posts.[23] A comparable number of survivable Russian strategic warheads could wreck no less comprehensive devastation on the United States.

In the post–cold war era a latent mutual threat of such proportions seems excessive, except as an insurance policy. At these force levels, assuming no rupture occurs in U.S.-Russian relations and Russia does not return to its authoritarian past, deterrence is surely overdetermined. A strong case could be made for even deeper reductions. It is worth noting that Chairman Reed and the other members of General Butler's commission, while declaring themselves comfortable with a force of "5,000 treaty warheads," did not reject outright any strategic force posture except for a "minimum deterrent concept of only a hundred or so weapons on hand."[24] The group's list of objections to such a low number, even if the objections are valid (and they are disputable), do not apply to the proposed force level of 1,000 strategic warheads. The primary objections stemmed from the group's judgment that a minimum deterrent force of 100 weapons permitted too little targeting flexibility and dictated an immoral and self-deterring policy of threatening to concentrate a retaliatory attack on the civilian population. There is of course no such targeting imperative, and at any rate a force of 1,000 strategic warheads could offer enormous targeting flexibility, as the earlier comments attest.

A number of reasonable designs for a balanced, resilient force structure composed of 1,000 strategic warheads have been proposed.[25] What is lacking is a presidential directive to guide the restructuring. Whether a smaller or larger arsenal is deemed adequate insurance, the extant presidential guidance written over a decade ago lacks relevance to nuclear requirements in the post–cold war era. New presidential guidance is needed.

Conventional Weapons in the Strategic War Plan

The future role of conventional weapons in strategic planning is an important question. On the one hand, the reduction and disengagement of conventional firepower in the European theater virtually eliminates the most important mission performed by conventional forces during the cold war. On the other hand, the rapid advances of conventional weapons technology in range, accuracy, and versatility—in short, in lethality—foreshadow a quantum leap in the role of non-nuclear forces in regional and international deterrence. This was graphically illustrated by the impressive performance of U.S. conventional technology during the Gulf War with Iraq, and it is abstractly illustrated by standard calculations showing that a modern cruise missile with a conventional high-explosive warhead has a lethality against a hardened point target equal to that of a nuclear warhead delivered by a Polaris submarine-launched missile.[26] (Recall that the Polaris force formed the backbone of the U.S. nuclear deterrent in the 1960s.)

The revolution in conventional weapons technology—"stealth" aircraft and missiles, precision-guided munitions (bombs and missiles) with pinpoint accuracy, and command-control-communications-intelligence systems—enables the West, particularly the United States, to use long-range strategic air power to threaten a vast array of *fixed* targets of a regional aggressor's military-industrial complex.[27] The Reed report goes further. It proposes to add to the single integrated operational plan an option to use conventional weapons to attack the Russians or others with the objective of laying "down a one-night attack so shocking to the recipient and so indicative of serious US intent that the triggering crisis would be re-evaluated in a different light."[28]

With respect to the U.S.-Russian strategic balance, this technological revolution raises possibilities for substituting conventional for nuclear weapons in the strategic war plans. Indeed, studies performed by the U.S. Strategic Air Command over a decade ago showed that many hundreds of Soviet targets in the U.S. SIOP could be successfully attacked by conventional weapons available then. A proposed plan for incorporating conventional weapons into the strategic war plan was not implemented, but its feasibility was certainly established. In the near future, however, the emphasis on conventional strategic power seems destined to expand. In early 1993 a wing of B-1 bombers will be fully converted from nuclear to conventional missions.

Such substitutions deserve consideration as a means to denuclearize strategic deterrence. But this force option is primarily available only to the United States, because of its technological lead and wealth, and the force's operational appearance is bound to be perceived as a new threat to Russia. Even if the objective is to reduce reliance on nuclear weapons for strategic deterrence, and not to seek strategic superiority by exploiting advantages in conventional weapons technology, the development will be viewed as threatening to Russia. Indeed, this emergent threat already looms large in Russia's new military doctrine.[29]

The Day-to-Day Strategic Mission

With the end of the cold war and a rising concern about nuclear proliferation and accidental or unauthorized use of weapons, the wisdom of keeping thousands of widely dispersed nuclear weapons in a launch-ready configuration is dubious. Continuously operating thousands of forces on so short a fuse in peacetime, as is the current practice, results in a constant projection of large-scale threat that is not only reminiscent of the cold war but also the source of significant tension between the strategic organizations. The vigil increases the risk of unauthorized use and carries the vestigial impulse to generate maximum strategic capability in a crisis and to place the capability on a hair trigger susceptible to discharge on false warning. This U.S.-Russian posture also sets a poor example for the world. It exaggerates the symbolic importance and practical military utility of nuclear weapons and encourages fledgling nuclear states to adopt comparably dangerous operational practices.

The commitment to attack opposing strategic forces that has traditionally driven the rapid reaction postures on each side could be reduced by a presidential directive that lowers requirements for damage expectancy. It also can be and certainly should be constrained in operational terms. Although the trends in strategic force modernization and arms control are already promoting this goal—for example, by encouraging greater reliance on mobile forces that confound the opponent's counterstrategic targeting—it could be better served by a wide range of negotiable constraints on operational activities. A new presidential order is needed to rationalize and guide the imposition of such constraints.

"ZERO" ALERT RATES. Lowering the alert levels of nuclear forces would alleviate the danger of their accidental or unauthorized use. The United States and Russia should aspire to remove all forces from nuclear alert—"zero alert."[30] A study should be performed to define options for reducing alert levels in stages. A two-stage plan of implementation has merit. In the first stage, both parties would take off alert all nuclear forces slated for elimination under the START I and START II agreements. The study should evaluate the merits of immediately taking this step on a reciprocal basis, with no monitoring stipulations beyond the verification regime established to enforce the START agreements. In the second stage, the parties would take off alert all nuclear forces. This step would entail reciprocal reductions by the charter nuclear weapons states—France, Britain, and China—and a stringent regime of international verification.

Land-based ballistic missiles could be taken off combat alert in the same way as the 450 Minuteman II and 503 Soviet ICBM forces were stood down to concur with the Bush-Gorbachev initiatives of September and October 1991. Reversing the steps to generate these forces back to combat status would have taken approximately twenty-four hours or more to complete. As for the submarine forces, combat readiness can be lowered by adopting a "modified" alert status. Submarines on modified alert, which is the normal status for half the U.S. SSBN force at sea at any given time in peacetime, require a minimum of eighteen hours after leaving port to complete the complex procedures—for instance, the removal of flood plates from the launch tubes and the installation of vital electronic components into the fire-control system—that enable them to assume a launch-ready disposition. Submarines on "modified" alert would remain invulnerable to attack, but they could not mount a strike for at least eighteen hours if the preparatory procedures had not been previously accomplished. For SSBNs on permanent "modified" alert with warheads on board, verification would be facilitated by cutting back to a single-crew concept and operating the SSBNs in the way attack submarines (SSNs) are operated—that is, by making numerous port calls and reducing the time spent at sea from two-thirds to one-third.

The warheads for the strategic forces could also be removed to extend the time required for returning them to combat status. As long as the warheads could be protected from attack, the launchers and missiles would remain viable reserve forces, because each side's prompt counterstrategic threat to the other side's silos and submarine launch tubes would also be removed. The key challenge would be to devise a means of timely verification to ensure that neither side could gain a decisive head start in generating its strategic capability. The participation of international bodies in conducting continuous on-site inspection of warhead stockpiles would help meet this challenge.

Multilateral negotiation and verification of severe operational restrictions on the nuclear postures would mark a notable and controversial departure in arms control, but the potential benefits are large enough to merit serious consideration. Such restrictions would certainly set an example of responsible custodianship for the rest of the world to follow.

NUCLEAR EXERCISES. U.S. and Soviet nuclear operations during exercises have been provocatively ambiguous on occasion. Officials of the former Soviet Union have been especially disturbed by the Global Shield exercises conducted since 1979 by the Strategic Air Command, whose scale and realism often caught the serious attention of the Soviet command and control system.[31] The United States regarded Soviet naval exercises involving unusual SSBN activities to be potentially threatening during the 1980s. Nuclear exercises may also provoke extra alarm because of errors committed. For instance, mistakes occasionally resulted in the United States disseminating actual nuclear launch orders instead of exercise launch orders.

Realistic practice of full-scale nuclear attack by either side against the other has become a vestigial ritual that ought to be abolished. It would not only tarnish the new cooperative relationship between the old adversaries but would also sow some operational suspicion and invite an operational response. Such activity would perpetuate a sense of nuclear confrontation at a time when the ascendant goal on both sides is to reduce the scope and intensity of combat alert operations.

The START I agreement obliges the parties to notify each other "no less than 14 days in advance about the beginning of one major strategic forces exercise which includes the participation of heavy bomber aircraft

to be held during each calendar year."[32] The parties should further agree
to specific curbs on nuclear exercises that embody the alert constraints
discussed earlier. For instance, the MX and SS-18 forces taken off alert
under those terms would not be brought to combat status as part of an
exercise. A low ceiling on the number of SSBNs that can surge out of
port within twenty-four hours and a low ceiling on the number of heavy
bombers that can take off and simulate bomb runs during an exercise
are also desirable as confidence-building measures.

COUNTERSTRATEGIC RECONNAISSANCE ACTIVITY. Discussions between
U.S. and Russian officials could be helpful in specifying ways to regulate
surveillance to preclude the effective targeting of systems (command and
control and force) that depend on mobility and covertness for their survival. Space-based and undersea reconnaissance have growing significance as the strategic portfolios shrink and rely increasingly on land- and
sea-mobile forces. Such reconnaissance activities are especially sensitive
topics, but room exists for the parties to suggest restrictions that would
promote operational stability.

Reliance on Launch on Warning and Warning Sensors

Despite the obvious dangers, the reaction times of the nuclear postures
grew shorter and shorter during the cold war. The command systems
geared themselves to launch on warning. Retaliation after ride-out was
an abstract idea in the theory of stability but not a viable option in the
real world. As a practical matter, the susceptibility of command systems
to disruption, the mutual vulnerability of each side's silo-based forces,
and the commitment to strategic weapons targeting created a strong bias
on both sides for extremely rapid reaction to evidence of impending
attack—*in effect a launch-on-warning posture for both sides.*

The fact of having established and refined these rapid reaction postures during the cold war will remain a residual danger in the U.S.-
Russian strategic nuclear relationship. It should not be ignored just because the strategic confrontation has ended. Lengthening the reaction
times of the command and control systems would be promoted if the
counterstrategic mission was brought under the operational constraints
discussed earlier. In a serious crisis, however, the systems would very
likely adopt a rapid reaction posture—that is, nuclear forces would be

generated to launch-ready status, and both sides would prepare to fire them on tactical warning.

This residual danger should gradually diminish as relations continue to improve; meanwhile it can be mitigated by pursuing increasingly secure (invulnerable) command systems and forces. Beyond that, both sides share a strong interest in improving the performance of early-warning systems. The emphasis should be put not on improving positive detection of a massive deliberate attack—a cold war function of warning systems designed to support rapid reaction or literal launch on warning. Improvements should instead emphasize (1) reducing the chances of false alarms and thereby providing extra assurance that an attack is *not* under way, (2) ensuring that a small-scale accidental or unauthorized attack is detected and identified as such were it to occur, and (3) helping monitor the testing of ballistic missiles to verify compliance with arms agreements.

A related function, which is an increasingly important priority, is to monitor the launch activities of third countries that are developing or deploying ballistic missiles. This proliferation has a growing potential to directly threaten the nuclear superpowers as well as to strain their early warning systems. It might increase the risks of false alarms and thus aggravate the problem of nuclear inadvertence.

Cooperation to improve early-warning performance would be beneficial. Among other ideas, some combination of acoustic, infrared, and optical sensors could be placed at ICBM fields, with the processed signals sent simultaneously to the early-warning centers on both sides, to provide mutual reassurance that each side's ICBMs remained in their silos.[33] Also, a direct communications link could be established between the North American Aerospace Defense Command headquarters and its Russian counterpart (the PVO Strany Center for Analysis of Space and Missile Situation) so that the key military officials responsible for early-warning and attack assessment might quickly confer to clarify ambiguous situations. At present, the two sides have no capability to establish a channel of communications and to exchange information within a short period of time, and certainly not within the thirty-minute flight time of an intercontinental missile.

The deployment of stealth technology, designed to confuse opposing warning systems, should be strictly limited at very small levels of deployment. Also, the patrol zones of ballistic missile submarines in particular could be circumscribed in ways that improve attack early warning performance. For instance, submarines could be excluded from patrol areas that are poorly covered by existing warning systems—notably, far northern Arctic waters for Russian SSBNs and certain Pacific ocean zones for U.S. SSBNs.

Warning system assets should be the focus of greater investment, and explicit arrangements should be made for mutual protection of these assets, most notably an agreement prohibiting the testing or deployment of dedicated antisatellite weapons and a ban on all space weapons. Although antisatellites are not high priorities in current defense programs— the U.S. Congress sharply limited the ASAT budget, and the Strategic Defense Initiative Organization cut the budget for one technology with a primarily ASAT application, the free electron laser—the time is ripe to turn this lull into a permanent ban on the activity.

Last, each party ought to closely examine the procedures for threat evaluation that have been institutionalized by its early warning organization. These procedures should be subject to top-level civilian oversight and decisions made on the requirements for dual-sensor detection and other such issues. In particular, a high-level review should be conducted to determine whether a high-confidence threat evaluation by the North American Aerospace Defense Command should require the presence of nuclear detonations, especially under normal peacetime conditions, and require the detection of nuclear delivery vehicles by at least two different sensors during a crisis. NORAD's current standards of evidence are substantially lower.

Joint Early-Warning Center

A jointly manned (U.S., Russian, and affiliated nations) early-warning center could be established to improve missile and space monitoring. The basic mission of such a center would be to detect every ballistic missile launch that occurs anywhere in the world, and to provide to the key command posts of the participating nations, as rapidly as possible, a report that identifies the time of launch, launch site and country of origin, missile type, trajectory, and point of impact. The center could also monitor and report on events in outer space that might present a danger to a member state. It could be tied into space- and ground-based sensors and receive some data directly from them, and could receive other data from the principal early-warning processing centers, particularly NORAD in the United States and the Center for Analysis of Space and Missile

Situation in Russia. Communications linking the duty staffs of the center with those major national facilities should be established to provide a way to clarify ambiguous events.

Among its tasks, the joint center would monitor not only the launches of ballistic missiles by the established nuclear powers but also those of proliferator states whose programs pose direct threats to U.S. allies, U.S. forces overseas, and the territory of Russia and other states participating in the center. Cooperative warning would be valuable for monitoring and responding to the combat use as well as the developmental testing of these missiles. Of particular value in this regard would be the radars that cover the Middle East. The Lyaki radar in Azerbaijan, for instance, detected SCUD missiles fired by Iraq toward Israel during the Gulf War, and real-time access to this data might have provided the United States with better SCUD launch detection and impact point predictions than it was able to produce on its own.[34]

The main benefit, however, is that joint monitoring of ballistic missile launches, whether conducted by the established nuclear powers or the proliferator states, is important as a way to alleviate the problem of nuclear inadvertence caused by erroneous early warning. The object is to prevent false alarms and increase mutual assurance that a nuclear missile attack is not under way. Joint operations that combine the surveillance assets of the participants, and accumulate data and experience, promise to serve this goal better than any individual operation could.

Which nations should staff the center? In principle, it seems appropriate to invite the participation of states that are already partners in existing missile early-warning operations. Those states that participate in actual operations—such as Canada, a full partner in NORAD—should be invited to join, as should states that permit early-warning systems to operate on their territory—such as Great Britain, the host nation for a ballistic missile early-warning radar tied to NORAD. By this principle, quite a few states in the CIS could become members, along with the United States, Canada, Great Britain, Australia, and Denmark. In addition, it seems reasonable to bring in all states that currently possess nuclear armed missiles, and perhaps also the members of the Missile Technology Control Regime and members of the Conference on Security and Cooperation in Europe, which produced the recent "open skies" agreement.

Warning reports issued by the early-warning center might also be sent to the proliferator states testing ballistic missiles and their regional rivals.

Such quick dissemination of launch information would increase the transparency of the rivals' programs and mitigate the effects of false alarms produced by the rivals' own warning systems.

Security of Command and Control Systems

During the four decades of the cold war the nuclear superpowers proliferated strategic weapons in the name of deterrence, according to which rationally calculating decisionmakers would never initiate an attack on an opponent capable of delivering a severe punitive blow in retaliation. This logic on which the prevention of nuclear war was presumed to hinge unfortunately suffered in the translation from theory to practice. The burden of retaliation fell on complex strategic organizations whose basic coherence was severely threatened by opposing nuclear forces. Command systems remained vulnerable despite huge investments to protect them. In the U.S. and Soviet cases, their functions could have been severely disrupted by the effects of a few hundred weapons at most. On available evidence, analyzed theoretically according to conservative principles, a well-designed first strike using 1990 forces could have demolished a victim's command centers and their communications tentacles. Literal decapitation might not have resulted, but strategic organizations feared that their retaliatory plans would be so disrupted that it would be intolerable to ride out an attack.

This vulnerability, which is partly responsible for the rapid reaction postures that carry risks of nuclear inadvertence during a crisis, is far less consequential in the post–cold war era, yet it remains a latent problem that should not be aggravated by continuing efforts to threaten strategic command posts and communications. The parties should end programs of research and development designed to counter each other's command and control. Earth-penetrating nuclear weapons designed to destroy deep bunkers and disrupt communications should be prohibited.

Nuclear Weapons and PALs

An important safeguard against unauthorized use of nuclear weapons are permissive action links (PALs) or coded switch systems. A PAL is an electromechanical coded lock on a warhead that requires an essentially unbreakable code to be inserted before the warhead will explode.[35] For bombers and missiles, similar devices known as coded switch systems can be used on the launcher or delivery vehicle. Such systems prevent, for instance, the bomb racks from dispensing their stores or prevent the beginning of a missile's terminal countdown to launch. Codes for PALs or coded switch devices are not held by the individual weapons commanders but are distributed by higher authority only when nuclear weapon employment has been legitimately authorized. The locks provide a physical barrier to accidental or unauthorized employment.

By the end of the 1970s almost all land- and air-based U.S. tactical nuclear weapons were equipped with PALs, and all strategic bombers and missiles assigned to the Strategic Air Command were equipped with PALs or coded switch systems, or both. The Air Force rejected the use of PALs in favor of coded switch devices for the B-1 bomber in order to save money, whereas the U.S. Navy has resisted the imposition of any such device. There are no PALs or coded switch devices on the submarine ballistic missile force, or for that matter on most other naval nuclear weapons. Certain naval weapons such as the submarine-launched cruise missile and all antisubmarine warfare weapons have been equipped with PALs,[36] but the protection is removed when the vessels carrying them go to sea on mission. Navy policy evidently calls for restoring PAL protection when the vessels complete their missions, return to port, and transport weapons to storage depots on land.[37]

Most Russian nuclear forces—all strategic weapons and most tactical weapons—must receive unlock codes from higher authority, without which the weapons cannot physically be dispatched or detonated. The unblocking system for their ICBMs is especially sophisticated in that only those weapons designated for immediate launch need be unlocked, and after a short period they are automatically locked up again if for any reason they had not been launched as planned. The U.S. unblocking system lacks this sophistication. However, many Russian strategic weapons, such as air- and sea-launched cruise missiles and most tactical weapons, lack sufficient PAL protection. In those cases the primary safeguard is on the container or launcher rather than on the weapon itself.

Whenever possible, all nuclear weapons remaining in the active inventory should be equipped with PALs that are integral to the warhead itself, and all others should at least have the protection of a coded switch device for the launcher. All other nuclear weapons without exception should be retired and dismantled. The fall 1991 Bush-Gorbachev initiatives earmarked for destruction most of the weapons that lack modern safeguards of these types. The residual weapons lacking the devices should be either equipped with them or destroyed. The parties need to exchange information on the status of their respective inventories and establish standards with which to evaluate the effectiveness of existing technical safeguards. Weapons that fail to meet the requisite standards would, by mutual agreement, be immediately inactivated (taken off alert) and slated for eventual destruction.

This recommendation is important insofar as it sets a high standard of technical safety for the proliferator states to meet. The existing nuclear states should also make PAL technology available to others without exception. This is one nuclear technology that should be exported.

Russian Nuclear Anarchy and U.S. Crisis Policy

As argued in chapter 3, the U.S. command and control system could be better prepared to deal with a nuclear crisis in the former Soviet Union. If Russian nuclear control convulses under the strain of a coup or other internal pressures, U.S. reaction should be designed to help restore its cohesion. The situation might pose an increased nuclear threat to the West, but it would warrant reassurance and assistance from the West. The danger would probably be not an increased risk of deliberate attack but a danger of illicit or inadvertent use of Russian forces. U.S. nuclear restraint would be more constructive than an aggressive reaction under such circumstances. Raising the alert level of U.S. nuclear forces to increase the salience of deterrence, for instance, would be misguided. Such a move could be counterproductive because it would create pressure on the Russian system to maintain high combat readiness or even elevate it at a time when Russian alert levels should be lowered to restore strict negative control.

The United States thus needs to develop a contingency plan tailored for a nuclear crisis in the former Soviet Union that puts severe strain on the Russian command and control system and produces abnormal nuclear activity. U.S. planners could design a specific option for U.S. military forces, including nuclear forces, that involves prudent but nonprovocative alert responses. Key elements of the U.S. government—intelligence, crisis management, diplomatic, and federal disaster relief agencies—should also coordinate plans for an emergency of this kind. The U.S. government should hone its ability to distinguish abnormal Russian nuclear activity reflecting difficulties of internal control from unusual activity reflecting preparations to launch a deliberate attack. To this end, the government of Russia and the United States should outline the emergency measures that each might invoke. The discussion might begin with Russian officials explaining the operational steps taken to enhance nuclear weapons security and control during the 1991 coup attempt. The parties could also explore the possibilities for communications and joint actions to be taken in the midst of a domestic Russian nuclear crisis.

Emergency Disabling of Weapons

Nuclear weapons, launchers, delivery vehicles, and storage facilities could be rigged to allow them to be quickly disabled in such emergencies as terrorist assaults. The Russians apparently have moved quite far down this path. The parties should have technical discussions of the feasible options and agree to implement them comprehensively. Certain of the devices could be jointly developed and produced. Among the desirable options is one that would permit higher authorities to disable weapons systems by remote radio control in the event that local custodians were overpowered and unable to perform the task. In a similar vein, special counterterrorist response teams could be formed on both sides and trained to conduct joint operations if either side requests assistance. The efforts along these lines could be further facilitated by sharing intelligence on threats to the nuclear systems posed by terrorist-like groups.

"Command-Destruct" Devices

If all these measures fail to prevent the inadvertent employment of one or more nuclear weapons, steps could be devised that mitigate the consequences. Apart from reducing the number of warheads carried by each delivery vehicle, measures could be developed to disable weapons before they reach their destination.

The Accidents Agreement signed by the Soviet Union and the United States in 1971 actually obliges each side to develop such measures.[38] Each side not only must notify the other in the event of an unintentional nuclear act that might ignite a nuclear war,[39] but must also take steps that protect the other from damage. The second sentence of article 2 states: "In the event of such an incident, the party whose nuclear weapon is involved will immediately make every effort to take necessary measures to render harmless or destroy such weapon without its causing damage."[40]

A command-destruct system offers a solution. Almost the only practical way to cope effectively with a missile launch after its has occurred is for the country of origin to destroy its own missiles or warheads before impact and detonation. The United States has not developed this capability for nuclear-armed strategic weapons, but to do so is technically feasible by using *active* command-destruct systems similar to those used by range safety officers to destroy errant test missiles, or by using *passive* systems that would energize a self-destruction mechanism on board a missile a few seconds after launch if that missile had not previously received an appropriate coded signal allowing it to fire. Russia might readily incorporate the passive system into its missiles, because a sizable portion of its combat-ready strategic missile forces is already equipped with on-board sensors and an explosive charge designed to blow up the missiles automatically if they stray from their proper trajectory during an authorized strike. Such a system could be modified to deal with unauthorized or accidental launches. As Richard Garwin notes, "Buried inside the missile, such a system could not readily be disconnected by the operating crews, and it could be arranged so that an attempt to disconnect it would irrevocably disable the missile (as is the case with the more modern U.S. PALs)."[41]

The characteristics of the two variants of such a destruct-after-launch (DAL) system, one passive and one active, and the pros and cons of each, are examined by Sherman Frankel.[42]

Crisis Communications

Communications in crisis circumstances need to be improved. In 1987 the United States and the Soviet Union signed an agreement establishing Nuclear Risk Reduction Centers in Washington and Moscow. These centers contribute little to crisis management, since their primary task is to exchange routine information pertaining to two arms control agreements. The centers could play a much larger role in the handling of a crisis. Enlarged and linked to other nerve centers such as the Crisis Management Center of the National Security Council, they could assume responsibilities for fulfilling the obligations of the Accidents Agreement of 1971.

Independent and Joint Study of Nuclear Safeguards

Congressional legislation required the U.S. secretary of defense to establish a Fail-Safe advisory committee to "consider all aspects of existing and recommended positive measures for safety, security, and control of nuclear weapons, as they relate to assured execution of national policy and the prevention of unauthorized use of these weapons."[43] Also, Congress has mandated that the Defense Department submit a report to Congress evaluating the recommendations that PALs be installed on all nuclear forces at sea and that devices allowing for post-launch destruction of strategic missiles be installed on the pertinent weapons systems.[44] Former congressman Les Aspin (now secretary of defense) and Senator Sam Nunn have been especially active in pushing for stronger nuclear safeguards on both U.S. and Russian weapons. As chairman of the House Armed Services Committee, Aspin also sponsored an independent evaluation of the safety of the U.S. nuclear stockpile—for instance, the danger of accidental explosion during the operational handling of nuclear weapons.[45]

The Russian leadership should be no less active in identifying, evaluating, and correcting deficiencies in the surety of its nuclear weapons. It is indeed particularly urgent that flaws in safety and safeguards be remedied in view of the specter of social disintegration hanging over the former Soviet Union.

The results of such independent studies by the two security establishments should be exchanged and discussed. The Fail-Safe Committee, which is expected to recommend phasing in PALs on U.S. ballistic missile submarines, should brief the Russian defense minister and general staff on its findings and recommendations. Classification requirements will necessarily impose some limits on the discourse, but a constructive collaboration leading to new ideas and technical innovations can readily be envisioned. Investigators could delve deeply into command system operations to identify potential sources of accidents, miscalculations, misperceptions, or unauthorized use of nuclear weapons.

Along with jointly evaluating the quality of existing safeguards, it would be useful to consider whether standards of nuclear surety should be raised to counteract the diminishing priority of nuclear combat effectiveness in the post-cold war era. For instance, the prevailing U.S. standard for evaluating the need for PALs assumes the existence of only one cognizant agent or unstable individual with access to a given nuclear weapons area ("no lone zone"). Evaluation rests on the assumption that one such insider tries to sabotage, capture, launch, or otherwise exploit his position of trust. It would be illuminating to evaluate existing safeguards against more stringent criteria—for instance, to consider the threat to negative control posed by *two* conspiring insiders.

The United States and Russia could also benefit from joint research into methods for assessing the safety and reliability of nuclear weapons other than nuclear testing. Progress along this front could help pave the way to a comprehensive test ban.

The Russian government is likely to endorse and cooperate in such joint endeavors. Its leaders have always had a penchant, bordering on an obsession, for preserving strict operational control over nuclear weapons. They are clearly not complacent about recent developments that raise questions about nuclear safety and security. The political revolution in the former Soviet Union has created serious problems of nuclear weapons control, but it has also brought previously taboo subjects into the public domain for serious examination.

Principles for Political Nuclear Command

It is strongly in the West's interest to ensure that a single nuclear command structure is preserved within the former Soviet Union. This interest could be pursued in joint discussions to define the principles of political control over Russian nuclear forces. At a minimum, it could offer the basis for reassurance. Beyond that, the United States might appreciate the value of modifying its own nuclear command structure, which is now far more decentralized than its counterpart. The principles that emerge from the joint endeavor could guide efforts on *both* sides to strengthen political control.

Nuclear Alert and Release Authority

Concern over nuclear authority stems largely from an examination of the U.S. command and control system. Such concern may be less for the Russian system because of its high degree of centralization.

Although designed to deal with cold war nuclear contingencies, the U.S. nuclear command and control system has been carried over into the post–cold war era. From the standpoint of organization, planning, and mission requirements, the old system is essentially intact. It stands substantially removed from the political revolution in U.S.-Russian relations. One cannot fail to notice a fundamental, vestigial, inconsistency between the autonomy of the U.S. system and the international political context in which it operates.

The United States evolved a chain of authority over nuclear combat operations that was, and is, heavily skewed toward *decentralization*. Decentralization extends to the custody of codes needed to fire nuclear weapons. A large part of the U.S. strategic and tactical nuclear arsenal is unrestrained by PALs or other technical unlock devices, and those that are so equipped can be enabled for use by many sources within the military chain of command. Numerous military nodes possess all the authorization and enabling codes needed to implement nuclear war plans. Some of them also have contingent delegation of authority (so-called pre-positioned national command authority) to execute the plans in a communications outage or in other events that isolate the strategic forces from the national political authorities.

A case can be made for revoking all such predelegations and for centralizing authority over alerting activity. Such arrangements are vestiges of the cold war that should be subjected to presidential scrutiny and modified as appropriate.

Conclusion

In the Soviet Union it was said that the past was always changing; only the future was certain. Entrenched political forces constantly revised Soviet history to suit their interests while maintaining their stranglehold on the destiny of the nation. In the former Soviet Union the future holds both profound change and continuity. The political revolution within the Soviet bloc brought the cold war to an abrupt end, but it also created possibilities for nuclear anarchy. As the world celebrated the end of the traditional nuclear rivalry, it realized that the disintegration of the USSR carried nuclear risks of a different kind. Nuclear proliferation and loss of control over nuclear weapons replaced the old fear of premeditated attack.

The former Soviet nuclear command and control system provided the continuity needed to prevent nuclear anarchy during a difficult transitional period. The military remained steeped in the political culture of strict top-down control. It managed to preserve the cohesion of the nuclear command and control system during a coup attempt and other social, political, and economic distress.

The nuclear difficulties, real and imagined, experienced recently in the former Soviet Union have had a sobering effect on governments bearing responsibility for the safe operation of nuclear weapons. The United States and Russia in particular learned to better appreciate their common interest in preventing nuclear inadvertence.

Their responsibility extends beyond the narrow aim of ensuring the security of nuclear weapons based in the former Soviet Union. It extends to the operational postures they carried over from the past. Some features of these postures—notably, their predisposition to rapid reaction—run unnecessary risks of operational instability.

Responsible nuclear custodianship requires that the nuclear super-powers address these anachronisms. The root causes of the nuclear stances adopted during the cold war deserve further reflection. The steps required to alleviate the dangers lurking in today's command and control systems need to be defined and then jointly taken. An example of responsible custodianship needs to be set for the rest of the world.

Notes

Chapter One

1. The author is indebted to John Steinbruner for his contribution to this introduction, which draws heavily on points he developed in Bruce G. Blair and John D. Steinbruner, *The Effects of Warning on Strategic Stability,* Brookings Occasional Papers (Brookings, 1991).

2. John Steinbruner, "Beyond Rational Deterrence: The Struggle for New Conceptions," *World Politics,* vol. 28 (January 1976), pp. 231–32.

3. The seminal expositor of "the threat that leaves something to chance" is Thomas C. Schelling, *The Strategy of Conflict* (London: Oxford University Press, 1960). See especially chapter 8.

4. See, for instance, Matthew Bunn, "The ABM Talks: The More Things Change . . . ," *Arms Control Today,* vol. 22 (September 1992), pp. 15–23.

5. Serge Schmemann, "Gorbachev Matches U.S. on Nuclear Cuts and Goes Further on Strategic Warheads," *New York Times,* October 6, 1991, p. 1.

6. See "Ambassador Robert L. Gallucci: Redirecting the Soviet Weapons Establishment," interview, *Arms Control Today,* vol. 22 (June 1992), pp. 3–6.

7. For an excellent review that is rich in information and insight on this and related topics, see Christopher Paine and Frank von Hippel, eds., *Report on the Fourth International Workshop on Nuclear Warhead Elimination and Nonproliferation,* held in Washington on February 26–27, 1992 (Federation of American Scientists and Natural Resources Defense Council, March 1992).

8. "Protocol to the Treaty between the United States of America and the Union of Soviet Socialist Republics on the Reduction and Limitation of Strategic Offensive Arms," reprinted in *Arms Control Today,* vol. 22 (June 1992), pp. 34–35.

9. "Letter to President Bush from Ukrainian President Leonid Kravchuk," Kiev, May 7, 1992, reprinted in *Arms Control Today,* vol. 22 (June 1992), p. 35. See also "Letter to President Bush from Chairman of the Belarusan Parliament Stanislav Shuskevich," May 20, 1992, and "Letter to President Bush from Kazakh President Nursultan Nazarbayev," May 19, 1992, both reprinted in *Arms Control Today,* vol. 22 (June 1992), pp. 35, 36.

287

10. For a contrasting view, see Kurt M. Campbell and others, *Soviet Nuclear Fission: Control of the Nuclear Arsenal in a Disintegrating Soviet Union,* CSIA Studies in International Security 1 (Harvard University, Center for Science and International Affairs, November 1991), pp. 3–4. It is argued that established launch procedures "bear only indirectly on the question of how missiles might be launched" improperly.

11. One pathbreaking study is Stephen M. Meyer, "Soviet Nuclear Operations," in Ashton B. Carter, John D. Steinbruner, and Charles A. Zraket, eds., *Managing Nuclear Operations* (Brookings, 1987), pp. 470–531. Other valuable sources include David Holloway and Condoleezza Rice, "The Evolution of Soviet Forces, Strategy, and Command," in Kurt Gottfried and Bruce G. Blair, eds., *Crisis Stability and Nuclear War* (Oxford University Press, 1988), pp. 126–58.

12. A highly respected social scientist, Donald Campbell, minces no words: "All scientific knowing is indirect, presumptive, obliquely and incompletely corroborated at best." Donald T. Campbell, "On the Conflicts between Biological and Social Evolution and between Psychology and Moral Tradition," *American Psychologist,* vol. 30 (December 1975), p. 1120. Although Campbell overstates the case, strategic analysis could enhance its reputation by embracing his wisdom. Alas, the field often bows to strong pressures to show not the slightest epistemic humility. As in any field that straddles science, policy, and politics, the temptation to overreach is unusually strong. High demand for unwaffled answers creates a market for study products that package immature theories as final, easily digestible truth.

13. An excellent source is *Nuclear Weapons Safety,* Report of the Panel on Nuclear Weapons Safety of the House Committee on Armed Services, 101 Cong. 2 sess. (Government Printing Office, December 1990), report 15. See also Scott D. Sagan, *Organizations, Accidents, and Nuclear Weapons* (Princeton University Press, forthcoming).

14. Among the best current treatments of civil-military relations are Timothy J. Colton and Thane Gustafson, eds., *Soldiers and the Soviet State: Civil-Military Relations from Brezhnev to Gorbachev* (Princeton University Press, 1990); David Holloway, "State, Society, and the Military under Gorbachev," *International Security,* vol. 14 (Winter 1989–90), pp. 5–24; Condoleezza Rice, "The Party, the Military, and Decision Authority in the Soviet Union," *World Politics,* vol. 11 (October 1987), pp. 55–81; Stephen M. Meyer, "How the Threat (and the Coup) Collapsed: The Politicization of the Soviet Military," *International Security,* vol. 16 (Winter 1991–92), pp. 5–38; and Harry Gelman, *Gorbachev and the Future of the Soviet Military Institution,* Adelphi Papers 258 (London: Brassey's for the International Institute for Strategic Studies, Spring 1991).

15. Sagan, *Organizations, Accidents, and Nuclear Weapons;* and Peter Douglas Feaver, *Guarding the Guardians: Civilian Control of Nuclear Weapons in the United States* (Cornell University Press, 1992).

Chapter Two

1. Evidence to the contrary is just beginning to come to light. Sagan cites recently declassified U.S. documents indicating that U.S. intelligence agencies

detected an increase in the alert level of Soviet nuclear forces during the 1962 crisis. Scott D. Sagan, *Organizations, Accidents, and Nuclear Weapons* (Princeton University Press, forthcoming). Raymond Garthoff recently found authoritative corroborating evidence in the archives of the Central Committee (personal communication).

2. This discussion is largely based on information provided by people who served in the Soviet strategic rocket forces (SRF).

3. The SRF had been organized a year earlier, but this branch had only a few experimental missiles (mostly at Baikonur) capable of delivering some nuclear warheads. Interview.

4. Representative of the comments in the academic literature are the following: Richard K. Betts, *Nuclear Blackmail and Nuclear Balance* (Brookings, 1987), p. 120; Paul Bracken, *The Command and Control of Nuclear Forces* (Yale University Press, 1983), p. 223; Richard Ned Lebow, *Nuclear Crisis Management: A Dangerous Illusion* (Cornell University Press, 1987), p. 67; Raymond L. Garthoff, *Reflections on the Cuban Missile Crisis*, rev. ed. (Brookings, 1989), p. 65; Marc Trachtenberg, *History and Strategy* (Princeton University Press, 1991), pp. 253–58; and Marc Trachtenberg, "The Influence of Nuclear Weapons in the Cuban Missile Crisis," *International Security*, vol. 10 (Summer 1985), pp. 156–61.

5. See Trachtenburg, "Influence of Nuclear Weapons," p. 159.

6. According to Chairman Nikita Khrushchev's speech delivered on December 12, 1962, which Western analysts generally consider to be highly inaccurate and misleading, "The Soviet government instructed the U.S.S.R. Defense Minister to put the entire army of the Soviet Union, and above all the Soviet intercontinental and strategic missile troops . . . strategic aviation and naval forces, in a state of combat readiness. Our submarine fleet, including atomic submarines, took up positions as instructed. A state of heightened combat readiness was proclaimed for the ground forces, and the discharge from the Soviet Army of the older contingents of the strategic rocket troops, the antiaircraft troops, and the submarine fleet was postponed. The armed forces of the Warsaw Treaty countries were also placed in full combat readiness." "Krushchev's Report on the International Situation—1," *Current Digest of the Soviet Press*, vol. 14 (January 16, 1963), p. 5.

7. Betts, *Nuclear Blackmail and Nuclear Balance*, p. 120.

8. See Sagan, *Organizations, Accidents, and Nuclear Weapons*, for newly unearthed evidence of U.S. awareness of Soviet nuclear alerting during the crisis.

9. Interview.

10. The ICBMs in the operational arsenal were based around Baikonur. New bases elsewhere were under construction, and some were partially operational. ICBMs were being located at places beyond the range of U.S. Jupiter missiles in Turkey. The Soviets were also deploying mobile missiles to increase their chances of surviving attack. Interview. The inventory of operational intercontinental missiles did not exceed "about twenty," according to General Volkogonov, as reported in Garthoff, *Reflections on the Cuban Missile Crisis*, p. 206. Garthoff estimates twenty-four to forty-four (pp. 207–08).

11. The bombers were required to achieve reaction times that were shorter than the flight times of Jupiter missiles launched from Turkey; the time of flight

of those missiles was quite long because of the trajectories they were designed to fly. Interview.

12. See, for instance, the statement cited by Betts, *Nuclear Blackmail and Nuclear Balance,* p. 120.

13. Information about this particular alert was provided largely by a defector from the Soviet SRF. His account was confirmed and enlarged upon by another person who served in the SRF.

14. Interview with Western source. All other descriptive material for this alert came from Soviet sources.

15. Interview with Western source.

16. Interview.

17. Interviews with Western sources.

18. Henry Kissinger, *White House Years* (Little, Brown, 1979), p. 622.

19. See Barry M. Blechman and Douglas M. Hart, "The Political Utility of Nuclear Weapons: The 1973 Middle East Crisis," *International Security,* vol. 7 (Summer 1982), pp. 132–56. The authors portray the U.S. nuclear alert as an exercise in the "manipulation of the risk of nuclear war. . . . In effect, the U.S. actions said to Soviet decision-makers: 'If you persist in your current activity, if you actually go ahead and land forces in Egypt, you will initiate an interactive process between our armed forces whose end results are not clear, but which could be devastating. Moreover, the United States feels so strongly about this issue that it is prepared to participate in this escalatory process until our objectives are achieved' " (pp. 146–47).

20. An excellent treatment of the *security dilemma* is Robert Jervis, *Perception and Misperception in International Politics* (Princeton University Press, 1976), esp. pp. 58–113.

21. In the family of rational choice models to which the spiral model belongs, people or states obey by rote mathematical laws of utility maximization. The rationality assumption and a necessary utility calculation preordain the outcome, from which no escape exists. In similar fashion, nonrational models of individual choice typically specify lawlike mechanisms that in effect deny the existence of volition. Seeking cognitive consistency, for instance, actors see only what they expect to see, and if presented with ambiguous or discrepant information, they assimilate it by rote to preexisting beliefs.

22. Among the best treatments of organizational determinants of crisis behavior is the meticulous analysis in Scott D. Sagan, "Nuclear Alerts and Crisis Management," *International Security,* vol. 9 (Spring 1985), pp. 99–139.

23. On former defense secretary Robert McNamara's view of the appropriateness of existing nuclear plans, Henry S. Rowen wrote: "[McNamara] apparently also came to believe that the task of preplanning nuclear options was a hopelessly difficult one because the contingencies in which weapons might be used were so unpredictable that nuclear planning could be done only when the contingency arose." Henry S. Rowen, "Part III: Formulating Strategic Doctrine," in Commission on the Organization of the Government for the Conduct of Foreign Policy, *Appendices,* vol. 4, app. K (Government Printing Office, June 1975), pp. 231–32.

24. See John D. Steinbruner, "Choices and Trade-offs," in Ashton B. Carter, John D. Steinbruner, and Charles A. Zraket, eds., *Managing Nuclear Operations*

(Brookings, 1987), pp. 535–54. This section also draws on Bruce G. Blair, "Alerting in Crisis and Conventional War," in ibid., pp. 75–120.

25. When unfolding events in a crisis drive target coverage below the prescribed level, the system triggers preprogrammed actions designed to return the value to the tolerable range. This can also occur during peacetime if a sudden degradation of target coverage is experienced. For instance, the U.S. command and control system dramatically increased the alert rate of the SAC bomber force in the late 1960s when it discovered that most of the Polaris SSBN force was carrying warheads with defective fuzes that disabled the warheads. Interviews with Western sources.

26. Its approach to successful adaptation strikes one as Darwinian: response variation is the raw material, and natural selection is the directing force. The system busily reformulates objectives and tailors operational plans to support them in the hope that the emerging stratagem coincides with a niche in the conflict ecology. It does not blindly resort to a pat response, but instead scans a wide range of political and military objectives, integrates them into a new formulation of security policy, and devises a custom-made plan of operations. Strategic target coverage may or may not be a major factor in the planning process.

Chapter Three

1. Damage expectancy is the probability that the desired level of damage will be achieved against each target or set of targets. It can also be expressed as a norm, or requirement. As an objective calculation of capability, damage probability is the product of several probabilities: $DE = PK \times PTP \times PLS \times PRE$, where PK is the probability of destroying—or killing—the target; PTP is the probability of penetrating air defenses; PLS is prelaunch survivability (probability that systems survive enemy preemptive actions); and PRE is the probability that systems function reliably. For elaboration of the formula and the underlying factors that affect the various probabilities, see Theodore A. Postol, "Targeting," in Ashton B. Carter, John D. Steinbruner, and Charles A. Zraket, eds., *Managing Nuclear Operations* (Brookings, 1987), pp. 373–406.

2. The other major target base—the People's Republic of China—was removed from the SIOP in 1982–83, five years after normalization of political relations. Interview with former senior U.S. military officer.

3. The major categories during the 1980s were nuclear forces, other military targets, leadership, and war-supporting industry. Norms were also doubtless stipulated for major options and suboptions in the SIOP.

4. This "decision" process in large organizations is artfully explained in John D. Steinbruner, *The Cybernetic Theory of Decision: New Dimensions of Political Analysis* (Princeton University Press, 1974).

5. A short list of such functions includes diplomatic signaling, bargaining, control of escalation, confidence building, limitation of damage inflicted on society and military installations by enemy strikes, denial of enemy military objectives, limitation of direct and collateral damage to enemy society, maximum

protection of offensive forces from enemy attack during conventional and nuclear hostilities, and nuclear war termination.

6. I am indebted to John Steinbruner for the points made in this paragraph.

7. Author's estimates and interview with former senior U.S. military official.

8. The best scholarly account of the largely futile efforts from the Kennedy through the Reagan administrations to incorporate LNOs into the operational command and control system is the penetrating and important book by Janne E. Nolan, *Guardians of the Arsenal: The Politics of Nuclear Strategy* (Basic Books, 1989).

9. The weapons in question were originally carried exclusively by a small number of Minuteman missiles. Later on, the assignment became more evenly balanced among the Minuteman forces, the SSBNs, and the air-launched cruise missiles on board strategic bombers. Interview with former senior U.S. military officer. LNOs were programmed operationally for the first time in the mid-1970s under the banner of the Schlesinger doctrine. SAC, however, allowed some LNOs to consist of a hundred or more weapons. Interview with former SAC officer. According to Nolan, very small options were finally incorporated in the nuclear war plans in concrete operational terms in the late 1980s. Ibid., pp. 248–61.

10. On the other hand, procedures were developed to allow in principle for rapid planning and implementation of limited nuclear options or ad hoc missions by drawing Minuteman, submarine, or bomber weapons out of the strategic reserve force account. Assuming a pliant military, it would not have taken long to replan the missions and execute the forces. Replanning bomber mission portfolios took about five hours. Minuteman III retargeting took as little as thirty minutes per missile (many hours for the entire force because of sequential processing in each squadron and parallel processing among squadrons) for those units equipped with a device known as command data buffer. SSBN retargeting took only a few minutes because of extensive on-board computer capacity. These estimates apply to retargeting against targets that were not previously stored in the missile's memory. Each missile normally stored several preprogrammed targets in memory, any of which could be selected in seconds. Informal interviews.

11. For a thorough and incisive critique of civilian oversight of strategic war planning, see Nolan, *Guardians of the Arsenal*.

12. For a primer on the construction of the SIOP, see Mark D. Mariska, "The Single Integrated Operational Plan," *Military Review*, vol. 52 (March 1972), pp. 32–39.

13. Typically, the SIOP was overhauled every two years; minor revisions were made every six months.

14. Access was limited to those persons in the chain of combat command and their designees; the president and the secretary of defense were the only civilian officials in this chain.

15. Nolan, *Guardians of the Arsenal*, p. 255.

16. Ibid., p. 256.

17. See Richard H. Ellis, "Strategic Connectivity," in *Seminar on Command, Control, Communications and Intelligence*, Incidental Paper (Harvard University, Center for Information Policy Research, Program on Information Resources Pol-

icy, Spring 1982), p. 5. This authority derived from JCS guidance issued in 1959 allowing each commander of a unified or specified command "to establish at any time their own DEFCON [defense condition] appropriate to circumstances . . . based upon their own estimate of the situation." Joint Chiefs of Staff, JCS-977405, May 18, 1960, Records of the U.S. JCS, Record Group 218, National Archives.

18. As a result of the September 1991 Bush initiative, the strategic bomber force was relieved of the requirement to be ready for immediate takeoff in peacetime. Such changes in the peacetime posture, however, did not affect the basic responsibility of senior commanders to protect their strategic assets through generation and protective dispersal should threat conditions warrant such action.

19. Specific alert measures associated with various levels of U.S. defense condition are discussed in Bruce G. Blair, "Alerting in Crisis and Conventional War," in Carter, Steinbruner, and Zraket, eds., *Managing Nuclear Operations*, pp. 75–120. Alert levels and associated steps for NATO and U.S. forces assigned to the defense of Western Europe are described by Paul B. Stares, *Command Performance: The Neglected Dimension of European Security* (Brookings, 1991), pp. 114–21.

20. I am indebted to Sagan for sharing his painstaking research with me.

21. Gen. Thomas D. White, letter to Gen. Thomas S. Power (declassified), November 22, 1957, Thomas D. White Papers, Box 41, 1957 Top Secret General File, Library of Congress, p. 1.

22. I can personally attest to the complete absence of predelegation of release authority at the level of ICBM launch control crews. Numerous discussions with bomber and SSBN crew members reinforce the judgment that predelegation did not reach the level of individual commanders of strategic forces.

23. White, letter to Gen. Power, p. 2.

24. CINCPAC ADMINO, memo to Chief of Naval Operations (CNO) (declassified), August 8, 1957, no. 4551, p. 2.

25. CINCPAC ADMINO, memo to CNO, pp. 2–3.

26. Gen. Horace M. Wade, *U.S. Air Force Oral History Interview*, K239.0512-1105 (Albert F. Simpson Historical Research Center, Office of Air Force History, Headquarters USAF, Maxwell AFB, AL, October 10–12, 1978), p. 308.

27. *Department of Defense Appropriations for 1961*, Hearings before the Subcommittee of the House Committee on Appropriations, 86 Cong. 2 sess. (Government Printing Office, 1960), pt. 7, p. 69.

28. General Lauris Norstad, *U.S. Air Force Oral History Interview*, K239.0512-1116 (United States Air Force Historical Research Center, Office of Air Force History, Headquarters USAF, Maxwell AFB, AL, February 13–16; October 22–25, 1979), pp. 321–22; quotations on p. 322.

29. *Memorandum to the President, Policies Previously Approved in NSC Which Need Review*, NSC Meetings 1961 (January 30, 1961), folder 2, box 313, National Security Files (NSF), John F. Kennedy Library (JFKL), Boston; as quoted in Scott D. Sagan, *Moving Targets: Nuclear Strategy and National Security* (Princeton University Press, 1989), pp. 142–43, 217.

30. Carl Kaysen in a conversation with the author.

31. Prepared statement of Vice Adm. Gerald E. Miller, U.S. Navy, Retired, in *First Use of Nuclear Weapons: Preserving Responsible Control,* Hearings before the Subcommittee on International Security and Scientific Affairs of the House Committee on International Relations, 94 Cong. 2 sess. (GPO, 1976), p. 55.

32. Harold Brown, *Thinking about National Security: Defense and Foreign Policy in a Dangerous World* (Boulder, Colo.: Westview Press, 1983), p. 79.

33. Interview with former senior U.S. defense official. Another interview disclosed that the legitimate successors to the president, whether issued identifying codes or not, were tracked continuously by the Presidential Emergency Operations Center located in the basement of the East Wing of the White House. This center was under the Office of Emergency Operations (OEO), which was responsible for continuity of government plans and operations—that is, reconstitution of government and installment of a successor president. Interview. As of the end of 1991, the OEO was headed by a two-star officer who reported to a retired three-star officer serving as the military aide to the president. Interview.

34. For good discussions of the delegation issue, see Paul Bracken, "Delegation of Nuclear Command Authority," in Carter, Steinbruner, and Zraket, eds., *Managing Nuclear Operations,* pp. 352–72; Laurence J. Legere and Judith E. Corson, "Presidential Succession and the Authority to Release Nuclear Weapons," Research Paper 537 (Arlington, Va.: Institute for Defense Analyses, August 1969); Library of Congress, Congressional Research Service, *Authority to Order the Use of Nuclear Weapons (United States, United Kingdom, France, Soviet Union, People's Republic of China),* prepared for the Subcommittee on International Security and Scientific Affairs of the House Committee on International Relations, Committee Print, 94 Cong. 1 sess. (GPO, 1975); and Kurt Gottfried and Bruce G. Blair, eds., *Crisis Stability and Nuclear War* (Oxford University Press, 1988).

35. Interview with former senior U.S. defense official.

36. These codes were occasionally misplaced, as when Reagan's card containing them was put aside in the hospital after the attempt on his life (Ronald Reagan, *An American Life* [Simon and Schuster, 1990], p. 257); or when Carter's clothing containing them was sent to the dry cleaners (interview with U.S. military officer).

37. This contrasts with the Soviet arrangement (discussed extensively in the next chapter), in which the necessary codes were split up and controlled by at least two different organizations; for instance, the chief of the general staff and the commander in chief of the strategic rocket forces normally must have each generated part of the complement of codes needed by the individual firing units. No single command post, let alone several, possessed all the requisite codes needed to initiate a strategic strike, although special provisions existed to enable certain high-level facilities to fire the strategic forces in retaliation for a strike that destroyed key posts. Finally, the Soviet system eschewed vertical (down the chain of command) delegation of nuclear release authority. It was anathema.

38. Interview with former senior U.S. military officer.

39. See John Steinbruner, "An Assessment of Nuclear Crises," in Franklyn Griffiths and John C. Polanyi, eds., *The Dangers of Nuclear War,* A Pugwash Symposium (University of Toronto Press, 1979), pp. 34–49.

40. A declassified report by the USAF Historical Division notes: "Many USAF actions already were underway prior to the discovery that the Soviet Union was emplacing ballistic missiles in Cuba." For instance, "the increasing seriousness of the Cuban situation during the summer of 1962 alerted the Tactical Air Command to the necessity of preparing a well-planned, thoroughly coordinated tactical air offensive to be launched against Cuba well in advance of an airborne assault and amphibious landing. . . . By 10 October TAC forces had already commenced training exercises at McCoy, MacDill, and Homestead AFB's and the build-up of war readiness materiel at these bases had begun." "Thus, the advent of the crisis—triggered by perhaps the most important USAF reconnaissance flight in American history [the U-2 photosurveillance flight of 14 October]—found the Air Force in a somewhat advanced posture to support the Cuban contingency." USAF Historical Division Liaison Office, Headquarters USAF, "The Air Force Response to the Cuban Crisis," Top Secret (declassified) 1963, pp. 5, 21.

41. Many examples are presented in Scott D. Sagan's important study *Organizations, Accidents, and Nuclear Weapons* (Princeton University Press, forthcoming).

42. The most authoritative recent disclosure of the number of Soviet targets in the SIOP gives a range of 5,000 to 10,000 as of late 1991. See Thomas C. Reed, "The Role of Nuclear Weapons in the New World Order," briefing, Joint Strategic Target Planning Staff/Strategic Advisory Group, Strategic Deterrence Study Group, October 10, 1991, p. 23. The upper end of this range was probably closest to the actual number before the Moscow coup and the subsequent disintegration of the USSR. After the breakup, the SIOP-92 planning exercise plausibly eliminated thousands of "desired ground zero" aimpoints, particularly non-Russian, nonstrategic infrastructure targets.

43. Interviews with former senior U.S. military and defense officials, and author's estimates. This range of damage expectancy apparently had its origin in the Eisenhower administration. A civilian consultant involved in target planning at the time recalled that the established requirement of 90 percent damage expectancy was reduced to 70 percent at the behest of President Eisenhower. Subsequent planning worked within the 70–90 percent range.

44. Military planners excuse thousands of nuclear weapons from SIOP assignments. By disqualifying these weapons, they limited the creditable means of achieving target coverage. The exclusion of theater nuclear weapons and nuclear sea-launched cruise missiles, for example, jettisoned their contributions to SIOP target coverage, even though they constituted a very large force (thousands of weapons, formerly forward deployed but later put largely in storage in accordance with the Bush initiative of September 1991) whose likely targets would have extensively overlapped the target set assigned to the SIOP forces. (Many hundreds of SIOP targets were also included in theater nuclear strike plans, but SIOP planners assumed that U.S. theater nuclear forces would have completely failed to accomplish their mission.) The potential contribution of conventional weapons was also completely discounted. Classified studies performed in the early 1980s by the Strategic Air Command showed that conventional weapons, such as non-nuclear cruise missiles carried by long-range bombers, could contribute sub-

stantially to target coverage, particularly to coverage of weakly defended Soviet targets east of the Ural Mountains. Rivalries within the Air Force quashed the idea. Interview with former senior U.S. military officer.

45. A senior U.S. adviser asserted in an interview that the U.S. SIOP did indeed include a specific preemptive option during the late 1980s.

46. Barton Gellman, "U.S. Military Took Precautions: Officials Were Braced for Profound Changes in Strategic Posture," *Washington Post,* August 24, 1991, p. A22.

47. Ibid.

48. Quoted in ibid.

49. Allegedly threatening changes in the Soviet nuclear posture during the coup attempt were reportedly discovered several months after the fact, when U.S. intelligence agencies sifted through the previously recorded data. See Bill Gertz, "U.S. Missed Soviet Nuke Alert in Coup," *Washington Times,* May 12, 1992, p. A1.

50. Reed, "Role of Nuclear Weapons," p. 15.

51. Ibid., p. 16.

52. Ibid., p. 17.

53. Ibid.

Chapter Four

1. Raymond L. Garthoff, *Deterrence and the Revolution in Soviet Military Doctrine* (Brookings, 1990), pp. 158–59.

2. Ghulam Dastagir Wardak and Graham Hall Turbiville, Jr., eds., *The Voroshilov Lectures: Materials from the Soviet General Staff Academy,* vol. 1: *Issues of Soviet Military Strategy* (Washington: National Defense University Press, June 1989), p. 83. See also p. 237, which states that "strategic action in a nuclear war should comprise . . . massive use of nuclear missile armaments, particularly strategic nuclear weapons, to maximally weaken enemy strategic nuclear forces and destroy enemy war production capabilities, disrupt governmental control functions, and destroy enemy armed forces' groupings."

3. Interview with U.S. defense official.

4. Quotation from Col. D. Samorukov and Col. L. Semeyko, "The Increase of Efforts in Nuclear Warfare Operations," *Voyennaya mysl',* no. 10, 1968, FPD 0084/69, August 29, 1969, p. 52, as cited in Joseph D. Douglass, *Soviet Military Strategy in Europe* (New York: Pergamon Press, 1980), p. 122. In the secret General Staff Academy course materials of the mid-1970s, the view expressed is that nuclear war plans must be "constantly reviewed, readjusted, and modified as needed, according to changes in the military and political situation," and moreover that "political reasons may affect the selection of areas of the TSMAs [theaters of operations] for action, the selection of countries to be hit by nuclear strikes, or nations not to be attacked or temporarily not to be attacked by nuclear weapons." Wardak and Turbiville, eds., *Voroshilov Lectures,* vol. 1, pp. 271, 266.

5. Ghulom Dastagir Wardak and Graham Hall Turbiville, Jr., eds., *The Voroshilov Lectures*, vol. 2: *Issues of Soviet Military Strategy* (Washington: National Defense University Press, December 1990), p. 29.

6. For discussions of these categories, see John Erickson, "The Soviet View of Deterrence: A General Survey," in Stephen J. Cimbala, ed., *Soviet C³* (Washington: AFCEA International Press, 1987), p. 419; Joseph D. Douglass, Jr., and Amoretta M. Hoeber, *Soviet Strategy for Nuclear War* (Stanford, Calif.: Hoover Institution Press, 1979), pp. 58–66; and William T. Lee and Richard F. Staar, *Soviet Military Policy since World War II* (Hoover Institution Press, 1986), p. 149.

7. The U.S. approach to targeting allowed for little adaptive reprogramming. Except for local reprogramming of bomber sorties at the target area, involving on-site damage assessment and crew choice between primary and secondary targets, the U.S. system handled random reliability failures and other uncertainties by using prior probability distributions and by redundant cross-targeting instead of reprogramming. A knowledgeable officer in the Soviet strategic rocket forces told me that Soviet strategic planners took a similar tack because the surfeit of available weapons permitted such an uneconomical allocation. Interview.

However, an alternative algorithm was acknowledged to be a far more efficient way to allocate weapons to targets, and it may have partially guided the targeting scheme in use. On paper this algorithm enables a Soviet planner to achieve the same probability of damage using about one-third to one-half the number of warheads required by the U.S. approach. To illustrate, let us assume that the U.S. planners require a 90 percent level of damage expectancy against a set of 100 Soviet targets. Suppose that the strategic weapons available for use against these targets have an individual PK (probability of kill) of 90 percent, an expected reliability of 80 percent, and a 100 percent probability of prelaunch survival and air defense penetration. Since the allocation of only a single weapon against a given target would result in an insufficient damage expectancy (72 percent, the product of PK times PRE, which falls short of the required DE of 90 percent), the U.S. planner must allocate another weapon. This cross-targeting of two weapons produces a joint DE of 92 percent for a given target. (Note that the probability that the target survives the first weapon is 28 percent [1 minus 72 percent]; the probability that it would survive both the first and second weapon is about 8 percent [28 percent × 28 percent], and hence the DE against that target is 92 percent [1 minus about 8 percent].) For the set of 100 Soviet targets, the U.S. planner allocates 200 weapons and thus expects to meet and somewhat exceed the established DE requirement.

The Soviet planner recognizes the wastefulness of this allocation. He reasons that if the U.S. planner's assumptions are correct, the allocation of 100 weapons against 100 targets will result in the arrival of 80 weapons, each with a PK of 90 percent, at their targets. For the vast majority of targets the DE requirement will be satisfied by one-on-one targeting. The remainder—the 20 targets that were not struck in the initial salvo because 20 out of the 100 allocated weapons proved unreliable—can be covered by an operational reserve force. Assuming that identifiable launch failures account for most of the incomplete target coverage, a

Soviet planner can plan to launch an operational reserve of 20 weapons in a second salvo, of which 80 percent, or 16 weapons, each with a PK of 90 percent, reach their targets. That leaves 4 targets unstruck, which requires the planner to have yet another 4 weapons set aside for use in a third salvo. In total, the Soviet planner having perfect information on his own missile force's performance need allocate only 124 weapons to achieve the desired DE (90 percent) against all 100 targets.

To conclude, the Soviet planner seeks to compensate for actual reliability failures as they occur, using operational reserves, and theoretically achieves the DE requirements with 38 percent fewer weapons than his U.S. counterpart allocates. The U.S. planner achieves a slightly higher average DE (92 percent), but expends substantially more weapons in the process. Furthermore, the U.S. planner achieves a skewed DE distribution against the 100 targets by using expected rather than actual reliability failure distributions. His allocation of 200 weapons results in a 99 percent DE against 64 targets, a 90 percent DE against 32 targets, and a 0 percent DE against 4 targets. The U.S. algorithm thus produces overkill for the majority of targets, while allowing a small fraction of the targets to be missed altogether.

8. This lesson was applied to the organization of the strategic forces: both the weapons and the command system. With respect to command, the idea of reserves translated into redundant control points and communications. The importance attached to surplus forces and command elements has been given formal scientific status and validation, notably in R. Ashby's concept of variety, to which legions of Soviet military analysts subscribe. Ashby's law of requisite variety implies that reserves of information (read command channels) and physical characteristics (read surplus forces) are necessary to adapt to random disturbances of the magnitude and variety encountered in military operations. This law was the guiding principle used in designing Soviet automated control systems in particular and Soviet control systems in general. The significance of this idea is better appreciated by noting that the Soviets considered the comprehensive automation of weapons systems and troop control to be the third and last stage—often called the 'cybernetic' stage—of the revolution of military affairs. (The advent of nuclear weapons and long-range missiles for delivering them were the first and second stages.) See W. Ross Ashby, *An Introduction to Cybernetics* (Methuen, 1984), especially chap. 11; and Ashby, *Design for a Brain: The Origin of Adaptive Behaviour* (London: Chapman and Hall, 1978).

9. A typical rendition of this theme is the following: "Strict centralization of control . . . is necessary in order to make it possible for higher authority, in short time periods, to make a decision and direct all efforts of subordinate troops toward achievement of the assigned objective and to subordinate their actions to a single aim and plan. . . . The greatest degree of command and control centralization will take place while completing the most complex missions in critical situations; the initiative of subordinates is aimed mainly at carrying out assigned missions in the shortest possible time with the least amount of losses and expenditure of material resources." P. K. Altukhov and others, *Fundamentals of the Theory of Troop Control* (Voyenizdat, 1984), translated in *USSR Report: Military Affairs*, JPRS-UMA-84-022-L (November 15, 1984), pp. 42–43.

10. See Robert P. Berman and John C. Baker, *Soviet Strategic Forces: Requirements and Responses* (Brookings, 1982), p. 18.

11. Interview. For more information on ICBM command and control during the coup attempt, see *Command and Control of Soviet Nuclear Weapons: Dangers and Opportunities Arising from the August Revolution,* Hearing before the Subcommittee on European Affairs of the Senate Committee on Foreign Relations, 102 Cong. 1 sess. (Government Printing Office, 1992).

12. Wardak and Turbiville, eds., *Voroshilov Lectures,* vol. 2, p. 39.

13. "The decisive means of achieving the goals of modern war are rocket and nuclear weapons with their unlimited effective range and tremendous destructive capabilities. This requires maximum centralization of control of the principal nuclear rocket weapons in the Supreme Command, particularly in the initial period of the war, for here and only here is it possible to decide correctly and most effectively questions concerning the objectives of nuclear strikes, targets for destruction, the power of warheads and means for delivering them to the targets, the type of explosive effect and the time for the delivery of such strikes, and finally the issuing of orders or signal dispatches. Only here can the authority be placed for pressing the button to activate the principal weapons of war. The Supreme Command has thus become not only a directing organ of supervision but also the immediate executor of principal missions of the armed conflict." General Major N. Komkov and Colonel P. Shemanskii, "Certain Historic Trends in the Development of Troop Control," *Military Thought,* no. 10 (October 1964), p. 13, as cited in Lee and Staar, *Soviet Military Policy since World War II,* p. 56.

14. According to the secret Voroshilov lectures, direct command and guidance of the armed forces in wartime "is conducted by the Supreme High Command [VGK] through its main executive organ (*glavnyi organ upravleniia*), i.e., the General Staff." With respect to the strategic forces in particular, the lectures state: (1) "The Supreme High Command will directly control the Strategic Rocket Forces (through the General Staff or commander-in-chief of the Strategic Rocket Forces)"; (2) "Long-Range Aviation is a means of the Supreme High Command"; and (3) "Nuclear rocket submarines are means of the Supreme High Command," meaning directly under the control of the VGK. Wardak and Turbiville, eds., *Voroshilov Lectures,* vol. 2, pp. 22, 24, 27, 32.

15. Skip-echelon was a basic tenet of Soviet central command arrangements. The secret Voroshilov lectures say that "the Supreme High Command has the authority to assign missions directly to formations and large units without observing the established channels of control. The commanders-in-chief of the affected Services of Armed Forces are informed later about the missions assigned." Ibid., p. 32.

16. Ibid.

17. Interview with Soviet military source. The CINC Navy (Admiral Chernavin) acknowledged the subordination of his SSBNs to the SRF in wartime. See "Chernavin—the New C-in-C of the Soviet Navy," *Jane's Defence Weekly,* January 18, 1986, pp. 61–62.

18. Interview with Soviet military source.

19. Interview with former Soviet military officer. See also Statement of Bruce G. Blair, *Command and Control of Soviet Nuclear Weapons,* Hearing, p. 7.

20. The respective alert orders were complex, and the originators frequently sent erroneous messages that later had to be canceled. Interview with U.S. defense official.

21. The bombers may have been placed on combat ground or airborne alert for some unspecified period of time during the mid-1980s, according to one interview with U.S. government analysts.

22. Wardak and Turbiville, eds., *Voroshilov Lectures*, vol. 1, p. 229.

23. Ibid., pp. 191–95.

24. The secret course materials of the Voroshilov academy explain that alerting may proceed "on the basis of the General Staff's special directive (*osobaia direktiva*) that specifies concretely what measures are to be taken, by whom, and when." Ibid., p. 215.

25. During the 1968 SRF alert, which moved SS-5 units to 'increased' readiness, target instructions were retrieved from an envelope and technical personnel began to compute missile fuel requirements, engine calibration parameters, and so forth. Interviews with former Soviet military source.

26. For instance, constant readiness in the 1960s required the old SS-5 rockets of the SRF to be kept horizontal without fuel and warheads; increased readiness entailed mating the missiles with warheads (as was done during the 1962 SRF alert and the 1968 invasion of Czechoslovakia); and full readiness called for bringing them to the vertical position and fueling them. Once fueled the missiles could have been launched in twenty-two minutes after receiving a fire command, compared with about one to two hours for missiles at "increased" readiness. Interview with former SRF technician.

27. "In case of limited time, the Armed Forces are brought directly to a level of full combat readiness through notifying units and subunits by combat alert (*boevaia trevoga*) and by open and parallel execution of all measures and actions ensuring the readiness of troops for the accomplishment of assigned combat missions. At the same time, in accordance with additional instructions, the dispersal of forces and means are achieved, combat support elements deploy, the delivery of nuclear rounds is effected, and other actions are taken as the situation may require." Wardak and Turbiville, eds., *Voroshilov Lectures*, vol. 1, pp. 191–92. According to a 1965 Soviet military dictionary, "a combat alert is given by the senior commander, either as a command, or by a pre-arranged signal transmitted through communications channels, or otherwise." *Dictionary of Basic Military Terms: A Soviet View* (U.S. Air Force, 1976), p. 23, entry 174.

28. Wardak and Turbiville, eds., *Voroshilov Lectures*, vol. 1, p. 181.

29. Ibid., p. 190.

30. This discussion, as well as subsequent description, of Soviet nuclear commands is largely based on interviews with a former Soviet SRF officer.

31. See statement of Gennadi A. Pavlov, *Command and Control of Soviet Nuclear Weapons*, p. 5.

32. Interview with Soviet military officer.

33. "Strategic Directive of Stavka (SHC for Strategic Operations in the Western Theater of Military Operations)," Moscow, 1984; to be published as part of Voroshilov lectures series.

34. Interview with U.S. defense analysts, who further asserted that this authorization sometimes came from theater TVD headquarters.

35. Wardak and Turbiville, eds., *Voroshilov Lectures*, vol. 2, p. 33.

36. Multiple confirmations of an order also may have been necessary within a given organization such as the SRF. In the 1968 SRF alert that raised the combat readiness of SS-5 missiles in the SRF army headquartered at Smolensk, SS-5 battalions received orders from SRF headquarters in Moscow (via high-frequency radio), which were repeated via secure teletype links from Smolensk as well as Moscow. According to the defector on duty at the time, all three of these messages were necessary to validate the alert order. Interview with former SRF technician.

37. Wardak and Turbiville, eds., *Voroshilov Lectures*, vol. 1, p. 194.

38. Igor Fesunenko, "'Who's Who' Program with Dmitry Yazov, USSR Defense Minister and Marshal of the Soviet Union," Moscow Central Television First Progam Network, March 30, 1991, in Foreign Broadcast Information Service (FBIS), *Daily Report: Soviet Union*, April 1, 1991, p. 30.

39. It was functionally similar to an order given by the U.S. president to the senior U.S. military officials in the nuclear chain of command, an order whose legality could be established by using the identifying codes that the president (and some successors) carried on his person. If the U.S. president identified himself properly, his orders were considered legal.

40. " 'Nuclear Briefcase' Designer Interviewed," *Komsomolskaya Pravda*, January 28, 1992, p. 2, in FBIS, *Daily Report: Central Eurasia*, January 29, 1992, pp. 7–12. A six-person special unit from the Ninth Directorate of the general staff accompanied them and operated the portable equipment (lap-top computer size). A three-person unit from the general staff provided communications. See "Gorbachev Did Not Have Control of Nuclear Forces during Putsch," *Nezavisimaya Gazeta*, August 21, 1992, pp. 1–2, in FBIS, *Report: Central Eurasia*, August 30, 1992, p. 15.

41. Interview with a former SRF officer, who said the early-warning center also notified the CINC SRF. Another recent account asserted that the center notified the president, the general staff, and the central command posts of the services of the armed forces. See A. Dokuchayev, "A Bridle for 'Nuclear Racers,' or the Missile-Attack Warning System," *Krasnaya Zvezda*, September 27, 1990, 1st ed., p. 2., in *JPRS Report: Central Eurasia: Military Affairs*, October 15, 1990, pp. 53–55.

42. Interview with former Soviet SRF officer. This list of successors, if it ended here, was much shorter than the list of U.S. presidential successors, which ran from the president to the vice president, Speaker of the House of Representatives, president pro tempore of the Senate, and on through the entire cabinet. The parallel chain of U.S. pre-positioned national command authorities with emergency powers to order the release of nuclear forces further expanded the pool of U.S. officials who had the potential power legitimately to initiate U.S. nuclear strike operations. For further discussion, see Walter Slocombe, "Preplanned Operations," in Ashton B. Carter, John D. Steinbruner, and Charles A. Zraket, eds., *Managing Nuclear Operations* (Brookings, 1987), especially p. 133.

43. The organization was called *SIGNAL*, which is not to be confused with the *Signal* communications network discussed elsewhere. Interview with former Soviet SRF officer. See "Gorbachev Did Not Have Control of Nuclear Forces."

44. This statement is probabalistic rather than categorical, because one knowledgeable Soviet military source said that the supreme command had the option to send a special preliminary command to subordinate commanders that gave them conditional authority to launch the forces in the event of massive nuclear explosions on Soviet territory and a communications outage. Another equally knowledgeable Soviet military source dismissed this, saying it would never have been contemplated, on the grounds that top leaders feared that if nuclear authority was even provisionally delegated, they could not get it back. Interviews with two former SRF officers.

45. Such an arrangement seems to have been implicitly advocated by a former CGS who publicly voiced dissatisfaction with legislation enacted by the Soviet Congress on the grounds that it failed to vest the Soviet president (then Gorbachev) with sufficient authority to order the use of nuclear weapons single-handedly in an extreme emergency. Not long before the coup the CGS, whose complicity during the coup led to his dismissal, complained that had he been given the opportunity to speak to the Congress of People's Deputies, he would have proposed adding the following right to the president's powers: "in the event of enemy nuclear attack, the right to personally make the decision and issue the authority to use nuclear weapons as a retaliatory measure." "Important Step in Military Building," *Krasnaya Zvezda*, March 16, 1990, p. 2, in FBIS, *Daily Report: Soviet Union*, March 19, 1990, p. 88.

46. See Marina Chernukha, "The Nature of the Disagreements between Ukraine and the Chief Command of the CIS Joint Armed Forces on Strategic Nuclear Armaments," Moscow INTERFAX, July 17, 1992, in FBIS, *Daily Report, Central Eurasia,* July 17, 1992, pp. 2-3.

47. CINC Commonwealth Marshal Evgenii Shaposhnikov stated as recently as November 17, 1992, that he, and not Russian defense minister Grachev, was still in command of the strategic nuclear forces, though he stressed that it was "illogical" to exclude Grachev from the chain of strategic command. Doug Clarke, "Shaposnikov Commands Strategic Forces," *RFE/RL Daily Report,* no. 222 (November 17, 1992), p. 1. In reality, Grachev probably had already replaced Shaposhnikov in this role by early September. Grachev and the Russian CGS had by then moved into the general staff headquarters housing the nuclear war room. Shaposhnikov and his entourage simultaneously moved out to the headquarters of the defunct WTO. Interview with Russian analyst. In late September, Shaposhnikov began to advocate giving Russia sole control over the launch of strategic nuclear forces and over their dismantling. Belarus and Kazakhstan reportedly accepted the proposal; Ukraine rejected it completely. John Lepingwell, "Shaposnikov Calls For Russian 'Statehood' for Nuclear Weapons," and John Lepingwell, "Ukraine Rejects Increased Russian Control of Nuclear Weapons," both in *RFE/RL Daily Report,* no. 189 (October 1, 1992), p. 1.; and John Lepingwell, "CIS Heads of State to Discuss Nuclear Weapons Control," *RFE/RL Daily Report,* no. 195 (October 9, 1992), p. 1. By mid-October Shaposhnikov reportedly

relinquished control over all but Ukrainian strategic forces to the Russian SRF, while retaining a mediating role between Russia and Ukraine. John Lepingwell, "Summit Produces Mixed Results on Nuclear Weapons Control," *RFE/RL Daily Report,* no. 196 (October 12, 1992), p. 1; and John Lepingwell, "Commander of CIS Strategic Deterrent Forces Removed," *RFE/RL Daily Report,* no. 197 (October 13, 1992), pp. 1–2. The ascendance of Grachev over Shaposhnikov was further suggested by President Boris Yeltsin's statement on November 10, 1992, that all strategic forces belong to Russia and are controlled by the Russian president and defense minister. Stephen Foye, "Yeltsin on Nuclear Arsenal; Defense Production," *RFE/RL Daily Report,* no. 219 (November 12, 1992), pp. 1–2.

48. Wardak and Turbiville, eds., *Voroshilov Lectures,* vol. 2, p. 33.

49. Before this execution phase of the operation began, the supreme command could conduct a last-minute strategic *maneuver* that entailed changing targets and allocations of nuclear weapons: "Now maneuver is interpreted above all as an organizational and quick shift or redistribution of previously planned nuclear rocket strikes . . . usually carried out in accordance with the plan and under the leadership of the Supreme High Command. Large groupings of strategic rocket troops, the air forces, PVO Strany troops, naval forces and ground troops can participate in it. It is carried out both within the theaters of military operations and among several theaters. The chief content of strategic maneuver is the redirection of nuclear strikes." General Major S. Begunov, "The Maneuver of Forces and Matériel in an Offensive," *Military Thought,* no. 5 (May 1968), pp. 42–43, as cited in Lee and Staar, *Soviet Military Policy since World War II,* p. 235, note 47; quotation on pp. 57–58. According to Lee and Staar, the initial strategic maneuver of most forces was likely to occur during the crisis period prior to the onset of hostilities. Ibid., p. 235, note 46.

50. Actually the general staff released a direct command as a code with three equal parts, one for each branch of the strategic triad. The code was processed separately by the CINC SRF and then electronically sent back to a general staff node, which integrated the CINC SRF and general staff code inputs before disseminating it to the forces. This procedure points up the CINC SRF's importance relative to the navy and air force. Interview with former SRF officer. A different description of the nuclear launch procedure that implies a process by which the permission and direct commands are combined and sent to the launch crews as a string of ciphers (three from the president, three from the defense minister, and three from the affected nuclear CINC) is found in Yu. Kardashevskiy, "In Whose Hands Is the 'War Button'?" *Argumenty I Fakty,* no. 52 (December 1991), p. 2, in FBIS, *Daily Report: Central Eurasia,* January 6, 1992, p. 17. This questionable description implies that the president and defense minister codes are physically required by the launch crews for them to fire their weapons.

51. Interview with U.S. defense analysts.

52. Interview with SRF officer.

53. "There is the necessity to establish close interaction among all Services of the Armed Forces participating in a strategic action and centralized control by the Supreme High Command. The need for continuous interaction and central-

ized control of Armed Forces' strategic actions is important and must be met, since . . . strategic missions in each TSMA [theater of operations] and in each operation can only be accomplished if they are coordinated in the interest of the common goal. . . . The application of the principle of centralized control of strategic actions should ensure constant and flexible control of the Armed Forces." Wardak and Turbiville, eds., *Voroshilov Lectures,* vol. 1, pp. 243–44.

54. Wardak and Turbiville, eds., *Voroshilov Lectures,* vol. 2, p. 33.

55. Interview with U.S. defense analyst.

56. Interviews with U.S. government analysts.

57. Typically a pair of emergency communications rockets were launched, one from Tyuratam and one from another remote test site, on lofted trajectories that intersected each other as the missiles flew in opposite directions. Interviews with U.S. defense analysts.

58. Links to the fields east of the Urals were less dependable than land-line cable; those links consisted of microwave, high- and low-frequency radio, and satellite radio communications. Interviews with U.S. defense analysts.

59. The only SS-17s still in operational service in late 1992 reportedly were a division at Valday, midway between Moscow and St. Petersburg. The SS-17s were slated to be phased out over the next two years. See Doug Clarke, "Kokoshin on Strategic Rocket Forces," *RFE/RL Daily Report,* no. 220 (November 13, 1992), pp. 2–3.

60. The U.S. ERCS missiles—presumably now deployed in Minuteman III silos (previously deployed in Minuteman II silos at a SAC base in Missouri, all of which were deactivated in late 1991)—definitely could not be used to send fire signals directly to unmanned ICBMs. (For a discussion of the 1991 deactivation, see Susan Turley, " 'When We Speak, the World Listens' Motto Ends with System Deactivation," *Emergency Rocket Communications System,* A *Missouri Warrior* supplement, October 18, 1991.) The U.S. ERCS missiles merely transmitted a voice-recorded launch message to combat crews in other Minuteman control posts, strategic bombers, Navy SSBN communications relay planes, and so forth. The U.S. ERCS were normally loaded and fired by local launch crews after receiving a SIOP attack order from higher authority. In the event of the destruction of local launch centers, SAC airborne command posts positioned within line-of-sight range of the ERCS detachments (about 200 miles for an aircraft at 32,000 feet altitude) could load and fire the rockets by remote commands sent over UHF radio to the isolated, unmanned silos. See Bruce G. Blair, *Strategic Command and Control: Redefining the Nuclear Threat* (Brookings, 1985), pp. 166–69, 193–200. They also could do this at Defense Condition 3 or higher, when circuitry that normally blocks airborne access to the silos was tacitly turned off by the local launch crews in the underground control centers. (It is tacit because peacetime procedures called for these crews periodically to send computer commands to the Minuteman silos which block airborne access for a set amount of time measured in hours; at Defcon 3, the procedures no longer applied and after the short-time delay established by the last computer command, airborne access was unblocked.) It was technically feasible to modify this arrangement so that U.S. central command posts in the Washington vicinity could gain access to ERCS

missiles, in order to load and fire them, via satellite or other long-range communications.

61. Interviews with U.S. defense analysts and former Soviet SRF officers. See *Command and Control of Soviet Nuclear Weapons,* Hearing, p. 19.

62. Those who doubt the feasibility of unlocking missiles by such means should note that the United States installed an analogous system, though less centralized, on its Titan II missile force deployed between the 1960s and early 1980s. Wing and alternate wing command posts at Titan II missile bases, upon receiving a valid launch order, physically actuated switches that in effect unlocked the missiles throughout the wing and thereby configured them to accept the subsequent launch commands of SAC crews manning the individual missile sites. Under normal conditions, the SAC crews were physically incapable of firing their missile unless and until both the primary and alternate wing posts took positive actions to unlock the missiles. The reader should appreciate the potential to substitute higher level command posts for the wing posts in order to further centralize the release of safeguards against unauthorized launch. This could have been done easily from a technical and organizational standpoint.

63. Interview with former SRF officer.

64. Soviet military sources equated this SRF communications system with the 465L SAC Automated Command Control System used in the Minuteman ICBM system.

65. Interview with former Soviet SRF officer.

66. V. Litovkin, "Army General Yu. Maksimov: 'One Republic Cannot Maintain a Nuclear Shield,'" *Izvestiya,* August 30, 1991, p. 3, in FBIS, *Daily Report: Soviet Union,* August 30, 1991, p. 80.

67. David Remnick, "Alcohol Said to Fuel Coup by Gang of 8," *Washington Post,* August 30, 1991, p. A29.

68. Litovkin, "Army General Yu. Maksimov," p. 81.

69. See *Command and Control of Soviet Nuclear Weapons,* Hearing, p. 8.

70. Unique "biophysical" input from Gorbachev was supposedly necessary to activate his equipment. Some speculate this could involve retina scans or fingerprint readers. See Les Aspin, "A New Kind of Threat: Nuclear Weapons in an Uncertain Soviet Union," White Paper, House Armed Services Committee, Washington, September 12, 1991, p. 2. Aspin quotes the former Soviet CGS, Vladimir Lobov, as stating "that the system includes 'biophysical' safeguards." Russian sources suggest something far less sophisticated—for instance, a PIN number and a signature.

71. "Gorbachev Did Not Have Control of Nuclear Forces"; and A. Krayniy, " 'I Kept the Codes under My Pillow': Was There Any Real Danger of Starting a Nuclear War during the Putsch?" *Komsomolskaya Pravda,* August 31, 1991, p. 1, in FBIS, *Daily Report: Soviet Union,* September 10, 1991, pp. 1–2.

72. Interview with former Soviet SRF officer. See also *Command and Control of Soviet Nuclear Weapons,* Hearing, pp. 8–9.

73. " 'Nuclear Briefcase' Designer Interviewed," p. 7.

74. See Michael Dobbs, "Russia, Ukraine Both Claim Control over Black Sea Fleet," *Washington Post,* April 8, 1992, p. A16; and Steven Erlanger, "Ukraine

Finds 'Active Independence' despite Military and Other Obstacles," *New York Times,* September 6, 1992, p. 18.

75. The highly enriched uranium in the warheads can be diluted for use in commercial nuclear power reactors. The HEU in the Ukrainian strategic missiles alone has an estimated commercial market value of about $180 million. The United States has agreed to buy as much as 500 tons of HEU from dismantled warheads in the former Soviet arsenal. The FSU may possess upwards of 1,000 tons in its total arsenal. Serge Schmemann, "Ukraine Asks Aid for Its Arms Curb," *New York Times,* November 13, 1992, p. A10; Fred Kaplan, "Ukraine Officials Tying Missile Removal to Aid," *Boston Globe,* November 16, 1992, p. 1. This amount is consistent with a total inventory estimated by a Russian military officer to be 47,000 warheads (55,000 produced, and 8,000 eliminated, during the cold war). Interview.

76. "Further on Ministers' Actions," Moscow INTERFAX, July 3, 1992; "Shaposnikov Disagrees with Ukrainian Claims," Moscow ITAR-TASS, July 3, 1992; Yevgeniy Zherebenkov, "More on Shaposnikov's Comments," Moscow Radio Rossii Network, July 3, 1992; Andrey Naryshkin, "Results of Meeting Reported at News Conference," Moscow ITAR-TASS, July 4, 1992; Ivan Akkuratov, "More on Meeting's Results," Moscow Mayak Radio Network, July 4, 1992; all in FBIS, *Daily Report: Central Eurasia,* July 6, 1992, pp. 9–11.

77. Statement of Russian Deputy Foreign Minister Sokolov during meeting with Western visitors in October 1992.

78. Interview with former SRF military officer.

79. "Ukrainian Official on Plans for Warheads," Moscow INTERFAX, July 6, 1992, in FBIS, *Daily Report: Central Eurasia,* July 7, 1992, p. 3.

80. By November 1991 Marshal Shaposhnikov and Soviet experts had provided detailed briefings on nuclear command and control procedures for Ukrainian security officials. For instance, they had been briefed on a three-minute and ten-minute timeline for issuing the preliminary and direct commands, respectively. Interview with a U.S. adviser to Ukrainian government.

81. Marina Chernukha, "The Nature of the Disagreements between Ukraine and the Chief Command of the CIS Joint Armed Forces on Strategic Nuclear Armaments," Moscow INTERFAX, July 17, 1992, in FBIS, *Daily Report: Central Eurasia,* July 17, 1992, p. 2.

82. Ibid.

83. Ibid.

84. Interview with former SRF officers.

85. Ibid.

86. Interview with a former SRF officer.

87. See Mark Frankland, "Ukraine's Stance on Nuclear Arsenal Stirs Fresh Worries," *Washington Times,* November 23, 1992, p. 7.

88. Chernukha, "Nature of the Disagreements," p. 3.

89. To monitor and, if necessary, enforce the execution of orders, a general staff team was normally present at major field headquarters. Also the chief of staff from the headquarters level down to division level was a general staff officer. In addition to these normal peacetime assignments, John Hines contends, the

general staff dispatched a "shadow" network of troop control officers whose reporting network was separate from normal, regular general staff channels. For instance, one-star generals in this network monitored division-level activities. Interview. See also John G. Hines and Phillip A. Petersen, "The Changing Soviet System of Control for Theater War," *Signal*, vol. 41 (December 1986), pp. 97–110. Lynn Hansen notes that this control apparatus followed a World War II tradition in which the Corp of Officers of the general staff were dispatched to complement and assist the higher-ranking Stavka representatives sent to critical sectors. Lt. Col. Lynn M. Hansen, "Appendix L: The Soviet Command Structure: From Party to Military District," in Hansen and Rex D. Minckler, eds., *The Soviet Military District in Peace and War: Manpower, Manning, and Mobilization* (Washington: General Electric Company-Tempo Center for Advanced Studies, Net Assessment Programs Office, September 28, 1979), p. L-12. Accordingly, a corp of general staff officers presumably resided at the major command posts of the strategic forces, while additional teams could have been dispatched in a crisis to lower-level echelons. This crisis dispersion of representatives would have helped ensure continuity of central control in the event of disrupted command channels.

90. The now-defunct MPA reported to the Central Committee and operated as an independent body within the Ministry of Defense with parallel echelons through the five components of the Soviet armed forces down to the level of companies, batteries, and naval vessels. "Political Control of the Soviet Armed Forces: The Committee of People's Control," Defense Intelligence Report DDB-2600-1279-78 (Bolling Air Force Base, Va.: Defense Intelligence Agency, April 1978), pp. 2–4. The chain of command for the MVD interior troops apparently ran from the Defense Council through the Ministry of Defense to the field units. See also James T. Reitz, "The Soviet Security Troops—the Kremlin's Other Armies," in David R. Jones, ed., *Soviet Armed Forces Review Annual*, vol. 6 (Gulf Breeze, Fla.: Academic International Press, 1982), pp. 302–17.

91. U.S. government officials interviewed for this book universally emphasized the dual-track character of Soviet communications with nuclear units. Reportedly, almost all main military channels were overlayed on the same carrier by a KGB channel.

92. "Gorbachev-Yeltsin Nuclear Control Agreement," Berlin ADN, October 13, 1991, in FBIS, *Daily Report: Soviet Union*, October 15, 1991, p. 38.

93. Mark L. Urban, "Order of the Red Banner Carpathian Military District," *Armed Forces*, February 1983, p. 54. Steven Zaloga also asserts that the KGB *osnaz* teams guarded the detachable nuclear warhead sections for tactical missiles such as the SCUD. The warhead section for a missile was carried in a special trailer and attached only prior to fueling and loading. Steven Zaloga, "Soviet Military Developments: Russia's 'Military Chernobyl'?" *Armed Forces Journal International*, vol. 128 (June 1991), p. 28.

94. Regarding transportation, David Isby elaborates: "The warheads are moved to the delivery systems in closed vans as part of small, heavily guarded convoys, often with light aircraft overhead to maintain communications. Alternatively, warheads may be delivered by helicopters with a close escort of gunships

and a top cover of fighters." David C. Isby, *Weapons and Tactics of the Soviet Army* (London: Jane's, 1981), p. 210. Movement in special railroad carriages at night was also presumably a Soviet practice.

95. Clearance from Moscow reportedly came to the nuclear storage sites through telephone, radio, or satellite links assigned to the KGB, links that paralleled the military communications lines. Walter Pincus, "Soviets' Posture Shifts as SS20s Deployed," *Washington Post*, October 25, 1983, p. A15.

96. The Third Directorate, also known as the Special Departments (*osobye otdely*), conducted military counterintelligence, protected all military secrets, including nuclear weapons secrets, granted all security clearances of military personnel, and ensured strict observance of security regulations and procedures in all branches of the armed forces. Amy W. Knight, "The KGB's Special Departments in the Soviet Armed Forces," *Orbis* vol. 28 (Summer 1984), p. 271. Special departments or case officers from those departments existed in all military installations down to the levels of regiments and battalions (the latter is the level of ICBM launch control centers, for example). Ibid., p. 269. See also Aleksei Myagkov, *Inside the KGB: An Exposé by an Officer of the Third Directorate* (Richmond, Surrey, U.K.: Foreign Affairs Publishing Company, 1976), pp. 20–22. One Western study based on interviews with Soviet defectors concluded that, at least until the late 1960s, these special departments had custody of nuclear weapons. John Barron, *KGB: The Secret Work of Soviet Secret Agents* (Reader's Digest Press, 1974), p. 10. Other analysis suggests that while the KGB's special departments clearly had some important collateral relation to nuclear weapons custody and control, the main KGB stewards in charge of controlling stockpiles belonged to 'Section K' of the Ninth Directorate, a directorate that was also responsible for protecting the leadership and guarding key party and government buildings. Mark L. Urban, *Soviet Land Power* (Hippocrene Books, 1985), pp. 66, 71. According to Reitz, such KGB special objective guards (*Okhrana Osobykh Ob'ektov*)—or OOOs, as opposed to the OOs in the special departments—may have been technically trained for the handling and storage of nuclear munitions, whereas the portfolio of the more civil-oriented KGB counterintelligence personnel (OOs) seemed ill suited to custodial responsibilities. Reitz, "Soviet Security Troops," pp. 300–02.

97. "Interview with Bronislav Omelichev," *Defense Science*, August 1989, p. 14.

98. See Christopher Paine and Thomas B. Cochran, "Kiev Conference: Verified Warhead Controls," *Arms Control Today*, vol. 22 (January–February 1992), pp. 15–17. Paine and Cochran identify the special custodial unit as the Twelfth Directorate of the Defense Ministry, but in interviews Russian military officers asserted that this unit belonged to the general staff.

99. According to Stephen Meyer, "aircraft nuclear payloads [are] held separately in special storage sites guarded by KGB troops." Stephen M. Meyer, "The Soviet Theatre Nuclear Force Posture: Doctrine, Strategy and Capabilities," in Jeffrey D. Boutwell, Paul Doty, and Gregory F. Treverton, eds., *The Nuclear Confrontation in Europe* (London: Croom Helm, 1985), pp. 179–80. Meyer is among many U.S. analysts who have said that the KGB guarded warheads near the bomber airstrips.

100. William A. Burhans, "Operation 'Anadyr'—Backdrop to the 1962 U-2 Shoot Down," *Journal of Electronic Defense,* July 1990, pp. 26, 43, based on A. Dokuchayev, "Operation Anadyr'," *Krasnaya zvezda,* February 4, 1990, p. 2.

101. The defector knew only that these personnel were assigned to a nearby but totally separate bunker complex, were not SRF personnel and never mingled with SRF personnel, managed the nuclear warheads, and reported through a non-SRF chain of command. He considered it implausible that they were KGB.

102. "Since the Strategic Rocket Forces, the long range aircraft from the Air Forces and the nuclear submarines of the Navy must always be on the alert, with nuclear weapons in place, it would appear that KGB special guards must be with these forces. They also would be with other elements of the Soviet Armed Forces that have tactical nuclear capabilities." William Fontaine Scott, "Survival in the Nuclear Age: An Examination of a Soviet Concept," Ph.D. dissertation, George Washington University, 1974, p. 123.

103. Meyer, "Soviet Theatre Nuclear Force Posture," p. 180.

104. This claim is reported by Andrew Cockburn, *The Threat: Inside the Soviet Military Machine* (Vintage Books, 1984), p. 298. Cockburn told the author that the source of this information is a former U.S. government official who wished to remain anonymous.

105. "Close-up on ICBM Command and Control," *Jane's Defence Weekly,* February 6, 1988, p. 225.

106. Each SS-20 regiment reportedly was guarded by a KGB OSNAZ battalion equipped with BTR-70/80 armored transporters. War alert information and weapon-use authorization was provided by a "KGB communications alert company." "Further Details Released on SS-20 Saber Missile," *Jane's Defence Weekly,* vol. 9 (January 30, 1988), pp. 182–83. See also Steven Zaloga, "Soviet INF Forces," unpublished paper, 1988, on which the article in *Jane's* is based.

107. Interview with U.S. defense analyst.

108. Discussions with Sergei Zamascikov at the Rand Corporation.

109. Interview. This officer claimed that this KGB activity was abolished after the 1991 coup failed, and that nuclear custody became an exclusive responsibility of the general staff. His comment about the KGB is confirmed in "Tactical Nuclear Warheads Said to Have Been Removed from Baltic States," *Report on the USSR* (RFE/RL Research Institute, December 1991), vol. 3, p. 36.

110. KGB units accompanied his submarine on some but not all of the voyages his vessel made into the North Atlantic during the late 1970s to early 1980s.

111. A. Gorokhov, "Za pul'tami strategicheskikh," *Pravda,* May 29, 1985, as cited in Stephen M. Meyer, "Soviet Nuclear Operations," p. 492, note 56.

112. A senior Soviet general staff officer also said during an interview that the custody of the unlock codes for the strategic forces used to reside below the level of the general staff. This function was centralized in the fairly recent past. Similarly, a U.S. government analyst interviewed for this study disclosed that unlock codes for the strategic rocket forces were once held at the level of army SRF headquarters (there were six SRF armies, each one notch below the level of the CINC SRF in the pecking order) and disseminated from there to the ICBM launch crews. Special general staff detachments would presumably have resided at army headquarters in this case. Such decentralized arrangements for the cus-

tody of the codes was probably necessary for older models of ballistic missiles— SS-4s, SS-5s, SS-6s, SS-9s, and SS-11s—whose control systems were primitive compared with those of the newer classes. Extensive automation was introduced into the control systems of the SS-17s, SS-18s, and SS-19s. This streamlining allowed for greater centralization of control, with unlock codes placed under the jurisdiction of the chief of the general staff.

113. Major-General Geli Batenin, "Is Nuclear Terrorism Likely in the USSR?" press release, Novosti Press Agency, May 15, 1990.

114. Interview with a participant in the discussion.

115. Testimony presented May 8, 1990, as quoted in George Leopold, "U.S., Soviets Raise Concern Over Sea-Based Nuclear Security," *Defense News,* May 21, 1990, p. 6.

116. Interviews with Soviet military officers.

117. A contrary account cites Soviet navy sources who claimed that special safeguards requiring the insertion of a special code into a nuclear torpedo warhead prevented the unauthorized detonation of these weapons. See "Test Models of Small Submarines Described in Connection with 1981 Incident" [book abstract], *Izvestiya,* January 28, 1992, no. 23 (23597), p. 6.

118. Interview with participant in the meeting.

119. Conversation with the author in January 1992. See also Allen Levine, "Soviet General Says Unrest May Spark Nuclear Terror," *Atlanta Constitution,* October 16, 1991, p. 2.

120. Christopher Hanson, "Tensions Ease, but Nuclear Risk Lurks," *Seattle Post-Intelligencer,* June 6, 1990, pp. A1, A5.

121. A single short launch order would trigger the firing of U.S. SLBMs. The U.S. launch procedures were as follows. An order to launch would arrive encrypted at the radio room. The radioman alerted the officer of the deck who ordered the entire crew to battle stations. A two-person team responsible for validating the launch order convened in the radio room, where they may have been joined by the ship's captain and executive officer. The two-person team opened a dual-lock safe using combinations known only to themselves. They retrieved the presidential authenticators. If the launch message contained a code that exactly matched the authenticators, the team deemed the order valid; the captain and the executive officer also had to inspect and validate the codes. (This may have been performed in the control room rather than the radio room.) From the main control room, the captain informed the entire crew over the intercom that a valid order to launch had been received from the National Command Authority. The executive officer confirmed this fact over the telephone to the ship's missile control officer. Using a key retrieved by him from his safe (secured by a combination lock known only to him), the captain threw a switch that activated the ship's fire-control system. Simultaneously the executive officer removed, from a safe with a combination known only to him, a set of keys needed by missile technicians for arming the gas pressure release mechanisms on each missile tube designated for launch by the order. (The two-man control team provided the captain and executive officer the targeting information they needed from the order.)

Once launch preparations were complete, the missile control officer unlocked a safe with a combination known only to him, retrieved the actual missile firing pistol and, in accordance with the launch schedule specified by the original message and the standing war plan, pulled the trigger as each missile's light designated it was ready. This entire validation and launch procedure took about fifteen minutes. There were no external controls to physically prevent the launch of SLBMs. All safeguards were internal to the ship. Similar descriptions of U.S. SSBN launch procedures are found in Gerald Marsh, "Skirting Human Error: The Navy's Missile Launch System," *Bulletin of the Atomic Scientists,* vol. 43 (January–February 1987), p. 38; and Richard Whittle, "Ready for the Unthinkable," *Dallas Morning News,* May 25, 1986, pp. 1A, 18A.

122. S. Guk, "Robot at the Nuclear Control Panel?" *Izvestiya,* January 6, 1988, p. 5, in FBIS, *Daily Report: Soviet Union,* January 7, 1988, pp. 1–3.

123. Interviews with other knowledgeable Soviet sources have confirmed this account. See Victor Litovkin, "Inside a Russian Atom Sub," *We/My,* vol. 1 (March 1992), pp. 1, 2.

124. Interviews with former Soviet SSBN crew member.

125. *Weapons Proliferation in the New World Order,* Hearing before the Senate Committee on Governmental Affairs, 102 Cong. 2 sess. (GPO, 1992), p. 19.

126. This highly centralized release of unlock codes became possible after automatic equipment was introduced in the early 1980s. Previously the six SRF army headquarters probably controlled the unlock codes, which reportedly consisted of six-digit codes inserted into the launch panels by the missile battery commander. Interview with former SRF officer.

127. For representative statements, see V. Ostrovsky, "Army Gen Maksimov [commander in chief of the Strategic Rocket Forces] on Aspects of Military Doctrine," *New Times,* December 26, 1986, pp. 12–14, reprinted in JPRS-UMA-87-024, April 13, 1987, pp. 5–8; and N. Belan, "Masters of Strategic Missiles," *Sovetskaya Rossiya,* November 19, 1989, p. 3, in FBIS, *Daily Report: Soviet Union,* November 27, 1989, pp. 106–07. The chief of staff of the SRF put the matter as follows: "I repeat, historians of the nuclear missile forces have not recorded prerequisites for unauthorized actions." A. Gorokhov, "The Rocket Age," *Pravda,* February 21, 1990, 2d ed., p. 6, in FBIS, *Daily Report: Soviet Union,* February 23, 1990, p. 88.

128. V. Shcherban, "19 November Is Rocket Forces and Artillery Day," *Izvestiya,* November 19, 1987, p. 3, in FBIS, *Daily Report: Soviet Union,* November 27, 1987, p. 73. This proves very little or nothing. It is worth noting that U.S. ICBM launch crews were also trained to thwart unauthorized launch attempts despite the protection of coded switch devices that required input from higher authority before missiles could physically be fired.

129. Interview with former SRF officer.

130. Two-person launch crews (two SRF line officers) performed the essential procedures at the battalion control centers. These actions were monitored closely by higher authority and were coordinated with the two other battalion centers in a given regiment that provided redundant backup launch capability for each other. Interviews with former SRF officers. In the U.S. case the control proce-

dures for Minuteman launch were as follows: two-person SAC crews at underground launch control centers received the SIOP execution order. (The same SIOP message went to all the nuclear forces, including SSBNs and bombers.) The crews removed sealed authenticators and launch keys from a dual-lock safe (this step was already accomplished in the event of prior alerting) and compared the message codes with the authenticators. If they matched, the crew treated the order as a valid direct command from the president and convened a telephone conference with four other launch crews in their fifty-missile squadron to confirm the order's validity and coordinate launch procedures. If it was confirmed, the crew dialed unlock codes contained in the launch order into its "enable panel" and fired the missiles. In contrast to the Soviet system, which allowed weapons to be unlocked in a variety of groupings, the U.S. system used, for SIOP purposes, a universal unlock code—a single eight-digit unlock code unlocked the entire contingent of U.S. Minuteman missiles, including those to be withheld from launch according to the SIOP order. There were, however, individual unlock codes for non-SIOP strategic missions, such as limited nuclear options (LNOs).

Missiles began to lift off within four minutes after the crew received the SIOP message, and within seconds after the crew turned keys to issue the fire signal. In the absence of unlock codes, the "enable panel" was designed to prevent the launch center from transmitting a valid fire signal. The enable panel had been installed in Minuteman units in the 1960s, but Strategic Air Command did not activate its use until the late 1970s. When it was activated, unlock codes were needed to fire the missiles. If this blocking function was somehow compromised and a single crew succeeded in sending a fire signal to the squadron's missiles, an intrasquadron computer-based communications net immediately warned the other crews that an unauthorized launch was in progress. These crews vetoed the illicit command via computer control. (This was the main safeguard before unlock codes began to be used in the 1970s.) If two crews sent the fire signal, nothing could be done to stop the launch.

131. The West took the opposite approach to nuclear site security in Europe. It worried less about the Soviets being able to find and target nuclear storage sites in Europe than it did about terrorist attempts to capture weapons.

132. The number of nuclear warheads stored outside Soviet territory had probably always been very small. In the mid-1980s the main stockpiles inside Soviet territory assigned to the Soviet army were reported to be located around Kaliningrad, Klaipeda, and Kaunas in the Baltic republics (by 1990 evidently all nuclear munitions had been removed from the Baltics and relocated to other republics out of concern for security in this area of civil unrest); Nevel in Belarus; Lvov, Ivano-Frankovsk, Berdichev, Kharkov, and Odessa in Ukraine; Ulan Ude and Chita in the Transbaikal; Baku in the Caucasus (reportedly evacuated in 1990 during ethnic strife in the region, though a Soviet general asserted that nuclear munitions were never stored there and that the nearest nuclear stockpile was in the northern Caucasus); and around Vladivostok on the Pacific coast. Nuclear weapons storage facilities at Chita also served the strategic rocket forces, as did installations at Novosibirsk and Sverdlovsk. Nuclear weapons for the Soviet navy were sited on the Kola Peninsula, in the Crimea, in Vladivostok, and in

Petropavlovsk. Site locations taken from Urban, *Soviet Land Power*, p. 66. See also U.S. Department of Defense, *Soviet Military Power, 1986* (March 1986), p. 101. Quasi-official Soviet reports and Western reports of the relocation of nuclear weapons from areas of civil and political turmoil are Michael Dobbs, "Soviet Says Warheads Moved from Ethnic Sore Spots," *Washington Post*, September 28, 1990, p. A1; "Nuclear Weapons Removed from Baltics," *Washington Times*, May 22, 1990, p. A8; "Soviets Deny Having Moved Nuclear Arms," *Washington Post*, October 4, 1990, p. A43; Bill Gertz, "Lithuania Home to Biggest Soviet Nuclear Arsenal," *Washington Times*, April 23, 1990, p. A1; Bill Gertz, "Soviet Arms Safe from Civil Strife, CIA Director Says," *Washington Times*, February 14, 1990, p. A1; William J. Broad, "Upheaval in the East: Specter Is Raised of Nuclear Theft," *New York Times*, January 28, 1990, p. 12; and Bill Gertz, "Soviet Rebels Storm an A-Bomb Facility," *Washington Times*, February 19, 1990, p. A1.

133. This cooperative Russian-Ukrainian operation is described in detail in R. Jeffrey Smith, "Ukraine Plans to Speed Removal of A-Weapons," *Washington Post*, December 20, 1991, p. A1; R. Jeffrey Smith, "Ukraine Rigs A-Weapons to Ensure Safe Transfer," *Washington Post*, December 25, 1991, pp. A1, A26; and R. Jeffrey Smith, "Ukraine Minimizes West's Nuclear Fears," *Washington Post*, December 25, 1991, p. A26.

134. Smith, "Ukraine Minimizes West's Nuclear Fears." According to a U.S. government analyst, the disabling of warheads involved removing tritium bottles from each warhead before shipping them to Russia. Interview. The arming and fusing mechanisms on the warheads also could have been readily disabled in the field.

135. Interview with former Russian SRF officer.

136. One possible exception concerns an alleged effort by an international environmental organization to negotiate the purchase of a SCUD warhead from a general staff custodial unit based in East Germany. Reportedly, the transaction was scheduled for August 1991 but fell through when the unit and its wares were abruptly transferred back to the Soviet Union, according to persons involved in the scheme. Interview.

137. Doug Clarke, "Tactical Nukes Removed from Fleet," *RFE/RL Daily Report*, no. 216 (November 9, 1992), p. 2.

138. Russian defense minister Pavel Grachev recently confirmed this step. See John Lepingwell, "Grachev Reports Missiles outside Russia off Alert," *RFE/RL Daily Report*, no. 199 (October 15, 1992), p. 1. See also "CIS Strategic Nuclear Weapons outside Russia," Fact Sheet, Arms Control Association, Washington, November 4, 1992.

139. In January 1992 a Russian general told the author that nuclear weapons for strategic bombers would be relocated to Russia by July 1992. Another Russian general said in March 1992 that these weapons had been removed to "army storage facilities," but the location of such facilities was not disclosed. Interviews.

140. Interview with Russian military officer.

141. Interview with former SRF officer.

142. Interview with U.S. government analyst.

143. Interview with Russian military officer.

144. Ibid.

145. Interview with Russian analyst, who attributed these numbers to a Russian general.

146. Interview.

147. Interview.

148. "Ukrainian Official on Plans for Warheads," Moscow INTERFAX, July 6, 1992, in FBIS, *Daily Report: Central Eurasia*, July 7, 1992, p. 3.

149. Andrey Naryshkin, "Ukraine Disagrees with Strategic Forces Issue," Moscow ITAR-TASS, July 3, 1992, in FBIS, *Daily Report: Central Eurasia*, July 6, 1992, p. 8. See also Chernukha, "Nature of the Disagreements," pp. 2–3.

150. An SRF officer told the author that the combat readiness of strategic missiles had become very difficult to maintain because of shortages of equipment, supplies, and foodstuffs. Interview. The difficulty of maintaining missile forces at a high level of combat readiness is sometimes forgotten. The U.S. Minuteman force probably requires relatively less maintenance than Soviet ICBMs because of its reliable guidance system and solid fuel propulsion, yet its breakdown rate of approximately 1 percent a day (author's estimate) means that the alert rate would fall practically to zero in a few months if maintenance were suspended. Assuming a 2 percent a day breakdown rate for Soviet ICBMs, less than half the force would be operable after a month if maintenance were suspended.

151. In the majority of such regions, the non-Russian population constituted less than 50 percent. The portion of indigenous non-Russian ethnic groups varied widely from a low of 1 percent in the Khanty and Mansi autonomous district (West Siberia) to more than 80 percent in the republic of Dagestan (North Caucasus). Interview with Alexander Pikaev, Brookings, December 1992.

152. Ibid.; and *START: Treaty between the United States of America and the Union of Soviet Socialist Republics on the Reduction and Limitation of Strategic Offensive Arms*, signed in Moscow on July 31, 1991 (U.S. Arms Control and Disarmament Agency, 1991), pp. 157, 171.

153. See *START*, p. 200; and Robert S. Norris, "The Soviet Nuclear Archipelago," *Arms Control Today*, vol. 22 (January–February 1992), p. 28.

154. Interview with Russian SRF officer. See also "Comparison of U.S. and Russian Nuclear Cuts," Fact Sheet, Arms Control Association, Washington, September 1, 1992.

155. Author's estimate based on a number of sources, including Ivo H. Daalder, "Cooperative Arms Control: A New Agenda for the Post-Cold War Era," CISSM Papers I, Center for International Security Studies at Maryland, School of Public Affairs, University of Maryland at College Park, October 1992, p. 26.

156. This represents a reduction from an estimated 11,012 Soviet strategic warheads in September 1990 to 3,000 Russian strategic warheads by 2003. Under START, Russia's inventory would drop to 6,163 by the end of the seven-year implementation period. "Past and Projected Strategic Nuclear Forces," Fact Sheet, Arms Control Association, Washington, September 3, 1992.

157. Interview with U.S. government analyst. A Russian military officer estimated the cumulative number at 8,000 in an interview in early 1992.

158. Christopher Paine and Thomas B. Cochran, "Kiev Conference: Verified Warhead Controls," *Arms Control Today*, vol. 22 (January–February 1992), p. 16.

159. Sverdlovsk-44, Arzamas-16, and Chelyabinsk-65. Foye, "Yeltsin on Nuclear Arsenal; Defense Production," p. 1. Chelyabinsk-65 was the main facility for dismantling. Interviews with former SRF officer and U.S. government analyst. For a description of these and related facilities in the Russian nuclear weapons complex, see Norris, "Soviet Nuclear Archipelago," pp. 24–31.

160. Interview with former SRF officer.

161. Author's estimate.

162. Interview with former SRF officer.

163. Interviews with former Soviet military officers. The existence of this system was first revealed to the author during an interview with a Soviet official in 1989. See Bruce G. Blair and Henry W. Kendall, "Accidental Nuclear War," *Scientific American*, vol. 263 (December 1990), p. 58. Follow-on interviews with Soviet officials established that this passive destruct system was used extensively in combat missiles and also test missiles instead of range safety officers. One Soviet expressed the view that on-board technology was more reliable than these officers who might, for example, fall asleep on the job.

164. This tension would be greatly eased by a strategy of preemption: if an early firm commitment to unleash the Soviet nuclear arsenal were made, nuclear safeguards would immediately assume secondary importance. The command system would intentionally shed peacetime restraints, and a failure of negative control during this transition would obviously not be as catastrophic as a failure that occurred while the adversaries were still trying to avoid war.

165. Bruce J. Allyn and James G. Blight, "After Missile Crisis, Game of Chicken Went On: Closer Than We Knew," letter to the editor, *New York Times*, November 2, 1992, p. A18.

166. "The Hundred-Day Nuclear Cruise," *Krasnaya Zvezda* (*Red Star*) (November 6, 1992), p. 2. It is also doubtful that the general staff would have sent such an order unless Khruschev as well as the defense minister gave permission.

167. Brezhnev pledged, "The Soviet Union is assuming the obligation not to be the first to use nuclear weapons." L. I. Brezhnev, "The Second Special Session of the UN General Assembly," *Pravda*, June 16, 1982, p. 1, as cited in Garthoff, *Deterrence and the Revolution in Soviet Military Doctrine*, p. 85.

168. Marshal D. Ustinov, "To Avert the Threat of Nuclear War," *International Affairs*, vol. 9 (September 1982), p. 14.

169. Marshal D. F. Ustinov, "Strengthening the National Defense Capability of the Soviet Union: An Undertaking of the Party and the Entire Population," JPRS 82960 (February 28, 1983), pp. 133–34.

170. Bill Gertz, "KGB Halts Lookout for U.S. Nuclear Attack," *Washington Times*, November 28, 1991, p. A9; and "U.S./Soviet Tension," p. 7.

171. "U.S./Soviet Tension," p. 6.

172. These developments are discussed in greater detail in chapters 5 and 6.

173. Gen. Army D. T. Yazov, *Na strazhe sotsializma i mira* (On guard over socialism and peace) (Moscow: Voyenizdat, 1987), p. 32, as cited in Garthoff, *Deterrence and the Revolution in Soviet Military Doctrine,* p. 124.

Chapter Five

1. See Bruce G. Blair, *Strategic Command and Control: Redefining the Nuclear Threat* (Brookings, 1985).

2. See the assessment using strategic exchange calculations in Michael M. May, George F. Bing, and John D. Steinbruner, *Strategic Arms Reduction,* prepared in cooperation with the Lawrence Livermore National Laboratory (Brookings, 1988).

3. Reassurance and threat are the twin requirements of stable deterrence. The former refers to an implicit promise never to initiate a strategic attack; such reassurance may be necessary in a crisis to calm a nervous adversary lest his fear of enemy attack impel him to strike the first blow. The latter refers to the flip side, which conveys a stern warning: an aggressor will be severely punished for striking the first blow. Whichever side breaches the social covenant will suffer annihilating retaliation by the victim.

4. A representative example of the conservative bias on the U.S. side is the 1982 testimony by James P. Wade, Jr., then the principal deputy under secretary of defense for research and engineering and the individual most responsible for planning U.S. strategic command modernization during the early 1980s. His presentation conveys the impression of invulnerable Soviet nuclear command and control, notwithstanding the vast uncertainty permeating the issue. See *Department of Defense Appropriations for 1983,* Hearings before a Subcommittee of the House Committee on Appropriations, 97 Cong. 2 sess. (Government Printing Office, 1982), pt. 4, especially pp. 462–63. Regarding the U.S. system, a relatively known quantity to him, Wade says: "A very key uncertainty in the deterrent equation is the ability of our C^3 [command, control, and communications] system to survive a Soviet first strike, and thereafter be able to get the necessary messages out to our forces to respond, to retaliate. That is an imponderable, but it is something we are very worried about." Ibid., p. 544.

5. Albert Wohlstetter and Richard Brody, "Continuing Control as a Requirement for Deterring," in Ashton B. Carter, John D. Steinbruner, and Charles A. Zraket, eds., *Managing Nuclear Operations* (Brookings, 1987), p. 156.

6. Ibid.

7. Interviews with U.S. military officials.

8. Interviews with U.S. government analysts.

9. U.S. defense officials argued that the U.S. nuclear arsenal was "minimally effective" against such targets. See Warren Strobel, "U.S. May Redesign Nuclear Missiles to Hit Buried Targets," *Washington Times,* March 31, 1988, p. 1. The Defense Intelligence Agency reportedly asserted that "deep underground facilities for the top national leadership probably guarantee their survival in case of a

protracted conflict." Hardened facilities for the rest reportedly ensured that "a large percentage of the wartime management structure could survive the initial effects of a large-scale US nuclear attack." Edgar Ulsamer, "Gains and Gaps in Strategic Forces," *Air Force Magazine*, September 1985, p. 131.

10. Lawrence K. Gershwin, statement in *Soviet Strategic Force Developments*, Joint Hearing before the Subcommittee on Strategic and Theater Nuclear Forces of the Senate Committee on Armed Services and the Subcommittee on Defense of the Senate Committee on Appropriations, 99 Cong. 1 sess. (GPO, 1986), p. 17.

11. Ibid.

12. According to one scholar, a separate option for discretely attacking "Soviet command and control centers and systems" had been built into the SIOP that went into effect in July 1962, and had been preserved through subsequent SIOP revisions during the 1960s and early 1970s. See Desmond Ball, "U.S. Strategic Forces: How Would They Be Used?" *International Security*, vol. 7 (Winter 1982–83), p. 34. These plans included a separate option for targets in Moscow, providing at minimum a de facto leadership option because the top political and military headquarters were located there. An interview with a former SAC director of operations confirmed the existence of thirty-five SIOP plans within the overall SIOP at the time (late 1960s), one of which excluded the Soviet National Command Authorities from direct attack.

13. Interview with former SAC targeting official.

14. This level of Soviet government was roughly comparable to a county seat in the United States.

15. Director of Central Intelligence, *Soviet Civil Defense*, NI 78-10003 (Central Intelligence Agency, July 1978), p. 8.

16. Author's estimates based on interviews. See the discussion later.

17. As Lt. General Kelly H. Burke testified in 1982, "There has been a change in priorities. . . . the various studies that have been done on this in the last few years have all tended to affirm the scholarly view, that the thing that deters the Soviets most is to put at risk that which they value most, and typically the top of that list is their leadership. Right below it is their power projection capability, and then their urban industrial base, and I think this started really about the first year of the Carter Administration, and I think each year has moved a little more towards that set of priorities." *Department of Defense Appropriations for 1983*, Hearings, pt. 4, pp. 552-53. Testifying on behalf of MX procurement in 1985, General Charles A. Gabriel, the Air Force chief of staff, noted the missile's indispensability in killing hardened "command and control nodes and leadership targets. A lot of them may be even more important than the silos that we will have to go after." *Department of Defense Appropriations for 1986*, Hearings before a Subcommittee of the House Committee on Appropriations, 99 Cong. 1 sess. (GPO, 1985), pt. 2, p. 398.

18. That Soviet nuclear forces competed strongly with Soviet leadership for targeting priority comes through clearly in 1986 testimony by the Commander in Chief General Larry D. Welch of the Strategic Air Command. According to him, Soviet nuclear forces represented the number-one "priority target class" among

"the four classes of strategic targets," identified earlier as Soviet nuclear forces, other military targets, leadership, and urban-industrial base. Statement of Gen. Larry D. Welch, *Department of Defense Authorization for Appropriations for Fiscal Year 1987,* Hearings before the Senate Committee on Armed Services, 99 Cong. 2 sess. (GPO, 1987), pt. 4, pp. 1562–63. Interviews with recently retired former senior SAC officers confirm the roughly equal priority of Soviet nuclear forces and leadership in SIOP targeting. These officers point out, however, that coverage of all four target sets was so extensive that none appeared to lack weapons allocations. One could not examine the SIOP and deduce any clear-cut difference in priority across the categories. In fact, the SIOP was built in such a way that no category dominated another. One top SAC official, however, asserted categorically that counterforce targeting received the highest priority in U.S. strategic planning.

19. Thus a requirement had been levied to develop third-generation nuclear weapons and earth-penetrating warheads and to deploy them on delivery vehicles that could be withheld during a protracted nuclear war but yet be always available and reliably linked to higher authority for prompt, effective attack on Soviet command should the need arise. R. James Woolsey advocated the use of a mobile or shell-based ICBM for this purpose. See note 30.

20. The paramount importance of command and control survival was a theme running prominently through the gamut of Soviet military writings throughout the postwar era. A unique new source of information on Soviet military doctrine—lecture notes taken in 1973–75 by a student at the prestigious Voroshilov General Staff Academy—that has recently become available elaborates on the theme: "the probable enemy will focus particularly on conducting all types of reconnaissance to detect, locate, and disclose our control systems," and "anticipates the delivery of nuclear strikes on our command posts, signal centers, communication links, and other elements of signal communication to foil or significantly interrupt control of the Armed Forces at strategic, operational, and tactical levels." "Nowadays, secrecy of control of the Armed Forces must be ensured well in advance of wartime, because in the absence of a pre-established secret system, control in modern wars becomes meaningless." Ghulam Dastagir Wardak and Graham Hall Turbiville, Jr., eds., *The Voroshilov Lectures: Materials from the Soviet General Staff Academy,* vol. 2: *Issues of Soviet Military Strategy* (Washington: National Defense University Press, 1990), pp. 38, 37–38, 39.

21. To wit, the then chief of the Soviet navy's general staff wrote in 1982 (as translated by Drew Portocarrero): "The opponent will strive to disorganize the work of the means of control, communication and observation, and to protect his own radio-electronic means. Without exaggeration, it can be said that the course and outcome of armed struggle depend on how much commanders of all levels master questions of conducting radio-electronic struggle. It is known that foreign preparations for the struggle are accorded primary importance." Admiral V. Chernavin, "High Training Is the Basis of Combat Readiness," *Morskoy Sbornik* (Naval Digest), no. 11 (November 1982). As commander of the Soviet navy, Chernavin wrote in 1987 that "combat logic shows that the enemy will always seek, first of all, to put the command and control system out of action." "New

Requirements for the Navy," *Strategic Review*, vol. 15 (Summer 1987), p. 98, excerpted from V. Chernavin, "To Teach What Is Necessary in War," *Morskoy Sbornik*, no. 1 (January 1987).

22. The guidance issued under former defense secretary Caspar Weinberger's signature is quoted as instructing U.S. planners to ensure that "United States strategic nuclear forces can render ineffective the total Soviet and Soviet allied military and power political structure through attacks on the political and military leadership." Quoted in Richard Halloran, "Weinberger Angered by Reports on War Strategy," *New York Times*, August 24, 1982, p. B8.

23. Gen.-Maj. R. Simonyan, "Multi-variant Plans of Aggression: The Pentagon's Strategic Aims," *Red Star* (March 24, 1987), p. 3.

24. *Department of Defense Authorization for Appropriations for Fiscal Year 1987*, Hearings, pt. 4, p. 1592.

25. Edgar Ulsamer, "In Focus . . . The Chernobyl Backlash," *Air Force Magazine*, vol. 70 (August 1987), pp. 21–25.

26. Citing the Pentagon's planning guidance, Minister of Defense Dimitry Ustinov charged in 1982 that Pershing II missiles "will be aimed primarily at Soviet government and military command centers and also at our intercontinental ballistic missiles and other strategic targets." Quoted from excerpts published in Leon Gouré and Michael J. Deane, "The Soviet Strategic View," *Strategic Review*, vol. 11 (Winter 1983), p. 85. The commander of the Soviet strategic rocket forces, Marshal Vladimir Tolubko, similarly argued that by deploying Pershing II missiles, U.S. planners "hope to deliver the so-called 'decapitating' strike on the USSR." See Yuriy Teplyakov, "Constantly on Alert," *Moscow News*, July 8, 1984, p. 5, in Foreign Broadcast Information Service (FBIS), *USSR International Affairs: United States and Canada*, July 12, 1984, p. A1. Other Soviet critics underscored the missile's mission of attacking "command posts of strategic nuclear missile forces," and its payload of nuclear warheads "intended to penetrate dozens of meters into the ground. . . . to hit specially protected underground installations." See, respectively, Don Oberdorfer, "Soviet Says U.S. Missiles May Violate Pact," *Washington Post*, January 25, 1984, p. A18; and "Threat to Europe: Threat to the World," Moscow Television Service, April 20, 1985, in FBIS, *USSR International Affairs: Arms Control and Disarmament*, May 1, 1985, p. AA12. See also Raymond L. Garthoff, *Détente and Confrontation: American-Soviet Relations from Nixon to Reagan* (Brookings, 1985), pp. 881–83. Another Soviet charge alluded to Soviet reliance on launch on warning and to the potential of Pershing II to thwart the tactic: "the time required for a 'Pershing-2' to fly to its assigned target would be roughly five to six minutes, not the 25–30 minutes it would take an ICBM. This would give rise to the temptation to launch them by surprise in the hope that the other side would not be able to launch its missiles in retaliation before aggressor missiles reach its territory." Major General R. Simonyan, "The Pentagon's Nuclear Ambitions," *Agitator armii i flota* (Agitator of the army and navy), no. 1 (January 1982) [as translated by JPRS 81446, Aug. 4, 1982, p. 3].

27. The Pershing II would have been able to reach the SS-19 fields in the Ukraine as well as key SRF army headquarters and strategic bomber headquar-

ters for a long-range air aviation army. The U.S. missile would also have threatened the strategic intermediate high command headquarters of the Western TVD commander (Marshal Nikolay V. Ogarkov), whose main command post was located at Legnica, Poland, and backup command post was at Minsk. The Warsaw Pact commander's (Viktor G. Kulikov) command posts were also within range; his main command post was at Frankfurt on Oder near the East German–Poland border, with a backup at Lvov. Last, the Pershing II possessed the range to reach nearly all the way to Moscow itself. National command posts for the top leadership, such as one located in Kuntsevo, a short distance to the west of Moscow, were presumably considered, not unreasonably, to be within the lethal radius of the weapon.

28. The test warhead penetrated "through 22 feet of solid rock." Dan Stober, "Earth-penetrating Warhead Experiment Called Successful," *San Jose Mercury News,* October 20, 1988, p. B4.

29. For authoritative statements on the weapons program see the testimony of Robert Barker, Assistant to the Secretary of Defense for Atomic Energy, *Hearings on National Defense Authorization Act for Fiscal Years 1988/1989—H.R. 1748 and Oversight of Previously Authorized Programs, Department of Energy National Security Programs,* before the Procurement and Military Nuclear Systems Subcommittee of the House Committee on Armed Services, 100 Cong. 1 sess. (GPO, 1987), p. 55; Lawrence W. Woodruff, "Operations Research and Strategic R & D Planning," *Phalanx* [Bulletin of Military Operations Research], vol. 21 (March 1988), pp. 1, 3–4. See also David J. Lynch, "SAC Readies New Warhead Requirement," *Defense Week,* vol. 7 (December 8, 1986), pp. 1, 14; "Industry Observer," *Aviation Week and Space Technology,* vol. 126 (February 16, 1987), p. 11; Charles W. Corddry, " 'Earth Penetrator' Missile Proposed for Deep Strikes," *Baltimore Sun,* June 11, 1987, p. 3; "Maneuverable, Penetrating Nuclear Warhead Expected," *Defense Electronics,* September 1987, p. 13; Howard Silber, "U.S. Working on Warheads to Hit Soviets Underground," *Omaha World-Herald,* September 27, 1987, p. 1; and Strobel, "U.S. May Redesign Nuclear Missiles."

30. R. James Woolsey advocated the use of a mobile or shell-based ICBM for delivering earth-penetrating weapons. In evaluating candidate delivery systems he argued that "such a weapon should not be employed, however, on any system, such as a silo- or garrison-based ICBM, that might be used hastily at the beginning of a nuclear exchange—thus destroying initially any party on the other side that might be able to negotiate an end to the war. Placing such a weapon on a bomber would be better, but the questions about bomber survivability . . . mitigate the deterrent effect of any such bomber-based system. Submarine survivability is excellent, but it would be preferable to have such earth-penetrating weapons based in such a way that they could be employed singly, not on systems such as submarines for which there are military incentives to use all available weapons on the platform at one time and for which two-way communications are difficult. The most desirable system . . . is a mobile or shell-game based ICBM, so that if a war should begin, a surviving national command authority could let the Soviets know that it had available at any time, with good command and

control, the ability to launch a weapon that could with great certainty arrive at and destroy the most precious Soviet assets." R. James Woolsey, "U.S. Strategic Force Decisions for the 1990s," *Washington Quarterly,* vol. 12 (Winter 1989), p. 82.

31. Marshal Tolubko, commander of the SRF, laid out a scenario for U.S. preemptive nuclear attack using third-generation weapons in an article published in 1983: "The U.S. Administration has set its scientists the task of creating new, 'third generation' bombs (the first generation being the atom bomb and the second the hydrogen bomb) with an intensified electromagnetic pulse. The hope . . . is simple: by means of the simultaneous surprise detonation of several such bombs at an altitude of 400–450 km above the Soviet Union's territory to totally destroy our communications control system and temporarily deprive us of the possibility of swiftly delivering a retaliatory strike; and then, exploiting this pause, to carry out a massive strike using the entire might of the American triad (ground-, sea-, and air-launched missiles)." Naum Mar, "Roads to Victory," *Literaturnaya Gazeta,* no. 18 (May 4, 1983), p. 12, in FBIS, *USSR International Affairs: Disarmament/START/MBFR,* May 3, 1983, p. AA4.

32. These descriptions of Soviet nuclear exercises are composites based on incomplete material collected during interviews for this study. Owing to sketchy information some details may be incorrect and the interpretation may be no closer to and perhaps further from the truth than alternative interpretations.

33. This account of the exercise up to the point of SIOP impact closely matches a scenario described in a Soviet book published in the same year that the exercise was conducted. The Soviet author's scenario has been summarized by an American analyst as follows: "[The] scenario depicts a war with a long conventional phase, where dual-capable aircraft play an important role. The picture painted is one of a conventional air campaign, with enemy bombers operating in the theatre and entering Soviet airspace on deep-strike missions. At a point, they initiate a nuclear attack, but the USSR is unable to recognize the transition, and has no warning. It is thus deprived of any chance of pre-emptive action, and must absorb a nuclear strike before retaliating." Rose E. Gottemoeller, *Land-Attack Cruise Missiles,* Adelphi Papers 226 (International Institute for Strategic Studies, Winter 1987–88), pp. 18–19. The Soviet work in question, as cited by Gottemoeller, is Aleksey Arbatov, *Voyenno-strategicheskiy paritet i politika SShA* (Military-strategic parity and U.S. policy) (Moscow: Izdatel'stvo politicheskoy literatury, 1984), p. 97. Gottemoeller (p. 52) notes Arbatov's interesting assertion that his scenario was "closer to reality" than one in which ballistic missiles strike first and bombers lumber in later.

34. Two separate accounts of this exercise differ slightly on the character of the initial Soviet response. Both accounts agree it was a minimal response. One version, however, claimed the Soviets simulated the employment of 250 theater nuclear missile warheads plus some aviation sorties, but no ICBM or SLBM warheads.

35. If instructions for preparing and arming missiles for launch had been sent previously, the final launch order could be transmitted in about four minutes. The final order could have been very short—consisting of a single word alone or

together with a date-time group—but the required number of repetitions length-ened the transmission period. However, according to a former Soviet SSBN of-ficer, launch orders could be transmitted in less than one minute. As discussed in chapter 4, a direct command to SSBNs normally involved both the general staff and the CINC Navy.

36. The West started jamming the Soviet fleet broadcast network five hours before the British submarine opened fire, but apparently the jamming was inef-fective.

37. By this time a full U.S. SIOP attack had begun, and the Soviet leadership faced bigger problems. Their decision to launch on warning is analyzed in the next chapter.

38. This exercise reaction time of seventeen minutes compares with estimates given by a former SSBN crew member ranging from nine to fifteen minutes. Interview.

39. Reportedly the first time the airborne naval command staff communicated directly with Soviet SSBNs was in 1983. "News in Brief: Soviet Airborne Com-mand Posts Exercised," *International Defense Review,* vol. 16 (June 1983), p. 755. Transmitting at the high-frequency band of the radio spectrum, signals do not penetrate water, which implies the use of submarine antennas that float on the water's surface. The Soviet's Bear-J aircraft are superior for this mission, but these aircraft disappeared from the exercise after supporting the earlier Delta I strike. The Bear-J planes were a recent addition to the Soviet inventory and normally operated in tandem with Soviet Delta IV- and Typhoon-class ballistic missile submarines, which in exercises never launched in conjunction with strikes by the land-based SRF forces. This implied that they would be held in reserve during a strategic exchange and would receive any eventual launch orders through the Bear-J channel.

40. Author's estimate.

41. *Department of Defense Appropriations for 1984,* Hearings before a Sub-committee of the House Committee on Appropriations, 98 Cong. 1 sess. (GPO, 1983), pt. 8, p. 316.

42. Statement of Lawrence K. Gershwin, *Soviet Strategic Force Developments,* Joint Hearing, p. 17.

43. The size of the personnel roster for the general staff alone was immense. The main operations directorate alone had a very large staff.

44. *Department of Defense Appropriations, Fiscal Year 1978,* Hearings before the Senate Committee on Appropriations, 95 Cong. 1 sess. (GPO, 1977), pt. 1, p. 17.

45. U.S. Department of Defense, *Soviet Military Power: An Assessment of the Threat, 1988* (April 1988), p. 61.

46. Ibid., pp. 59–62.

47. Ibid., p. 60.

48. Richard D. DeLauer, "Emerging Technologies and Their Impact on the Conventional Deterrent," in Andrew J. Pierre, ed., *The Conventional Defense of Europe: New Technologies and New Strategies,* Europe/America 5 (Council on Foreign Relations, 1986), p. 56n.

49. Interviews with U.S. government analyst.

50. U.S. Department of Defense, *Military Forces in Transition, 1991* (1991), pp. 40, 43.

51. The KGB allegedly built the facilities and communications reserved for party and government officials, while military construction units built the military command facilities. Interview with U.S. defense consultant.

52. Every ministry is reported to have had a primary and alternate facility, the latter described as a "hardened bunker facility of enormous extension." *Department of Defense Authorization for Appropriations for Fiscal Year 1983*, Hearings before the Senate Committee on Armed Services, 97 Cong. 2 sess. (GPO, 1982), pt. 7, p. 4673. See also *Department of Defense Appropriations for 1984*, Hearings, pt. 8, p. 316; and William E. Burrows, *Deep Black: Space Espionage and National Security* (Random House, 1986), pp. 7–8.

53. *Department of Defense Appropriations, Fiscal Year 1978*, Hearings, pt. 1, p. 16.

54. U.S. Department of Defense, *Soviet Military Power, 1988* (April 1988), p. 59; *Department of Defense Authorization for Appropriations for Fiscal Year 1983*, Hearings, pt. 7, p. 4673; and *Department of Defense Appropriations for 1984*, Hearings, pt. 8, p. 316.

55. Interview with U.S. defense consultant.

56. A high-ranking Soviet defector, Arkady N. Shevchenko, divulged this fact in *Breaking with Moscow* (Knopf, 1985), p. 208.

57. Interview with former U.S. government analyst. According to the interview, U.S. monitoring of this exercise, including eavesdropping on the telephone links to the limousines, was abruptly thwarted because of a compromising leak to a columnist who published a story in the middle of the exercise.

58. Interviews with U.S. government analysts. Interview material indicates that communications between the supreme high command and the operations directorates of the general staff and the SRF utilized KGB channels. It is commonly asserted that KGB channels ran from the top to the bottom of the Soviet nuclear chain of command, through which political authorities could exercise direct control, independent of the military command structure. As discussed in chapter 4, special sections of the general staff actually managed this separate channel of control. Also, the specialized *Kazbek* channel became operational in the early 1980s. It was to be used by the supreme command to give permission to employ nuclear weapons. See chapter 4 for further discussion of the Soviet's dual-channel control of nuclear operations.

59. U.S. Department of Defense, *Soviet Military Power, 1988*, p. 61. U.S. analysts generally believe that top political authorities who relocated to remote facilities outside the Moscow area would have exercised nuclear command through KGB links back to the primary and alternate command posts in the Moscow vicinity. After the early 1980s the *Kazbek* system was available to dispersed national command authorities for the purpose of sending nuclear release authorization to the nuclear CINCs and the general staff. The U.S. arrangement is similar. When the U.S. national command authorities and presidential successors travel outside Washington, the White House military office sets up commu-

nications links back to the Pentagon, the location of the primary command post of the National Military Command System, through which the National Command Authorities (NCA) would exercise nuclear release authority. Backup communications would link the NCA to alternate command posts of the National Military Command System (NMCS) (the underground alternate at Ft. Richie, the national emergency airborne command posts, the national ground mobile command posts) in the event of an enemy attack that destroys the Pentagon's war room.

60. U.S. Department of Defense, *1991: Military Forces in Transition* (September 1991), pp. 40, 43.

61. Desmond Ball, *Soviet Signals Intelligence (SIGINT)*, Canberra Papers on Strategy and Defence 47 (Canberra: Australian National University, Research School of Pacific Studies, Strategic and Defence Studies Centre, 1989), p. 12.

62. Interviews with former Soviet weapons designer and U.S. government analyst.

63. Director of Central Intelligence, *Soviet Civil Defense*, p. 3.

64. Samuel Glasstone and Philip J. Dolan, eds., *The Effects of Nuclear Weapons*, 3d ed. (U.S. Department of Defense and U.S. Department of Energy, 1977), pp. 253–57.

65. This calculation is based on ibid.

66. This revised calculation and others derived from the new formula, which are presented below, are unclassified. They were provided to the author by a U.S. Department of Defense analyst.

67. Interview with former senior SAC officer.

68. According to U.S. specialists who have examined Soviet technical research in the area of underground structures vulnerability, the Soviets developed at least four different models of the cratering effects of nuclear weapons, and the results of these models vary enormously (by 200 to 300 percent). This represents a high level of uncertainty. According to one specialist, bibliographic references of particular interest are A. M. Basovskaya and L. Ye. Basovskiy, *Povysheniye prochnosti podzemnykh sooruzheniy* (Increasing the strength of underground installations) (Moscow: Nedra, 1982); I. Ya. Dorman, *Seysmostoykost' transportnykh tonneley* (Seismic stability of transport tunnels) (Moscow: Transport, 1986); M. V. Kurlenya and V. Ye. Mirenkov, *Metody rascheta podzemnykh sooruzheniy* (Methods for designing underground structures) (Novosibirsk: Nauka, 1986); G. M. Lyakhov, *Volny v gruntakh i poristykh mnogocomponentnykh sredakh* (Waves in soils and multicomponent media) (Moscow: Nauka, 1982); and P. S. Mironov, *Vzryvy i seysmobezopastnost' sooruzheniy* (Explosions and seismic safety of structures) (Moscow: Nedra, 1973).

69. All the estimates that follow assume that a buried command post would suffer severe structural damage unless its depth exceeded one and one-half times the apparent crater radius and that severe impairment of equipment and occupants would occur unless the facility's depth exceeded two and one-half times the apparent crater radius. This is of course a simplification, but there is evidence to support it, and the Soviets have assumed this relationship in some of their studies. This assumption was pointed out by a U.S. analyst specializing in the

vulnerability of deep Soviet command posts. He cited, among other Soviet studies, an open source that corresponds closely to confidential material: V. G. Ma-
likov, *Shakhtnyye Puskovyye Ustanovki* (Launching silos) (Moscow: Voyenizdat,
1975). Another simplification concerns the soil varieties found in the Moscow
vicinity. According to the U.S. Defense Department, the Moscow basin consists
largely of wet soft rock. The new formula is therefore applied to this specific soil
variety. The old formula inconveniently clumps wet soft rock and wet soil into
the same category. For purposes of computation the old formula treats them as
equivalent geological materials.

70. The B-53 bomb was brought out of retirement several years ago to serve
this mission, in an evident scramble to replace the high-yield (7.4-megaton) warheads retired from the inventory when the Titan II ICBM was phased out. "U.S.
Puts Old H-Bomb out on Line," *Daily Progress* (Charlottesville, Va.), August
5, 1987, p. A9.

71. Oleg Penkovskiy, *The Penkovskiy Papers,* trans. Peter Deriabin (Avon,
1965), p. 333.

72. A Soviet military officer who defected to the West in the 1970s placed the
location of the Soviet wartime supreme command post at Zhiguli near Kuybyshev.
"In Zhiguli tens of kilometres of tunnels have been cut, hundreds of metres deep
into the granite monolith and command posts, communications centres, stores
and shelters have been built for those who will control the gigantic armies during
a war." He also claimed that a corps of national air defense forces and a division
of the KGB were stationed there to protect the facility. Viktor Suvorov, *Inside
the Soviet Army* (Macmillan, 1982), p. 155. This description is consistent with
Albert Wohlstetter's suggestion that Soviet command fortifications be hypothe-
sized as "1,000 feet deep in a spot unknown within a radius of, say, tens of miles."
Albert Wohlstetter, "Between an Unfree World and None: Increasing Our
Choices," *Foreign Affairs,* vol. 63 (Summer 1985), p. 988. Another reputable
analyst surmised that the Volga Military District headquarters at Kuybyshev
would have "become an alternative supreme command post for the entire Soviet
Army." David C. Isby, *Weapons and Tactics of the Soviet Army* (London: Jane's,
1981), p. 26. The use of specially prepared command posts of military districts
by the supreme high command was revealed in the secret lectures of the Voroshilov General Staff Academy. Ghulam Dastagir Wardak and Graham Hall Turbiville, Jr., eds., *The Voroshilov Lectures,* vol. 1: *Issues of Soviet Military Strategy*
(Washington: National Defense University Press, June 1989), p. 304. A U.S.
government analyst interviewed for this study confirmed the existence of an
alternate supreme high command post at Zhiguli.

73. Whereas available weapons created craters and ruptured the earth surrounding an underground command post to cause damage, the earth-penetrating
nuclear warheads under development exploited a phenomenon known as "ground
coupling," which magnifies the underground shock effects of nuclear explosions.
See "Maneuverable, Penetrating Nuclear Warhead Expected," p. 13; and Lynch,
"SAC Readies New Warhead Requirement," p. 1.

74. Clemens Range, "NATO Digs Itself In on the Ruhr," *Die Welt,* April 4,
1988, p. 4.

75. Ibid. The U.S. Strategic Air Command employed such high-frequency "pop-up" transmitters at squadron launch control centers in the Minuteman fields. These were slated for replacement by buried antenna plots modeled after Soviet deployments (discussed later). See Eyring Research Institute, "Eyring Survivable Antennas: MHFARS," ERI Doc. 900-0020, Rev. C. (Provo, Utah, April 1987).

76. Various interviewees identified them as B, D, and E type antennas with frequencies ranging from medium to high to very high. They used a combination of troposcatter links and sky- and ground-wave modes of propagation. The ground-wave mode was by far the least susceptible to disruption from nuclear effects, but its range was short—approximately 100 miles. The United States also exploited this mode to a limited extent. A medium-frequency ground-wave link connected the launch control centers at one of the Minuteman III ICBM wings with their missile silos, augmenting the underground cable connections. Interview with U.S. defense contractors.

77. See Freeman G. Lee, "High Frequency Tactical Antennas Go Low Profile," *Signal,* vol. 41 (November 1986), pp. 27–35.

78. Interviews with U.S. government analyst and U.S. defense contractor.

79. Eyring Research Institute, "Eyring Survivable Antennas: Blast Hardened Series," ERI Doc. 900-0019, Rev. A (Provo, Utah, April 1987), p. 6.

80. U.S. Department of Defense, *Soviet Military Power, 1985* (April 1985), p. 28.

81. *Department of Defense Authorization for Appropriations for Fiscal Year 1983,* Hearings before the Senate Committee on Armed Services, 97th Cong. 2 sess. (GPO, 1982), pt. 7, p. 4675. Polmar identifies the cruisers as two *Sverdlov*-class light cruisers. Norman Polmar, "Thinking about Soviet C³," *NATO's Fifteen Nations,* vol. 24 (October–November 1979), p. 38.

82. Converted to a command ship configuration in 1972, the cruiser *Zhdanov* was intended to be the Pacific Fleet command ship, and the cruiser *Senyavin* was the Black Sea command ship for the Atlantic side. The Soviets also converted two old Golf-class submarines for use as communications relays in theater naval roles. Jim Bussert, "Soviet Navy Communications," *Jane's Soviet Intelligence Review,* vol. 2 (March 1990), p. 140. See also Polmar, "Thinking about Soviet C³," p. 38.

83. The largest Soviet naval exercises in the 1970s, called Okean-70 and Okean-75 for the years they were held, "appeared to rely on command being exercised directly from the Main Naval Staff in Moscow, even to the extent of co-ordinating simultaneous air attacks on targets in both the Atlantic and Pacific Oceans." Large naval exercises in the 1980s involving conventional operations at sea apparently allowed some of the direct control of the main naval staff to be shifted to the Sverdlov cruisers with new flagship facilities. R. van Tol, "Soviet Naval Exercises 1983–85," *Naval Forces* vol. 7, no. 6 (1986), pp. 22, 23. See also Desmond Wettern, "Stretching the Bears Claws: Soviet Exercise '83," *Navy International,* vol. 89 (September 1984), pp. 518–24.

84. Interviews with U.S. government analysts. In 1979 the U.S. chief of naval intelligence characterized the Soviet airborne command posts as "archaic" and as serving essentially as communications relay aircraft. *Department of Defense*

Appropriations for 1980, Hearings before the Subcommittee on the Department of Defense of the House Committee on Appropriations, 96 Cong. 1 sess. (GPO, 1979), pt. 6, p. 143. Sources interviewed believed the Coots were likely to be replaced by newer transport aircraft, such as the wide-bodied, IL-86 or IL-96 jet aircraft. According to some reports the Soviets began to fly modern jet aircraft in the role of national airborne command posts. Norman Polmar claimed the Soviet version of the national emergency airborne command post used Ilyushin-62 and Il-76 turbojet aircraft. Polmar, "Thinking about Soviet C³," p. 40. A U.S. naval intelligence officer said as recently as 1988 that the dedicated airborne command post for strategic naval staffs was an IL-22 Coot, an archaic plane that he expected to be augmented and eventually replaced by the IL-96 over the next decade. Edward D. Sheafer, Jr., "The Threat Expands, Expands," *Wings of Gold,* Summer 1988, p. 20.

85. The airborne command posts attached to the individual SRF armies would normally have performed this polling function, but if they became disabled the task fell to the higher level SRF airborne command post and the SRF army representatives on its battle staff. Interview with U.S. government analysts.

86. More Bear-Js were being built; the total inventory was expected to reach twelve. Interview with government analyst.

87. Base locations are discussed in G. Jacobs, "Soviet Strategic Command and Control and the Tu-142 'Bear J,' " *Jane's Soviet Intelligence Review,* vol. 3 (April 1, 1991), pp. 161–64.

88. Interviews with U.S. government analysts and former military officials.

89. This general staff organization was directly subordinate to the supreme high command, and its activity would have been interpreted as a sign of Soviet concern about the possibility of war. Its activity was an early tip-off of major Soviet exercises and would have been an early strategic warning indicator in time of crisis. Interview with former U.S. government analyst.

90. Interview with U.S. government analysts.

91. U.S. Department of Defense, *Soviet Military Power* (September 1981), p. 55.

92. These armies occupied six regions of the Soviet Union, though most missile fields were spread along the trans-Siberian railroad. The types of missiles and missions associated with the six armies are discussed at length in Robert P. Berman and John C. Baker, *Soviet Strategic Forces: Requirements and Responses* (Brookings, 1982), especially pp. 14–18.

93. For the locations of divisional headquarters, see U.S. Department of Defense, *Soviet Military Power, 1990* (September 1990), map foldout.

94. A battery consisted of a single launcher (silo or transporter-erector-launcher for fixed and mobile ICBMs, respectively). For a precise breakdown of ICBM deployment patterns, see *START: Treaty between the United States of America and the Union of Soviet Socialist Republics on the Reduction and Limitation of Strategic Offensive Arms,* signed in Moscow on July 31, 1991 (U.S. Arms Control and Disarmament Agency, 1991), pp. 152–70.

95. Each regiment has three battalions, and each battalion had three batteries. Ibid., pp. 170–75.

96. See U.S. Department of Defense, *Soviet Military Power,* 1981, p. 55. See

also Michael MccGwire, *Military Objectives in Soviet Foreign Policy* (Brookings, 1987), pp. 489–92.

97. This setup was comparable to a Minuteman launch control center that commanded a flight of ten missiles.

98. Interview with former U.S. government analyst. Similarly five Minuteman flights formed a squadron of fifty missiles, any or all of which could be launched by any of the five redundant launch control centers in the formation. See Blair, *Strategic Command and Control,* p. 87. The Soviet deployments varied considerably more. In some units there were four, six, or more potential launch control points. Typically the nearest two neighboring launch posts provided redundant backup control for the primary battalion post. Interview with former SRF officer.

99. The Soviets surely worried that prospective U.S. missile defenses threatened to be quite effective in dealing with the ragged firing of residual ICBMs by the surviving battalion launch centers. The Soviet planner's worst nightmares presumably included this scenario of a judiciously aimed decapitation strike and active defenses against the attrited Soviet forces that were eventually launched in retaliation.

100. SS-11 units = 335; SS-13 units = 40. Author's estimates based on International Institute for Strategic Studies, *The Military Balance, 1990–1991* (London: Brassey's, 1990), p. 34.

101. See Berman and Baker, *Soviet Strategic Forces,* pp. 14–21, 98. The SS-11 variable range deployments were credited with theater as well as intercontinental capability on the basis of evidence from testing and communications intercepts during SRF exercises. Interview with former U.S. government analyst. See also Lawrence Freedman, "The Dilemma of Theatre Nuclear Arms Control," *Survival,* vol. 23 (January–February 1981), p. 10, note 19.

102. U.S. Department of Defense, *Soviet Military Power, 1990,* pp. 48–54.

103. *Allocation of Resources in the Soviet Union and China—1981,* Hearings before Subcommittee on International Trade, Finance, and Security Economics of the Joint Economic Committee, 97th Cong. 1st sess. (GPO, 1982), pt. 7, p. 199.

104. Meyer, "Soviet Nuclear Operations," pp. 494, 495.

105. Interview with U.S. government analyst.

106. Author's estimates.

107. *Allocation of Resources in the Soviet Union and China—1977,* Hearings before the Subcommittee on Priorities and Economy in Government of the Joint Economic Committee, 95th Cong. 1 sess. (GPO, 1977), pt. 3, p. 134.

108. Interviews with U.S. government analysts.

109. *Allocation of Resources in the Soviet Union and China—1977,* Hearings, pt. 2, p. 77.

110. Interviews with U.S. government analysts.

111. According to interviewed U.S. analysts, the Soviet airborne command posts that support national, CINC SRF, and SRF army commanders lacked the capability to fire ICBMs directly by remote radio control. However, Soviet SRF officers indicated that their airborne command posts could remotely fire (at a range of about 200 miles) an ERCS missile, which in turn could transmit the

firing signals directly to the unmanned ICBM launchers. One such source further indicated that the airborne command posts were able to transmit fire signals directly to the ICBM launchers in special circumstances but that the procedure was extremely complex and could be performed only when coordinated with the activities of other launch centers.

For the United States, airborne launch control centers were the primary back-ups to the underground launch control centers. In a crisis, airborne launch control centers would have initiated patrols in each of the six regions of Minuteman deployments to back up the ground crews. Some but not all of these SAC aircraft possessed all the codes necessary to issue valid launch orders to the ground crews, replete with unlock codes. They could also have bypassed the ground crews and sent fire signals directly to the unmanned missile silos after a high alert was declared. Safeguards on board the aircraft were largely procedural except in the case of the portion of the airborne fleet that acquired unlock codes only upon receiving a launch message from higher authority. See Blair, *Strategic Command and Control*.

112. Meyer attributed launch capability to local ground mobile command centers. "Soviet Nuclear Operations," p. 507. U.S. government analysts interviewed for this study doubt that ground mobile command posts have any direct launch capability.

113. The quantitative methods used herein are discussed in Bruce Blair, *Strategic Command and Control*, app. A and app. B. The hypothetical attack strategy is standard and involves no reprogramming of strike assets. The specific assumptions and data inputs for this book are available from the author.

114. Interviews with U.S. government analysts.

115. U.S. Department of Defense, *Soviet Military Power, 1990*, pp. 51–52.

116. U.S. Department of Defense, *Soviet Military Power, 1988*, p. 47.

117. Interview with U.S. government analyst.

118. SS-20 bases (divisions) often consisted of four or five regiments (each with nine batteries). SS-25 bases varied widely in size and probably closely resembled the SS-20 deployment patterns. For the locations of all the SS-20 regimental operating areas, see "Further Details Released on SS-20 Saber Missile," *Jane's Defence Weekly*, January 30, 1988, pp. 182–83. For the location and deployments of SS-25s in 1991, see *START*, pp. 170–74.

119. *Strategic Force Modernization Programs*, Hearings before the Subcommittee on Strategic and Theater Nuclear Forces of the Senate Committee on Armed Services, 97th Cong. 1 sess. (GPO, 1981), p. 16.

120. Their operating range in practice probably closely approximated that of the SS-20s, which was substantially more restricted than the figures given above. A typical SS-20 regimental operating area was reportedly only about fifteen to thirty miles in length and even smaller in width. "Further Details Released," p. 183.

121. Interview with former U.S. government analyst.

122. Bill Gertz, "U.S. Satellites Detect Marked Increase in Mobile Soviet ICBMs," *Washington Times*, October 14, 1988, p. 6. Another report says the first SS-24 rail-mobile deployment began in 1987 near Archangel in northern Russia.

Steven J. Zaloga, "Land-Based Logic Drives Soviet Mobile ICBM Effort," *Armed Forces Journal International,* vol. 126 (November 1988), p. 28.

123. U.S. Department of Defense, *Soviet Military Power, 1990,* map foldout.

124. *START,* pp. 174–75.

125. This paragraph draws on an interview with a U.S. defense analyst.

126. Interview with former U.S. government analyst.

127. For instance, a new six-channel HF-VHF radio system connected locomotives with regional traffic management authorities. In the late 1980s the ministry of railroads was also fielding a new automated traffic data management system that used wire-line and microwave relay. Interview with U.S. defense analyst.

128. Author's estimate based on *START,* p. 123; and Serge Schmemann, "Gorbachev Matches U.S. on Nuclear Cuts and Goes Further on Strategic Warheads," *New York Times,* October 6, 1991, p. 1. An estimated 30 missiles and 300 warheads were deployed in 1990.

129. SSBN deployments were 6 Typhoon (120 missiles); 6 Delta IV (96 missiles); 14 Delta III (224 missiles); 4 Delta II (64 missiles); 18 Delta I (216 missiles); 1 Yankee II (12 missiles); 12 Yankee I (192 missiles). The total force was 61 SSBNs (924 missiles). IISS, *Military Balance, 1990-1991,* p. 34. The seventh Delta IV SSBN was launched in 1990 according to U.S. Department of Defense, *Soviet Military Power, 1990,* p. 53. SSBN base locations are identified in *START,* pp. 183–85.

130. Northern Fleet SSBN deployments were 6 Typhoon; 9 Delta I; 4 Delta II; 5 Delta III; 6 Delta IV; 6 Yankee I; and 1 Yankee II. The total force was 37 SSBNs with 576 missiles. Author's estimates. The major submarine bases in the region were identified (with photos) by Tomas Ries and Johnny Skorve, *Investigating Kola: A Study of Military Bases Using Satellite Photography* (London: Brassey's, 1987), pp. 55–63. Polyarnyy base housed much of the SSBN flotilla and included many submarine bunkers blasted into the cliffsides (p. 58). The other main SSBN base was Gremikha, which was believed to have had a large underground SSBN tunnel. The START I agreement signed in 1991 contains a statement by the USSR that its underground structures near submarine bases were not accessible to waterborne craft from adjacent waters. *START,* p. 277.

131. SSBN deployments are 9 Delta I; 9 Delta III; and 6 Yankee I. The total force was 24 SSBNs with 348 missiles. Author's estimates.

132. The operational readiness of Soviet SSBNs apparently held more or less constant at this level during the decade of the 1980s, except for exercise surges in the early part of the decade and a slight elevation in peacetime combat patrol rates lasting for a couple of years beginning in 1984, as a Soviet response to U.S. deployment of Pershing II and GLCM forces in the NATO theater. The 1980 average at-sea rate was reportedly 13 boats out of about 60, or about 22 percent. Ian Bellany, "Sea Power and the Soviet Submarine Forces," *Survival,* vol. 24 (January–February 1982), p. 5. Oral comments by U.S. Navy sources in January 1985 asserted that at the time about 25 percent of Soviet SSBNs were at sea on any given day, and another 25 percent probably were on alert in port. John M. Collins, *U.S.-Soviet Military Balance 1980–1985* (McLean, Va.: Pergamon-Bras-

sey's, 1985), pp. 54n, and 33, n. 7. An analyst interviewed in 1987 said the normal Soviet SSBN deployment was two Yankee-class boats in the western Atlantic (in a box just east of Bermuda, about 1,400 miles from Washington, D.C.) and two in the eastern Pacific, plus one or two Delta class in the northern Atlantic and one or two in the northern Pacific patrol areas (with a Typhoon-class boat sometimes in the Arctic region). This represented an alert rate of about 15 percent if a relief SSBN was normally in transit to each coastal box. In July 1986 the director of U.S. naval intelligence told an audience at a symposium that the Soviets maintained about 15 percent of their submarines on "combat patrol," another 35 percent on "combat duty" in some condition of availability to sortie, and the remaining 50 percent in "operational reserve" (25 percent) or "reserve" (25 percent) status. Remarks of Rear Admiral W. O. Studeman at 4th Annual Symposium of the Naval Submarine League, Alexandria, Virginia, July 10, 1986. In 1984 the Soviets augmented the Yankee deployments off each U.S. coast with Delta-class submarines that previously patrolled only near their home ports. The Soviets dispatched at least one additional Delta SSBN and perhaps as many as two or three to each coastal patrol box. Fred Hiatt, "More, Newer Soviet Subs Seen Off U.S.," *Washington Post,* January 27, 1984, p. A23; Robert C. Toth, "Advanced Soviet A-Subs Move to North Atlantic, Navy Secretary Asserts," *Los Angeles Times,* February 15, 1984, p. 13; Richard Barnard, "Ships Collide at Sea, Some Soviet Subs Evade Navy as Admiral Toughens ASW Policies," *Defense Week,* March 26, 1984, p. 4; and Thom Shanker, "Arms-Race Strategy Surfaces," *Chicago Tribune,* July 3, 1984, sect. 4, p. 11. Reports of ten or twelve Yankee- and Delta-class SSBNs operating at sea in the NATO area alone (north and west Atlantic waters) in 1985 pointed to an unusually high SSBN alert. "Soviet Submarine Strength—Latest Figures," *Jane's Defence Weekly,* March 16, 1985, p. 442. By late 1987 the Soviets ended continuous SSBN patrols off the U.S. coasts, and U.S. intelligence officials predicted that henceforth the patrols would occur on an irregular basis. John H. Cushman, Jr., "U.S. Asserts Soviet Shifts Nuclear Subs to Europe," *New York Times,* March 13, 1988, p. 19; Norman Black, "Soviet Nuclear Subs Resume Patrols Off U.S. East Coast," *Washington Post,* August 8, 1988, p. 19; and "Developments in Submarine Forces," *Jane's Defense Weekly,* November 12, 1988, p. 1233.

133. Berman and Baker, *Soviet Strategic Forces,* pp. 36–37.

134. Unlike the United States, which assigned two complete crews to each submarine (the so-called blue-gold team concept), the Soviets apparently had only one crew per SSBN. *Department of Defense Appropriations for 1983,* Hearings, pt. 4, p. 570.

135. See "Statement of Rear Admiral John L. Butts, U.S. Navy, Director of Naval Intelligence, before the Seapower and Strategic and Critical Materials Subcommittee of the House Armed Services Committee on the Naval Threat," February 28, 1984. Butts sums up, *"the goal of this readiness philosophy is to achieve a maximum force generation capability"* (p. 11). Rear Admiral Studeman's estimates of 15 percent "combat patrol" and 35 percent "combat duty" suggests an overall quick surge rate of 50 percent of the SSBN force, which could have been achieved in a matter of hours. An additional 25 percent on "operational

reserve" could have been put to sea in a matter of days or weeks. These figures are consistent with Admiral Gorshkov's claim that "70% of the Soviet Navy put to sea in 21 days." "Soviet Submarine Strength—Latest Figures," p. 442. Other analysts offer comparable figures. Meyer estimated an on-station surge rate of 50 percent, increasing to 75 percent within three weeks. Meyer, "Soviet Nuclear Operations," p. 507.

136. Interview.

137. He also participated in test missile launches from dockside at least twice during his service.

138. Private conversation with Russian military officer.

139. Suvorov, *Inside the Soviet Army,* p. 84.

140. Interview with former SSBN officer.

141. A "high level of dedicated SSN escort" reportedly accompanied Typhoon and Delta IV SSBNs for example when they left port. "Developments in Submarine Forces," p. 1233.

142. Interview.

143. The U.S. Navy, for instance, kept a surveillance vessel just outside the Northern Fleet bay to monitor Soviet ship deployments. Interview with former U.S. government analyst.

144. According to Western sources an attack submarine (SSN) often "rode shotgun" during the seventy-eight-day period of combat patrol. One-half to two-thirds of the SSBN missions apparently enjoyed this escort service. Interviews. However, a former SSBN crew member asserted that SSBNs on full combat patrol never interacted with SSNs or any other friendly vessel. Apparently SSBNs at sea often interacted with SSNs when performing training and other missions while off-alert or on modified alert. The former crew member did note that once or twice during a combat patrol an SSBN made prescheduled passes at predetermined undersea locations and that friendly SSNs often sat silently at those passes to ensure that the Soviet SSBN was not being trailed by an enemy attack submarine. In wartime this would be a point of ambush.

145. Interview with former SSBN officer.

146. Account of former SSBN crew member.

147. Acoustic boat-to-boat communications have a maximum reliable range of about twenty nautical miles. This was a detectable and exploitable procedure for purposes of localizing Soviet SSBNs and SSNs, though such sonar communications could have been encrypted and hence difficult to decipher. Hydroacoustic communications involving Soviet submarines is discussed by William J. Ruhe, "Submarine Communications," *Naval Forces,* vol. 3, no. 1 (1982); and Phoenix, "Soviet Submarine Command and Control," *Submarine Review,* January 1985, pp. 28–36. Excellent technical descriptions of sonar communications and virtually the entire gamut of methods used in strategic nuclear communications are found in Ashton B. Carter, "Communications Technologies and Vulnerabilities," in Carter, John D. Steinbruner, and Charles A. Zraket, eds., *Managing Nuclear Operations* (Brookings, 1987), pp. 217–81.

148. Bradford Dismukes, "The Pro-SSBN Mission of the Soviet Navy's General-Purpose Forces," Memorandum, (CNA) 81-0931.09 (Alexandria, Va.: Center for Naval Analyses, June 12, 1981), p. 7.

149. Tenders were available to load SLBMs into SSBNs in protected waters. Paul F. Herman, Jr., "U.S. and Soviet Strategic Nuclear Arsenals," *Signal,* vol. 42 (November 1987), p. 94.

150. Interviews with former SSBN crew member. This pattern was similar to the communications regime of U.S. SSBNs on modified alert at sea. U.S. SSBNs on full combat alert were required to listen continuously for emergency orders from the National Command Authorities.

151. A map of the Soviet Union showing the locations of the major naval LF and VLF transmitter stations is found in Bussert, "Soviet Navy Communications," p. 137.

152. Soviet LF, VLF, and other communications techniques are analyzed in Milan Vego, "Soviet Submarine Communications," *Signal,* vol. 42 (November 1987), pp. 65–73.

153. Interview with U.S. government analysts.

154. William J. Ruhe reported that the effective range of U.S. VLF stations was about 5,000 miles (for the Cutler, Maine, transmitter) or more (the Annapolis transmitter reached the Mediterranean Sea and the Indian Ocean). "Submarine Communications," pp. 38–39. By contrast, a British Royal Navy Captain (ret.) reported that VLF coverage reliably extends to only about 1,500 miles, beyond which the submarine must have resorted to other means such as satellite or HF radio. W. T. T. Pakenham, "The Command and Control of Submarine Operations," *Naval Forces,* vol. 6, no. 2 (1985), p. 54.

155. See testimony of the former director of U.S. naval intelligence in *Department of Defense Appropriations for 1985,* Hearings before the House Committee on Appropriations, 98 Cong. 2 sess. (GPO, 1984), pt. 2, p. 698. The ELF station began operation in 1983. Antony Preston and Malcolm Spaven, "Penetrating the Depths: An Overview of Submarine Communications," *Defence,* vol. 18 (July 1987), p. 412. For a thorough technical description of ELF communications to submarines, see Malcolm Spaven, "Communicating with Submarines," *Jane's Defence Weekly,* November 23, 1985, pp. 1152–55. Other reports that the Soviets operated a second ELF station in the Far East appear to be erroneous. Interviewees have confirmed that only one ELF site existed, although one analyst said in an interview that a mobile ELF transmitter may have been under development. Interviews with U.S. government analysts.

156. VLF itself was relatively slow. Its transmission rate was quite adequate for purposes of sending a short coded order—for example, a launch order—to SSBNs.

157. Interview with U.S. government analysts.

158. Author's estimates based on Vego, "Soviet Submarine Communications," pp. 65–73; and interviews with U.S. defense analysts.

159. Satellite outfitting of SSBNs began with the Delta-class boats. The Yankees were not backfitted. Interview with U.S. government analysts.

160. The U.S. strategic submarine force normally observes strict radio silence for its entire two-month period of alert patrol.

161. Interview with SSBN crew member.

162. A recent authoritative Soviet publication with a foreword written by S. G. Gorshkov, then admiral of the Soviet fleet, reinforces this judgment: "Getting

the signal for employing nuclear weapons to the performers on a timely basis is one of the important missions of the system for control of strategic submarines. While execution of this mission is not highly difficult for landbased or airbased weapons, it is a different matter for submarines: to ensure simultaneity of a strike by the maximum number of submarines the signal for them to employ nuclear weapons must be transmitted well ahead of the planned time. Here it will be necessary to consider not only the time it takes the signal to pass over communications means, but also the time necessary for submarines to occupy firing positions, to rise to near the surface under the established communications schedule, and to evade ASW forces as well as the time it takes to prepare navigation and missile systems for launching missiles." Nikolay Petrovich V"yunenko, Boris Nikolayevich Makeyev, and Valentin Dmitriyevich Skugarev, *The Navy: Its Role, Prospects for Development, and Employment* (Moscow: Military Publishing House, 1988), p. 171 (translated by U.S. Department of the Navy, Naval Intelligence Command). This assessment can be faulted for being too cavalier about the ease of control over the mission execution of other strategic forces, however. The air-based component in particular presented quite a challenge for command and control. Exercises during the 1980s pointed up the complexity of strategic bomber operations and the difficulty of integrating them into a combined-arms strike. For instance, the Soviet high command has had to cancel LDT orders and revert to launch-on-command arrangements for the SSBNs because the bomber leg failed to meet the scheduled launch-hour owing to adverse weather. Interview with U.S. government analysts.

163. Interview with former SSBN crew member.

164. Further, according to the SSBN crew member, each SLBM typically carried four to six decoys.

165. Victor Litovkin, "Inside a Russian Atom Sub," *We/My*, vol. 1 (March 1992), pp. 1, 2.

166. Interview with former SSBN officer.

167. According to Commander Ackley (retired), Yankee SSBNs lacked a ship inertial navigation system altogether. Richard T. Ackley, "The Wartime Role of Soviet SSBNs," *United States Naval Institute Proceedings,* vol. 104/6/904 (June 1978), pp. 38–39.

168. Interview with former U.S. government analyst.

169. It was thus misleading to assert, as senior defense officials sometimes did, that Yankee SSBNs could reach targets up to 1,800 miles away "while alongside their piers." Quoted in Cushman, "U.S. Asserts Soviet Shifts Nuclear Subs to Europe."

170. V"yunenko, Makeyev, and Skugarev, *The Navy*, p. 171.

171. U.S. Department of Defense, *Soviet Military Power, 1990,* map foldout. See also IISS, *Military Balance, 1990–1991,* p. 34.

172. U.S. Department of Defense, *Soviet Military Power, 1990,* p. 53; *START,* p. 224; and IISS, *Military Balance, 1990–91,* pp. 34, 223.

173. *Soviet Military Power, 1990,* map foldout; and IISS, *Military Balance, 1990–1991,* p. 34.

174. The START documents list the five bases as Uzin, Mozdok, Semipalatinsk, Priluki, and Ukrainka. *START,* pp. 200–01.

175. Located on the Kola Peninsula at Olenegorsk (the largest), Tiksi, Vorkuta, Mys-Schmidta, and Anadyr. A new base at Schagui under construction on the Kola also may have been intended to support heavy bombers, the Blackjack aircraft in particular. William M. Arkin and Richard W. Fieldhouse, *Nuclear Battlefields: Global Links in the Arms Race* (Ballinger, 1985), pp. 252, 258, 262, 263; "Soviet Notebook: Soviet Strategic Air Fleet," *International Defense Review*, vol. 20 (June 1987), p. 718; and Ries and Skorve, *Investigating Kola*, pp. 53–54, 64.

176. Simon Beavis, "Nato's Cold Shoulder," *Flight International*, vol. 127 (May 18, 1985), p. 33.

177. Interview with U.S. government analysts; and IISS, *Military Balance, 1990–1991*, p. 34.

178. Interview with U.S. government analysts.

179. *Allocation of Resources in the Soviet Union and China—1981*, Hearings, p. 199.

180. U.S. Department of Defense, *Soviet Military Power, 1983* (March 1983), p. 17, and *Soviet Military Power, 1984* (April 1984), p. 21.

181. Recall that the Soviet KGB was then under orders to search for evidence of an impending nuclear attack against the Soviet Union.

182. The time required to arm and fire AS-15s is estimated to have been about twenty minutes, counting the time used in transmitting codes to the aircraft. Interview with U.S. government analysts.

183. Though the evidence is inconclusive, Soviet exercises suggest that very few silo-based forces (about 10 percent) had been earmarked to be held in reserve during the initial strike. Second-echelon and reserve forces participating in follow-on strikes appeared to be concentrated in mobile land-, air-, and sea-based forces. U.S. employment plans apparently called for a larger fraction of silo-based forces to be withheld in circumstances short of an all-out exchange. Interviews with U.S. government analysts and author's estimates.

Chapter Six

1. *Department of Defense Appropriations for 1986*, Hearings before a Subcommittee of the House Committee on Appropriations, 99 Cong. 1 Sess. (Government Printing Office, 1985), pt. 2, p. 389.

2. Joint Chiefs of Staff (JCS), *Dictionary of Military and Associated Terms* (U.S. Department of Defense, January 1986), p. 204. The JCS defined tactical warning as follows: "1. A notification that the enemy has initiated hostilities. Such warning may be received any time from the launching of the attack until it reaches its target. 2. In satellite and missile surveillance, a notification to operational command centers that a specific threat event is occurring. The component elements that describe threat events are: *Country of origin*—country or countries initiating hostilities. *Event type and size*—identification of the type of event and determination of the size or number of weapons. *Country under attack*—determined by observing trajectory of an object and predicting its impact point. *Event time*—time the hostile event occurred." Ibid., p. 359.

3. Preemption involving forces used in a central strategic exchange was distinguished from first use of nuclear weapons. U.S. nuclear policy allowed for the first use of U.S. nuclear forces, including some strategic forces, in the context of a NATO effort to parry a Warsaw Pact conventional thrust into Western Europe.

4. Such an expectation would have been based on strategic warning, which the JCS defined as "a notification that enemy-initiated hostilities may be imminent. This notification may be received from minutes to hours, to days, or longer, prior to the initiation of hostilities." JCS, *Dictionary of Military and Associated Terms*, p. 346. The basis of this notification would have been various strategic warning indicators. During the late 1970s the list of indicators used to notify the U.S. National Command Authorities of possible imminent Soviet nuclear attack included the following items selected from a declassified JCS document (DJSM 19-77, January 6, 1977) and quoted verbatim:

General

• Information, warning, or statements from any source, however fragmentary or unsupported, that foreign sources will initiate hostilities against the United States, its allies, or any country.

• Widespread imposition of alerts within the foreign armed forces, or extensive cancellation or marked restriction of leaves for military forces or political/government powers.

• Changes in communications patterns which are judged to be significant indicators of the imminence of hostilities.

• Increased foreign intelligence collection activities, particularly relating to abnormal patterns noted in launch recovery or target coverage anomalies of space reconnaissance systems.

Missiles. Abnormal activity at known or suspected foreign missile launch, storage, or support sites.

Foreign Nuclear/Bacteriological/Chemical Weapons

• Large-scale withdrawal of nuclear, bacteriological, or chemical weapons from depots, movements of such weapons, or their release to the control of combat units.

Aviation

• Abnormal operations, developments, or preparations for flight activity by medium or heavy bomber or tanker aircraft, or by fighter/bomber units.

• Abnormal transport activity involving key staging bases, or nuclear or missile-associated sites.

Naval Forces

• Abnormal deployment of missile submarines.

Air Defense

• Widespread alerting of foreign air defense units, ABM complexes, SAM complexes, or fighter units.

• Unusual activity in operations of Early Warning/Space Defense Radars.

Civil Defense
• Sudden alerting of civil defense organizations, the civil population.
• Evacuation or relocation of key elements of the civil population such as government, technical and industrial personnel and workers, or of key military headquarters.

Other Critical Situations
• Instances of sabotage or large-scale attacks against US official installations.
• Imminence, or actual initiation of armed revolution, civil war, a coup, widespread sabotage, or major civil or military disturbances.
• Assassinations or severe molestation of key civil or military leaders.
• Sudden, or unannounced changes in top government leadership.
• Governmental decisions, or actions which could materially jeopardize vital US national interests in the political or military spheres.

5. The best analysis of the potential contribution of launch on warning to deterrence and stability in general, and Minuteman missile survivability in particular, is Richard L. Garwin, "Launch under Attack to Redress Minuteman Vulnerability?" *International Security,* vol. 4 (Winter 1979–80), pp. 117–39.

6. The high priority of Soviet military targets in the SIOP during the 1960s was no secret, but it nonetheless went generally unassimilated during the McNamara years. The rationale for a "no-cities" counterforce doctrine was clearly articulated by William Kaufmann, a key adviser to McNamara and the preeminent figure in the development of strategic policy during the Kennedy administration. See William W. Kaufmann, *The McNamara Strategy* (Harper and Row, 1964).

The groundbreaking scholarship on SIOP targeting is the work of Desmond Ball. His major contributions include *Politics and Force Levels: The Strategic Missile Program of the Kennedy Administration* (University of California, 1980); *Targeting for Strategic Deterrence,* Adelphi Papers 185 (London: International Institute for Strategic Studies [IISS], Summer 1983); "U.S. Strategic Forces: How Would They Be Used?" *International Security,* vol. 7 (Winter 1982–83), pp. 31–60; and "The Development of the SIOP, 1960–1983," in Desmond Ball and Jeffrey Richelson, eds., *Strategic Nuclear Targeting* (Cornell University Press, 1986).

Important official documents pertaining to SIOP targeting and strategy were located in archives, submitted for declassification, and published by David Rosenberg and Scott Sagan. See David Alan Rosenberg, " 'A Smoking Radiating Ruin at the End of Two Hours': Documents on American Plans for Nuclear War with the Soviet Union, 1954–1955," *International Security,* vol. 6 (Winter 1981–82), pp. 3–38; Rosenberg, "The Origins of Overkill: Nuclear Weapons and American Strategy, 1945–1960," *International Security,* vol. 7 (Spring 1983), pp. 3–71; and Scott D. Sagan, "SIOP-62: The Nuclear War Plan Briefing to President Kennedy," *International Security,* vol. 12 (Summer 1987), pp. 41–51.

Other especially valuable contributions to understanding the development of U.S. strategic policy are Fred M. Kaplan, *The Wizards of Armageddon* (Simon and Schuster, 1983); Lawrence Freedman, *The Evolution of Nuclear Strategy* (St.

338   NOTES TO PAGES 177–79

Martin's Press, 1981); Scott D. Sagan, *Moving Targets: Nuclear Strategy and National Security* (Princeton, 1989); John Newhouse, *War and Peace in the Nuclear Age* (Knopf, 1989); Janne E. Nolan, *Guardians of the Arsenal: The Politics of Nuclear Strategy* (Basic Books, 1988); John Prados, *The Soviet Estimate* (Dial, 1982); and Lynn Etheridge Davis, *Limited Nuclear Options: Deterrence and the New American Doctrine,* Adelphi Papers 121 (IISS, 1975).

7. The waning support in Congress for deploying mobile ICBMs reflected the improvement in U.S.-Soviet political relations and the growing pressure to cut spending on defense, not a philosophical retreat from the principle of survivable forces and second-strike operational practices.

8. Remark of General Burke in *MX Missile Alternatives,* Hearings before the Subcommittees on Military Construction Appropriations and Defense Appropriations of the Senate Committee on Armed Services, 97 Cong. 1 sess. (Government Printing Office, 1981), p. 85. The most interesting congressional discussions of launch on warning took place in the Senate Armed Services Committee under the astute examination of Senator Sam Nunn. Senator Nunn correctly discerned the growing reliance of the United States on prompt launch from the late 1970s through the mid-1980s. His persistent inquiry into the subject during committee hearings alas failed to elicit satisfactory responses from witnesses. The best colloquies occurred in hearings in 1981 and 1985. At the 1981 session, Nunn told Fred Iklé: "I am very concerned that a Soviet planner might very well conclude that America has given up on survivability of the land-based missile force and has gone to a launch-under-attack policy." *Strategic Force Modernization Programs,* Hearings before the Subcommittee on Strategic and Theater Nuclear Forces of the Senate Committee on Armed Services, 97 Cong. 1 sess. (GPO, 1981), p. 64. In 1985 Nunn again pursued the issue with the SAC commander, General Bennie Davis. The senator remarked: "We have always strived for a strategic retaliatory capability that would not require us to launch under attack that would permit us to ride out an attack and then retaliate with enough power to be able to have what we call true deterrence. Now, what I am saying is that it seems to me that we have come off the old policy and we are now relying as almost the first option, if not policy, on planning to launch under attack. . . . There is a lot of other discourse that indicates to me that we have moved the option in reverse and that riding out appears more and more to be the last option instead of the first option." *Department of Defense Authorization for Appropriations for Fiscal Year 1986,* Hearings before the Senate Committee on Armed Services, 99 Cong. 1 Sess. (GPO, 1985), pp. 3716–17, 3737.

9. *Department of Defense Annual Report, Fiscal Year 1979,* p. 53.

10. An excellent analysis of the problem of surprise attack and its remedies is Richard K. Betts, *Surprise Attack: Lessons for Defense Planning* (Brookings, 1982).

11. Such a combination of misconception and deception led U.S. and Israeli intelligence not to anticipate the Arab attack on Israel in 1973, even though both intelligence services had a good picture of Egyptian and Syrian military preparations. The failure stemmed from the rational assumption that Egypt would not

attack unless its prospects were militarily propitious, whereas Anwar Sadat actually sought a limited political objective. A similar rational misconception confounded the American government before the attack on Pearl Harbor.

12. Interviews with U.S. officials, including one assigned to the relevant intelligence desk at the time, indicate a complete absence of knowledge about the Soviet nuclear alert throughout the course of the crisis and long afterwards. A British government analyst interviewed for this study and Paul Nitze, deputy secretary of defense in 1968, recalled that the alert had been noticed, but their recollections were hazy on the point and further confirmation has not been obtained.

13. Interview. During the summer and fall of 1969, the Soviets conducted a war of nerves with China by raising the possibility of a nuclear strike on China, particularly Chinese nuclear facilities (their test site and threatening nuclear bases). The crisis reached peak intensity in early September and then subsided after high-level Soviet-Chinese discussion in mid-September. Significant tensions persisted for several more years, however. Raymond L. Garthoff, *Détente and Confrontation: American-Soviet Relations from Nixon to Reagan* (Brookings, 1985), pp. 208–11.

14. Interview with British intelligence analyst. Garthoff cites evidence indicating that Soviet bomber units staging out of Siberia and Mongolia had practiced attacks on targets made to resemble Chinese nuclear facilities. *Détente and Confrontation,* p. 209.

15. Paul Stares, of Brookings, obtained declassified but heavily censored U.S. documentation that indicates that SAC increased its operational readiness and sustained it for most of October. In a conversation with the then CINC SAC, I was told that the alert affected only the SAC bomber forces, and not the ICBMs. The CINC SAC believed, though he could not recall for certain, that the Sino-Soviet crisis precipitated the bomber alert. The SAC director of operations at the time told me that this alert may have been connected with the recently discovered problem of unreliable SLBM warheads on the entire Polaris SSBN fleet. Another possible explanation of the heightened bomber readiness is that the Soviets had initiated continuous SSBN patrols along the Atlantic coast of the United States for the first time in late 1969, and by 1970 had commenced similar patrols off the west coast. Robert P. Berman and John C. Baker, *Soviet Strategic Forces: Requirements and Responses* (Brookings, 1982), pp. 18, 58, 96. These patrols posed a major new threat to SAC bombers on runway alert (airborne alerts had been discontinued in 1968) because of the short flight time of the Soviet missiles. SAC thus had cause to increase its bomber alert posture to increase survivability and to send the message to Moscow that the new threat had not gone unnoticed. The bomber alert in effect tested Moscow's reaction to a qualitatively new dimension of U.S.-Soviet operational interaction.

16. Raymond Garthoff learned this during a conversation in October 1992 with former Soviet ambassadors Anatoly Dobrynin and Alexander Bessmertnykh. Both former Soviet officials recalled that they had been informed of the unusual SAC alert at the time.

17. Interviews with a current and a former U.S. government analyst.

18. Interviews with U.S. government analysts; and "Soviets Stage Integrated Test of Weapons," *Aviation Week and Space Technology,* vol. 116 (June 28, 1982), pp. 20–21.

19. In interviews U.S. analysts revealed that the Soviets sometimes hand-delivered the launch instructions to the weapons commanders, rather than transmitting them over communications channels, which were susceptible to intercept. These officials considered the hand delivery of instructions to be useful for very limited nuclear options but not practical for large-scale coordinated attacks. According to a senior military official the Soviet example inspired the United States to develop similar procedures for hand-delivering launch messages to the nuclear forces.

20. Gordievskiy's account is reported in Gordon Brook-Shepherd, *The Storm Birds: Soviet Postwar Defectors* (New York: Weidenfeld and Nicholson, 1989).

21. A U.S. intelligence analyst told me that top Soviet leaders did not take the warning seriously and that the entire incident was nothing more than Kremlin intrigue.

22. One U.S. intelligence analyst said the responses were authorized at a level "just below the top." Another analyst indicated that the disposition of some Warsaw Pact forces changed on orders from the Western TVD headquarters. These statements are consistent. However, a third analyst from the same intelligence agency claimed that the Soviets did not react militarily in any way. Three interviews.

23. There is reason to suppose that the NATO release procedures were subsequently revised to avoid any repetition of this snafu. These procedural adjustments probably involved tighter restrictions on the use of unsecure communications to request nuclear release approval from higher authority.

24. This summary was leaked to the press and widely circulated in the public domain. *U.S./Soviet Tensions,* SNIE 11-10-84 JX, p. 6.

25. Ibid., p. 1.

26. Interview with former U.S. government analyst. I checked this insider account of the alleged incident against the memory of the then CINC of the U.S. Atlantic command, who did not recall any such clandestine Soviet SSBN surge and strongly doubted it had taken place.

27. The fact that Western intelligence estimates of Soviet ICBM launch readiness varied greatly only supports the contention that strategic warning was problematic. From interviews with current and former U.S. government analysts the lowest estimate of the portion of the Soviet ICBM force maintained at launch-ready status was 10 to 15 percent; the highest estimate was about 80 percent. Most estimates fell into the middle of this range, or about 50 percent. All interviewees agreed that it was extremely difficult to gauge the day-to-day alert level of the silo-based ICBM forces from the fourth generation on (SS-17s, SS-18s, SS-19s, and SS-24s) or to detect changes in the levels. Those interviewees most familiar with Soviet operational practices were most comfortable with the lower estimates.

28. This trend was somewhat erratic. Indeed the first six-month period of the

training year beginning in December 1989 saw the tempo of Soviet nuclear exercise activity increase substantially. There were about ten major strategic force exercises during this short period, compared with one in 1989 and one in 1988. Interviews with U.S. government analysts. By all accounts, nuclear activity after 1990 greatly diminished.

29. The most complete, authoritative description of Soviet wartime nuclear operations in this theater is found in the secret course materials of the Voroshilov Academy. This material is of course dated (mid-1970s), and the scenario itself is only of historical relevance in light of the ongoing disengagement of Soviet forces from Germany and Poland and the completed withdrawal of forces from the rest of Eastern Europe. It nonetheless illuminates the issue of strategic warning and nuclear preemption.

30. Ghulam Dastagir Wardak and Graham Hall Turbiville, Jr., eds., *The Voroshilov Lectures: Materials from the Soviet General Staff Academy,* vol 1: *Issues of Soviet Military Strategy* (Washington: National Defense University Press, June 1989), pp. 257–313, 378.

31. Ibid., p. 262.

32. Ibid., p. 268.

33. Ibid., p. 271.

34. Ibid., p. 262.

35. "It is recommended that the initial nuclear strikes be launched simultaneously by all strategic, operational, and tactical nuclear forces and means. However, the Supreme High Command can take into consideration the decisive role of strategic nuclear forces in the initial strike, their high combat readiness, and the rapidity of their actions, and, for the sake of ensuring surprise or other purposes, launch the strikes of nuclear forces without waiting for preparations of front and fleet nuclear delivery means at the same time. Under such circumstances, on the signal of the Supreme High Command, the Strategic Rocket Forces and submarine-based rockets conducting combat missions on the sea launch their strikes first. They are followed by the nuclear strikes of Long-Range Aviation. To ensure surprise, Long-Range Aviation may start taking off from airfields simultaneously with the commencement of the launch of strategic missiles. . . . If at that time all operational-tactical rockets are not yet in full combat readiness, combat duty (on-call) rocket systems are first launched. Then the remaining rockets deliver their strikes as they get ready to do so." Ibid., p. 306.

36. For example according to the Voroshilov lectures an order could have conveyed the following information on the use of operational-tactical nuclear rockets: "Enemy sites are suppressed and destroyed in the following manner: nuclear weapons—by a 10 kiloton airburst; . . . a tank division—by a 20 kiloton airburst; a control post or a nuclear stockpile—by a 100 kiloton ground burst; a communications junction and control posts—by a 3 kiloton airburst; airfields and rear targets—by a 40 kiloton airburst. Launch preparation time is H minus 20, 20 minutes before launch time. The time for allocating nuclear and chemical munitions is 3 hours. P minus 3 hours." "Strategic Directive of Stavka," unpublished volume of the Voroshilov lectures, p. 12.

37. These items are taken from an unpublished volume of the lectures.

38. This so-called launch at designated time, or LDT, procedure, sometimes cited by Western analysts as evidence of Soviet planning for a first strike, was acknowledged in a recent Soviet military publication edited by the former admiral of the fleet S. G. Gorshkov. Nikolay Petrovich Vyunenko, Boris Nikolayevich Makeyev, and Valentin Dmitriyevich Skugarev, *The Navy: Its Role, Prospects for Development, and Employment* (Moscow: Military Publishing House, 1988); translation by U.S. Department of the Navy, Naval Intelligence Command, p. 171.

39. Interview with U.S. defense consultant. One of the main effects of this new option was presumably to extend the initial launch window by eliminating prescheduled launch delays originally designed to prevent fratricide at the targets.

40. At the risk of sowing confusion over terminology, launch on warning and launch under attack (LUA) were interchangeable terms in that both often referred to the dissemination of launch orders after receiving positive indications of enemy attack but before nuclear detonations from incoming weapons occurred. A distinction commonly drawn, however, was that LUA withheld launch authority until nuclear detonations had been detected. This is not to say that such authority would have been withheld until definitive evidence of massive damage had accumulated. The timing of LUA was in fact closer to the timing of launch on warning than to the timing of retaliation after ride-out.

41. *Department of Defense Appropriations for 1978,* Hearings before a Subcommittee of the House Committee on Appropriations, 95 Cong. 1 Sess. (GPO, 1977), pt. 7, pp. 154–55.

42. Ibid.

43. Interviews with former NORAD officers.

44. Ibid; and NORAD Regulation 55-10, Attachment 1, "NORAD/SHAPE Memorandum of Agreement for Exchange of Early Warning Information," May 30, 1980, annex A, p. 5. A partly declassified NORAD document dated November 30, 1980, describes the basis for inferring an attack: "Factors affecting confidence include: the frequency of false reports experienced or calculated for the system; independent reporting by two or more sensors or sensor systems that are consistent with the performance characteristics of the possible enemy weapons and the expected timing of the threat objects through each sensor's coverage; the ability to identify the launch locations of threat objects and determine the consistency of these locations with known or probable enemy deployment; the magnitude and multiplicity of the threat reports; and the consistency of the threat reports with intelligence estimates of the international political and military status." Aerospace Defense Command, *ADCOM Command and Control System Master Plan* (Peterson Air Force Base, Colo., November 30, 1980), p. 3–13.

45. *Our Nation's Nuclear Warning System: Will It Work If We Need It?* Hearings before a Subcommittee of the House Committee on Government Operations, 99 Cong. 1 sess. (GPO, 1986), p. 82.

46. There were thousands of anomalous signals every year from sensors that required urgent attention and evaluation. From 1977 through 1984, the only period for which official information has been released, NORAD annually per-

formed an average of 2,598 routine assessments of unusual warning indications, about 5 percent of which required further evaluation of the possibility of a missile threat to North America. Letter (February 13, 1985) from NORAD headquarters to the Center for Defense Information.

47. Two such incidents occurred in each year from 1978 to 1980, according to NORAD (letter HQ NORAD, dated 2–13–85). No false alarms leading to nuclear alerts occurred from 1981 through 1984, the last year of available official data.

48. Letter HQ ADCOM, April 13, 1981. The author thanks Jeff Richelson for providing this information.

49. These propositions and their implications are developed in the following chapter.

50. *Department of Defense Appropriations for 1978,* Hearings before a Subcommittee of the House Committee on Appropriations, 95 Cong. 1 Sess. (GPO, 1977), pt. 7, p. 153.

51. Interview with U.S. government analyst.

52. Note that this scenario excludes any Soviet SLBM tactics that theoretically could have used X-rays from high altitudes explosions to pin down Minuteman forces even before a missile attack conference got under way. A similar timeline with a good discussion of the lead times needed by ICBMs to escape damage during their boost phase is found in John D. Steinbruner, "Launch under Attack," *Scientific American,* vol. 250 (January 1984), pp. 37–47.

53. This section is based on interview materials with military officers posted to NORAD during the 1980s.

54. Procedures doubtless existed for the president to inquire into the basis of the NORAD's assessment during the missile attack conference. A so-called black book was produced for former president Jimmy Carter (carried by the president's military aide in the so-called football briefcase) to simplify the SIOP decision process. This book could have contained guidance to assist the National Command Authorities in determining whether NORAD's assessment stemmed from dual-sensor reports or some other combination of warning and intelligence. This book was passed down to succeeding presidents.

55. An interesting illustration of precisely this error occurred in the Soviet early-warning system in a peacetime context. A. Dokuchayev, "A Bridle for 'Nuclear Racers' or the Missile-Attack Warning System," *Krasnaya Zvezda,* September 27, 1990, p. 2, in Joint Publications Research Service (JPRS), *Soviet Union: Military Affairs,* October 15, 1990, pp. 53–55.

56. This characterization is developed further in chapter 7.

57. During their ascent to high altitude (several hundreds of miles), the rockets would have entered the satellites' field of view, but by then they would have nearly completed their powered boost phase. After their engines shut off, the missiles become too cool for satellite infrared sensors to detect.

58. See *Recent False Alerts from the Nation's Missile Attack Warning System,* Committee Print, Report of Senator Gary Hart and Senator Barry Goldwater to the Senate Committee on Armed Services, 96 Cong. 2 sess. (GPO, 1980).

59. Wardak and Turbiville, eds., *Voroshilov Lectures,* vol. 1, p. 246; and vol. 2: *Issues of Soviet Military Strategy* (Washington: National Defense University Press, December 1990), p. 3.

60. For a thorough review of the evolution of Soviet nuclear doctrine from the post–World War II era to the present, see Raymond L. Garthoff, *Deterrence and the Revolution in Soviet Military Doctrine* (Brookings, 1990). See also Michael MccGwire, *Military Objectives in Soviet Foreign Policy* (Brookings, 1987).

61. V. Popov, "Some Problems with Surprise," *VM,* no. 12 (1951), pp. 17–21, cited in James M. McConnell, "The Soviet Shift toward and away from Nuclear War-Waging," working paper, Center for Naval Analysis, Alexandria, Va., 1983, p. 137.

62. N. Pukhovskiy, "The Creative Nature of Soviet Military Science," in B. S. Lyalikov and P. A. Sidorov eds., *Marksizm-leninizm o voyne, armii i voennoy nauke* (Moscow, 1955), p. 107; and V. Vasilenko, "The Reactionary Essence and Aggressive Nature of Imperialist Military Ideology," in ibid., p. 213, cited in McConnell, *Soviet Shift,* p. 137.

63. Marshal of the Tank Troops P. A. Rotmistrov, "On the Role of Surprise in Contemporary War," *Voyennaya mysl',* no. 2 (February 1955), pp. 14–21. See also an unsigned editorial article "On Some Questions of Soviet Military Science," *Voyennaya mysl',* no. 3 (March 1955), pp. 3–18, cited in Garthoff, *Deterrence and the Revolution in Soviet Military Doctrine,* p. 42.

64. See Raymond L. Garthoff, *The Soviet Image of Nuclear War* (Washington: Public Affairs Press, 1959), pp. 64–73; Garthoff, *Soviet Strategy in the Nuclear Age* (New York: Praeger, 1958), pp. 84–87; and H. S. Dinerstein, *War and the Soviet Union* (Praeger, 1959), pp. 24–25, 76–77, 187–211.

65. P. A. Rotmistrov, "The Causes of Modern Wars and Their Distinguishing Features," *Kommunist vooruzhennykh sil,* no. 2 (January 1963), p. 30; S. N. Kozlov, M. V. Smirnov, and others, *O Sovetskoy voennoy nauke* (Moscow, 1964, 2d ed.), p. 347; N. M. Nikol'skiy, *Osnovnoy vopros sovremennosti: problema unichtozheniya voyn* (Moscow, 1964), p. 367; V. Sokolovskiy and M. Cheredni-chenko, "The Military Art at a New Stage," *Krasnaya Zvezda,* August 28, 1964, pp. 2–3; and V. Larionov and I. Glagolev, "Soviet Defense Might and Peaceful Coexistence," *International Affairs* (Moscow), no. 11 (1963), p. 32, cited in McConnell, *Soviet Shift,* p. 6.

66. Maj. Gen. I. Anureyev, "Determining the Correlation of Forces in Terms of Nuclear Arms," in Stephen J. Cimbala, ed., *Soviet C³* (Washington: AFCEA International Press, 1987), p. 131. The actual response time from receipt of launch orders to Minuteman missile lift-off was three minutes.

67. Wardak and Turbiville, eds., *Voroshilov Lectures,* vol. 2, p. 35.

68. Ibid., vol. 1, pp. 182–84.

69. Soviet concern over the possibility of surprise was expressed in the secret course materials:

In modern times, the main attack means of the enemy in the TMSA [con-tinental theater of operations] are: the air forces, tactical and operational missile troops kept in a high state of combat readiness, organized ground and aviation groupings deployed in the theater, American submarine-based nuclear rocket squadrons [assigned to NATO], and U.S. operational naval forces deployed in important areas of the ocean (seas) and on islands. . . . Therefore, most of the actions formerly taken during the phase of direct preparation for war, which required a considerable amount of time, today are taken in peacetime in contemporary times under the cover of different forms of combat training, maneuvers, and field exercises and are constantly and gradually expanded into full preparation for war. Moreover, in modern times the direct preparation for war will be conducted in a short period of time, showing very little indication of the enemy's real intentions. However, the enemy will have to take a series of preparatory measures, each indicating specific evidence of actual intentions. The main indicators in this connection will be the following:

—deploying and organizing control systems and control centers to guide tactical aircraft to land-based targets;

—removing nuclear rounds from depots, moving them to air bases, and finally arming the aircraft with nuclear ammunition;

—launching airborne command posts and testing their performance;

—changing routine radio-electronic reconnaissance posts of air defense systems, supporting their transition to a state of continuous manning, and deploying additional posts in depth;

—deploying combat and transport vehicles of the ground forces, supplying the ground forces with POL, distributing nuclear rounds, moving out rocket troops for deployment, and deploying command posts;

—placing air defense means in a combat-ready status and testing the control system;

—resupplying naval ships with all types of material, moving them out of bases to deploy and disperse them, and moving out aviation strike forces (aircraft carrier task forces) from their bases and deployment on airfields;

—deploying submarines to positions from which they can launch missiles within six to eight hours;

—evacuating commercial ships from seaports and internal seas of Socialist countries.

Most of these indicators may not be disclosed. However, sometimes the disclosure of a few specific indicators may play a decisive role in determining enemy direct preparation to launch his attack." Wardak and Turbiville, eds., *Voroshilov Lectures*, vol. 1, pp. 293–94.

70. Ibid., vol. 2, p. 35.

71. V. D. Sokolovskiy, *Soviet Military Strategy*, 3d ed. (Crane, Russak, 1975), p. 391.

72. Marshal N. I. Krylov, "The Nuclear Missile Shield of the Soviet State," *Voyennaya mysl'*, no. 11 (November 1967), p. 20. See also Maj. Gen. N. Vesendin and Col. N. Kuznetsov, "Contemporary War and Surprise," *Voyennaya mysl'*, no. 6 (June 1968), p. 42; and Gen. Army S. P. Ivanov, "Soviet Military Doctrine and Strategy," *Voyennaya mysl'*, no. 5 (May 1969), p. 47, cited in Garthoff, *Deterrence and the Revolution in Soviet Military Doctrine*, p. 78.

73. Wardak and Turbiville, eds., *Voroshilov Lectures*, vol. 1, pp. 181, 190.

74. Pictures taken by U.S. photoreconnaissance satellites of SS-11 silos with their lids removed during maintenance of the fuel tank apparatus (fuel tanks were emptied and refilled approximately once a year) suggested this conclusion to some western analysts. Interview with former U.S. government analyst.

75. These exercises involved SS-11 forces launched after the initial salvo. Ranking SRF officers flew along with control personnel, presumably affiliated with the general staff, in helicopters to the launch locations to coordinate activities by ground crews responsible for arming and firing these operational reserve missiles. Interview with former U.S. government analyst.

76. "Secretary of Defense Statement on FY1971 Defense Programs and Budget," before the House Armed Services Committee, March 2, 1970, p. 62, cited in Matthew Partan, *Soviet Assessments of U.S. Early Warning Technology Programs,* Research Report 86-1 (MIT Center for International Studies, August 1986), p. 13.

77. The Defense Intelligence Agency provided an estimate of "about seventeen minutes" for Soviet Hen House ground radar warning. Testimony of Gordon Negus, *Hearings on Military Posture and H.R. 1872,* House Committee on Armed Services, 96 Cong. 1st sess. (GPO, 1979), pt. 3, bk. 1, p. 121.

78. A. B. Krasnov, "The Early Warning System: Means and Prospects of Development," *Voyennaya mysl',* no. 4 (April 1969), p. 86, cited in Partan, *Soviet Assessments,* pp. 26, 60.

79. Wardak and Turbiville, eds., *Voroshilov Lectures,* vol. 2, p. 104.

80. The Voroshilov lectures also noted that twenty to twenty-five minutes of advance warning of the flight of enemy ballistic missiles would allow for air defense means to organize the repulsion of the attack. Ibid., vol. 2, p. 105.

81. Col. Gen. V. N. Karpov, "On the Theory of Soviet Military Strategy," *Voyennaya msyl',* no. 10 (October 1979), p. 25. See also G. A. Trofimenko, "Some Aspects of U.S. National Security Strategy," *SShA: Economika, politica, ideologiya,* no. 10 (1970), p. 26; General Major A. Slobodenko (of the General Staff Academy), *Voenno-strategicheskie teorii imperilazma i ikh kritika* (Moscow, 1971), p. 16; V. F. Tolubko (SRF Cinc), *Raketnye voyska* (Moscow, 1977), p. 34; N. Petrov, "Futile Strategy," *Soviet Military Review,* no. 8 (1982), p. 45; A. Slobodenko, "Strategy of Nuclear Adventurism," *Mezhdunarodnaya Zhizn,* no. 10 (1982), p. 102; Yuri Yartsev, "Notes for the Occasion: They Better Think Twice," *Literaturnaya gazeta,* October 27, 1982, p. 14; A. Arbatov, "Strategy of Nuclear Imprudence," *Kommunist,* no. 6 (April 1981), p. 106; and R. G. Bogdanov, "Limiting and Reducing Strategic Arms—the Heart of International Security—Is a Problem of Paramount Importance," *SShA,* no. 5 (1981), p. 12, cited in McConnell, *Soviet Shift,* pp. 142–43.

82. "The Leninist Conception of War and the Present," *Kommunist vooruzhennykh sil,* no. 20 (October 1973), p. 35, cited in Garthoff, *Deterrence and the Revolution in Soviet Military Doctrine,* p. 83.

83. Garthoff, in ibid., p. 83, cites Col. Ye. Rybkin and Col. S. Dmitriyev, "V. I. Lenin and the Essence Character, and Types of Wars," *Voyennaya mysl',* no. 1 (January 1975), p. 66.

84. According to Garthoff, ibid., p. 83, Rybkin wrote that the Soviet military

had been "guided by the instructions of the Central Committee of the CPSU that the Soviet Union shall not be the first to employ nuclear weapons . . . at the same time, the Soviet armed forces should be ready and prepared for any nuclear 'escalation.' "

85. This evaluation of exercises is based on interview material. This view was disputed by some U.S. analysts, who cited as primary evidence of Soviet retention of preemptive options the strategic exercises in which launch orders with future execution times—the so-called LDT procedure—were relayed to Soviet SSBNs, which then initiated the strategic exchange scenario. This practice occurred on a number of occasions, most recently in 1989. One such exercise during the 1980s was described in chapter 4. In the exercises, a Soviet SSBN received its launch instructions and fired several hours later according to the designated time. Several minutes later, the Soviets launched a massive salvo of ICBMs. Those analysts who portrayed this sequence as preemptive regarded the initial Soviet SSBN launch as a well-designed precursor strike against the adversary. Those who contested this view believed the opening SSBN salvo represented a simulated Western SSBN precursor attack, an event that then triggered the immediate dissemination of launch authorization to Soviet ICBM forces under a policy of launch on warning. The charitable interpretation saw Soviet strategy as defensive and retaliatory, whereas the other view saw it as offensive and preemptive.

86. Soviet perceptions of the increasing danger of war, and Soviet strategic responses to reduce their vulnerability to surprise attack, are detailed in *U.S./ Soviet Tensions*. See also the thorough analysis of this war scare by Michael MccGwire, *Perestroika and Soviet National Security* (Brookings, 1991), especially pp. 380–92.

87. See Garthoff, *Détente and Confrontation*, pp. 780–85.

88. There are several related causes of signal reflection and backscatter: the actual missile (or aircraft) body, the ionized plume of rocket engines, or other ionospheric disturbances that result from the passage of missiles through the ionosphere.

89. Stations for monitoring U.S. launches were built near Chernobyl in the western USSR and near Komsomolsk-na-Amur in the far eastern USSR; Chinese launches were monitored by a station at Nikolayev near Odessa. The history of OTH radar development and deployment by the USSR is spotty, but useful references include the superb analysis in Partan, *Soviet Assessments*. Other valuable sources are U.S. Department of Defense, *Soviet Strategic Defense Programs* (1985), p. 13; and U.S. Department of Defense, *Soviet Military Power* (1985), p. 45.

90. See Partan's review of the Soviet technical literature in *Soviet Assessments*.

91. E. K. Bragin and A. G. Kubarev, *Protivoraketnaya oborona* (Moscow: Voyenizdat, 1966), pp. 57–58; A. I. Leonov, *Radiolokatsiya v protivoraketnoy oborone* (Moscow, Voyenizdat, 1967), p. 86; A. B. Krasnov, "The Early Warning System: Means and Prospects of Development," *Military Thought* (April, 1969), p. 86; and N. F. Shibayev, *Bor'ba s raketami* (Moscow: Voyenizdat, 1965), p. 68, cited in Partan, *Soviet Assessments*, p. 41.

92. I. I. Anureyev, *Oruzhie protivoraketnogo i protivokozmicheskogo oborona*

(Moscow: Voyenizdat, 1971), pp. 140–41, 296–302, cited in Partan, *Soviet Assessments*, p. 43.

93. Wardak and Turbiville, eds., *Voroshilov Lectures*, vol. 2, pp. 104–05.

94. Steven J. Zaloga, "Former Soviet ABM Chief Mocks USSR's Ballistic Missile Defenses," *Armed Forces Journal International*, October 1990, p. 29.

95. "Front Line: Report from the Missile Attack Early Warning System Command Center," *Pravda*, April 15, 1991, p. 8, in Foreign Broadcasting Information Service, *Soviet Union: Daily Report*, April 18, 1991, p. 29.

96. Except where noted, the details of the Soviet spaceborne launch detection system presented in this section are taken from the following sources: *Soviet Space Programs: 1976–80*, Senate Committee on Commerce, Science, and Transportation, 99 Cong. 1 sess. (GPO, 1985), pt. 3, pp. 1076–85; Nicholas L. Johnson, *The Soviet Year in Space, 1982* (Colorado Springs: Teledyne Brown Engineering, 1983), pp. 18–19; and subsequent annual reports by N. L. Johnson on the *Soviet Year in Space* (*1981*, pp. 20–21; *1983*, pp. 29–30; *1984*, p. 30; *1985*, pp. 37–38; *1987*, pp. 66–68; *1989*, pp. 77–79; and *1990*, pp. 81–85).

97. Partan, *Soviet Assessments*, pp. 55–66.

98. U.S. Department of Defense, *Soviet Military Power, 1984* (GPO, 1984), p. 32.

99. Russian scientists from the military-industrial complex recently told me that geosynchronous satellites had become the linchpin of early warning but that assessment could not be verified from official U.S. publications.

100. U.S. Department of Defense, *Soviet Military Power: An Assessment of the Threat, 1988* (GPO, 1988), pp. 44–45.

101. M. Rebrov, "The Logic of Large Numbers," *Krasnaya Zvezda*, July 29, 1989, p. 3.

102. "Front Line," p. 29.

103. Interviews with former U.S. government analysts. These analysts described the themes of several subsequent training years: launch under attack (1983); Western surprise attack and Soviet launch under attack (1984); protracted nuclear warfighting—thirty to sixty days with reconstitution (1985 and 1986); nuclear force survival during protracted conventional war, protecting silos from commando assaults and testing endurance of mobile SS-20 missile units (1987); initial period (first several hours) of strategic nuclear war (1988); nuclear warfighting and reconstitution (1989); and nuclear warfighting with commitment of strategic reserves, and war termination (1990).

104. The publicly available details of this exercise appear in "Soviets Stage Integrated Test of Weapons," *Aviation Week and Space Technology*, vol. 116 (June 28, 1982), pp. 20–21.

105. Interview with U.S. government analysts.

106. Ibid. This direct link probably involved the issuance of the direct command through the Signal communications network. See chapter 4.

107. This discussion of exercises in 1984 and 1988 is from interviews with U.S. government analysts.

108. John D. Steinbruner, "Launch under Attack," *Scientific American*, vol. 250 (January 1984), pp. 37–47.

109. Interview with Russian designer, and Robert P. Berman and John C. Baker, *Soviet Strategic Forces* (Brookings, 1982), p. 143. Meyer cites Marshal Ogarkov's writings as a source for the claim that the PVO was responsible for all early warning systems associated with missile or air attack. Stephen M. Meyer, "Soviet Nuclear Operations," in Ashton B. Carter, John D. Steinbruner, and Charles A. Zraket, eds., *Managing Nuclear Operations* (Brookings, 1987), p. 481.

110. Meyer, "Soviet Nuclear Operations." There is some evidence suggesting the PVO main headquarters in Moscow was largely devoted to administrative matters and that the command center outside Moscow was the main operations center. David R. Jones, "Air Defense Forces," in Jones, ed., *Soviet Armed Forces Review Annual* (Academic International Press, Florida, 1982), p. 140. The Soviet-influenced Egyptian air defense system is so organized, with the main operations complex located deep within a mountain in the Cairo suburbs near the overall PVO headquarters. Ibid., p. 171. In this vein, it is worth noting that the command decision to shoot down the KAL Flight 007 was alleged to have come from the duty officer (a colonel general) at PVO operations center in Kalinin, though an effort was made by the Far East air defense district deputy commander to contact the PVO commander in Moscow. Seymour M. Hersch, *The Target Is Destroyed* (Random House, 1986), pp. 231–32.

111. U.S. early-warning satellite and most ground radar systems sent data directly to the Pentagon's war room and another national command center as well as to the Strategic Air Command headquarters at the same time as they sent the data to NORAD. Many U.S. and Russian analysts told me that Soviet attack early warning went directly to the top politico-military leadership. This direct link might have bypassed the PVO command facilities to facilitate rapid notification of the supreme command and other top commanders, or it might have simply routed the sensor data automatically through the Center for Analysis of Space and Missile Situation to higher authorities, allowing attack notification and assessment to occur in parallel and simultaneously at the key headquarters.

112. See the analysis of Desmond Ball and Robert Windrem, "Soviet Signals Intelligence (Sigint): Organization and Management," *Intelligence and National Security*, vol. 4 (October 1989), especially pp. 651–55.

113. Such strikes did not interfere with the launch of Soviet strategic rocket forces during the transit of U.S. ICBMs.

114. Early-warning facilities outside of Russia included Mingechaur (Lyaki) in Azerbijan; Baranovichi in Belorus; Sary Shagan in Kazakhstan; Skrunda in Latvia; and Mukachevo, Nikolayev, and Sevastopol in Ukraine.

115. Dokuchayev, "A Bridle for 'Nuclear Racers,' " p. 55.

116. Benjamin S. Lambeth, *The State of Western Research on Soviet Military Strategy and Policy* (Santa Monica, Calif.: Rand Corporation, 1984), pp. 40–41.

117. Karl F. Spielmann, *Prospects for a Soviet Strategy of Controlled Nuclear War: An Assessment of Some Key Indicators* (Arlington, Va.: Institute for Defense Analyses, 1976), p. 100.

118. Garthoff, *Deterrence and the Revolution in Soviet Military Doctrine*, p. 116.

119. Ibid., p. 120.

120. Ibid., pp. 123–27.

121. Ibid., p. 125.

122. Interview by *Moscow News* with Major General Boris Surikov, as reported by *Bulletin of the Atomic Scientists*, vol. 46 (June 1990), p. 47.

123. A. Gorokhov, "The Rocket Age," *Pravda,* February 21, 1990, p. 6, in FBIS, *Daily Report: Soviet Union,* February 23, 1990, p. 88.

124. Garthoff, *Deterrence and the Revolution in Soviet Military Doctrine,* 126.

125. Interview with former SRF officer.

126. Interview with U.S. government analysts.

127. Lambeth, *State of Western Research,* p. 42.

128. Spielmann, *Prospects for a Soviet Strategy of Controlled Nuclear War,* p. 103.

129. "Important Step in Military Building," *Krasnaya Zvezda,* March 16, 1990, p. 2, in FBIS, *Daily Report: Soviet Union,* March 19, 1990, p. 88.

130. This point is credited to Cristann Gibson by Steven M. Meyer, "Soviet Nuclear Operations," pp. 485–86.

131. Ibid., especially pp. 152–53.

Chapter Seven

1. Sections of this chapter draw heavily on points developed by John Steinbruner in Bruce G. Blair and John D. Steinbruner, *The Effects of Warning on Strategic Stability,* Brookings Occasional Papers (Brookings, 1991). Contributions to this work by Richard L. Garwin are gratefully acknowledged. See also an excellent similar study, M. Elisabeth Paté-Cornell and Paul S. Fischbeck, "Bayesian Updating of the Probability of Nuclear Attack," Stanford University, Center for International Security and Arms Control, November 1990.

2. The model changes the assessment according to Bayes's formula for conditional or contingent probabilities. Lawrence D. Phillips, *Bayesian Statistics for Social Scientists* (London: Thomas Nelson and Sons, 1973), pp. 56–68.

3. The vantage point of a commander is the inverse of the designer's perspective. The designer conceives enemy attack scenarios and engineers a warning apparatus capable of detecting attack under the postulated conditions while filtering out false indications generated under other conditions. The designer thus defines the problem as providing warning if an attack occurs and preventing warning if an attack does not occur. By contrast a commander defines the problem as one of determining whether an attack is occurring if warning systems have reported one, and whether an attack is not occurring if warning systems have not reported one. The commander judges whether an attack is under way given warning, whereas the designer estimates the probability of warning given attack. Moreover the commander judges whether an attack is not under way given no warning, whereas the designer estimates the probability of no warning given no attack. In short the commander occupies the hot seat. The interpretive tasks of operators are not only more complex but are also the inverse of the designer's.

Stated in terms of formal logic, their inverse perspective on the warning problem can be expressed as follows (the symbol "|" stands for "given"):

Designer's Calculation: Estimate the probability of (warning | attack), and

(no warning | attack) [or type I error], and

(no warning | no attack), and

(warning | no attack) [or type II error].

Decisionmaker's Calculation: Estimate the truth of the hypothesis of:

(attack | warning), and

(attack | no warning), and

(no attack | no warning), and

(no attack | warning).

4. This estimate represents degrees of belief in the hypothesis "an attack is under way."

5. The rule is Bayes's formula for conditional or contingent probabilities.

6. "It is this feature of Bayes' theorem that saves Bayesian statistics from being wholly subjective. Initially subjective opinion is brought into contact with data through the operation of Bayes' theorem, and with enough data differing prior opinions are made to converge. This comes about because the prior opinions become less and less relevant to posterior opinion as more and more data are observed. Prior opinion is swamped out by the data, so that posterior opinion is controlled solely by the data. For a Bayesian, this is the only way in which data can 'speak for themselves'." Phillips, *Bayesian Statistics,* p. 78.

7. The most thorough review of this subject is Robert Jervis, *Perception and Misperception in International Politics* (Princeton University Press, 1976). Other valuable analyses with particular relevance to crisis decisionmaking are John D. Steinbruner, *The Cybernetic Theory of Decision: New Dimensions of Political Analysis* (Princeton University Press, 1974); and Richard Ned Lebow, *Between Peace and War: The Nature of International Crisis* (Johns Hopkins University Press, 1981); and Richard K. Betts, *Surprise Attack: Lessons for Defense Planning* (Brookings, 1982).

8. Jervis's treatment is among the fairest in this regard because he appreciates that "it is difficult to specify when a person is being 'too' closed-minded." Jervis, *Perception and Misperception,* p. 177. His balanced treatment of the issue stems in part from his implicit application of Bayesian logic to the case study material under consideration.

9. Bayes's theorem is applied as follows, (the slash symbol, "|" stands for "given"):

Definitions:

Prob (Attack|Tactical Warning) = $P(A|W)$

Prob (Attack|No Tactical Warning) = $P(A|NW)$

Prob (Tactical Warning|Attack) = $P(W|A)$ = 1 − Prob (Type I error)

Prob (Tactical Warning|No Attack) = $P(W|NA)$ or Type II error

Prob (No Tactical Warning|Attack) = $P(NW|A)$ or Type I error

Prob (No Tactical Warning|No Attack) = $P(NW|NA)$ = 1 − Prob (Type II error)

Prior: Initial subjective expectation of an attack is Prior (A)
Posterior: Subjective expectation of an attack after either receiving or not receiving tactical warning is Post (A)

Formulas:
Given tactical warning is received during warning report period:

$$\text{Post (A|W)} = \frac{P(W|A) \, \text{Prior(A)}}{P(W|A) \, \text{Prior(A)} + [P(W|NA)(1 - \text{Prior(A)}]}$$

Given tactical warning is *not* received during report period:

$$\text{Post (A|NW)} = \frac{P(NW|A) \, \text{Prior(A)}}{P(NW|A) \, \text{Prior(A)} + [P(NW|NA)(1 - \text{Prior(A)}]}$$

10. During the most tense phase of the Berlin crisis in the summer of 1961, President John Kennedy reportedly remarked that "there was one chance out of five of a nuclear exchange." Arthur M. Schlesinger, Jr., *A Thousand Days: John F. Kennedy in the White House* (Houghton Mifflin, 1965), p. 395. During the Cuban missile crisis of 1962 Kennedy believed by his own account that the odds of war were "somewhere between one out of three and even." Quoted in Theodore C. Sorensen, *Kennedy* (Harper and Row, 1965), p. 705.

11. Theodore Jarvis, Jr., and Cindy L. Williams, "Comments on Richard Garwin's Letter of 3 May," memo to C. A. Zraket, president of MITRE, MITRE Memorandum D40-M247 (June 2, 1989), p. 2.

12. Interview with former senior U.S. and Soviet defense officials. That Soviet leaders were never falsely notified that an attack might be under way was credited to the Soviet requirement for dual-sensor confirmation. Ground radar detection was required to confirm satellite detections.

13. The implications of the state of internal consensus on the gravity of a crisis extend well beyond the narrow issue of tactical warning interpretation. The way in which national policy and military operations interact is affected. If military organizations fail to understand the assessments, expectations, and intentions of national policy officials, then their precautionary alert operations may not be properly aligned with the way in which the core security problem has been framed by the apex of government. See chapter 3.

14. An argument can be made that certain types of strategic warning were not more ambiguous and less reliable than tactical warning indications. For example, communications intercepts revealing the dissemination of enemy launch instructions were arguably less ambiguous than blips on a radar screen indicating missiles in flight.

15. Jarvis and Williams, MITRE memorandum, p. 2.

16. This calculation of unsuccessful adaptation is based on formulas used by W. Ross Ashby to illustrate the probability of successful adaptation by complex systems. The points of our illustrations are exactly the opposite, but the math is identical. W. Ross Ashby, *Design for a Brain: The Origin of Adaptive Behaviour* (London: Chapman and Hall, 1978), pp. 150–52.

17. The basic scenario for this degradation involved the launch of a small contingent of SLBMs whose warheads explode at high altitude several minutes later, producing electromagnetic pulse effects that damaged space- and ground-

based tactical warning sensors. The initial launch might have been detected by an intact warning system, but the subsequent sensor damage might have prevented follow-on confirmation and assessment of this precursor attack as well as detection and assessment of any salvo of ICBM forces that followed on the heels of the SLBM launch.

18. As discussed in the previous chapter, NORAD assessment procedures did allow that the loss of a tactical sensor due to presumed hostile action could be counted as a positive indication of attack.

Chapter Eight

1. Representative Les Aspin, "From Deterrence to Denuking: Dealing with Proliferation in the 1990s," House Armed Services Committee, February 18, 1992, p. 5.

2. For a review of some of the academic analyses, see Bruce G. Blair, "Targeting and Deterrence," in Rose Gottemoeller, ed., *Strategic Arms Control in the Post-START Era* (London: Brassey's for the International Institute for Strategic Studies, 1992), pp. 161–75.

3. Pentagon officials sent a rewrite of NSSD 13 to President Bush's national security adviser, Lt. General (ret.) Brent Scowcroft, in August 1991, but it went nowhere because of the Moscow coup. Interview with U.S. defense official.

4. According to one recent unofficial estimate, the target base shrunk from about 12,500 aimpoints in late 1988 to 10,000 (1990), 8,000 (early 1991), and 5,000 (post-Soviet breakup). A further reduction of about 2,000, leaving a residual target base of 3,000 aimpoints, was projected after the Bush-Yeltsin summit in June 1992 lowered the ceiling on strategic inventories to 3,000 to 3,500 warheads on each side by the year 2003. Within the various target categories, substantial reductions evidently reflected the decline in Soviet power projection (other military targets), such as airborne and military transport deployments, the changing nature of government within Russia and the former Soviet Union (leadership), and the lower priority of basic industry like metallurgy and steel compared with finished military products like tanks (war-supporting industry). See William M. Arkin, "How Much Isn't Enough?" draft paper prepared for a Center for Strategic and International Studies study, "Nuclear Weapons after the Cold War," September 17, 1992. If the Reed report is any indication, the extent of U.S. targeting of transportation and energy infrastructure also decreased because of a growing ability to identify critical nodes in the networks. Thomas C. Reed, "The Role of Nuclear Weapons in the New World Order," briefing for the Joint Strategic Target Planning Staff/Strategic Advisory Group, Strategic Deterrence Study Group, October 10, 1991, p. 14. Furthermore, the task of suppressing air and missile defense systems to facilitate bomber and missile offensive penetration probably requires fewer weapons because of the disruption of defensive system operations caused by the breakup of the Soviet Union.

5. Reed, "Role of Nuclear Weapons," pp. 13–14.

6. Interview with defense analyst.

7. Reed, "Role of Nuclear Weapons," p. 16.

8. Ibid., p. 13.

9. This thesis is advanced in lucid and compelling arguments by Morton H. Halperin, *Nuclear Fallacy: Dispelling the Myth of Nuclear Strategy* (Ballinger, 1987).

10. Interview with U.S. defense analyst.

11. I am indebted to John Steinbruner for his contribution to this section, which draws heavily on points he developed in Bruce G. Blair and John D. Steinbruner, "The Effects of Warning on Strategic Stability," Brookings Occasional Papers (Brookings, 1991).

12. R. Jeffrey Smith, "Officials See Shift in Ukraine's Nuclear Position," *Washington Post,* December 19, 1992, p. 10.

13. Interview with Ukrainian official. The United States has offered Ukraine only $175 million for denuclearization.

14. See Sam Nunn and Richard Lugar, "Still a Soviet Threat," *Washington Post,* December 22, 1992, p. A21.

15. Peter Grier, "US Effort to Aid Ex-USSR in Disarming Bogs Down," *Christian Science Monitor,* January 13, 1993, p. 1.

16. This position is advanced in "Nuclear Non-Proliferation and the Former Soviet Union," in Ad Hoc Working Group on Non-Proliferation and Arms Control, *Non-Proliferation and Arms Control: Issues and Options for the Clinton Administration* (January 1993), p. 9.

17. See Serge Schmemann, "Ukraine Finds Nuclear Arms Bring a Measure of Respect," *New York Times,* January 7, 1993, p. A1.

18. This section relies on information from an unpublished briefing by Victor E. Alessi, director of the Office of Arms Control and Nonproliferation, Department of Energy, "Activities Involving the Former Soviet Union (FSU)," January 11, 1993; and Grier, "US Effort to Aid Ex-USSR."

19. The groundbreaking scientific work and policy analysis in the areas of warhead dismantlement and fissile materials disposal have been performed since 1985 by Frank von Hippel in collaboration with many of his colleagues at Princeton, the Federation of American Scientists, the Natural Resources Defense Council, and Russian research centers. The important studies produced by this group endeavor include Theodore B. Taylor, "Verified Elimination of Nuclear Warheads," *Science and Global Security,* vol. 1 nos. 1, 2 (1989), pp. 1–26; Frank von Hippel and others, "Stopping the Production of Fissile Materials for Weapons," *Scientific American,* vol. 253 (September 1985), pp. 40–47; F. von Hippel and R. Z. Sagdeev, eds., *Reversing the Arms Race: How to Achieve and Verify Deep Reductions in the Nuclear Arsenals* (Gordon and Breach, 1990); Frank von Hippel and others, "The Elimination of Nuclear Warheads," *Scientific American* (forthcoming); Federation of American Scientists, *Ending the Production of Fissile Materials for Weapons, Verifying the Dismantlement of Nuclear Warheads: The Technical Basis for Action,* a study prepared in collaboration with the Committee of Soviet Scientists for Global Security and the Center for Program Studies of the USSR Academy of Sciences (Washington, June 1991); and Frans Berkhout

and others, "Disposition of Separated Plutonium," *Science and Global Security,* vol. 3 (1992), pp. 1–53.

20. Similar and additional preconditions for reductions to 1,000 strategic warheads on each side are enumerated by the Committee on International Security and Arms Control of the National Academy of Sciences, *The Future of the U.S.-Soviet Nuclear Relationship* (Washington: National Academy Press, 1991), pp. 27–31.

21. Reed, "Role of Nuclear Weapons," pp. 9–10.

22. Author's estimates. A congressional study estimates that the current arsenals of these countries total about 1,500 (700, 500, and 300) warheads. U.S. Congressional Budget Office (CBO), *The START Treaty and Beyond* (October 1991), p. 118.

23. Ibid., pp. 21, 14–15.

24. Reed, "Role of Nuclear Weapons," pp. 12, 10.

25. Good examples are CBO, *The START Treaty and Beyond,* especially pp. 38–39, 174–75; Harold Feiveson and Frank von Hippel, "Dismantling the Doomsday Machine," *Technology Review,* vol. 95 (May–June 1992), pp. 61–69; and William W. Kaufmann, *Assessing the Base Force: How Much Is Too Much?* (Brookings, 1992), especially pp. 31–47, 77–81.

26. See Gennady K. Khromov, "Limitation of Cruise Missile Technologies: A Road to Strategic Stability," in Gottemoeller, ed., *Strategic Arms Control in the Post-START Era,* p. 179.

27. A list of potential targets threatened by the latest generation of conventional weapons delivered by air would include "military command bunkers, communications sites, air defense radars, airfields (including parked aircraft in or out of hardened bunkers), research and production facilities for weapons of mass destruction, oil refineries and distribution systems, electrical power plants and switching stations, logistics centers, railroad and auto bridges (if combat in the invaded country were ongoing), the political leadership, military support industries, and other economic structures." Albert L. Latter, Ernest A. Martinelli, and Roger D. Speed, *Conventional Strategic Deterrence,* UCRL-ID-111265 (Livermore, Calif.: Lawrence Livermore National Laboratory, August 1992), p. 4.

28. Reed, "Role of Nuclear Weapons," p. 16.

29. See Mary C. Fitzgerald, "Russia's New Military Doctrine," *RUSI Journal,* vol. 137 (October 1992), pp. 40–48.

30. An earlier version of this far-reaching proposal appeared in Bruce G. Blair and Henry W. Kendall, "Accidental Nuclear War," *Scientific American,* vol. 263 (December 1990), pp. 53–58.

31. See V. Pokrovskiy, "Air Forces: 'Global Shield' Exercise," *Zarubezhnoye voyennoye obozreniye,* no. 12 (December 1981), pp. 47–50, in JPRS, *Perceptions, Views, Comments,* 81754, September 13, 1982, pp. 65–68; Ye. Chugunov, "The United States: Counting on Preparations for Nuclear War," *Zarubezhnoye voyennoye obozreniye,* no. 4 (April 1984), pp. 7–11, in JPRS, *Foreign Military Affairs,* JPRS-UMA-84-053, August 4, 1984, pp. 63–75; and Henry M. Narducci, "Strategic Air Command and the Alert Program: A Brief History," Office of the

Historian, Headquarters Strategic Air Command, Offutt Air Force Base, Nebraska, April 1, 1988.

32. *START: Treaty between the United States of America and the Union of Soviet Socialist Republics on the Reduction and Limitation of Strategic Offensive Arms,* signed in Moscow on July 31, 1991 (U.S. Arms Control and Disarmament Agency, 1991), p. 248.

33. In the words of an early proponent of this idea, Richard Garwin, "This could be achieved by mounting small, specialized radio transmitters on each silo cover, generating an [unbreakable] code that would be relayed by a normal communications satellite to . . . the other side. . . . Arranged so that the communication would cease if the transmitter (or silo cover) were moved, the system would give continuing assurance that ICBM's were not on the way. This would not be, in truth, a warning system but a confidence-building measure, since the transmitter could readily be destroyed or disabled, thus denying any possibility of report of actual launch. But if a signal stopped, and especially if many stopped at once, the ICBM owner would be highly motivated to explain how this had happened, in order to avoid the presumption of launch." Richard L. Garwin, Prepared Statement, in *The START Treaty,* Hearings before the Senate Foreign Relations Committee, 102 Cong. 2 sess. (Government Printing Office, 1992), pt. 1, p. 139.

34. "U.S.-C.I.S. Cooperation in Ballistic Missile Global Launch Detection and Early Warning," summary of a meeting held at Stanford University, Center for International Security and Arms Control, May 8–9, 1992, p. 4.

35. Useful background on PALs is found in Peter Stein and Peter Feaver, *Assuring Control of Nuclear Weapons: The Evolution of Permissive Action Links* (Lanham, Md.: University Press of America, 1987); Donald R. Cotter, "Peacetime Operations: Safety and Security," in Ashton B. Carter, John D. Steinbruner, and Charles A. Zraket, eds., *Managing Nuclear Operations* (Brookings, 1987), pp. 17–74; and Dan Caldwell, "Permissive Action Links: A Description and Proposal," *Survival,* vol. 29 (May–June, 1987), pp. 224–38.

36. Cotter, "Peacetime Operations," p. 50.

37. A similar practice—configuring weapons with PALs but keeping them unlocked as a matter of policy whenever the weapons carriers go on alert—exists for many SAC bomber weapons. The bombs themselves are equipped with PALs that are typically used only when the bombs are put in storage. When they are loaded onto alert bombers (note that the United States ceased bomber alert operations in September 1991), which are not internally equipped such that the combat crews can unlock the PALs in flight upon receipt of a war order containing the codes (for example, the B-1 bomber), the PAL codes are inserted into the bombs during alert "prepping" on the ground. The PAL protection is thus removed from the bombs themselves. Although the bomber crew is impeded by coded switch devices that prevent the racks in the bomb bay from releasing their loads until codes from higher authority are received, the bombs themselves are not safeguarded and could be usable if they fell into irresponsible hands. Much of this section is taken from Bruce G. Blair, "Strengthening Nuclear Safeguards through Arms Control," in *The Future of Arms Control: New Opportunities,*

report prepared for the Subcommittee on Arms Control, International Security and Science of the House Committee on Foreign Affairs by the Congressional Research Service, Committee Print, 102 Cong. 2 sess. (GPO, April 1992), pp. 89–106.

38. "Agreement on Measures to Reduce the Risk of Outbreak of Nuclear War between the United States of America and the Union of Soviet Socialist Republics," September 30, 1971, reprinted in Barry M. Blechman, ed., *Preventing Nuclear War: A Realistic Approach* (Indiana University Press, 1985), pp. 193–95. I am indebted to Professor Sherman Frankel of the University of Pennsylvania for pointing out this information.

39. Article 2, sentence 1, states: "The Parties undertake to notify each other immediately in the event of an accidental, unauthorized or any other unexplained incident involving a possible detonation of a nuclear weapon which could create a risk of outbreak of nuclear war." Ibid., p. 194.

40. Ibid.

41. Garwin, Prepared Statement, in *START Treaty,* Hearings, p. 138.

42. See Sherman Frankel, "Aborting Unauthorized Launches of Nuclear-armed Ballistic Missiles through Postlaunch Destruction," *Science and Global Security,* vol. 2 (1990), pp. 1–20.

43. "Committees: Establishment of the Nuclear Fail-Safe and Risk Reduction Advisory Committee," *Federal Register,* vol. 55 (December 3, 1990), p. 49940.

44. See Title XIV, part D, section 1441, of the 1991 Defense Authorization Act Conference Report: "Conference Report on H.R. 4739, National Defense Authorization Act for Fiscal Year 1991," in *Congressional Record*, October 23, 1990, pp. H11935–H12046 (discussion of PALS on p. H11998).

45. See *Nuclear Weapons Safety*, report of the Panel on Nuclear Weapons Safety of the House Committee on Armed Services, Committee Print 15, 101 Cong. 2 sess. (GPO, December 1990).

Index

359